THE SPECIAL CHILD IN THE LIBRARY

THE SPECIAL CHILD IN THE LIBRARY

Barbara Holland Baskin
and Karen H. Harris, editors

American Library Association
Chicago 1976

Library of Congress Cataloging in Publication Data
Main entry under title:

The Special child in the library.

  Includes bibliographies and index.
  1. Libraries, Children's—Addresses, essays,
lectures. 2. Exceptional children—Addresses,
essays, lectures. I. Baskin, Barbara Holland,
1929– II. Harris, Karen H., 1934–
Z718.1.S64 027.62′5 76-21268
ISBN 0–8389–0222–7

Contents

Introduction

Increasing interest has been evident lately in the myriad problems involved in providing library service to exceptional children. Major professional journals have devoted entire issues to the subject; symposia and workshops have been held; and a steady stream of articles has appeared in current serials. In addition, legislation has established and financed centers and funded research related to this problem. Reports of these efforts are so widely scattered in the journals and proceedings of many academic disciplines that keeping informed of important developments is a major challenge for the concerned professional.

Communities are moving away from homogeneous classroom grouping. The growing interest in multilevel classrooms, individualized instruction and related administrative arrangements has presented librarians with groups and classes containing a wide variety of abilities and talents. Now that many special education programs are attempting to integrate their students as fully as possible within the regular classes, the range within a given group will be broader than ever. Thus, the librarian must be prepared to modify the library to meet the needs of those children with serious sensory, intellectual, emotional, and physical differences who require specific attention. The librarian will need to investigate such areas as adaptations to the total environment, innovative changes in equipment and technology, enabling legislation, dissemination networks, sources, material development and utilization, specifically focused programming, and other information which will maximize knowledge, sensitivity, and skill in responding to the special needs of the exceptional child.

The primary and fundamental problem created by the special child's use of the library centers upon the setting in which library experiences take place. The structural environment has two equally critical components: accessibility to, and physical elements within, the library or media center itself. Unfortunately, many libraries have been designed without consideration for ease of entrance to the premises, in effect excluding utilization by the disabled. Within the library, size, structural design, acoustics, lighting, storage space, furnishings, and other such factors will prove critical variables affecting optimum usage for the handicapped. The works selected offer practical ideas both for design standards and modification of existing structures.

Advances in technology have succeeded in partially compensating for some disabling conditions. Media have proved effective in achieving a variety of educational goals. They have been used to increase motivation, to facilitate learning experiences, and, in some dramatic instances, to provide the child access to data using sensory modalities which would otherwise have been underutilized in the learning process. The librarian, as a media specialist, must be aware of the full spectrum of available facilitating equipment and creatively use this technology to respond to the unique needs of the special child.

Recent enabling legislation and subsequent supportive funding have permitted the establishment of regional instructional materials centers to provide for the development, evaluation, and dissemination of materials for use in programs of special education. Legislation has extended to the physically handicapped many of the services formerly available only to the blind including vast stores of equipment as well as materials. Special interest groups, such as the Lighthouse for the Blind, National Easter Seal Society, and various federal and state agencies also provide a multitude of materials and services. The librarian, functioning as a resource person, needs to become acquainted with these organizations and their procedures for providing services.

The selection of materials for exceptional children is predicated on a clear understanding of each child's functional level, how the disability interferes with optimal learning, and what kinds of materials are available which would capitalize on the child's assets and bypass, if possible, the disabilities. Materials for gifted children need to provide intellectual and aesthetic challenges and still be relevant to the chronological and social age of the child. The media specialist must be aware of sources, material modification procedures, and specialized materials such as captioned films for the deaf and talking books for the blind or physically handicapped. The librarian must scrutinize the collection for such items as high-interest, low-vocabulary books for the retarded, large-print books for the visually impaired, and potentially therapeutic stories for the emotionally disturbed.

Even the most outstanding collection is of limited value unless it is fully utilized by children, faculty, and library staff. It is imperative for the librarian to be alert to varied uses of mediated instruction and to the multisensory possibilities of such tools. The collection should be made enticing, especially for those children who are unschooled in library use or who have had prior negative experiences in learning settings. As these children begin to find personal pleasure and academic success, the library will be newly reevaluated as a source of excitement and fulfillment.

Ultimately the assessment of a library rests on the quality and extent of its program. Many librarians have been able to modify standard activities such as reading guidance, storytelling, and puppetry to the unique needs of the exceptional. Often novel programs have been devised to involve the special child with the library. New alliances between other faculty and school library personnel have been established for diagnostic purposes and for mutual prescriptive planning. In sum, the library program must be redesigned to supplement curricular goals, encourage recreational reading, provide stimulation and pleasure, and teach how information can be used for problem solving and enhancement of understanding for all children, including those with exceptional needs.

In the past, bibliotherapy has been practiced primarily by institutional librarians. As disturbed and maladjusted children are returned to a regular school setting, it is important that the school librarian assist in the continuing normalization of the child. Studies available on bibliotherapy indicate that it has a significant contribution to make in the remediation of emotional disorders and the social adjustment processes. This is not to imply that librarians act as clinicians, but rather that they become contributing team members in the provision of therapeutic support. Included in this collection are some theoretical discussions and clinical reports of bibliotherapeutic activities.

Much can be learned from librarians in non-school settings. Institutional librarians often find themselves in a situation which contains its own set of restrictions and opportunities. For example, because of the defined focus of responsibility of each setting, e.g., a state school for the deaf or a youth correctional facility, librarians often develop a collection and program solely directed to that one exceptionality. Their success with specific materials and programs can be highly instructive for school librarians.

Public libraries have also successfully reorganized their outreach plans to extend their talents and offerings to special groups. Their work with specialized books, media, and programs can serve as a source of models and ideas.

The public school librarian, in most instances, has had little exposure to information relating to the adaptations necessary to adequately serve the exceptional child. Because of progress in technology and the increasing level of involvement of the special child in the library program, the librarian needs to have readily available a handbook which will cogently present a philosophical base for procedures, a compendium of information on materials, examples of creative, unusual and effective programs, and guidelines for environmental modifications.

This book of readings is offered in the hope that the new practitioners, in addition to experienced librarians who wish to increase their knowledge and competency vis à vis the exceptional child, will find herein exciting ideas and the means to implement them. The right to read must be extended to include all children.

PART 1

Structure, Design, and Ambience: Components of the Physical Environment

The physical plant provides a setting within which the library program can function, with the structural components serving as enabling or limiting factors. Traditional library concerns with the physical plant involve size, layout, functionalism, ambience, and comfort: Will the library accommodate enough students at any one time? Will it have appropriate areas for the variety of activities which are regularly scheduled, e.g. story-telling, research, conferences? Does the interior design promote the success of the library program? Is it an inviting, stimulating place? Are the systems which control temperature, light, and sound conducive to optimum utilization? These are the basic questions the librarian should use to assess the environment.

These considerations, while critical, are not sufficient to respond adequately to the needs of the exceptional child. Accessibility to and mobility within various activity centers of the library must be judged by new standards, if the physical plant is to be fully usable by special children. Split-level floor plans and narrow passageways are insurmountable obstacles to the wheelchair-bound student. More stringent acoustical and lighting standards are imperative if the hearing-impaired or partially seeing child is to function well. In addition, concerns for safety become an especially high priority factor when blind, deaf, or physically handicapped children are library patrons.

Environmental modifications responsive to the needs of special children and the elimination of architectural barriers often have salutory results for nonhandicapped users as well. Improved lighting clearly benefits everyone. Carpeting provides acoustical control, safety, and improved appearance for all users of the library.

Librarians, architects, and administrators must be aware of those factors which interfere with successful school participation by the disabled child. Such factors should be eliminated—but in a subtle manner which preserves and maintains the dignity of each child insofar as possible. Separate entrances, specially designated areas, and other such alternatives which label or separate are offensive to children who seek to diminish the differences between themselves and their nonhandicapped peers.

It is imperative that the librarian bring informed judgment to bear on recommendations for environmental change. In instances where goals for the improvement of setting are in conflict, the librarian will need to order priorities in favor of humanistic over administrative and even aesthetic demands. A further complication is that many handicapped children are highly dependent. The interior design

5

and layout should promote growth in self-help skills and any obstacles to independent functioning by the special child must be reduced.

Moreover, the physical environment should be examined for its potential to provide enriching, expanding, and stimulating experiences. Thus, the setting should not be regarded as merely a passive or nonrestrictive factor, but needs to be evaluated in terms of its potential as an active facilitating agent in the educational process.

It is distressing to note that in a survey of articles dealing with educational adaptations for the special child, even minimal attention to the role of the library or to library design is conspicuously wanting. In fact, those articles in this chapter which are specifically directed to the school library were solicited, since recent periodical and textbook literature on facilities for the exceptional child ignores the library completely or assumes the library has no unique problems. The unspoken premise seems to be that all academic instruction takes place in the classroom and the critical potential of the library is simply not factored into physical plant planning or modifications. Librarians will clearly need to be aggressive in asserting their role in the total educational structure and demand inclusion at every level of planning; early input into architectural and interior design is critical.

The articles in this section focus on the specific environmental adaptations required in library settings. Such adaptations are designed to facilitate service to the emotionally disturbed, the visually impaired, the hearing handicapped, and the physically disabled. Robertson has drafted some constructive suggestions for developing a therapeutic environment in which an emotionally disturbed child can function. She also pinpoints the means to achieve this goal. The purpose of her article is double-barreled: to specify modifications in the setting which can aid in reducing undesirable behaviors and to guide the librarian in changing the disturbed child's perception of the library as hostile territory to that of a place of succor and warmth.

Kirk reviews some of the critical reading problems of the visually impaired and suggests specific responses the librarian can make which are based on the varying visual capabilities and needs of the students. She analyzes how the physical elements of the library can be used to extend instructional and communication possibilities for students with visual problems. Since informational input for these youngsters is processed primarily through their aural and haptic senses, suggestions for capitalizing upon these alternative instructional channels are discussed.

Drawing on her own experience in library and media work with hearing deficient children, Batt describes how the structural components of the library impinge on the learning problems of auditorily handicapped users. She also suggests some ways to function within the physical plant, particularly in relation to the manipulation of spatial elements in the library in order to maximize communication and efficiency.

Velleman's extensive experience in library design and management of a learning center for the severely physically handicapped student is demonstrated in her contribution. Many obstacles precluding full library utilization by students in wheelchairs or on crutches can be avoided by other librarians, provided close attention to her recommendations for modifying the library environment is given.

The expansion of libraries into instructional materials centers was an important development in the education of the exceptional child because it opened up the possibility of mediated differential channel input and varied reinforcement of cognitive concepts. The Special Experience Room takes the next dramatic step of creating an entirely new stimulating milieu for learning. A multisensory locale surrounds, engulfs, envelops the child— simulating the sounds, sights, smells, and temperature of the setting being studied. Ray presents the rationale and development of such a room in a school which serves a variety of disabled populations in an integrated setting, and Dailey reports on the operational aspects of this rich center for mediated learning.

The synergistic consequences of uniting instruction, media, and architecture in the library/media center are tremendously exciting. These authors suggest some tempting models to the librarian who is eager to welcome exceptional children to the library and seeks means to insure that they can use the center profitably, comfortably, and pleasurably.

Impact of the Physical Environment on the Emotionally Disturbed and Socially Maladjusted Student

PATRICIA ROBERTSON

The concept of an "emotionally disturbed student" evokes an endless variety of prejudices and images in the average individual. Some immediately imagine a wild-eyed, aggressive person who takes out his hostilities on everyone and everything around him. Others picture a morose, depressed individual, affected by what Hippocrates termed "black bile."

Actually, the emotionally disturbed or socially maladjusted student may manifest only a few, or at the other extreme, a wide variety and intensity of symptoms within this range. The Mental Status Examination of the Missouri Division of Mental Diseases, for instance, cites a partial checklist of possible symptoms:

Facial Expression—can be sad, expressionless, hostile and angry, or anxious and worried.
Motor Behavior—can be composed of pacing and hand wringing, mannerisms, posturing, repetitive acts, angry outbursts, compulsive acts, or ritualistic acts.
Mood and Affect—sad about pleasant things, elated about sad things, shows silliness, flat (no fluctuations) affect, labile affect, mood elevated, or mood depressed.
Delusions (if any)—of grandeur, of reference, of influence, of persecution, of worthlessness, of passivity, nihilistic ideas, somatic delusions.
Hallucinations (if any)—visual, auditory, tactile, gustatory, or olfactory.
Manifestations (if any)—clouding of consciousness, short attention span, inability to concentrate, poor recent memory, poor remote memory, amnesia, dissassociation.[1]

How are these abnormal behavior symptoms manifested in the classroom and in the library? E. M. Bower has made a checklist which is excellent:

1. Day dreams almost incessantly and very few school activities hold his interest.

2. Extremely impulsive and/or hyperactive. There is a quality of driveness to the hyperactivity.
3. Demonstrates a very short attention span and poor ability to concentrate. Rarely seems to finish assigned tasks. He may or may not perform adequately at the task but habitually never seems to finish.
4. Inability to tolerate frustration—tends to seek immediate reward or gratification; has difficulty waiting for his turn when some activity demands it.
5. Excessive requests to go to the bathroom.
6. Overly impatient for snack and lunch time to come; frequently asks when it will be time to eat.
7. Destructive with his own, peers' or school property.
8. Inability to accept limits or restraints and will not or cannot abide by the general rules.
9. Overly exhibitionistic; craves attention and the limelight.
10. Compulsively ritualistic in work or behavior, e.g. the child who must tap the teacher's desk four times each time he passes her.
11. Tends to be extremely rigid in the way he performs various tasks; or consistently tries to straighten or fix things which he insists are unbalanced, inharmonious, or misplaced.
12. Resistant to changing to new activities and in general adjusts poorly to new situations.
13. An inability or unwillingness to handle even the most minor of responsibilities. Burdened by excessive doubts; indecisive and unable to make decisions.
14. Chronically fearful, apprehensive, or depressed.
15. Will deny vehemently when caught doing something he is not supposed to do. Will insist he did not do it even when caught "red-handed."[2]

In designing library space and equipment to accommodate the wide variety of possible manifestations of emotional disorders, first the needs reflected by these behaviors must be precisely analyzed. Then the librarian may decide upon specific design objectives for the areas and the facilities of the library. This paper, therefore, will focus upon these four major issues: (1) What are some of the library behaviors typical of emotionally disturbed students? (2) What library responses do these behaviors require? (3) What are our library design objectives for emotionally disturbed and socially maladjusted students? (4) What environmental impact can we hope to achieve for these students?

Library Behaviors

Examine first the activities of Student A. One day, he might enter the library, immediately seeking a table with other students. He might want to discuss schoolwork with them, or to plan a project. His appearance is bright, animated; perhaps he is even a bit pressured in his speech, and somewhat overactive. Several days later, the same student might enter the library, quietly shuffling his feet and seemingly dragging himself along. He looks up slowly, choosing a quiet carrel away from the other students. He opens a book and stares at it, but he isn't reading. At this time, his needs in the library are in direct contrast with his needs of the previous few days.

Student B, on the other hand, swaggers as he enters the library, picks up a recent magazine and seeks any area that is somewhat isolated. He may even move his chair so that his back is against the wall. The librarian may notice that this student's everyday activities seem to require more space than the average person. If anyone invades his "territory," an aggression or hostility response may be made. For instance, if another student jostles student B's chair, that small act might cause a confrontation.

Student C has the appearance of a robot, with a "glass wall" in front of his eyes. At times, he seems to be lost in thoughts of his own. This student may be an intense reader; often he seems to block out reality by his immersion in book after book.

Student D apparently lives his life in high gear. He trips over his own shoe lace as he enters the library; he knocks down several magazines as he reaches for one; although he sits down, he seems to be continually in motion. His attention span is limited, to say the least. Records may reveal that this student has managed to get into continual fights at school; his school record chronicles one disciplinary action after another. His reading age is often extremely low in comparison to his chronological age.

Student E may look and act, much of the time, like the typical "boy next door." The majority of the time he is friendly, alert, intelligent, and perfectly behaved—perhaps too perfectly behaved. One day he might be observed in the corner of the reference area, viciously ripping sections out of the encyclopedias.

Students A through E are merely composites of some of the types of emotionally disturbed and socially maladjusted students who might be encountered in a specialized library setting.

Needs

Each of these students reflects individual environmental adaptations, but all share some common elements of need:

1. The need for an atmosphere which affords them a sense of acceptance and respect for their individual worth and self esteem. (However, note that acceptance of the *individual* does not mean acceptance of disturbed or deviant *behavior*.)
2. The need for a variety of activities which they can pursue in a library setting. Some of the students may be primarily auditory in their learning modality; others may learn best visually, or even kinesthetically. The library should provide a variety of support for the multiple levels of literacy or multiple modalities of learning which the students manifest.
3. The need for adequate space for each student. Some recent studies upon prisoners indicate that they seem to need more space than average individuals, but little research has been done with emotionally disturbed individuals in this light. This is an area for additional controlled psychological research. The experience of this author, however, seems to indicate that additional unshared space in a library for emotionally disturbed students is a definite asset.
4. The need for adequate supervision. State regulations vary, but the maximum teacher-student ratio is usually one to fifteen or less.
5. The need for both quiet study areas and areas for quiet discussions with other students.

Objectives

What are the library objectives for these emotionally disturbed students? The librarian must remember that in this specialized setting, he or she plays a dual role: that of librarian and that of therapist. The objectives, therefore, center around four focal points: establishing a therapeutic environment, a safe and efficient environment, a varied, multimedia environment, and an efficient technical processing area.

Developing a therapeutic environment. One of the greatest challenges is establishing a warm, cheerful atmosphere in the specialized, institutional library area. Psychiatrists include these factors in their definition of a "therapeutic environment," and the general public considers this a favorable ambience, or atmosphere. Several elements are usually involved: decorations which counteract the "institutional look" and emphasize a homelike atmosphere are helpful. Plants, comfortable chairs, and student paintings or craft works are additionally valuable.

It is important to establish and to maintain a climate of security for these students—a security which is both emotional and physical. This can be accomplished partially by regular routines, and by an accepting attitude and stability on the part of the staff members. From the environmental aspect, a similar security must be maintained; for instance, adequate notice should be given before any physical changes in library arrangements are made.

Finally, a general attitude should be established which anticipates positive change and growth for the student. Success should be built into the learning devices in the area, for instance. Equipment should be purchased which is easily mastered and operated and can withstand strenuous use. Colors should be happy, but calming; displays and bulletin boards should focus on the positive.[3]

Developing a safe and efficient environment. In addition to the specialized therapeutic considerations, the librarian must be concerned with safety regulations and efficiency factors which are common to many types of libraries. In summary form, these factors could be listed as accessibility, safety and efficiency, lighting, and sound control.

The location should be in a relatively quiet area which is convenient for staff and students. Consideration should also be given to the entrance for physically handicapped students and for the movement of book carts and other materials to various areas of the school or wards.

Architectural and design factors which are particularly important are the floor loads and the air-conditioning facilities. Floor loads should be well within structural allowances. The live load for shelving and books, for instance, should be from 150–175 pounds per square foot.[4] Air-conditioning should be provided, if possible, with individual thermostatic level for the library areas.

Proper quality and quantity of illumination for the varied areas should provide nonreflective patterns of lighting which will provide flexible arrangement of furnishings and equipment. For study purposes, 70 footcandles of light are desirable; for ordinary reading, 30 footcandles will suffice. For detailed technical work, as in the processing area, 70 footcandles of light are again necessary; in addition, 70 footcandles of light are needed at the circulation desk. Stack areas, however, need only approximately 30 footcandles of light. An additional electrical consideration is that an adequate number, capacity, and proper placement of electrical outlets be installed for audiovisual equipment, for electric typewriters, and for technical processing equipment.[5]

Sound control is especially important. Acoustical treatment of ceilings, floors, draperies, and partitions is desirable. Serious consideration should be given to carpeting the library reading area; it provides sound control as well as enhancing the aesthetic appearance of the area.

Developing a varied, multimedia environment. During the planning process, consideration should be given to definition of behavioral objectives for the various library areas. Each library will establish a different set of these learning objectives, but here are some general guidelines.

A reading area for quiet study, reading, and reference work should have two components: one for those who read best in an isolated, distraction-free area, and those who read and study best when they have others surrounding them. Carrels are an effective screening and distraction-free area for the first type of reader. Tables, especially round tables, are convenient for group areas. Comfortable large furniture for reading areas might also be included. This helps to establish a comfortable, therapeutic environment.

Basic furnishings include a circulation desk, a card catalog, periodical shelving, vertical files, bulletin board areas, and typewriters for technical services. At Southeast Louisiana Hospital, considerable interest was expressed by the students in using a typewriter and in learning to type. If a place in or near the technical services can be designated as a student typing area, this might be a definite advantage. Care must be taken, however, to make sure that the area is adequately supervised by the technical staff members, and that the noise from the typing area does not carry to other adjacent areas.

Audiovisual equipment will be defined by the behavioral objectives set by each library; however, here are a few possibilities. For 16mm film utilization, the library will need one or more projectors, storage racks, carts, extra reels, and screens. A wall-mounted screen and a film showing and previewing area in the library area are extremely helpful. In planning the room, care should be exercised to specify placement for maximum viewing potential of the wall-mounted screen. Formulas for this are available in many audiovisual manuals. For records, the library will need record players, headsets, storage racks, and cleaning cloths. Cassette recorders are also useful both for music and for taping conferences.

Slide productions require slide projectors, storage cases for slides, camera for production, and lights. For filmstrips, storage racks, a rear screen filmstrip viewer, and/or a classroom filmstrip projector will be needed. The rear screen models are designed for carrel use in full light.

Miscellaneous equipment should include clocks, a telephone, a photocopier, and possibly an opaque projector and talking book machines. At Southeast Louisiana Hospital, an induction loop system was also installed, which provided students with the choice of reading while listening to music without disturbing the students who wished to have silence. The induction loop system utilizes wireless headsets, so it is additionally advantageous for those students who are fearful of wires. In addition, the headsets can be worn anywhere in the induction loop area, so that there is little of the "crowding factor" which is usually prevalent when a jack box attached to a record player is employed.

The students at Southeast Louisana Hospital also used a simple slide camera on a stand for production of slide shows. These were valuable both as a bibliotherapy tool and as a therapeutic device providing ego support for those students.

Developing an efficient technical processes area. Technical processes must have adequate lighting, ventilation, sound control, and privacy. The librarian's office may be combined with the technical area; care must then be taken to provide adequate supervision of the location, and to secure the room when not in use by the staff.

There are some additional considerations which pertain especially to libraries for the emotionally disturbed and socially maladjusted student. Traffic flow is an important consideration. It is vital to post signs which clearly indicate areas which are off limits and which list the rules and regulations of the library. Some students, especially at first, will be too reticent to ask questions; they will remain inactive rather than risk being vulnerable to criticism. Others will ignore the signs until reminded. In either case, the signs function as a means of information for the student.

It is extremely important that the design of the library provide for complete visual supervision of all areas by the staff members. Librarians should be especially wary of stack areas which are not in the line of immediate vision. The security of having the areas supervised will offset many problems before they arise.

Design of the furniture should be sturdy. Avoid entrance doors with glass panels, desks with glass tops, windows that are immediately adjacent to seating areas. Permanent audiovisual equipment should be mounted to the furniture for safety and efficiency. Machinery should be carefully supervised at all times.

Environmental Impact

According to Samuel A. Kirk, "Emotionally disturbed children are characterized by inner tensions and anxiety, and they display neurotic and psychotic behavior."[6] Socially maladjusted students, on the other hand, are usually "unmanageable in the home, generate problems in the school, are retarded in educational achievement, and are destructive, quarrelsome, and socially immature," but they have a lack of the anxiety which characterizes the emotionally disturbed.[7] The library, if it is properly designed, can be a truly therapeutic environment for these students. The stability, calmness, and happiness generated by a favorable ambience in the library can be significant factors in calming the inner tensions and anxiety of the disturbed student. The variety of activities can gently but persuasively lead the socially maladjusted student toward learning on his own level. The library environment itself can act as a favorable influence toward establishing meaningful reading guidance, bibliotherapy, and individualized programming.

NOTES

1. Missouri Division of Mental Diseases, *Mental Status Examination* (Jefferson City, Mo.: The Division, July 1970).

2. E. M. Bower, "Primary Prevention of Mental and Emotional Disorders," *American Journal of Orthopsychiatry* 33:832 (October 1963).

3. Dorothy Merenes and Louis J. Kainosh, *Essentials of Psychiatric Nursing*, 7th ed. (St. Louis, Mo.: C. V. Mosby Co., 1966), p. 56.

4. Hospital Library Standards Committee, Association of Hospital and Institution Libraries, American Library Association, *Standards for Library Service in Health Care Institutions* (Chicago: The Association, 1970), p. 16.

5. Ibid.

6. Samuel A. Kirk, *Educating Exceptional Children*, 2nd ed. (Boston: Houghton, 1972), p. 391.

7. Ibid., p. 391.

Designing Desirable Physical Conditions in Libraries for Visually Handicapped Children

EDITH C. KIRK

Most school systems throughout the country have either enlarged or enriched their library programs or replaced them with instructional materials centers. They afford a full range of print and nonprint materials with equipment for their utilization. Visually handicapped children have much to gain from these innovations.

The libraries have become extensions of the classroom for all children in the school. The visually handicapped, as well as others, are scheduled to spend part of each day in reading, studying or experimenting. The diversity of materials stimulates the children's interest in reading, satisfies their curiosity and broadens their horizons, thus fulfilling their informational and recreational needs.

Beginning at the kindergarten level, the librarian becomes acquainted with each child—his ability and interests, his instructional needs, and his skill in using the materials.

The visually handicapped constitute the smallest group of exceptional children. Jones and Collins established their number as about one in every 1,000 of the school-age population.[1] The great majority of these children are not blind, but partially seeing and may vary in their amount of useful vision. Their corrected visual acuity is 20/70 or less; that is, their visual efficiency is 64 percent of normal or less. Even so, vision is their main avenue of reading and of acquiring an education. The remainder of the children are blind or so greatly limited in vision that they must read braille or listen to tapes and records. Occasionally a child of very low vision will read both print and braille.

Physical conditions, materials and aids that facilitate the act of reading for the visually handicapped will be described and the librarian's role in assisting and guiding these children will be analyzed.

It is widely suggested that the library or materials center be located on the first floor of the school building; this makes it easily accessible to all children. It is also recommended that sufficient light be provided so that every child can read with ease and comfort. While 70 footcandles of evenly distributed and diffused light may be sufficient for some activities, as much as 150 footcandles may be needed by certain low-visioned children. This additional light can be provided by high intensity lamps to be used at desks or tables. The typical, modern school library should provide conditions suitable for both reading and study by the visually handicapped.

Following are characteristics of a library well adapted to the visually handicapped:

1. The library is in a relatively quiet part of the building away from outside noises and distractions, such as the school playground or heavy traffic. It is carpeted and has acoustical tile to reduce sounds within the library. Drapes are also helpful in this respect provided they do not cut out needed light.
2. The level of illumination within the room is increased by means of walls of pastel colors, white ceilings, bulletin boards with light backgrounds, gray-green or blue-green chalkboards, and dull-finish furniture, and floors and carpeting which are light in color.
3. The area surrounding the child's visual task, such as the table top and floor when he is reading, is not less than one-third the physical brightness of the task itself. A small contrast helps prevent eye fatigue.

4. Desks with adjustable tops are provided for the partially seeing. If not, either desk or floor easels are available. All enable the child to bring a book close to his eyes yet maintain a comfortable, upright posture. Sighted pupils should be encouraged to hold their books up when reading. Tinker states:

Printed material should be sloped at about 45 degrees from a flat table or desk top for most effective reading. Lowering the slope of the page by only 15 degrees from the 45 degree position reduces reading efficiency. When a book is flat on the table, the loss of efficiency is severe.[2]

5. The desk or table top which the blind child uses for reading is flat and large enough to support his braille book, and no higher than his elbow level when he is seated.
6. Carrels have ample table top space and electrical outlets. One child goes to a carrel to use a cumbersome visual aid which requires additional light, another views a filmstrip, and still another reads aloud to a blind classmate. The carrel provides a degree of privacy and comfort for the visually handicapped and enables them to avoid distracting other students in the library.
7. Easily accessible shelves are reserved for large type and braille books. If several visually impaired students use the library, large type and braille dictionaries and even encyclopedias are available to them.
8. Some easily accessible storage space, such as a small cupboard or a few shelves, is handy for easy storage of supplies by the visually handicapped. These might include a Braillewriter, special paper for writing braille, a desk easel and magnifiers.

Also, the librarian can give aid to the visually handicapped by modifying certain activities. The librarian does the following:

1. Makes library signs large and clear enough to be seen easily by using a pen which makes broad, heavy lines on paper of contrasting color. For smaller signs, the librarian may well use a typewriter with large type, 12 to 14 points. Signs which refer to books and material which a blind student uses, should be written in braille and located within easy reach.
2. Arranges bulletin board displays with large pictures and little detail. Pictures outlined in dark colors with a felt-tip pen are more easily seen as are strong, contrasting colors. Three-dimensional

objects on bulletin boards make it possible for the blind student to obtain information by touch.

3. Constructs displays and exhibits with large objects, some three-dimensional, that can be both seen and examined by touch. Displays with few objects rather than many are less confusing, and more easily comprehended.

In addition, many of the materials and equipment found in modern libraries, if carefully selected, can enhance the learning opportunities of the visually limited. The following are examples of superior materials:

1. Maps and globes that have definite outlines and distinct colors.
2. Tapes and recordings that are color coded for the partially seeing and have braille notations for the blind.
3. Filmstrips and previewers that low-visioned children can use in dark areas.
4. Science models, such as human organs or systems, accompanied by tapes or cassettes that describe and explain the models.
5. Programmed instructional material with print and characters large enough for the children to see.
6. Standard typewriters for blind children to use in carrying out their written assignments. (Most blind children start to learn touch typing when they reach the fourth grade.)

It is important for the librarian to help the visually handicapped child to know the location of materials and equipment and how to use them. It is even more vital to help in the guidance and personal growth of these children and to assist them in developing good habits of reading for information and as well as for pleasure.

Before the child enters the library for the first time with his peer group, the librarian or an aide should show and explain the layout of the room. The explanation should include such points as the classification and arrangement of print and nonprint materials, the location of special equipment, carrels, the librarian's desk or office and adjacent conference rooms. Many partially seeing students have vision adequate enough to use the card catalog if given occasional assistance by the librarian. Clear speech and specific directions are especially helpful to the child of limited vision.

The child's special teacher should give the librarian pertinent medical information and recommendations concerning factors such as lighting, assessment of vision, and use of optical aids. (In school systems without a special teacher, the classroom teacher must assume this responsibility.)

As the librarian creates an atmosphere of acceptance for all children, the normally sighted will accept and learn how to help the visually handicapped if asked. Moreover, the librarian should expect the visually handicapped to participate in discussions and activities which challenge their abilities. Some children require much motivation and encouragement to hold and promote their interest. They also need much support in developing their ability to progress in school.

The librarian has the opportunity to observe the behavior of children in a variety of learning situations. Thus, he can know when a child becomes fatigued from reading and needs a change of eye focus or when a child needs to move about the room in order to see things clearly. The librarian can guide certain children in selecting books which have specific bibliotherapeutic goals.

The librarian should provide a wide variety of tapes, cassettes and records for the children's use. This will increase their auditory perception and listening skills, and enable them to assimilate much more material than when reading either large type or braille. Young children can dictate stories on tapes rather than writing them.

The librarian's role should vary with partially seeing and blind children. Generally speaking, the partially seeing usually are not as well accepted by others as are the blind. This is probably due to the fact that low vision is not always evident. However, good librarians know that some of these children must hold the reading material very close to their eyes, others walk overcautiously, and still others fail to see objects not directly in their line of vision. Lowenfeld states that the marginal position of the partially seeing manifests itself in their increased anxiety and insecurity as compared with the blind and seeing.[3] Thus, librarians, as well as other school staff members, need to make strenuous efforts to help the partially seeing build a positive self-concept.

Low vision is much more of a handicap to some children than to others. Two children with exactly the same visual acuity often have very different reactions to their handicap. One child may progress satisfactorily in the regular school program, whereas another needs to be assigned to a special education teacher who can give him individual instruction and provide special aids.

However, certain procedures are helpful for all types of low-visioned children:

1. Provisions for a wide variety of books of appropriate difficulty and adapted to the child's needs, and the encouragement of free reading, which is essential if the student is to read with understanding and enjoyment.
2. The selection of reading materials with clear type and illustrations, adequate leading, wide margins,

good quality paper and clear, black type on white or off-white paper.

3. Guidance, especially for young children, in choosing books with type large enough for them to read with ease. Some library books for lower elementary children have large enough type for the partially seeing to read. As these children advance through school, some learn to read regular size type without magnification. Others must use a magnifier.

4. Definite attention to good reading habits with regard to lighting and posture, and allowing certain children to hold the book close to their eyes in order to see the print. Children may need help in finding a place within the room where they can see best.

5. Assistance to the child in using special corrective glasses or low vision aids as instructed by his professional eye specialist.

6. Extra guidance in observation and visual discrimination.

7. Assistance in adjusting the rate of reading to the situation; for example, skimming for general impressions or reading intensively and thoughtfully for evaluation.

8. Plenty of time to complete the reading of a chapter or a book. Partially seeing children usually do both oral and silent reading more slowly (from two to five times) than do other children. Extend the length of time so that a book may be charged out, if necessary.

Most blind children are not totally without vision, but have light perception or light projection, or can recognize nearby gross forms or objects. Some have a limited amount of color vision. Information about extent of vision should be reported by the special teacher to the librarian. Even small amounts of vision help the child in finding his way about the library or materials center.

A blind child should have many more firsthand experiences than other children in order to learn and understand. The child should be encouraged to touch and handle objects; for example, a touch story with shells, stones, and twigs. He should talk and ask questions about them rather than merely listen. This procedure will enable him to develop many more true concepts relating to his environment and thereby help him anticipate ideas as he reads.

Extraneous noises are very distracting to blind children in a study situation. Whenever possible, they should read or work in a quiet part of the room and wear earphones as they listen to recorded material.

In order to save the librarian's time, a blind student who has been assigned considerable research should bring a sighted reader with him to the library. Such a

reader can locate the materials and then read to the student as he takes notes in braille.

Some children who come to the library may have such low vision that they are considered borderline between partially seeing and blind. They are able to read ordinary or large print provided they have sufficient light and use special optical aids. These children may also benefit from reading braille.

The conditions and practices discussed will assist visually handicapped children to adjust, accomplish, and achieve. As the teachers associated with the blind and partially seeing are able to place them in classrooms and libraries having the best physical conditions and well stocked with appropriate instructional materials and children's literature, these children will make steady progress and begin to overcome their academic problems.

NOTES

1. John W. Jones and A. P. Collins, *Educational Programs for Visually Handicapped Children* (Washington, D. C.: Govt. Print. Off., 1966), p. 23.
2. M. A. Tinker, *Legibility of Print* (Ames, Iowa: Iowa State Univ., 1963), p. 265.
3. Berthold Lowenfeld, ed., *The Visually Handicapped Child in the School* (New York: Day, 1973), p. 48.

BIBLIOGRAPHY

Bernardo, Jose R. "Architecture for Blind Persons," *New Outlook for the Blind* 64:262–65 (October 1970).
Cogan, David G. "Lighting, Eyestrain, and Health Hazards," *Sight-Saving Review* 38:73–76 (Summer 1968).
Crouch, C. L. "Comment on 'Lighting, Eyestrain, and Health Hazards,'" *Sight-Saving Review* 38:76–83 (Summer 1968).
Freund, Elizabeth D. "Touch and Learn," *New Outlook for the Blind* 61:223–26 (September 1967).
National Society for the Prevention of Blindness. *Helping the Partially Seeing Child in the Regular Classroom.* New York: The Society, 1965.
Jones, John W., and Collins, A. P. *Educational Programs for Visually Handicapped Children.* Washington, D.C.: Govt. Print. Off., 1966.
Kaufman, John E., ed. *The Standard Lighting Guide.* 5th ed. New York: Illuminating Engineering Society, 1972.
Lowenfeld, Berthold, ed. *The Visually Handicapped Child in the School.* New York: Day, 1973.
Peabody, Ralph L., and Birch, Jack W. "Educational Implications of Partial Vision," *Sight-Saving Review* 37:926 (Summer 1967).
Tinker, M. A. *Legibility of Print.* Ames, Iowa: Iowa State Univ., 1963.

The Hearing Impaired Child in the Library

SR. DORIS BATT

A child who has a hearing problem is a unique individual who looks and acts normally, usually has normal intelligence, but is a child who does not hear. Such a child may enter the library and, unless he* is pointed out or speaks, might not be noticed. A concerned librarian, then, needs to be sensitive to the specialized instructional requirements of this child and plan for appropriate adaptations to the total environment.

A deaf child, or a child with a profound hearing loss, communicates by means of speechreading, sign language, fingerspelling, or a combination of these. Sight is his prime mode of obtaining information; therefore no obstruction between him and a speaker should be permitted, since this diminishes his ability to receive information. A child who has only a partial hearing loss needs to be physically near the speaker when communication is taking place so that he can capitalize on whatever usable hearing he has.

Deafness affects both the child's language acquisition and speech production. A deaf child, who has never heard his mother's voice, cannot speak until he is taught each individual letter and sound first. Every word must be taught through imitation and the tactile method which is a slow process and demands great patience. A child must feel the teacher's face and then try to imitate the various facial movements which cause sounds and words to materialize. There is nothing wrong with a deaf child's vocal chords; he simply does not know how to use them until he is taught. Each word must be taught with pictures, real objects if possible, or direct experience, all of which are interpreted in simple language.

A deaf child coming into the library would understand what was being said through speechreading; that is, looking at the speaker's face, reading his lips, watching his facial expressions, and assigning meaning to these elements. He would have begun to speechread at a very young age, seeing the same word on a teacher's lips hundreds of times before recognizing it or being able to attach meaning to it. Speechreading instruction is more efficient when accompanied by pictures or the real object. Since only 60 percent of what is said can be detected through observation of lip movement, every consideration to maximizing the visibility of the speaker must be given. Anyone speaking to a deaf person must spend time and speak slowly and distinctly, but without exaggerating the facial movements.

*Throughout this article and subsequent ones, the masculine pronoun has been used to refer to students and either the masculine or feminine pronouns to refer to librarians. The usage, then standard, was for succinctness and should be understood to refer to both sexes.—Ed.

The language performance of a deaf child is lower than that of his age peers. His sentence structure is very simple. He cannot grasp long sentences or complex meanings. He cannot express complicated information or make long explanations. The simpler the information and the shorter the explanation, the easier it is for a deaf child to understand.

Usually the hearing impaired child wears a hearing aid. This does not mean that he can understand the sounds that he is able to hear, but it does mean that any sound that is made is picked up and amplified by the hearing aid. Studies seem to indicate that every deaf child has some residual hearing and is capable of having this small amount stimulated. In some cases, a hearing aid helps the child a great deal by increasing the possibility that he will be able to distinguish sufficient sounds to identify separate words. In other cases, the hearing aid merely amplifies sound, enabling the deaf child to hear or feel vibrations, although below the level at which he can distinguish words. The usefulness of such devices varies among individuals depending upon the amount and nature of hearing loss. Therefore, the speaker must deliberately place the child nearby when communicating with him, in order to give him every possible chance of understanding. A deaf child will not hear the speaker if his back is turned; eye contact must be established before any message or communication with him can occur.

With this background information, the librarian can proceed to consider those physical components of a library which would help a deaf child experience success and gratification through his library experiences.

When the deaf child comes to the library for a story hour, the librarian should be aware of his problem and of the techniques of communicating with him. She must be sure he is sitting directly in front of her at eye level. It is difficult for any child to continually have to stretch his neck to see. The light should be shining on the librarian's face, not the child's, since her face must be well lighted and as visible as possible. If there are windows in the library, the librarian should so position herself that the child is not facing the windows. The light should be coming over the child's shoulder. If there are no windows, artificial lighting should be sufficiently bright and glare-free. Fluorescent lighting is preferred. Drapes are often used to keep out bright sunlight and minimize glare, as well as to provide acoustical control.

Story hours need not necessarily be restricted to books. Filmstrips, movies, slides, records, tapes, and video materials may also be used. When filmstrips or slides are used the room is usually in darkness. The librarian must be sensitive to the visual needs of the speechreader in her group. As mentioned previously, she should be facing the child with a light on her face and hands. Enough light may be reflected on the face of a person sitting or standing next to a projection screen so that additional illumination is unnecessary. If there is any need for communication, the speaker would be in position to be seen, and the deaf child could readily turn to her for further comment. The opaque projector is often used to show pictures in a book to hearing children but has serious limitations for use with the auditorily handicapped child. Its use requires almost total darkness and unfortunate positioning of the librarian in relation to the projected image and the child. The overhead projector is the preferred equipment since it can be used in a fully lighted room with the librarian standing in front of the children and adjacent to the screen.

Acoustical problems always arise when accommodating the needs of a deaf person. Carpeted rooms are better than those with wood or tile floors. Carpets absorb sounds, reduce noise levels and enhance the deaf child's ability to pick up speech sounds. Acoustical ceilings and wall baffles are recommended when additional sound control is desirable. Squeaky floor boards, noisy chairs, or shuffling feet are distractions and such extraneous sounds should be eliminated whenever possible. Music should not be played in the background since a deaf person finds it very difficult to distinguish between background sound and the important message. Because of the exhausting effort required to hear, the child will often seek relief by excluding all sounds. Auditory communication should not take place under a balcony or near posts, as there is a great possibility that vibrations or echoes would interfere with comprehension. The deaf person has difficulty following a conversation because the speaker changes continually within a group. By the time he finds out who is speaking, much of the message is over and he soon begins to get discouraged. Group members should be made aware of the deaf child's problem and encouraged to include him whenever possible.

The library should be located in a quiet area of the school where there is little distraction because of noise. An ideal setup within a library would be to have the entire room amplified by means of audiometric equipment known as loops. When utilizing the loop system, the teacher wears a microphone connected to an amplifier. The child, using his hearing aid, is able to pick up sounds through the looped room or area. Since many libraries have found a multitude of applications for the loop system for nondeaf children, such systems will be in increased usage and thus available to both populations. It is possible for the librarian to have an auditory trainer or a piece of audiometric equipment on a table in front of her and have the deaf child wear earphones in order to hear the amplified sound. This has helped considerably when only one or two children within the group were deaf.

There are now available in many libraries sections devoted to different media. One corner may have tables set up with audio equipment where individuals can go,

put on earphones and listen to stories without disturbing others. Can a deaf child gain by this? It depends on the amount of hearing deprivation each child has, but with pictures, with the book in which to follow along, and with guidance, a child can take advantage of this material to some extent.

Libraries also have study carrels where filmstrip projectors are set up along with viewers, video screens, 8mm movies, and earphones. This arrangement gives the individual child an opportunity to learn independently and at his own pace. Students can become much more involved in research and study through mediated instruction. The hub of education often centers around the library. It is the information center of the school and as such must be made available to every student.

If the librarian is aware of the techniques needed to work with a deaf child, the child will grow in his learning capacity because of all the resources abundantly available to him. Face to face story hour need not then be the totality of the library program for him.

To instruct any child in library skills is an important job of teacher and librarian. This can be accomplished through prominently displayed charts and posters or by the use of a multitude of instructional aids designed for this purpose. A deaf child has critical informational needs and thorough knowledge of reference tools is essential for his academic success.

The librarian must be cognizant of safety procedures for the deaf child. Warning bells for fire drills may go unheeded. Flashing red lights should supplement bells or buzzers. When extraordinary circumstances arise, the librarian must take into account the needs of her exceptional children. Attention to the special procedures, both in crises and in daily practice will insure a safe, stimulating, and fulfilling library experience.

Library Adaptations for the Handicapped

RUTH A. VELLEMAN

Recent developments in the education of exceptional children have placed emphasis on the necessity of bringing a much larger number of these children into the mainstream than had been thought possible in the past. It is an indisputable fact that school and public libraries are indispensable to the educational process. However, libraries must be architecturally designed to be accessible to disabled students.

The sole aim of this article, therefore, is to describe

the architectural adaptations incorporated in the Human Resources School Library, with the hope that many of these ideas will be helpful to both school and public libraries planning to change their present facilities to better accommodate the disabled.

The Human Resources School in Albertson, Long Island, has over 200 students with physical disabilities and special health problems. The school is one of the few which offer a nursery through grade-twelve program with a full academic high school curriculum leading to college or advanced vocational training. In his book, *The School* (Erikson, 1964), the school's founder, Henry Viscardi, Jr., recorded the story of its beginnings. The development and goals of the Human Resources School Library have been described by the author in articles printed in *School Library Journal* (September 1966), *Rehabilitation Literature* (May 1971), and *School Libraries* (Summer 1971).

In designing the library, the primary objective was to demonstrate that disabled children do not need extensive adaptation of the normal environment in order to function successfully. Necessary adaptations are based upon the fact that many disabled students are in wheelchairs and will have trouble reaching the lowest as well as the highest library shelves. High pile carpeting, narrow doors, steps or door sills, and a cluttered floor plan will impede the mobility of wheelchairs.

Room Facilities

The Human Resources School Library is a warm, comfortable, centrally located room. Central location enables all students to reach the library easily. An attractive wood burning fireplace, the focal point of the room, provides a pleasant background for story hours. A picture window offers a view of the interior greenhouse adjacent to the science laboratory. The library thus avoids being a confining enclosure by offering an open atmosphere—a feeling which is important to children who spend much time confined at home.

The size of the library has more than doubled as a result of recent expansion. This enabled us to remodel it to create a true school library media center. One section of wall opposite the greenhouse window has been eliminated providing a large L-shaped area. At the end of the enlarged area are windows, one of which has been converted into a door leading to a patio which is used on good days for storytelling. Another window has been reduced to a height of 18 inches from the floor so that wheelchair-bound students can look out.

Shelving Requirements

Perimeter wall shelving is most desirable for wheelchair students. When book stacks are used it must be remembered that at least 30 inches and preferably 5 feet of space between stacks is needed to permit passage of wheelchairs. In Human Resources School Library walnut perimeter wall shelving has been combined with free-standing yellow steel shelving with wood end panels.

The enlarged library is now wide enough to permit the aisle shelving to create alcoves for multilevel individualized and group work. Shelves are staggered and spaced 15 feet apart, permitting an 8-foot center aisle area.

Experience has taught us that the lowest shelves are difficult for the wheelchair bound students to reach, therefore aisle shelving is the standard T-base shelving obtainable from all library furniture suppliers. A height of 5 feet for book shelves should not be exceeded, although in many cases this may not be practical because of space limitations. Multicolored, free-standing 3-foot high steel book shelving is arranged in an L around the fireplace to delineate the storytelling area.

Furniture

Library furniture consists of three 29-inch high apronless tables, an optimum height to accommodate wheelchairs. A 23-inch high primary table accommodates groups of young children in smaller wheelchairs. No special furniture is required since any table can be used with wheelchair-bound students as long as they do not have wide aprons or pedestal leg supports. While some wheelchair students prefer to sit on regular chairs, most remain in their wheelchairs. When serving a large wheelchair population it is not feasible to have more than half the number of chairs ordinarily required in the library. Occasionally, an older student of small stature will find low stools at the primary table useful.

Whenever a student is limited by an exceptional disability, a special standing box or small table can be used. Although no other special furniture is needed, librarians can work with the administration, parents and medical staff to provide specialized equipment for specific needs.

Card Catalog

The most important piece of equipment in the library is, of course, the card catalog, a 12- or 15-drawer cabinet placed on a wood or aluminum frame base. In order to make the card catalog low enough to be completely accessible to students in wheelchairs, one section can be placed on a special 16-inch-high base. This can be made to order by any library furniture supplier. Extra drawers must be provided by adding another base and placing the card catalogs side by side, rather than on top of each other. Space does become a problem when several cabinets are needed. However, complete accessibility of the information in the card catalog to handicapped students can be achieved by using the 16-inch high base consistently.

Storage

Expanded library space has allowed for an additional storage area for our hardware and software media collection. Software is stored in standard commercial cabinets and open record cases. The only unusual features are low bases without crossbars for cabinets to make them completely accessible.

One 12-foot wide wall has specially built cabinets to house all media hardware. These cabinets consist of wide closet areas where 16mm and overhead projectors on portable stands can be stored. Shelving provides space for smaller items like filmstrip and filmloop projectors, cassette and reel-to-reel tape recorders and record players. While only some students in wheelchairs are able to wheel 16mm projectors to classrooms, most can check out and carry smaller pieces of equipment.

To display periodicals with the greatest possible accessibility, wall panels with extending individual periodical holders have been hung at optimum height to suit special needs of our population. In order to conserve space and for easy access, back issues of periodicals are on microfiche. Standard microfiche readers with average to high lens magnification can be easily used by students who have full or partial hand use. Two-drawer lateral files which are most accessible to wheelchair-bound students are used to house vertical file material.

Other Work Areas

The book preparation area has been expanded to include work space for servicing media production equipment. Low apronless counters accommodate students in wheelchairs. A sink in the corner of this area has been made accessible by placing the drain at the back of the sink and cutting away the cabinet below it.

The media area of the library is equipped with an overhead screen and four wet carrels. These commercially made carrels were purchased in 48-inch widths rather than the usual 36-inch width to allow comfortable leg space for wheelchair-bound students.

Special Features

The floor is covered with an institutional-grade tackless acrylic carpet which has a tight weave (looped through the back) and a thick jute backing. No padding is used and the carpet is cemented to the floor. This floor covering is most advantageous to both the wheelchair population and those ambulatory students who use crutches and braces. For libraries without carpeting, a nonskid vinyl floor covering is desirable.

Thresholds consist of metal strips with gripper edges to provide level entrances into the library. Doors should be light-weight and should have see-through panels, lever handles rather than knobs, and kick-plates. Human Resources School is experimenting with double swinging library doors with one side the entrance (swinging in) and one the exit (swinging out). When funds are available, electric-eye doors, preferably side-sliding, are best for a wheelchair population. Other features include light switches at lower than usual height.

Temperature

Since Human Resources School is air-conditioned, the library does not have a problem with temperature control. This is an important factor. Some students are highly susceptible to respiratory illnesses and it is desirable to avoid drafts and extreme temperatures.

Equipment Needs

Modifications in equipment for disabled students are minimal in cases where students have some hand control. For students with arm and hand disabilities, automatic page turners or reading stands may be required but it has been our experience that automatic page turners are relatively expensive and not very successful. For students whose arm or hand disabilities are not so severe as to require automatic page turners, publications of the American Heart Association and the British Red Cross Society include descriptions of inexpensive ways of constructing page turning equipment. More expensive commercial models are listed in *Reading Aids for the Handicapped,* prepared by the Association of Hospital and Institution Libraries of the American Library Association. This publication also lists reading aids such as talking books, large-print books and magnifiers for visually impaired students. *Aids to Independent Living* by Edward Lowman and Judith Klinger has sections on reading aids and special furniture. In its new library/media program, Human Resources School will be experimenting with portable, lightweight filmstrip projectors and cassette recorders which can be sent home with students along with nonbook curriculum materials.

Student Assistance

When handling a class of disabled students it is sometimes helpful to employ the buddy system, allowing ambulatory students to assist those in wheelchairs, and pairing students having good hand control with those with minimal hand usage. Group research can best be handled by removing the drawers of the card catalog and placing them on tables to avoid a crush of wheelchair traffic.

Make Your Library Accessible

Minimal architectural and room adaptations plus common sense will enable disabled students to participate in library activities which may otherwise be inaccessible to them. Most of the suggestions in this article can be incorporated into any traditional school library.

BIBLIOGRAPHY

American National Standards Institute. *Specifications for Making Buildings and Facilities Accessible to and Usable by the Physically Handicapped.* New York: The Institute, 1961.
Association of Hospital and Institution Libraries. *Reading Aids for the Handicapped.* Chicago: American Library Association, 1968.
Hoffman, Ruth B. *How to Build Special Furniture and Equipment for Handicapped Children.* Springfield, Ill.: Charles C. Thomas, 1970.
Lowman, Edward, and Klinger, Judith L. *Aids to Independent Living: Self-Help for the Handicapped.* New York: McGraw-Hill, 1969.

Creating Environments for Learning

HENRY W. RAY

The environment is a critical factor in determining what we can do toward helping children learn.

If we conceive of education or learning as primarily the memorization of information, the traditional "boxes" that have been the basic unit for learning or instruction are probably adequate for many children. If education is to carry children more deeply into stimulating their senses, arousing curiosity, stimulating inquiry and helping them to achieve significant perceptual growth, then the learning environment should be designed with such objectives in mind. The learning environment should contribute considerably to the achievement of the objectives.

Reprinted by permission from *The American Annals of the Deaf* 113:1076–85 (Nov. 1968).

In an attempt to improve education, many schools have been designed and built which, rather than focusing upon problems of learning and self-actualization, focus upon solving administration problems. We have so-called campus schools which are intended to house children from primary education through secondary education. We have schools where the classrooms are organized in clusters. We have schools with triangular shaped rooms. We have schools without interior walls separating classes. The variations are many. But the real environment, the environment the child encounters and which does much to shape his curriculum, is changed very little from what it has been for many years—not that men have not dreamed, designed and built exciting stimulating environments for learning. The world fairs, such as Expo and the recent New York World Fair, provided numerous examples. The IBM Building with its elevating "people wall" and multiscreen projections, the United States Building which mechanically moved you through a visualization of our country's history, The New York State Building with its 360° panorama motion pictures, and, at Expo, Labrynth, the Czechoslovakia Building, and Kaleidescope were unique. What do these kinds of ideas have to do with child development and learning?

The armed forces have been long noted for innovations in training. The Naval Devices Training Center at Port Washington, New York, has a facility for projecting an image which encompasses a large segment of a visual environment. The screen is a 22-foot diameter hemisphere, vertically standing. The projection material is taken and projected with a wide angle lens. Imagine, if you will, the inclusion in a school building of at least one room having this feature.

A variation of this scheme is used at the Fleischmann Atmospherium-Planetarium in Reno, Nevada, which is operated by the University of Nevada. In this room a projector equipped with a fisheye lens projects a hemispherical image. The original material, of course, would be taken with a fisheye lens.

Another type room utilizes the imagery reflected off a polished sphere located at floor level in the center of the planetarium. The original image is photographed off a similar sphere—consequently the camera is always a part of the picture. Students in the School of Architecture in the University of North Carolina were experimenting with this idea two years ago.

Another room which made possible the projection of a full circle of environment utilizes several motion picture projectors each of which projects part of an environment or situation. . . . In the United States an example of this idea can be seen in Disneyland. Eleven projectors convey to the audience a more complete feeling for the content being experienced. The idea was used at Expo and at the New York World Fair. One of the significant aspects of these special rooms and the experiences they provide is that the participant becomes really immersed or involved in the experience. There is a feeling of being in it.

In Warminster, Pennsylvania, a new elementary school was needed to relieve the pressure from the rapidly increasing population. The school district has special classes scattered about the district to meet the needs of the physically handicapped, slow learners, trainable and academically talented children. A decision was made to build a school which would centralize in one building all of these groups with the addition of attendance by the average student residing in the school area. The school environment was planned in great detail by teachers, special consultants, administrators, and the architect. The design which emerged and was constructed was based upon three learning centers. One center is a cafeteria/auditorium. Another center is a library. The third center is a special experience room. Each center has classrooms on the perimeter.

The design of the special experience room was the result of asking ourselves the question "What kind of a room would you want in order to do some desirable things with children that our present classroom designs do not permit?"

One desire was much more flexibility for the projection of images. For one thing, it was desirable to be able to project images on four walls simultaneously, thus, giving the child a better sense of environments and relationships existing in all environments. What is it like, for example, to be surrounded by sand dunes, or tropical forest, or great plains? A single, flat picture whether projected or not does not convey this kind of information. Or to be able to project and keep in view contrasting environments—one on each wall space—so that the student could observe for himself the differences that can be perceived in a variety of environments.

We wanted a ceiling projection area too. More of our environment than we realize is above our eye level. Our final design permits unlimited exploration of the overhead dimension.

We are interested in exploring verticality as a visual learning experience. Anyone who has stood at the base of a giant redwood tree, or the Washington Monument, or a city skyscraper and let his eyes move from the base to the top of the structure understands why this is a concern.

We had many other concerns in planning our special experience center. Our room will permit us to let images move. For example—a film shows a sea gull soaring over the water behind a ferry boat. The gull is sometimes high above the deck of the boat, and at other times it may be near the surface of the water. Given almost unlimited projection surface, our bird will no longer flap its wings within the confines of a relatively small screen. He can move freely about the room.

Our environment will permit projecting the northern or southern hemisphere as a map with the child inside the world looking out. We can project images simultaneously on this map hemisphere which demonstates some of the common dimensions of humanity. As an example, the small business man—the man with the cart—is a world wide phenomena. In Philadelphia he may be selling pretzels, in England oranges, in Afghanistan slices of sugar beet, in Japan turnips, in San Francisco flowers. Brought together as a unified idea, such experiences might help us achieve a higher level of humanism in education.

Our room will permit us to provide new experiences which might be helpful to children whose learning is impeded because of basic perceptual problems. As an example, how can a child be helped who cannot perceive embedded figures. Utilizing our projection facilities we plan to project slides in series which, starting with a simple well-known shape such as a cup, retains the cup figure in all slides, but each new slide in the series embeds the figure until in the final slide the cup is a deeply embedded figure. The point to be made is that each slide in the series can be held on the projection area after it is presented so that the child can go back and reinforce his imagery as necessary.

A number of loud speakers are spaced around the room and over the dome. We want sound to travel as well as images.

Odors can be sprayed into the room adding the sense of smell to certain learning experiences—if we can find a source of odors. You may recall the unique presentation of sight and smell the Coca-Cola exhibit offered at the New York World Fair.

Limited climate control will be possible. We will experiment with situations where heat, as in a southwestern desert or Florida subtropical forest, might be a significant factor in the overall perception of an environment.

School systems which have built planetariums with fixed furniture and fixed planetarium instrument and console have shortchanged themselves in terms of their ability to provide a broad range of learning experiences. I would like to see projected images low enough that children could touch them—at least the lower section of the projection.

We have not really advanced very far in our thinking concerning learning environments, whether they be for the common masses of students or those who have some physical and mental handicaps. In the special experience room, conditions are more ideal than most students in these groups have experienced. The trainable child, for example, will have an environment where some basic living skills can be experienced.

We need to search industry and technology and relate our findings to a more meaningful learning experience for all children. What can we do with foam rubber and plastics? Can the light transmission qualities of lucite be utilized to trigger lagging perception in seemingly hopeless learning cases?

What about the furnishings in the new environment? Unique items might be constructed of thin sheet plastic that are inflatable. We have available on the commercial market inflatable boats, inflatable furniture and inflatable works of sculpture.

It would be good to have rooms in which one entire wall is a rear projection screen. It would serve not only as an image transmitter but would lend itself to some unique shadow play experiences which could have great learning potential. Mixed images could be projected providing unusual perception stimulation and learning experiences.

Again speaking of furnishings—a teacher in Abington, Pennsylvania, secured one of the chairs used by Bell Telephone in their exhibit at the New York Fair. These chairs really "embraced" you—and had loud speakers on each side through which the exhibit was explained as one rode through in the chair.

Planning the environment to create the maximum learning opportunity for the child must also include full consideration of what the teaching-learning process activities will be.

A recent publication by the Georgia Department of Education states that the modern social science teacher will need facilities to plan, prepare and present:

assembly programs	guest speakers
bulletin board activities	illustrated lectures
cartoons	interviews
charts	lectures
class discussion	maps
club activities	models
collections	music
committee work	newspaper reading
debates	clippings
diagrams	discussions
dramatizations	notebooks
essays	objects, specimens
exhibits	outlines
field trips	pageants
floor talks	panels
forums	pictures
graphs	poems
posters	project charts
radio	readings
recordings	reports
simple visual aids	slogans
socio-dramas	sound filmstrips
sound motion films	stories

summarizations	surveys
television	tests[1]
time lines	

Most of the items on this list have environmental implications. If each area of learning were analyzed, unique requirements would be identified which should be considered in designing and building classrooms.

Buckminster Fuller had this to say about the learning environment, "With knowledge from today's behavioral science studies and the electrical exploration of the brain we have found that, if given the right environment and thoughtful answers to its questions, the child has everything it needs educationally from birth. It is possible to design environments within which the child will be neither frustrated nor hurt, yet free to develop spontaneously and fully without trespassing on others."[2]

Finally, attention is called to an article appearing in the *Saturday Review,* the issue of January 20, 1968.[3] The article, "The Chemistry of Learning," describes the effects of environment upon the problem solving power and brain growth of rats. The rats were placed in psychologically stimulating environments and in psychologically pallid environments. The rats in the innovative environment demonstrated greater problem solving ability and growth in brain weight than the rats in non-stimulating environments.

If so much can be done for the rats—what limits can we justifiably place upon ourselves in our thinking toward implementing the development and self-actualization of the child placed in our care?

NOTES

1. Georgia Department of Education, *The Social Science Laboratory* (Atlanta, Ga.: The Department, 1967).

2. Buckminster Fuller, *Conversations on the Arts* (Harrisburg, Pa.: Department of Public Instruction, 1967).

3. David Krech, "The Chemistry of Learning," *The Saturday Review* 51:48–50, 68 (20 Jan. 1968).

Media in the Round—Learning in the Special Experience Room

REBECCA F. DAILEY

A group of kindergarten children enter the large circular room with a domed ceiling. They sit in hushed anticipation on the carpeted floor, each child holding

Reprinted from *Teaching Exceptional Children* 4: 4–9 (1971) by permission of The Council for Exceptional Children. Copyright 1971 by the Council for Exceptional Children.

an unshelled peanut. The teacher turns on a projector and the screen—not just a regular 50-inch square screen but the entire 360 degree wall—becomes a maze of colors.

"Where are we?" the teacher asks, and the students watch intensely as she brings the projected image into sharper focus. Using their perceptions and imagination, the children enthusiastically offer their ideas:

"We're under the sea," suggests a dark haired boy. Then, remembering the peanut, "We're at a peanut factory!"

Carefully scrutinizing the colorful blur, a girl states, "I think we're in a grocery store."

As the picture grows more distinct, vague animal forms are detected.

"We're in a jungle!"

"It's a zoo!"

Seeing clearer forms of clowns and tents, several children exclaim in unison, "A circus, a circus!"

The children are surrounded with varying scenes of the circus. Sounds of circus music and noisy crowds permeate the room. The children continue to identify both visual forms and the sources of sound. "It even smells like a circus!" one boy triumphantly shrieks.

Learning experiences such as this occur daily in the Special Experience Room of the Everett A. McDonald Comprehensive Elementary School in Warminster, Pennsylvania. The school includes children with a wide range of educational abilities: physically handicapped, mentally retarded, learning disabled, and academically talented in addition to a large section of regular classes of children from the surrounding neighborhood. Supported in part by an ESEA Title III grant, the comprehensive school revolves around three learning centers— the library, an auditorium-gymnasium, and a unique room where sensory experiences form the core of the curriculum.

The creation of this Special Experience Room is largely the result of Henry Ray's concern with the development of children's perceptual abilities. Dr. Ray, the director of Teaching and Learning Resources for the Centennial School District, recognized the need for simulating a child's environment in order to provide him with sensory learning experiences which were previously impossible in the traditional classroom setting. An interview with Dr. Ray was conducted regarding the design and purposes of the Special Experience Room.

What are the unique aspects of the Special Experience Room? Dr. Ray: The room is circular, 40 feet in diameter, with a hemispheric dome. The floor is carpeted and contains no fixed furniture—instead, it contains movable back rests for the children to lean against. The entire wall above a couple of feet from the floor is projection area so that we have extreme flexibility in where we project images, how we project them, and the

number of multiple projections of an image which are possible. The room has climate control; that is, we can drop or raise the temperature of the room quite rapidly through the use of a very heavy duty air conditioning unit. The room also contains odor ducts through which smells from a variety of environments—bakery, stable, circus—can be introduced. We have sound equipment also—and the acoustics in the room are unusually good.

The room contains a planetarium instrument which can be lowered completely below the floor to permit full use of the floor space. The instrument is a very sophisticated one, allowing the observer to be on the moon looking back at the earth, as well as being on the earth looking out into space. We use basic equipment, such as carousel projectors, overhead projectors, lantern slide projectors, super 8 film, 16mm film. It's nothing exotic in terms of remote access or some of the more sophisticated types of recovery of imagery. Four lantern slide projectors together create the 360° projections.

None of our work is tied into tape-signal sort of things, because we find we need a lot of flexibility in using the projectors. We may have a program on transportation, for example. The timing or sequence of the projections would need to vary according to the needs of the particular group watching. Every mechanism of the Special Experience Room must be manually operated. A lot of people misunderstand this. They see the elaborate looking equipment and think we simply press a button and then sit back and watch our automatic program of slides and sound being absorbed by the kids. We maintain the flexibility of manual operation, because we want to use the room according to the needs of the kids—not program the kids to fit the design of the room. A major concern is to get the kids involved in the vision and sound experience. Kids do much of the talking. We raise questions for them, and so on, but it's a child-centered kind of thing. It's learning by inquiry and discovery.

Children often design the programs themselves. For example, one of the groups here was studying poverty, and they decided to do a project of visualization contrasting poverty and affluence. They went through hundreds of magazines and found pictures that symbolized both conditions. They tape recorded their own feelings about the two contrasting conditions to create certain background sounds.

Many of the high school students in the area have designed program content. The Special Experience Room is used by all the schools—elementary, junior high, and senior high—in the district.

How did the idea for the Special Experience Room develop? Dr. Ray: About 15 years ago, I became increasingly more concerned about the relationship between environment and learning. I became sensitive to how different environments change according to one's perspective. Things change even if you turn your head slightly. And I had a number of experiences where maybe I had seen a picture of say, the Eiffel Tower, but when I went to Paris and I saw it, it was so different, primarily because of the dynamics of the environment. And so I began wishing that in working with children I could show them pretty much all the visual information of the environment, show them the dynamics of the relationships—a perceptual context of things existent.

So when this comprehensive school was being planned, I brought up the idea that I had been harboring. At that time, however, it was a square room with stereophonic sound and a capacity for ceiling projections. I would have been very happy to have any kind of room that was unencumbered with bookcases and windows so the projection space could be large. Our superintendent, Dr. Everett McDonald, became very excited about the idea. He is a very creative person who has the philosophy that those people who have the jobs and are involved in the school should contribute to the planning.

What is the primary objective of the Special Experience Room? Dr. Ray: If I had to sum up a purpose using only a few words, it would be to increase a child's perception—and I use perception in a very broad sense, including social, environmental, and self-perceptions as well as more specific perceptions of color and shape. At this school we have what are considered by many as very elaborate facilities and equipment, but the idea behind it is the important thing. I think that any school can come within a reasonable approximation of the same kinds of things. The room isn't the key so much as having some place to project images effectively.

Of course, with the size of our projections, a child gets the feeling of actually being there instead of just looking at a picture. But in a regular classroom, you can project an image large enough so that a child can perform our shadow lessons, for example, which I'll tell you about later.

Also, rooms similar to the Special Experience Room can be created with far less expense. I know of a school in backwoods Appalachia in which a room incorporating the same ideas as ours was remodeled for about $7,000. A wooden frame was covered with canvas, and projectors were installed to poke through the canvas. The floor was carpeted and free of furniture.

The most important aspect of your program is not the design of the room but the idea of projecting visual images? Dr. Ray: It's not even the visual idea. It's a different educational philosophy. Unfortunately, for too long we've concentrated on the learning of facts as the focus of education. We have worshiped print. Too many schools are still *containment centers,* designed to house students while they memorize facts and figures. Many classrooms rely solely on print-verbal learning resources, teacher domination, and maintaining order.

What about developing awareness and sensitivity? Learning facts doesn't develop your powers of being human. In great literature, for example, it is not the absorption of the content facts that is important. More significant is the imagery, understanding, and emotions which the author can evoke. If we're going to develop the power to communicate in our children, we must work on the kinds of sensory and psychological elements that represent this communication power. Creativity and aesthetic appreciation are as important as the ability to add and subtract. We, as educators, have often verbalized this belief in the last few years—when are we going to permit our planning and budgeting to reflect it? This room is more important in terms of educational attitude than as a showplace for instructional technology.

What kinds of programs do you have? Dr. Ray: We have over 200 programs presently which have been developed by teachers, students, members of the project staff, and myself according to individual needs and problems. The programs are extremely varied in terms of both content and approach. For example, the complexity may range from a simple concept such as color awareness to an advanced unit on astronomy.

Let me tell you about some representative lessons. The development of a child's perceptual motor coordination can be enhanced through the use of flashlights on a darkened wall. The teacher (or another student) can project a light spot and have the children direct their individual beams of light onto the moving target. Another type of lesson involves shadows. The projection of a single light source in the center of an otherwise completely dark room enables the children to create and observe their own shadows. Concepts such as what causes shadows, differences in perspective (the closer to the projector, the larger the shadow), and effects of pantomime are only a few of the learning experiences possible with shadows.

A number of lessons on cultural study have been prepared with the primary purpose of contrasting and comparing cultures through the use of visual clues. For example, one lesson depicts variations in transportation in Afghanistan, Thailand, Hong Kong, and the United States. Music of the cultures is used, and the children are instructed that since they cannot speak the languages they must rely solely on what they see and hear. This experience can generate a number of activities such as the students writing letters "home" describing the cultures.

Visual imagery and symbology are developed through the study of projected slides of cloud formations, aerial views, and reflections and patterns seen in nature. From these, students can make comparisons with other natural phenomena, familiar objects, or mythological characters. Students are also instructed to visualize the setting or mood suggested by sounds or music in a darkened room. In addition, auditory discrimination can be developed through identifying changing sources of sound.

Another type of visual approach is to use a series of drawings which begin with a very incomplete image, say only two lines, and progress in steps to become the complete figure. Series of slides can also be used to teach sequencing and problem solving. For example, a series of four slides showing various stages of the setting sun can be incorrectly ordered to develop the child's concept of sequence. Teaching categorization and relationships —such as similarities and differences—is achieved through a limitless number of imagery lessons.

The curriculum development effort at the school has four major areas of objectives: information content (geography, history, science, math, spelling, literature), affective content (humanities, expression, creation, responsibility, self-actualization), skills content (technical writing, reading, numbers, language, listening, physical, problem solving, perception, memory), and recreation content (creativity, reading, theater, television, games, discussion).

The quality and scope of the lessons we use are a reflection of the commitment and ability of our project staff and teachers. If we conceive of education as the memorization of information, then the traditional methods that have been the basic unit for instruction are probably adequate. But if education is to increase sensory awareness, curiosity and inquiry development, and perceptual growth, then the learning environment and teaching objectives must be designed toward such objectives.

In recent attempts to improve education, many schools have been designed to focus more on alleviating administrative problems than problems of learning. We have variations of new school designs—campus schools, clustered classrooms, nongraded classes, and so on. But the real learning environment which the child encounters and which does much to shape his curriculum has changed very little from what it has been for many years.

Today, more than ever before, print is not the primary vehicle to learning. Approaches such as those used here more realistically reflect the needs of our children in the 70s.

PART 2

Selection Criteria: The Determinants of Choice

Librarians review a number of aspects of the school program as decisions are made in the selection of materials. Are these materials supportive of the academic program? Are they geared to the interests and capabilities of the school population accommodating both extremes of the ability spectrum? Is provision made for both breadth and depth in coverage of topics? Is the selection policy sufficiently flexible to be responsive to changes in user population and curriculum? Is consideration given to the recreational reading desires of the students? Is balance provided within budgetary restrictions? In sum, the librarian must conceptualize the total process: decisions relating to which book or medium to select for a child or a group must be made in tandem with a tentative plan for how it shall be used.

Additional considerations must be made in the selection of materials for exceptional children. Sensory, physical, emotional, and intellectual impairments interfere with the normal acquisition of knowledge. The experiential background which the handicapped child brings to school is often severely limited. Materials should be considered which address themselves to the modalities through which the child learns best and which compensate insofar as possible for the deprivations affecting his or her life. Materials should be evaluated for their motivational qualities, their multisensory components, their interest/ability ratio, their attention-span requirements, and their relationship to life styles. Visual considerations should be as significant as textual ones; clearly both elements should be age-appropriate.

Material selection in schools serving nonexceptional children is a relatively simple process. There is an abundance of selection tools and aids, the librarian has been educated to assess the needs of these children and the characteristics of the materials, and there is generally an abundance of items to choose from on almost every topic. A different situation exists when the librarian needs to select materials for the exceptional child. In some areas, the librarian is relatively well served. In recent years, many publishers have developed quantities of high-interest/low-ability materials which are useful in meeting the needs of retarded children. Lists abound of these materials and they are reviewed in many readily available journals. However, materials serving other disability populations are not reviewed as extensively, nor are they as widely available.

A variety of materials have been developed for some disabilities, e.g., the learning disabled, but they are classroom-specific, developed primarily for instructional purposes and thus not entirely suitable for library usage. Publication of large-print books has increased dramatically in recent years but the supply is still inadequate to meet minimal library demands. Selection for the gifted presents a particular challenge due to the frequently noted discrepancy between their social and emotional development on the one hand and their intellectual attainments and interests on the other.

Many educators feel that undue attention to the needs of the gifted is evidence of elitism and is therefore undemocratic, a bias which fortunately many librarians do not hold. Clearly, lack of attention to these exceptional children is a deprivation of their educational rights and needs. Usually, children with high abilities function fairly independently in the library; nevertheless the librarian should not abrogate the responsibilities of reading guidance in relation to them. The librarian will need to evaluate the reading styles, interests, and patterns of highly literate students and consider such moves as introducing them to useful source books and reference tools if they are ready, providing them with academically provocative books which stimulate them to reevaluate their thinking, and suggesting the independent use or production of media to reexamine an issue from a new perspective.

The high-ability child represents a population group which will probably not be as heavily affected by the mainstreaming phenomenon as other users. That is, they have been coming to the library for a long time. However, it is felt by many that these children have been underserved in the school and that this is a chronic, rather than a new, situation. Materials which illuminate and expand horizons need to be tactfully suggested; and literature and nonfiction which specifically tap into the gifted child's often well-developed abilities in humor and divergent thinking should be considered in the selection process.

Special mention should be made of one other group: children with learning disabilities. They are included in this section but are not represented quantitatively as much as other groups with special needs. Relevant information about the specific implications of learning disability and the library program are rare. To a large degree, this is a consequence of the relative newness of research and writing in this field. With the explosion of infor-

mation in this area, the librarian should be alert to forthcoming data about these children which will assist in the selection process. This is a particularly challenging situation since many of these children cannot read, yet test at average or above average levels.

Informed judgment about the implications of the disability as an instructionally significant entity as well as the uniqueness of the child is a sine qua non in the selection process. That is, the librarian should be aware of what learning implications (as a class defect) are imposed on the child automatically as a result of the problem. The nurse, psychologist, or child's homeroom teacher will be able to share information in those aspects of the disability which might impinge on the process of selecting appropriate materials.

Obviously, a prime source to consult in choosing materials is the affected child. The interests, needs, and skills of the child are often similar to those of age peers, but in many cases, these users differ greatly either as a function of their disability or as a result of their unique educational history. We do these children, particularly the older ones, a grave injustice when we exclude them from participating in the selection process.

It is clear that social attitudes, belief systems, and other external criteria impact on the selection policies of librarians. It is vital to examine these antecedents to selection to ascertain if choices are determined by user need or by selector bias. Preconception on the part of the selector is a deadly danger and inimical to the growth and maturation of the disabled user. When these decisions are made without regard for the prime needs of the reader, the library acts to undervalue the human needs of the special child.

Grannis deals with the issue of proscription in print and media selection and joins Kvaraceus in implying that the librarian should not arbitrarily impose moral judgment about the requisites of members of this group.

Grannis opposes those patronizing book selection policies which seek to protect the blind reader from tension-producing knowledge as well as from exposure to situations to which he or she could presumably not aspire. Thus, instead of opening up the constricted world of the blind, the censorious librarian acts as an inhibiting agent. Clearly, the blind may have difficulty in dealing with the content of some books—but so will their age peers. Such a protectionist book-selection policy is based on a cynical presumption on the part of the selector, namely that the presence of visual impairment is ipso facto evidence that the handicapped person will be excluded from the need to come to terms with such human problems as friendship, competition, loneliness, sexuality, and social conflict. If librarians operate with these preconceived formulations, it will diminish their ability to provide guidance, will restrict the options of the blind readers involved, and will prevent the development of open, humanistic relationships. Grannis discounts the possibility that the blind may have unique needs or demands which should be considered in book selection and implies that their content needs are identical to those of sighted users.

Although Johnson's article is limited to describing a single program, it is highly instructive to the perceptive librarian or teacher who is confronted with the reluctant, resistant student. The author addresses an omnipresent critical issue: when we add the numbers of students who won't read to those who can't, we have a sizable segment of the student population in many secondary schools. Data from numerous studies support the contention that adolescents resist reading because they remain unconvinced of the potential of the printed work to relate in any meaningful way to the world they know. Johnson astutely extracts from the adolescent culture that format and content which excite and involve. Her omissions are significant and raise critical questions: Where was the librarian? Why wasn't he or she involved in planning and enrichment activities? As diagnostic work with exceptional children is strengthened and enhanced by interdisciplinary input, so work with reluctant readers is accelerated and widened when affected faculty cooperate in the remediation process. The librarian can benefit from Johnson's suggestions on source material as well as from her adaptation of unconventional and sometimes oblique tactics used to convince illiterates of the relevance, importance, and pleasures of reading.

While Johnson addresses herself to the lack of relevance in reading matter, Boutwell examines other substantial facets of literature to which the diligent librarian should attend. Boutwell describes those factors which negatively impinge on the reading achievement of slow-learning students and suggests adoption of specific materials coupled with compensatory remediative behaviors. Reading matter must be carefully scrutinized for those salient components which determine readability. Structural simplicity is not the only criterion for selecting books for slow learners. The content must tempt the reader to risk the reading experience again. Boutwell predicts low achievement in all academic areas for the poor reader; however, he notes unevenness in performance is not unusual, and sometimes a special strength may even be exploited for reading improvement. The librarian must refrain from overgeneralizing about the limitations of the slow reader and persist in planning individualized prescriptive reading programs.

Irregularities in expected rate or performance in reading alter selection options but both are based on careful evaluation of the special capacities of the child in question. As Boutwell has highlighted certain aspects of selection for the slow or less efficient reader, Beswick points out some easily overlooked issues related to the gifted reader.

He states that certain subjects such as science are predictable areas of interest. The librarian must be cognizant of these interests, as well as the particular reading problems which often characterize this group. Surprisingly, he asserts that the child's intellectual assets can enhance or sabotage his reading. For example, the student's highly developed skimming facility can readily undermine comprehension as a consequence of reading too quickly and carelessly. In addition, the satisfaction derived from reading may induce the reader to use this talent as a shortcut or substitute for experience. Beswick suggests the types of material which should be made available to gifted children and delineates the qualities such materials should have. He warns against not providing sufficiently challenging books and supports erring on the side of difficulty—not a popular decision in some quarters. The author gives little counsel for book selection for the gifted underachiever. The needs of such children are making themselves felt, particularly in inner-city schools today, and the special library problems of these children need closer scrutiny and resolution.

Tuttle brings to the librarian's attention a critical caveat in planning for book or media selection for blind users: it is essential that this population not be categorized as a homogeneous group. The librarian must make recommendations to the visually impaired reader on the basis of the reader's own preferences and characteristics. This study urges that the librarian or reading consultant consider recorded, compressed speech as the medium of choice, especially if reading efficiency is desired. It is important to note that these findings are based on speed and comprehension of prose and it may be that technical or other nonfiction material is more readily learned through other instructional modes. An important variable is overlooked: one would assume from an efficiency point of view that teenage blind students would be able to use this mode for the long literature assignments which they receive in English and humanities. What needs to be examined, and is a central component of these subjects, is the level of enjoyment possible in the quality and expression of language when heard under conditions of compressed speech. A careful analysis of the priorities of the blind student should precede guidance in this area.

Both Tuttle and Luchow are included as examples of the type of research in the field which is indispensible in making purchase and planning decisions. They use two different user populations to indicate how pragmatic investigation in the field assists the librarian in sharpening selection skills.

Luchow makes a pioneering investigation into picture-book selection for learning-disabled children, an area often dealt with by librarians on the basis of intuition or extrapolation. Since the response rate in his study was low and other research criteria were omitted, the results are necessarily limited, but nonetheless important. The article contains an implicit challenge to validate these findings with other populations of the perceptually disturbed. The characteristics of materials for older children with learning disabilities are also in need of investigation. Luchow asserts that conventional trade books can be enjoyed by students with learning disabilities; contrived materials are consequently unnecessary if a careful analysis is made of both content and illustration. Although his inquiry is restricted to picture story books, similar evaluations must be extended to other genres, such as poetry and informational books, so that librarians can extract those resources which have high potential for this presently unserved group. Since work in this field is relatively new, librarians will need to be on the lookout for other additions to the professional literature which may confront these as yet unexplored questions.

Kvaraceus discusses the postulate that censorship can function as a deterrent to delinquent behavior. He contends that there are a multiplicity of factors governing response which have their origin in early childhood. Blaming books for behavior is simplistic since there is little evidence of a direct causal relationship between the printed word and overt action. People react to literature in a great diversity of ways—psychological predilection toward behavioral response is established long before reading skills are mastered. Reading may reinforce or challenge what already exists in a human personality, but instances of transformations are so rare as to be newsworthy. Kvaraceus acknowledges that books do play a very special role in everyday life but he seems to undervalue their potency as behavioral change agents. If they are a negligible force for evil, must we therefore conclude that they are also a negligible force for good? His contribution underscores that of other included writers in speaking against an obsessive concern with containment and restriction policies in the practice of book selection for exceptional patrons.

Philosophical Implications of Book Selection for the Blind

FLORENCE GRANNIS

If you believe that blind people cannot ride horses, you will not put books about horseback riding into braille, onto tape, and onto talking books. If you believe blind people cannot participate in swimming, dancing, bowling, you will not put books about swimming, dancing, bowling into braille, onto tape, and onto talking books.

It is said that philosophy bakes no bread, but conversely, without philosophy no bread is baked. All book selection is based on philosophy. If you are a parent choosing books for your children, you are likely to choose books that have the type of moral precepts you wish to inculcate in them. If you are a librarian or an educator, you will probably choose books that will help the children to stretch their minds, give them a fondness for reading, and give them a general background of knowledge. If you are a librarian for the blind, your book selection will reflect what you believe about blindness, about blind people, and about the role of the blind in society.

It has been said that book selection by its very nature is censorship; that since almost *no* library can have *every* book, the very process of selecting book *A* rather than book *B* constitutes censorship. It would be a rare thing for the book selector to choose books at random, eeny-meeny-miny-mo, every tenth book, or only books with green covers. Perhaps the result of his judgment would appear to be much the same thing if he lets the book salesman affect his judgment, or if he chooses subjects dear to his own heart (which all of us do to a certain extent), or if he chooses by format, size of type, appearance of volumes, etc. But usually the book selector chooses book *A* rather than book *B* because book *A* fits *his* concept of what his readers *want*, *should have*, or *will tolerate*. The book selector will probably not be conscious of it, but the books he *chooses* and the books he *rejects* will be determined by the way he sees his public.

I was once the head of a large general reading department of a public library. My predecessor, who had been in charge of the department enough years to really make an impact on its book collection, had taken into account that the community was a university town (and indeed it did have a college), and he had purchased heavily in the areas of the erudite and avant garde. There were almost *no* books for what I call Mr. Average Reader.

Reprinted by permission from the Dec. 1968 issue of the *Wilson Library Bulletin*. Copyright © 1968 by The H. W. Wilson Company.

This was not because he felt Mr. Average Reader should be ignored, but simply that he did not believe Mr. Average Reader existed in the sense that I did. Perhaps one could argue that who and what Mr. Average Reader was was purely a subjective judgment, but with my book selection, for my concept of Mr. Average Reader, the book circulation tripled and the nearly empty department became congested.

Book selection for the blind has always been based on the view the book selector has had of the blind reader. Let us draw up a profile of Mr. Blind Reader according to the way the average book selector has seen him.

Age: Over sixty
Education: Limited
Financial Status: Poor, on welfare
Mobility: Limited
Horizons (Experience of the world): Limited
Vocabulary: Limited
Employed: No
Religious: Yes

Here you have it: Mr. Blind Reader, as he has been seen by the book selector, is elderly, not very bright, has never done much with his life, his interests are very narrow, he is easily shocked, and books are pretty much a means of whiling away his time. That this is the way Mr. Blind Reader has been seen is not just supposition on my part. This is what has traditionally caused the heavy emphasis on the religious element in the book collection. This is what has traditionally caused the timidity in adding Balzac, Rabelais, Faulkner, Farrell, Henry Miller, Hemingway to the book collection. This is what caused one librarian for the blind to say, "You can't let them have just *any* books!" as she withdrew *Gone with the Wind* from her collection.

This librarian was genuinely concerned with the welfare of her patrons. She wanted to give *good* library service; she simply believed that it would be giving *bad* library service to release onto unsuspecting, innocent, sheltered, and to-be-sheltered Mr. Blind Reader torrid bedroom scenes such as those between Scarlet and Rhett in *Gone with the Wind*.

Of course, the book selector is a member of the general public, of society at large, and his view of Mr. Blind Reader is the view held by other individuals who will influence what Mr. Blind Reader's library service will be. The administrator has also seen Mr. Blind Reader as ignorant, helpless, inferior. Why else have the libraries for the blind traditionally been understaffed, underhoused, and underfinanced? Why has the person in charge traditionally been a sweet little old lady with little library skill, background, or knowledge that someone on the library board needed to find a spot for, or a querulous, cantankerous individual who could not be tolerated in any other department, but who should be employed? Isn't it because it has always been felt—and deeply and emotionally experienced—that *anything* is good enough for the blind, that they are mighty lucky to have *any* library service? Isn't this what prompted one administrator to say in my hearing, "We have to give *service* but we don't have to give *good* service"? This man was, in general, a first-rate administrator, and the library he directed for the sighted public was an outstanding one, because he had confidence in the worth of the sighted public. He simply felt that the blind who could never be first-class citizens (and this was his unquestioned belief) did not rate a first-class library. This man took for granted that the blind could never take their places in the community as self-supporting, contributing citizens.

Improvement in the caliber of book selection for the blind, and indeed in all library service for the blind, can only be brought about by improvement in attitudes toward the blind. There must be recognition that blind people are just people—some of whom want *Fanny Hill*, some of whom find *Fanny Hill* offensive; some of whom want Plato, some of whom find Plato boring; some of whom want Catherine Marshall, some of whom find Catherine Marshall insipid.

There must also be the recognition that given opportunity and proper training the average blind person can hold the average job in the average place of business, that he can be independent and self-supporting, and that it is vital for society as well as for the individual, that this status of independent self-support be brought about.

There is evidence that attitudes about the blind *are* improving, at least in certain areas. More and more blind people are employed in regular jobs. More people are questioning the whole concept of sheltered workshops. Blind and sighted alike are rejecting begging as an activity for the blind and welfare as a means of subsistence.

There is evidence, too, that libraries for the blind are improving. Robert Bray has consistently worked to upgrade the Division for the Blind of the Library of Congress, and all of the regional libraries. More and more of the regional libraries are headed by people with library school degrees. More and more libraries for the blind are beginning to get their fair share of their system's budget.

A great deal of education of the public and of the blind (for the blind are part of the public) is still needed. It is no accident that a large number of the individuals and groups who want to give to libraries for the blind want to give Bibles, until we are surfeited with them. It is no accident that it is very difficult to find transcribers who will braille the "naughty" books. Why was it that the prison inmate (convicted on a morals charge) objected to brailling the *Decameron*?

Why is it that in the world of the blind there are many religious organizations promoting and supplying materials of many denominations or no denomination at all, tracts, periodicals, hymns, etc., and so few promoting general culture, the best sellers, and "great books"? Why is it that blind people often do not want to be identified as blind, to be seen reading braille, or to be seen using a cane? That braille is often down-played as something on the way out, "too cumbersome to be useful," "too slow to be feasible"? That the words, "solely for the use of the Blind," in connection with the talking books often cause a rejection of the service by those with visual or physical disabilities? It is because it is thought that it is not respectable to be blind. Blindness is equated with darkness, ignorance, and inferiority.

It was early recognized that the reading needs of the blind have a wide scope, and the *Report of the Librarian of Congress* in 1932 states:

The blind represent a cross-section of the sighted population since blindness is no respecter of persons or of occupations so that this group has for the most part the same literary tastes as the sighted. But the handicap of blindness emphasizes to the utmost the necessity of having a wide variety of literature available since reading is the greatest source of profitable and recreational occupation open to them.[1]

And again, in the *Survey of Library Service for the Blind, 1956,* by Francis R. St. John:

Inasmuch as the interests and reading tastes of the blind are substantially the same as those of corresponding groups of sighted readers, the selection for the blind will be similar to that for the sighted; and one of the objectives of the program is to provide for the blind the same variety of reading matter which is available to the sighted.[2]

However, these book selection policies will only be paper policies as long as the book selectors reflect paternalism and condescension in their inner emotions.

By and large the needs of the blind reading public can be met by the approach I used in the public library, when I bought for Mr. Average Reader. Add the erudite and avant garde books my predecessor concentrated on and you have a balanced book collection.

Specifically, how do the libraries for the blind fare in book selection? In my comments I am totally disregarding hand-transcribed braille books and taped books. Taped books because many blind readers do not have access to tape recorders, and hand-transcribed braille books because there are so few copies of given books! (Our library in Iowa cuts off reserves on hand-transcribed books after we acquire enough for ten years. Many borrowers will die, or completely lose interest in the book, before they get it.)

Concerning book selection for the blind, the 1956 St. John *Survey* says:

The conclusion to be drawn from this checking of titles published in the Books for the Blind program with various standard lists is that the selection is of high standard and that there is good variety in certain of the more popular categories, such as fiction, literary classics, biography, and history, but that the material in scientific, technical, and specialized subject categories is thin. There is a serious lack in both talking book and braille titles in both scholarly and technical material. The selection policy has been to select the book that would appear to attract the largest number of readers rather than to try to build a well-rounded collection which could be used for information as well as for recreational purposes. In other words, the collection will supply the recreational and inspirational needs of the blind but it is obvious that it will not be of much help in meeting the demand for vocational information.[3]

St. John says further, "It is conceivable that many of the blind population do not use the libraries because they cannot find in them material they need."[4] Again, "A much broader selection of materials which will supply the vocational and professional needs of the blind is recommended."[5]

As yardsticks to measure the adequacy of book selection for the blind, I have chosen *1967 Hardbound Best Seller List,*[6] *Librarians' Choice—110 Significant Books from All Lands and Times,*[7] the *Fiction Catalog,*[8] and the *Standard Catalog for Public Libraries.*[9] Checking the books sent to the regional libraries by the Library of Congress with the 1966 supplement to the *Fiction Catalog* (I used the 1966 supplement so that there would be ample time for the production of the books), I find, of the 327 items checked, we have 70, or 21.41 percent, on talking books, and 22, or 6.73 percent, in press braille.

The preface of the *Fiction Catalog* says,

. . . the objective of the *Fiction Catalog* has been to provide its thousands of library purchasers with a list of adult fiction titles whose usefulness is vouched for by a representative group of experienced librarians and specialists of the highest professional standing, representing the needs and interests of libraries of various types and sizes in all parts of the country.[10]
. . . in accordance with the guiding principles of book selection adopted by the American Library Association . . . with emphasis on the usefulness . . . of each book.[11]

It is interesting to observe that today libraries for the blind have a smaller percentage of the books listed in standard book selection aids than they had in 1955, at the time of the publication of the St. John *Survey.* The St. John *Survey* indicated that 42.72 percent of the books listed in standard book aids were available in libraries for the blind.[12] Today the figure is 21.2 percent.

Let us break down *Fiction Catalog* listings further. The 1966 *Fiction Catalog* supplement has 69 books single starred for excellence, 10 books double starred for super-excellence. How many of these do we have?

We have Sholom Aleichem's *Old Country Tales,* Armstrong's *Dream of Fair Woman,* Barry's *Maximilian's Gold,* Benchley's *The Monument,* and 13 other books which have been single starred. We have Auchincloss's *The Embezzler,* Crichton's *The Secret of Santa Vittoria,* and four other books which have been double starred. Six of the 10 double starred and 17 of the 69 single starred—23 out of 79! Considering some of the titles that have been added during the past two or three years, this would seem to be rather damning.

Let us examine a few of the single star and double star books which have been omitted. Barth's *Giles Goat-boy* caused a considerable flurry in the world of sighted readers, and no wonder. The *Fiction Catalog* says of it, by quotation, ". . . there are many orgies and copulation explosions, as though Cecil B. DeMille were staging a new superdrama called 'incontinence'."[13] Graham Greene's *The Comedians* is double starred. In the words quoted by the *Fiction Catalog:*

This book concerns a back-slidden Catholic, a native of Monaco and owner of a run-down tourist hotel in Haiti; his affair with the German wife of a Latin American ambassador; and his involvement with a rascally British con man and an American Presidential candidate and his wife, in Haiti to propagate the cult of vegetarianism—most of them in varying degrees comedians on the stage of life.[14]

Surely blind people would enjoy this! Double starred Malamud's *The Fixer* is

. . . a study of human suffering in which the sufferer, a common ordinary man, manages to rise above his suffering and to remain alive when death seems easier, simply as a symbol of truth . . . The Christian reads these pages with a sense of shocked outrage as the worst accusations of the Middle Ages are hurled against the Jews in the present century, including, most horribly, that of ritualistic blood-murder.[15]

Do the blind need to be protected from this?

The preface to the *Standard Catalog for Public Libraries, 1966 Supplement* states

. . . the objective of the *Standard Catalog for Public Libraries* has been to provide a classified list of nonfiction titles whose usefulness is vouched for by a representative group of experienced librarians and specialists of the highest professional standing, representing the needs and interest of libraries of various types and sizes in all parts of the country.
. . . All inclusions in the *Catalog* and its Supplements are determined by the votes of the consultants; none by the publisher or editorial staff.[16]

Of the 400 items included in the 1966 supplement to the *Standard Catalog,* 47 are in talking books and 15 are in braille. Of the 36 single-starred books, 9 are in talking books and 2 are in braille. Of the 16 double starred books, 4 are in talking books and none is in braille. These books are, of all the nonfiction books published in the nation that year, the ones the book selection experts of the nation say should be in public libraries, large and small! How few were put in the libraries for the blind!

Let us quickly consider a few of the titles omitted. Double starred is Bernstein's *A Primer on Money, Banking and Gold*. The *Standard Catalog* says of this, "A clear, thorough, explanation of modern money and banking."[17] Double starred Cousteau's *Jacques-Yves Cousteau's World Without Sun* is described as "Narrative of man's first undersea colony in which a group of Oceanauts lived for a month in Continental Shelf Station No. 2 in the Red Sea."[18] Coon's single starred book, *The Living Races of Man*, where "The author 'traces the races of man from their five cradles at the end of the last glacial period to their present distribution.'"[19] Why should these books not be available for the blind?

Let us consider now the *1967 Hardbound Best Seller List*. There are 19 books on the list, 7 are in talking books, and one in braille. A few other of the books have excerpts or condensations in periodicals which are available on talking book, or in braille. Since this is a brief list, it is possible to go over it in its entirety.

Manchester's *Death of a President* has excerpts in *Look* Magazine, which is a talking book. Kazan, *The Arrangement* is not available. Styron, *Confessions of Nat Turner* is on talking book. Potok, *The Chosen* is on talking book. Uris, *Topaz* is excerpted in *Look* Magazine. Marshall's *Cristy* is on talking book. Wilder, *The Eighth Day* is on talking book. Levin, *Rosemary's Baby* is in braille. Wallace's *The Plot* is not available. Stewart, *The Gabriel Hounds* is on talking book. Sutton, *The Exhibitionist* is not available. Berne, *Games People Play* is not available. McKuen, *Stanyon Street* is not available. Kavanaugh, *A Modern Priest Looks at his Outdated Church* is on talking book. Levenson, *Everything but Money* is on talking book. Birmingham, *Our Crowd* is excerpted in *The Ladies Home Journal*, which is available in braille. Stearn, *Edgar Cayce: The Sleeping Prophet* is not available. *Better Homes and Gardens Favorite Ways with Chicken* is not available. Diller, *The Marriage Manual* is another book from the list that is not available.

Is there anything that the books which are not available have in common? Kazan, *The Arrangement* is a book with frank sex scenes. *Newsweek* says about *The Plot*:

Wallace has made the ultimate game. This one is about everything: the Kennedy assassination, the Sino-Soviet alliance, the Soviet-Sino split, the Anglo-Franco-Germano-Sino-Soviet-American rapprochement, the Profumo case, the publishing world, the fashion world, the newspaper world, gastronomy, wire-tapping, stripteasing.[20]

There we have it again—sex. *Library Journal* says of *The Exhibitionist*, "The novel is slick, determinedly sexy, well-constructed, very readable."[21]

Again, sex! Diller's *Marriage Manual* copes with sex in a different way. In a rollicking manner, Phyllis Diller points out some pitfalls to marriages and shows how to avoid them or correct them. *Better Homes and Gardens Favorite Ways with Chicken*: it is hard to see why this book has been left out, unless the book selectors have no faith in the cooking abilities of the blind. Certainly it is a first-rate book, and I am confident that when we have it hand brailled, it will be greatly in demand.

The libraries for the blind have done better in surveying their collection with *Librarians' Choice—110 Significant Books from All Lands and Times*. The most significant omissions are the works of Freud. Neither the talking book collection nor the braille collection has a single one of Freud's works. Darwin's *Origin of Species* is not represented. There is no significant history of modern art, such as Cheyney's, in either talking book or braille.[22]

To sum up—what does all of this mean? The libraries for the blind get more than 500 adult titles in talking book and press braille each year. A small percentage of these are the books listed in the *Fiction Catalog* and the *Standard Catalog*, the bulwarks and mainstays of librarians everywhere for book selection. They have far more of the books listed in *110 Significant Books* (though I have not checked to see *when* these books were added to the collection). There are many books on the *1967 Best Seller List* not in talking book and press braille. I do not mean to suggest that all of the 500 adult books added to the libraries for the blind each year should be *current* titles—obviously some should be standard works and classics missed from former years. I simply say the single starred and double starred books mentioned earlier should be included (unless there is an insuperable format problem such as a picture book). Also, the other *current* books put into braille and talking book should be of the caliber of the *Standard Catalog* and the *Fiction Catalog* and there should be a diminution of the trivial books.

Without going into a detailed analysis of the titles which *are* available and which *are* being added each year, I would point out that many of them would appear to be of doubtful value and still more of them would seem to reflect the standard misconceptions and stereotypes about blindness which I have already discussed. Consider for instance the following 10 titles:

Another Spring by Loula G. Erdman
Divided loyalties in Missouri during the Civil War years are the subject of an appealing novel. It depicts the helplessness of innocent persons displaced by the absurdities of war, but ends on a note of hope.[23]

The Best Is Yet to Be by Bentz Plagemann
A pleasantly relaxed account of a middle-aged couple who take a trip abroad after their only son is married. Even as tourists they become involved with young people, and the book ends as they hurry home, having learned that they are to be grandparents.[24]

A Crack in the Sidewalk by Ruth Wolff
Though the Templeton Family lived in a second-floor apartment surrounded by treeless concrete, they could escape every summer to the grandparents' home in the country. Linsey tells of her parents, her sisters and brothers, and how she found a way out through her talent for folk singing. This is a warm, wholesome story with a happy ending. . . .[25]

Days of Grass by Christian Herald
Readers weary of violence, cynicism, and pessimism will enjoy these stories, taken from the pages of the "Christian Herald." Differing in background and length, they are all affirmative in point of view, whether dealing with childhood, maturity, or old age.[26]

An End to Patience by Mary Durant
The title contains a neat pun, since this is the story of an amateur production of Gilbert and Sullivan, coached by a teacher in a boys' school. The various personalities of the cast and their interplay are well depicted and the whole thing is extremely entertaining without being at all heavy handed on the satire.[27]

Fair Is the Morning by Loula Grace Erdman
In this pleasant, wholesome, yet realistic story, a young teacher in a rural school finds challenge and opportunity aplenty. It gives an excellent picture of the teaching vocation.[28]

Here Come the Brides by Geraldine Napier
The bridal department in a fashionable Fifth Avenue department store is the scene of a diverting novel. Twenty-seven-year-old D'Arcy Evans, assistant buyer, can cope with all the crises except that of a new floor manager with unexplained power. In the end, however, the situation is straightened out and wedding bells will ring again.[29]

Little World Apart by Squire Omar Barker
A family ranch in New Mexico, before the first World War, is the scene of this pleasant, nostalgic story. Fourteen-year-old Jeff tells of roundups, hunting, school, picnics, and the small daily occurrences of a hard but rewarding life. The family relationships are especially memorable.[30]

The Marriage of Katherine by Dorothy Emily Stevenson
While happily honeymooning, Katherine and her second husband find themselves involved in all sorts of difficulties with other people. But Alex is a tower of strength to his bride and her three children. The Scottish setting and affirmative philosophy lend charm to the narrative.[31]

My Sky Is Blue by Loula Grace Erdman
When Jinny left her teaching job in the Middle West for a school in New Mexico, she found a very different life. The problems posed by a one-room school and her efforts to solve them make an absorbing story, with a romantic ending.[32]

Three Erdman and no Freud!

All of us tend to be defensive about book selection. The overwhelming reaction, when comments are made on which books we ḥave chosen and which we have rejected, is to defend ourselves and show why we really couldn't have done differently. The whole point of my thesis is that book selectors are just people in their social frameworks as everyone else is and as long as "the culture" says blind people are "different" and, in effect, less valuable, less able to participate and less able to pay their way, these attitudes will come through, consciously or unconsciously, in book selection for them. I haven't really softened my message greatly when I have said the book selectors have done the best they can within the framework of their situation, but I believe they have.

What to do about it? As I have said, all of us connected with book selection tend to be defensive and touchy in relation to which books we select. I believe some of the blind tend to be querulous, inaccurate, and negative in their criticism. Rather than complaining that the libraries are oversupplied with Zane Grey and don't have any *good* books, why not say precisely what is wanted? (Zane Grey is a good author for some reading needs.) If independent blind people and groups of blind will vocalize their reading desires and needs to the librarians, we will have gone one step further. We can only arrive, however, when the attitudes about the blind and of the blind are transformed so that it is recognized that blindness is merely a *characteristic* like many another, that blind people cannot be stereotyped and that their hobby reading needs, vocational reading needs, and recreational reading needs are just the needs of *people*.

NOTES

1. Library of Congress, *Report of the Librarian of Congress* (Washington, D.C.: Govt. Print. Off. 1932), p. 273.
2. Francis R. St. John, *Survey of Library Service for the Blind 1956* (New York: American Foundation for the Blind, 1957), p. 72.
3. Ibid., p. 81.
4. Ibid., p. 83.
5. Ibid., p. 103.
6. Alice P. Hackett, "The 1967 Hardbound Best Sellers," *Chicago Tribune Book World* (3 March 1968), p. 2.
7. M. Bloss and H. Terry, *Librarians' Choice—110 Significant Books . . .* (Milwaukee: Milwaukee Public Library, 1958).

8. *Fiction Catalog*, 7th ed. (New York: Wilson, 1961).

9. *Standard Catalog for Public Libraries, 1966 Supplement* (New York: Wilson, 1967).

10. *Fiction Catalog*, p. 5.

11. Ibid.

12. St. John, *Survey*.

13. "Book of the Month Club News," in *Fiction Catalog, 1966 Supplement* (New York: Wilson, 1967), p. 7.

14. *Library Journal*, in *Fiction Catalog, 1966 Supplement* (New York: Wilson, 1967), p. 21.

15. "Best Sellers," in *Fiction Catalog, 1966 Supplement* (New York: Wilson, 1967), p. 30.

16. *Standard Catalog*, p. 3.

17. *Library Journal*, in *Standard Catalog for Public Libraries, 1966 Supplement* (New York: Wilson, 1967), p. 24.

18. *Publishers' Weekly*, in *Standard Catalog for Public Libraries, 1966 Supplement* (New York: Wilson, 1967), p. 35.

19. *Cincinnati*, in *Standard Catalog for Public Libraries, 1966 Supplement* (New York: Wilson, 1967), p. 35.

20. *Newsweek*, 22 May 1967, p. 100, in *Book Review Digest* 63:277 (August 1967).

21. *Library Journal*, 15 November 1967, p. 4175, in *Book Review Digest* 64:325 (May 1968).

22. American Foundation for the Blind, *Talking Books Adult 1966–1967* (New York: The Foundation, 1968).

23. Ibid., p. 51.
24. Ibid., p. 52.
25. Ibid., p. 54.
26. Ibid., p. 55.
27. Ibid., p. 56.

28. Ibid., p. 57.
29. Ibid., p. 60.
30. Ibid., p. 63.
31. Ibid., p. 64.
32. Ibid., p. 66.

If It's Fun, It Can't Be Reading!

LAURA S. JOHNSON

Let us pretend for awhile today that this is the first Thursday after the first Tuesday in September. The ivy on the ledge outside our open classroom window grasps the sill and, finding support, surges with the color and vibrance of its nature as it seeks to move on into the room. We think of Dylan Thomas and the force that through the green fuse drives the flower. We feel, as we look at the ivy, that students too, given support, have a power for moving the way they were meant to go.

Yes, ivy's got a good thing going. Maybe there's something in it for us.

And now let our eye move inside the classroom, to the students sitting in front of us in even rows, five abreast. The reds, the oranges, and the greens of their

dashikis shout the way they'd like to be. Bright, full of life, ready to be a part of the scene. But their faces tell another story. These faces exude gloom; they register dislike; some even show hatred; all bear tight lines of tension, as if bracing to confront the worst again. Within this group there is no joy. Something has struck out. Perhaps I should begin by reading them *that* poem; then they'd have company in the misery of a lost ball game.

But they are depressed enough as it is. Why add to it? A November day does not glower more darkly nor sigh with greater vehemence than do most students in a Remedial Reading I class on the first day of school. For most of them, this is the eighth, ninth, or even tenth year they have been in a class labeled "poor reader." No wonder they are tired of the whole thing and have already called it quits. Their attitude says that though their counselor may have scheduled them into this course, they will be darned if they do anything while they are here.

My eye sweeps over them as I hunt for someone, or some thing, to open the way and let me in.

Zekiel, Abram, Hank, Bill, and Sue—on the back row.

No help there.

Each of them occupies a seat at the head of a row, and each has just crashed into the wall directly behind himself. Now in mock surprise and with abject consternation they all bounce back into line but with such force that they rebound to the wall.

This, I know, will go on until Bill's chair shoots off at a tangent and bumps Sue's chair. Then she will flop down onto the floor, pick herself up with a shriek, and head toward Bill with a karate chop. Anything to get him to look at her, or her to look at him—or me to look at all of them—anything goes in these first few moments when we meet and establish our lines of communication and territoriality.

But we could forestall all of this imminent disaster. We could go out and come in again. Let's do. But before we come back in, let's reset the stage and add something very significant in the way of props.

Let's place near the door an irresistible object. Say, a stack of fresh, daily newspapers. Just off the truck. We can still smell the printer's ink. It even rubs off on our hands. But that's good. It tells us that what we have here is alive—not old, not sterile, not yesterday.

With this fresh sight in front of them, the students enter the room and pause momentarily in disbelief. Then, following the instinctive urge to know what's going on, each picks up a newspaper. The next need is to find a place to sit down so that they can read. Right off, a group of boys grab some seats, rearrange them into a circle, and turn at once to the baseball scores.

I do not need to utter one word to them about reading for a purpose, nor do I need to tell them the importance of skimming, nor how to do it. They take care of oral reading spontaneously and without embarrassment. What they have got going for them already knows what to do—when it counts. Like the ivy, all the kids need is a sill to hang onto. For them, crucial battles are being fought out on Wrigley Field and in Shea Stadium. Once the scores are located and the standings figured out, their talk turns to the Cubs, the Mets, and the Baltimore Orioles. Their voices rise in the heat of argument. They refer to the text in the newspaper again and again for proof of their point of view.

In another part of the room a couple of girls sit off by themselves intent on Dear Abby. The distance between their understanding of her advice on personal problems and *Mr. and Mrs. Bojo Jones* (over on the bookrack) is not great. perhaps by the time the girls are juniors, they may even be able to comprehend *The Scarlet Letter*.

A few boys are deeply and solitarily absorbed in the opening pages of the newspaper. What *are* Nixon and Laird going to do about Vietnam? People say the war is going to last a long time, and these boys know the distance between fifteen and eighteen is only three short years. Not much time as the kid grows.

As I see my students satisfied and at ease by finding gratification for their desire to know, I am aware that they have brought their own readiness into the classroom. All I need do is recognize it, channel it, and sustain it. They sense something is coming their way, something that says "Yes" to them, rather than "No." Something's going on in reading class that they haven't run into before. Why, here in this one, you can read!

The following day, beside the stack of newspapers, the students find a pile of records.

"Hey, look! The Miracles!" Irene exclaims.

"You got to be kiddin'," says Bobbie.

"No, honest," she answers. "And to prove it, here's a record player."

"You mean we gonna jam today?" Billy breaks in.

"If you like," I say. "Today we are going to have a chance to listen and read."

The news is greeted with a clamor as I hand out dittoed sheets with the words of "Here I Go Again." Some students read the song in silence, others orally, and some begin to sing it. Somewhere in here, among the litany, the record player gets turned on and the impact of Smokey Robinson gathers them all into a union which ends with a sigh as the music dies away. A silence falls then, as if the audaciousness of it all is just too much of a good thing. It is suddenly broken by Sammy, tall, dark, and serious.

"How come?" he asks. "I thought we's sposed to be in a Readin' class. And jammin' ain't readin'."

"Man, you crazy," says Bo. "You readin', ain't cha?"

"Yeah," says Sammy slowly. "But this is fun. And if it's fun, it can't be readin'."

Well, can't it?

For most of them the daily newspaper soon becomes an absolute must. Likewise, the songs and the things they say and do when put on tape. These also become an important part of what they read.

The newspaper puts them into the habit of reading every day, a thing many of them have never done before. They gain a sense of continuity about events, too, as they read, for most major news stories extend over two or three days. This gives the students a chance to relate what's happening now to something which happened in the past as they read about it in history, or as something artistically conceived in literature, music, and art.

In this class, of course, there are a few students who cannot even read a newspaper. Their reading level is nil or else so low that even the sixth-grade vocabulary of the paper is beyond them. But I have something for them, too, so that they won't feel embarrassed or be left out because they are not reading like other students.

For them I have magazines. The student who can't read can always look at pictures and make it seem as if he is reading. And this is what he will do until such time as I can test him individually and know better how to help him. Our range of magazines is wide, with heavy emphasis on cars and sports for the boys, clothes and looks for the girls. Several copies of *Hot Rod* and *Sports Illustrated* have never been too many; and cartoon books about cars are really great. The girls go for *Teen, Seventeen, Jet*, and *Ebony,* and they couldn't care less about things mechanical or enervating.*

Along with the magazines and the newspapers, two spindles of paperback books are a great attraction for the better readers in the group. Once the newspaper urge for the day is satisfied, these better readers descend upon the paperback books like bees upon clover. Sports, humor, cars, and the supernatural offer the greatest attraction in this kind of reading. Ethnic fiction is popular, too, much more so than is nonfiction among this fifteen- and sixteen-year-old group. Most of them are not ready to take on remaking the world. Perhaps this will come later, tempered then by the degree to which they have succeeded in feeling respected as individuals.

Ready access to all of this reading material is very important, and we are generous in its availability to the students. Newspapers can be cut up or taken home when they are a day old. Magazines need to be noncurrent before they can be taken apart. I try to keep the books moving in and out, and yet still keep a good supply on hand, for the books are a very important part of the reading program. Many of the students come from homes that have no books. So I believe it is especially

---

*These differentiations are not as fixed as they once seemed to be. —Ed.

important for the students to be surrounded by them at school. And yet this presents a problem. For if, in this openness the books go out and do not come back, a part of our reading program disappears. For it to be effective, it must have something for everybody. We need to have all of its parts. The biggest culprit, so far as loss of books is concerned, turns out to be the nonreader.

But we can forestall this kind of thing if we offer the student something else first, something he'd rather have anyway. An analysis of why he takes and destroys a book he can't read supplies the remedy.

Let's say the boy takes *Stock Car Racer*, even though he can't read it. But it has an exciting picture of a car and a boy on the front cover. Gee! He'd like to own that car, and be that boy, and win that race! But he can't, really. He knows a dozen reasons why none of these things will ever happen. And yet, wouldn't it be great fun if he could just read the story and pretend for a while that it could happen?

So he takes the book for which he feels a real need—he wants to be, for a little while, the boy in the picture on the cover of that book. Possessing it, he feels good for another reason too. He sees the other fellows taking out books to read. He wants to do what they are doing. He doesn't want to look stupid, which is what will happen if he walks out without a book. So he picks *Stock Car Racer* off the rack.

The illusion is good while it lasts. He's like the rest of the kids, and he's winning the race! But as soon as he gets outside of the room, away from the other books and the kids and the teacher, the dream vanishes. That's when he pitches the book into the nearest wastebasket. Now if it only had some pictures, it might stand a chance of being looked at and perhaps of even making a trip back into the Reading Center. But without pictures, it will never return unless a perceptive janitor rescues it from the trash can and brings it back.

So what can the teacher do to cut down on this kind of loss and still have a paperback library? One of the things he can do is have enough magazines with pictures in them so that the poor reader will take them instead of the books. For unless he is totally illiterate, he can make some sense out of what he reads by looking at the pictures and by figuring out some of the words through context. After all, that is the way he learned to read Dick and Jane about ten years ago. He is simply carrying over a little longer into high school what he was exposed to in the first grade. So what if he misses a few things along the way, like the middles and the endings of words? That's nothing new for him. He's been making his way on pictures and by guessing for a long, long time.

But not just any picture.

Though his desire for pictures in magazines must be met, the magazines must look just as adult and respectable as the paperback books. A boy once put it very accurately to me when he said, "I like *True* magazine because it says right here on the cover it's a man's magazine." A statement like this emphasizes the young man's need to be treated as if he were an adult. And most of them can make a legitimate claim for this treatment. They look the part; they have jobs of a sort; a lot of them have transportation such as cars or bikes, and some even have a girl. So appeal to them should be made through adult-slanted materials. By reading materials which recognize their growing maturity, they achieve an improved self-image, and when this occurs through a reading class, they begin to feel more kindly toward reading. They discover that there is something in it for them.

When I sense that they are leaning this way, I have my first evidence that their attitude is changing in favor of the positive, that I have begun to score with them. For from the start, I have considered my first task with them to be one of changing their attitude about reading from negative to positive. Most of them have come to me with a strong antipathy for it, and until I disperse this, I cannot do much of lasting benefit for them. There is, of course, a great deal more I need to do, and will hope to get done; but changing their attitude so that they are willing to bring their power to bear on eliminating their reading problem must come first. I believe that until I can change their attitude toward reading, I cannot effect a permanent change in them. And this is what I am most concerned about.

I am primarily interested in what I can do that will have transfer value. I ask myself, "What will they do with reading after they leave my class?" And I answer, "If they are not moved to read on their own after they get out of my class, I have not done much to help them." I know that if they are to keep any gains they make in decoding in this class—if they are to improve at all in the skill of reading, they will have to be motivated to practice it. Unless they do this, daily and consistently and over a lifetime, the drills I can give them to raise their vocabulary achievement a few test points in June will not be worth a thing as transfer in the following September's test. They may not even register in that fall test because what they drilled on earlier did not become an integral part of their language pattern. And it did not become a part of that pattern because it was not rooted in an interest of theirs. So unused, unrelated, over a period of three months, the drills disappeared and the student had no carryover.

But worse than a poor showing testwise is the time the student could have been reading, finding out things he didn't know. For of course he didn't read because it had no pleasure for him. He had never found fun in it. So why do something so unpleasant if he did not have to?

For high school students I try to plan a reading program which emphasizes the pleasure and self-satisfaction in reading. I try to make it fulfilling rather than depleting.

The free ranging we begin through newspapers, magazines, and paperback books on the first day of class is continued on all the other days whenever a student finishes his assigned work and has some free time. But to assure every student's having some chance for free reading every day, each class period begins with ten minutes of reading; most students read the newspaper during this period. Once this habit becomes established, it is almost impossible to break. But who wants to? Who can justify not reading in Reading? I dare to predict a mutiny if we tried to begin a reading class now without a newspaper. I have had students from other classes stop by my room and beg for newspapers; I have heard them speak with regret of not being able to read in their classes. Somehow, it seems as though we ought to be able to do something about this.

At the beginning of the year, too, each student fills out an informal inventory on which he indicates his attitude toward reading and his preferences in it. This inventory does several things for both of us. It gives him an opportunity to state privately just what he really feels and thinks about reading. It tells him, too, that I am on his side because I have asked his opinion about what he wants to work with in this class.

And I discover, from what and how he writes, a great deal about his language patterns. This is important because I view reading as just one part of the total language process. I need to see reading in relation to a whole if I am to work with the part successfully. I must view reading in its relationship to the (1) subconscious or perceptive nature of the individual, (2) to the manner in which he speaks, (3) listens, (4) reads, and (5) writes. When I know his *total* pattern, I know more about him as a reader.

When I read what he writes, I know something of how words look to him when he reads. I know, too, something of how they sound to him when he listens. I discover that he is totally unaware of tense and of plurals; I see that phonetic spelling is the rule rather than the exception; I find odd combinations of consonants in his writing; I see him omitting vowels, structure words, and marks of punctuation; I find him reversing letters. I learn, in short, that for him, reading is an excursion into a foreign language, most of which he does not get because he does not recognize its printed form. What he has been able to learn rests mostly on what he has been able to pick up from listening and looking at pictures.

If he is to *read*, I must take him back to that place in the primary or intermediate grades where his missing techniques still await him; I must return with him to the place where, for a host of reasons, he either missed or rejected what he needed the first time around. But he must come willingly with me if he is to acquire it this time, for reading is not a skill easy to acquire. Now that he is fourteen, fifteen, or sixteen years old, he is psychologically not at all the person he was when he first encountered the code-breaking process.

Though he may need the same things at sixteen which he needed at age six, I cannot teach them in the same way. At age six he was still curious and eager to learn. Then he entered school, wanting to learn to read. He still thought he could find out what he wanted to know by reading. Also, as a child, he had a built-in love for repetition. This was the time when he liked to hear the same story over and over again. This was the time when he could still take the repetitive drills necessary for learning the shapes of letters, the sounds of consonants, and vowels, digraphs, blends, and the like. This was the time when his teacher could discover any ineptness in him and correct it.

But it was, unfortunately, also the time when she did not do this. Perhaps her class was so large that she couldn't get around to helping the children who were slower at catching onto the system for decoding. Or perhaps her teaching situation was so deprived that she could not do what she knew she ought to do. Perhaps the child himself brought handicaps to learning—perceptual, environmental, or otherwise. Whatever the reason for his lack of success in reading in the first grade, he kept falling further and further behind as he went on through the elementary school. With each passing year he took more verbal and emotional abuse from parents, teachers, and peers because of his failure. A lowered self-image, frustration, lack of motivation, and hostility thus become built into his personality so strongly that by the time he arrives in the ninth-grade reading class, I have more than just a decoding problem to solve for him. I need to be something of a counselor and a therapist as well.

From the very first day he enters that ninth-grade reading class he needs to meet some success and some pleasure. The best way for this to happen is to give him something to read or look at or listen to that interests him. Once he has become confident that he can count on finding these things in the reading classroom every day, he relaxes and becomes more willing to try decoding again. I make it more palatable to him, too, and more relevant by using newspaper and magazine materials as the basis for our drill materials. In fact, prefixes and suffixes may be more at home in an article on Operation Breadbasket than in the traditional reading workbook. Vocabulary words such as *hostile, deliberate,* and *incriminate* somehow make more sense and stick in the memory longer if taken out of a newspaper account of the Conspiracy Trial than if listed, out of context, in a word book.

Using the current and daily newspaper like this, of

course, requires my getting to school early before my first class so that I can go through the paper carefully enough to spot the one or two articles in it which I am sure will have most appeal to my students. Then I must quickly adapt these articles to the use I intend to make of them that day.

If, for example, I am working on comprehension and want students to recognize the logical order of ideas, I can copy onto Ditto stencils the beginning three or four paragraphs of an article, but I will not place them in sequence. I will put them in a scrambled order and ask the students to number them in 1,2,3,4 order. After they have done this, we will discuss the word clues and the idea clues which are present to help a reader know what comes first, then second, then third, and finally fourth. Again, paragraphs such as a local march on the City Hall for better housing are better materials for an exercise like this than some in a workbook about events totally unrelated to the students.

To help them see how much there is in the newspaper and in reading as an activity for them, each student is asked to make a scrapbook of clippings related to an interest of his. Over a three-week period, each student learns to select a topic—and for the really unmotivated ones this in itself becomes a major project. Once a topic is selected, the next step is to read, looking only for articles related to that one idea. Here the student practices reading for a purpose—skimming, categorizing, vocabulary, comprehension. He delves deeper and learns to ask questions about his reading, and he also provides answers for them. He may write a theme about his interest, or read a magazine article or a book relating to it. When he has finished his project, his scrapbook provides a graphic representation in print of something interesting to him.

Records offer him a strong inducement to read too. When a student brings us a pop record to play to the class, he also brings along the words which go with it. If it has no words, he provides them for the way it makes him feel when he listens to it. I type the words onto Ditto master sheets and produce copies for each student so that as he listens, he can also follow the words in print. Many students, learning to read this way, discover that in print many a word has sounds and letters which they do not know it has, judging from the way they say it and write it. For students whose native dialect is not standard English, this tape-listening-reading situation is very helpful. Of course, any materials that appeal to the students can be used this way: poems, stories, essays, plays, jokes—almost anything they want to bring and record can be transcribed into print to be read while they listen. For many students, this eye-ear connection has never been made before. For some, it is the road out of their reading problem.

Every Friday we have a reading review. It never takes the same form twice. Sometimes it is oral; sometimes it is written. One aspect of it has slowly but steadily grown in importance. To impress upon these so-called nonreaders their dependence upon reading, and also to demonstrate to them that they are not nonreaders, I ask them to list everything they can think of that they have read during the week. When we began this listing, most of the students said they never read anything. But questioning on my part soon showed them that they read more than they thought. Now their lists contain not only newspapers, magazines, books and history lessons, but also their journals for English, science lab reports, basketball schedules, marching band formations, menus, sales checks, price tags, street signs, prayer books, hymnals, candy wrappers, traffic tickets, and even a court summons. From their written reviews, I type excerpts and copy them to use again as reading when the material has been put on tape. The first time we did this, one student was so impressed by what she had done that she exclaimed, "Do you know? This is the first time I've ever been in print."

A comment so pointed and honest as this makes me realize anew the importance of recognition for the student who almost never has a chance to shine or excel in school. As a teacher of regular classes, I was always aware of those three or four very poor students who were scraping along at the bottom of the roster of thirty-five; but what does anybody ever have time to do for them? The papers and the reports and the meetings and the demands on the usual English teacher are so heavy that the poor kid who just can't keep up rarely gets the daily individual help he needs if he is ever to have a chance at all.

So though the taped-typed contribution of someone in a remedial reading class would look meager when viewed on the continuum of a regular English class, in the larger space which this remedial student has in his much smaller reading class, what he does begins to assume importance. And this feeling of importance, of being somebody, is what he must have if he is ever to pull himself out of the slough of failure in which he has been stuck for so many years.

Occasionally a few students will become so involved in a news event that they will want to carry on with it even after it leaves the front page. Two boys in one of my classes got into a terrific argument one day about Paul McCartney. Was he alive or was he dead? They squared off for a debate, but each asked for a week to get prepared. When their day came, each was ready with support he'd gleaned from a week of going through magazines, collecting pictures, and playing excerpts from several Beatles' albums. We taped the debate, included snatches of the songs; all of us listened carefully to the supposedly buried clues which proved, or disproved, that Paul is dead—or is still alive. Fortunately, for the debater who contended that Paul McCartney is still alive, *Life* magazine came out that week with a strong supporting article just at the right time. The class voted at the end of the debate, but the count was a tie. However, even though the decision was not clear, the popularity of Beatles' albums is still undisputed.

For me, however, the real issue was not Paul; mine was reading. Did they read or didn't they? Did they read on their own time? Was it spontaneous? Was it voluntary? Was it something they didn't have to do, but they did it anyway—because they wanted to?

I felt I won that one.

As the weeks go by and the students come to feel more and more that reading is something they must have in order to satisfy some deep inner need, I find myself becoming more and more involved with getting them what they want to read. Mitch, for example, has had me scouring every one of the five bookstores I patronize for books on cars. When I couldn't find any more, I channeled him into science fiction. This kick should hold him for awhile; but when I see it waning, I hope to have some indication from him of the next direction to take. From the start, Mitch has been the best reader in all of my classes, being about only one grade below level when he came. Perhaps he should not even have qualified for remedial reading because he was so good, when compared with the rest of the kids. But quickly I sensed his morale building qualities for me and the other students, furnishing as he did a shining example of what it was like to be a good reader. So I let him stay. Now he comes into class each day, breezes in five minutes through the assignment the other kids will spend twenty minutes on, and then spends the rest of his time off by himself in a corner reading. But, of course —this *is* a class in reading!

Sammy, who earlier in the year doubted the validity of a reading class that was fun, had a problem with words, which he finally got up nerve enough to talk about with me. He came up one day after class and asked, "Could you get me somethin' I always wanted to read?"

"Sure," I said. "What is it?"

"It's this thing about ice. I hear people talkin' about it." So the next day I handed him *Soul on Ice*. A week later he brought it back and sadly deposited it on my desk.

"What's wrong?" I asked. "Don't you like what Eldridge Cleaver has to say?"

"It's not that," he said. "It's just I can't read it. But that's the way it always is. Them great books always has them big hard words in them."

Knowing how disappointed he felt, and remembering that his news scrapbook was entitled "Black People Who Did Something Important," I gave him another paperback which I was sure he could read—a simplified version of Gordon Parks' *A Choice of Weapons*. He got it on a Thursday afternoon; the following Monday he brought it back and said happily, "Gee, that was great. What else have you got?" *Harlem Summer* was nearby, so he took that out. Again, he read it in less than a week. Next came an easy book on Frederick Douglass. This was followed by *Roosevelt Grady* and *South Town*.

Now, he is so eager to read, and so convinced of the benefit to him of reading extensively and on a level easy enough to give him no trouble with words, that he is following my suggestion of going to the young people's section of the public library to hunt for books for a fictitious sixth-grade brother. And I am willing to predict that Sammy's brother will hurry through sixth grade and graduate into junior high in record time, for Sammy has a great thing going. He's got himself. And he's going to move along and make up for lost time. And when the day comes that finds him reading *Soul on Ice,* it will happen, I think, because for him reading did become fun.

Motivating the Slow Learner

WILLIAM D. BOUTWELL

About five years ago an educator came to New York, at the invitation of a textbook publisher, bringing with him a plan and manuscript for a textbook series designed to serve three kinds of learners: the slow, the average, and the fast. The publisher, after examining the proposal, was not interested. His company, he said, was not interested in creating textbooks for the lower third of the school population.

We cannot entirely blame the publishers for being slow to create materials. For a very long time, the schools were not organized to serve the slow learner or the fast learner. Many are still not so organized. For a time, the proponents of progressive education argued that to organize classes homogeneously was undemocratic. The only thing a publisher could do, therefore, was to strike some kind of average in his published materials to match classes organized for the average student.

Within the last few years, great changes have occurred. Educators and parents now agree that it is more truly democratic to organize classes on the basis of ability so that students can be served with materials suitable to their reading levels and interests. In January 1964 superintendents of schools in the Great Cities Project called upon the publishers of this country to develop materials for the culturally disadvantaged slower learner (I use the term "culturally disadvantaged" because very frequently the child who comes from a culturally disadvantaged family is almost automatically a slower learner). The American Book Publishers Council and the American Textbook Publishers Institute held a joint meeting in which experts familiar with the problems of the culturally disadvantaged explained their needs to the publishers (*see Wilson Library Bulletin*, June 1964, p. 840).

As a result of these influences, many publishers have brought out new series of books for slow learners at various levels. Many more are currently being processed for publication. Scholastic Magazines, for example, responded to the requests of the school superintendents of large cities by creating a new magazine for the slow-learning teen-ager. By choosing subject matter close to their lives (job opportunities, current affairs, and mass media) and by using illustrations liberally and larger type, *Scholastic Scope* attracts the interest of these young people. By editing copy to fourth and fifth grade reading levels, Scholastic makes it possible for them to read without discouragement.

Lately, researchers have been attempting to isolate the problems of the slow learner. They are beginning to conclude, for example, that the IQ is only one factor in identifying the slow learner. There is more evidence that the IQ, as tested, is not a fixed, immutable ceiling. We are learning about the limitations imposed upon the slow learner by his environment, and we are beginning to understand what kinds of school experience he needs in order to succeed. For it is now quite clear that the kind of program that is suitable for the average student is not suitable for either the slower learner or the accelerated student.

Let us examine more closely two related aspects of this problem: the characteristics of the slower learner and the characteristics of the materials which the teacher can use to motivate the slow learner. The characteristics of the slow learner may be described as follows:

1. His capacity for schooling, even when gauged by new measures, is low. He is a poor reader and, since reading is the key to everything else, he is poor in math, social studies, etc.

2. He generally has a short attention span; therefore the materials put before him must be in very short units.

3. Because hardcover books look long and literally heavy, he tends to resist them. In experiments made in Boston, matched copies of titles in hardcover and paperback were placed side by side in the school library. Children from the lower economic levels almost invariably chose the paperback book because it appeared to be easier and shorter.

4. He usually comes from a family that has few, if any, books or magazines. It is almost invariably true that the slow learner has not been read to during his preschool years. The child who has had this experience will, almost certainly, be a reasonably good reader.

5. He needs to experience success. Because of his shortcomings in reading, failure becomes his daily companion in school. Certainly this is true when he is expected to keep up with the others. As a result, he finally gives up, as indeed would anyone who is faced with repeated failure. To motivate the slow reader at all, the materials placed before him must give him a chance to succeed.

6. He usually has a limited acquaintance with the world around him except for the distorted world that he sees on TV. In New York City and elsewhere, the Higher Horizons program has attempted to make up for this lack of first-hand knowledge by arranging for classroom trips to museums, zoos, theaters, and historic places. These trips open up to the child a larger world about which he is then motivated to read. He has visual images to match words on pages.

7. His oral expression is very limited. Therefore, one of the problems facing the teacher is to stimulate oral activities. In Cleveland last fall, I observed a teacher using a dual telephone equipped with a loudspeaker, supplied by the local telephone company. One child went out into the hall with one of the phones and "called" in to another student seated in the classroom. The child in the hall inquired about an advertisement for a baby-sitter from text in *Scholastic Scope*. The conversation was broadcast to the entire class and other pairs of students repeated the performance. Many were using a phone for the first time. This special kind of equipment for oral English exercises is obtainable from many local telephone companies.

8. His future is in the world of jobs and not in continued education. He is thinking about the jobs he hopes to get and hold. It is important for the teacher to provide him with materials geared to such interests. *Scholastic Scope,* for example, has described job opportunities in hotels, hospitals, telephone companies. Some easy-to-read job material appears in pamphlet form, but not much.

9. He is often an alienated child: alienated from his parents, from his teachers, and from his peer group. In Detroit and elsewhere, a personal diary has been used to enable such children to relate to at least one person—the teacher. Each child has a notebook diary supplied by the school, which is kept strictly confidential between teacher and pupil. Often, the student will write about his life in a way that he would not talk about to anyone else. This practice enables the teacher to know much more about the student as an individual.

The following are some of the things teachers should

consider when examining materials for use with the slow learner. These criteria are based on research which began at the University of Chicago in the early thirties.

Length of sentences: for the slow learner, sentences should range from ten to 15 words. There can, of course, be some variety, with some sentences longer or shorter than this range. The structure of the sentence should be simple: subject, verb, predicate, in that order.

Dependent clauses: there should be a minimum of dependent clauses and compound sentences, although the slow learner grasps the compound sentence more readily than *which, that,* or *because* clauses.

Verbs and verb forms: the slow learner likes simple tenses, such as the present and the past. He prefers the present tense because he tends to live more in the present and he sees experiences as existing in the present. The past drops out of sight and he cannot bring himself to contemplate his future. Material with strong verbs is desirable. Strong verbs put prose into motion. Variations of the verb *to be* should be avoided. They are simply teeter-totters: they go up and down but never stir from a fulcrum. Material that makes extensive use of other commonplace verbs, such as *has* and *make,* should also be avoided.

Hard words: although hard words differ according to the individual, they can usually be identified by noting the number of affixes: the more affixes the harder the reading. Generally, the word with many affixes presents a generalized concept. It lacks the hard visual reality of *house* or *bus*. The affix-ornamented word is a built-up word. Its central meaning is buried in a core surrounded by a shell of affixes. However, there are other words that are quite simple but become hard words because the spelling obscures their true sound. When the editor of *Scholastic Scope* visited a Harlem class, he listened to students reading from a short play which had appeared in the magazine. The students stumbled on the words *rough* and *tough,* although the words were certainly familiar enough. It was the spelling which confused them: *ough* does not look like the sound of *uf*.

Contractions and dialect: the child who recognizes the word *is* may boggle at the word *isn't*. Dialect is most difficult for the slow learner. Since he is just becoming used to words in their standard spelling, he has trouble recognizing words that depart from standard misrepresentation in our typical English spelling traps.

Conjunctions: the slow learner has difficulty with such words as *because, therefore,* and *if,* which require mental leaps backwards or forwards. For example, when the word *therefore* appears, he somehow must bring to the forefront of his mind a previous idea in an earlier sentence. Because the mental hurdle is too high, he gives up. He can manage time words such as *then* and *when,* but there should not be too many of these.

Conversational style: since speech is the one language that the slow learner employs reasonably well, the reading matter set before him should be closer to speech than to nonoral prose. Newspaper English, for example, is far from speech English.

Personal reference: as a rough measure, copy becomes readable if it contains eight to ten personal references (pronouns, names, father, mother, etc.) per hundred words. But pronouns should be placed close to the nouns to which they refer or the reader will be confused. Research clearly indicates that personal references humanize text. Young people think in terms of human beings rather than in terms of abstractions; therefore, the generous use of personal references does more to make text readable than almost any other single factor.

Is simplicity in writing enough to make material readable for slow learners? I think not. There is another factor, which may best be described as strategy: how do you get *through* to these boys and girls? Again, I offer a series of questions which should be asked about potential materials. They may be asked about teaching practices as well, for to separate teaching practice from the materials is impossible.

1. Are the materials preachy? Do they include references to *ought, must,* or similar injunctions? Are they patronizing? Do they reflect a "teacher-knows-best" attitude? Students have been preached at by parents and others and they resist it. They will, as Father John Culkin has said, "give you the mask."

2. Does the material repeat words? The slow learner welcomes a word that he knows as an old friend.

3. Is the reader involved as much as possible? Communication functions best when it is a two-way process. Material that poses questions, that pulls the reader into the communication act, succeeds. Easy quizzes, especially ones at which the youngster can succeed, are to be treasured. In Detroit's English S program for slow learners, tests have been developed which permit the students to achieve a perfect score. These tests are generally about TV personalities, advertising catch lines, or other facts well-known to young people.

4. Does the material relate closely to the lives and personal interests of teen-agers? Their world is the world of their school, their neighborhood, their youth club, their family, of movies and TV, and of the jobs that are just ahead. It is a world of personal growth.

5. Are the materials geared for the grade level? Material that may be suitable for seventh graders will not be acceptable to ninth graders. We have found, for example, that *Death Be Not Proud* is not popular with the former group but is enjoyed by the latter. At the junior high school level, especially, changes occur very rapidly. Materials, to be acceptable, must recognize these changes in child development.

6. Do the materials recognize separate boy and girl interests? There will be more male slow learners than

female, and their interests are quite diverse. Boys enjoy nonfiction and fiction about World War II. Both groups like mystery stories, although some stories will appeal more specifically to boys or to girls.*

7. Is the material humorous? Humor, of the right brand, will really motivate youngsters. Their type of humor is often corny, or as exaggerated and broad as *Mad* magazine. It will sometimes appear in comic strips or in books made up of cartoons.

8. Is the reading material tuned to the current teen hits? Movies and TV promote reading. Historical fiction and biography related to some current movie or TV series will lure readers.

It is important not to veto material for the slow learner merely because it grades out above his tested abilities. Never underestimate the slow learner's capacities. There countless is testimony to the fact that if a youngster finds the material of compelling interest, he will read a text two or three years above his rated reading level.

Youngsters cannot be pressed into a mold. If we find the material that will really appeal to them, they will surprise us. They will read with joy and understanding and will be motivated to read by that which moves them.

---

*These categories are not as fixed as they once seemed to be.—Ed.

The School Library and the Highly Gifted Child

NORMAN W. BESWICK

At first, the idea that the very highly gifted child might pose any particular educational or library problem is surprising. We are accustomed to considering the special needs of retarded children, and accepting them as a particular teaching challenge. We have plenty of experience in dealing with children of average ability, and those of rather more than average who can get through the selective barriers into grammar school level work. But what of the extremely bright boy or girl, consistently scoring 140 or more in intelligence tests and doing almost equally well in tests for creativity? How does such a child fare in our ordinary classrooms and around the shelves of our school libraries? In particular, how does he fare in the average primary school, with large classes and scattered book stock? A little reflection shows that these are not idle

---

Reprinted, with acknowledgments to Norman W. Beswick, Lecturer, Department of Library and Information Studies, Loughborough University of Technology, and *The School Librarian* (17: 349–55 [1969]), The School Library Association, Oxford, England.

questions. Many teachers have been just as concerned over the wasted potential of their brightest pupils, as over their more average classmates.

The highly gifted child seems to have many advantages. He is usually a little better in physical coordination, more obviously full of energy, even more talkative, often more attractive. He may have read three times as much as other children in his class, and usually has a large and unexpected vocabulary. Some gifted children show startling performances at early ages, like the child of seven who can already describe, in some technical detail, the nature and structure of a chromosome. Stimulated in class discussion, their minds may make astonishing leaps of intuition; they will see in a flash where the teacher is laboriously leading them, step by step, and they are bored long before he arrives.

Nonetheless, their intellectual ages are not matched by their emotional development; chronologically and emotionally, they are children. Some, aware of being different from their fellows, develop a defensive mask of apparent stupidity, and may even fail to master such basic skills as reading, until the right stimulus brings out their basic potential. For many, "the handicap of brilliance" is no exaggerated phrase. Disparity of development seems to occasion, or at least to accompany, personality problems, and boredom in class represents a regular hazard, temptation and stumbling block.

Brentwood College of Education has for several years been doing experimental work with highly gifted children from local primary schools, tutors and student volunteers working with small groups in a variety of activities in an attempt both to stimulate and enrich the children and to gain insight into their abilities and responses.[1] When Dr. S. A. Bridges, head of the Education department coordinating the work, invited the cooperation of the tutor-librarian, we began offering the children a variety of library-based activities, beginning in our new children's library.

In preparing to work with the children, it seemed sensible to make a study of the previous literature. It was found that very little had been specifically written about library work with the highly gifted, even in the U.S. with its thirty years' close study of such children. This seems a pity. It is not true that the very gifted child can manage entirely with library materials selected for his more average classmates, and few class teachers have the time to give the high-flier the stimulation and encouragement he needs. Indeed, in some ways this has the appearance of a special skill, as is work with the retarded. The library and its resources have a useful, possibly a crucial, role to play therefore, here, as with many other children. A study of what prominent authorities have said, on reading and the gifted, seemed worth attempting. What they proved to say adds to one's feeling when working with such children: that here is one special case of the species "child," half-formed and vulnerable, very much needing what we hope we have to give.

What the Pundits Say

The size of the problem can be seen from the characteristics these children have in common. First, of course, they are highly intelligent in the sense that they consistently score highly in both verbal and nonverbal intelligence tests. In their work they show exceptional intellectual ability, usually over a broad span of subject fields. Freehill writes:

They learn "how to learn" early and established learning patterns appear to persist. . . . Persons whose early education has been limited to the acquisition of facts tend to persist in memoriter kinds of learning, while those who have learned wisdom and critical thinking seem to persist in this more judgmental kind of activity. Though proofs are limited, it may be guessed that introductory school experiences are very significant in determining the qualities of judgment, creativity and scholarship which will mark adult life.[2]

This does not imply a corresponding degree of emotional maturity; a bright nine-year-old is still nine years old. Although high intelligence may enable a child to make an excellent adjustment to his environment, this cannot be taken for granted, and alienation, loneliness and bizarre behavior patterns are quite prevalent. So also are normal human weaknesses, like laziness and low standards of personal performance.

Very important to us is that every authority seems to unite in reporting their quite phenomenal reading ability and reading performance, other things being equal. Not only is there usually, as might be expected, a positive correlation between high IQ and reading skill, the gifted child himself places a high value on reading. Terman found that the gifted child is "an inveterate reader" (though not all inveterate readers are gifted). Walter Barbe says that, once the gifted child has turned from general reading to specialized topics,

The number of books read in this stage is almost unbelievable, and it is not uncommon to hear a gifted child say, "I've read *all* the books they have in the library about science."[3]

The Stanford studies indicated that gifted children of eight to nine read about three times as much as ordinary children of that age, and that junior-high-school gifted children read perhaps four times as much.[4] Moreover, like children's reading in general, their reading tends to be omnivorous. There is no problem, then, in "getting them to read." Ruth Strang cautions:

Occasionally a gifted child used reading as an escape. . . . Gifted children sometimes find the world of books more satisfying than the real world. Consequently they use reading as an escape from desirable physical activities or developmental tasks.[5]

Similarly, Bertha Friedman, writing in *Library Journal* of the bright child who is always being told, "You're always reading—why don't you go out and play?" adds that a child may be using reading, "to isolate himself from the group and thus cover up his fear of failure in group relationships."[6]

This is not something special to the gifted, and it may be that reading will in the long run prove actually therapeutic in helping a child to recover from emotional bruises. This is surely a good and desirable use of reading, so long as the alert teacher has the full situation in mind.

Brentwood tutors report that the children are good at skimming, an activity which in association with their famous leaps of intuition can lead to astonishing success and dismal catastrophe; intuition is not always right. Moreover, very extensive reading can give a sort of half-knowledge that gets in the way of true discovery. It depends what you are after. If a class is considering the properties of liquids, the object of the lesson may be to awaken awareness of the world about us, and critical observation. Johnny Brightchild, having already read, and half-understood, an advanced account in some library book, may perhaps be able to "get by" without doing any observation or critical thinking at all. The teacher is therefore a very important part (as it were) of school library stock, and equally important is the sort of book that challenges thought and demands a response. Moreover, there may well be many occasions when it will be educationally better for Johnny to have to put into his own words what he sees in a picture or slide or film, or hears on a tape or disc; a library experience limited to printed books is arguably unbalanced and incomplete.

Reading accounts of very gifted children, and the work done with them, one is struck by another emerging characteristic: the gifted child's typical system of values. There are particular subjects he is likely to favor, and particular books and interests he will readily ignore. J. Stanley Marshall quotes a class who were asked to think about, and write down, what they would most like to learn about as they prepared to go to the school library to do reading and research: "They were free to choose any topic they wished. Out of twenty-four . . . twenty chose topics in science."[7]

This theme is repeated again and again, and we have frequently found it true at Brentwood. It makes sense, too. Science is a subject where emotional immaturity is not in itself a handicap, and a child in advance of his years intellectually can progress happily in it. In contrast, there is some problem with certain types of imaginative literature, especially novels and stories. Robin Bateman's survey of ordinary grammar-school children's reading has already shown us that "sentimental fiction" goes badly with them.[8] Highly gifted children value it even less. Freehill noted that they read quite happily what he called "informational fiction" but read proportionately fewer books of what he called "emotional fiction." Perhaps few novels deal satisfactorily with the emotional side of the bright child's life, and he will lose interest certainly in what seems to him unintelligent behavior, except when it is mocked.

This goes hand in hand with the general question of social and moral awareness, the stimulation of which is one of literature's important functions. Perhaps one of the reasons why so many highly gifted children are behavior problems is that they have not developed, nor examined, their emotional natures and their understanding of other people. The gifted child is very much an individualist, and group experience is very important for him if he is to develop balance. This is where reading again has its place, if it can be chosen sensibly to entice him into a consideration of other people, moral choice, the depth of living. Mythical and religious literature can help, and so, on the other hand, can drama and science fiction (*Flowers for Algernon* is an example).[9]

Implications for Library Planning

"It is perhaps safe to say" (says Freehill) ". . . that no organized learning opportunity is more valuable than the library" in the education of the gifted; and William K. Durr goes so far as to suggest:

The gifted should have a stimulating learning environment which differs both qualitatively and quantitatively from that provided for other students.[10]

Even in such subjects as arithmetic, we find Foster E. Grossnickle writing: "The school library should be at the heart of the program for horizontal enrichment . . . in arithmetic for the gifted pupil."[11]

Thus in planning for work with such children, we need to consider quite carefully our library problems and policy. Tentatively, on a fairly brief practical acquaintance with their needs, I suggest that our selection policy might be summarized as follows: No one book will suffice; we need a great many. Range of subjects is more important than pupil numbers, so far as size of collection is concerned. There should be a variety of approaches within each subject. We certainly need many authoritative reference books, of the encyclopedia kind, and bibliographies are not inappropriate either. Magazines, brochures and pamphlets will be important (Freehill specifically suggests scientific magazines and industrial publications). A high proportion of the books should be imaginatively and intellectually stimulating and challenging. Polytopical books and interdisciplinary studies are useful. Many books chosen will have been originally intended for much older children or for adults. The most serious book selection problem will be with literature requiring a degree of emotional maturity.

In math and science, we need the big, glossy, well-illustrated reference books on the individual sciences, and plenty of books explaining, as provocatively as possible, individual topics. In math, series like "Exploring Mathematics on Your Own," published by Murray, take the child immediately into the heart of problems in numeration, topology, probability and other fields. In the physical and life sciences, books that excite imagination and wonder are important, for science is part of our imaginative and cultural life. Science histories and biographies, and the applications of science in medicine, technology, war and elsewhere, help the child to realize that not even astronomy works in a vacuum away from human responsibility.

Social sciences, history and geography will be valued by the gifted child especially where there is clear exposition not just of the subject matter but the method by which it is known: in history, not only "Jackdaws" and "They Saw It Happen," but books showing the controversial historian at work in current history; in social studies, weeklies and newspapers and (for instance) Peter Townsend's work on the problems of the aged, and plenty of political controversy.

Music, the arts, sports, hobbies and pastimes present no serious library problems, and there is some evidence that very bright children are quite happy to accept poetry if it is presented to them sensibly, free of sentimentality, with the accent on precision, shades of meaning, the fascinations of language. Properly chosen, indeed, poetry can play an important part in their emotional development, the verbal game aspect permitting examination of emotional areas sometimes shunned. Moral and philosophical studies are well covered, as is comparative religion, although I am somewhat discouraged by many of the books written for children and expounding the Christian faith—great care in selection is needed here.

In the realm of fiction, the problem is not with the junior ages, for whom there is plenty of good stuff. Hugh, aged just eight, has read *The Phantom Tollbooth*[12] many times and thinks it is the funniest book he is "ever likely to read." The opening of Rosemary Sutcliff's *Dawn Wind*, read to a group of very bright nine-year-olds, held them utterly spellbound, and her novels (usually thought advanced) have disappeared into their hand *en bloc*. Perhaps the problem of fiction for the teenage highly gifted might best be tackled from two opposite poles: first, through the standard classics, which can be presented as if they are purely "informational fiction," what-it-was-like-then, even though much social, moral and emotional discussion will in fact be taking place; and second, through the medium of science fiction. A child beginning with, say, Arthur C. Clarke may eventually come up against a wide and imaginatively literate range of speculation and insight; he might even reach to a book as superb in historical insights as Walter Miller's *A Canticle for Liebowitz.*[13]

There is very much we don't know. All human beings are mysterious, and the very highly gifted child is sometimes a complete enigma, watching the teacher behind inscrutably shining and restless eyes. How can we induce these children to develop that high personal standard which should be theirs and all too frequently is not? And how do we induce it without destroying in the process their opinion of their more ordinary classmates? When they can see what they think are the answers, in their intuitive heads, what a bore it is to them to have to write it all laboriously down, check it by tedious experiment, demonstration, or consultation of books–and how do we show the value? Few of those working with the children at Brentwood are confident they have the answers. When teachers say, "What a joy it must be to have really first-rate material to work with!" we are aware mostly of how infrequently we ourselves have kept up with the speed and patterns of their thought, and how often we have missed the point.

We have to hope for a lot from our libraries. We have tried, at Brentwood, to make sure that the children at least develop and practice the basic library skills, that they come in contact with as wide a range of books and resources as possible, and that the activities planned around the library are as varied and challenging as we can devise. The children are so individual that no book list of "suitable items" for them is likely to be much use, and there will be many teacher-librarians whose knowledge of children's and adult literature is such as to make any list an impertinence. The first task is simply to identify the problem and look hard at our planning and book selection. We might do worse than conclude with another quotation from William K. Durr:

While some books are too difficult even for the most gifted student, the teacher is more justified in erring on the side of difficult materials. . . . Careful avoidance of any reading materials which are "beyond the experience of the gifted" can lead us to assemble a sterile collection. While a reader must have direct or vicarious experience on which to build reading comprehension, we have not shared our students' experiences to the extent that permits a final, unequivocal rejection of books which seem beyond them. The areas familiar to today's children are frequently astounding to those of us who as children did not enjoy the wonderful proliferation of communication media they have. We must not limit opportunities to deepen their learning and broaden their horizons by timidly withholding books from them on the basis of inexperience.[14]

The highly gifted child presents a particular challenge to the school librarian and the teacher. The chances are high that there are a few examples, identified or quite unnoticed, in nearly every school.

NOTES

1. S. A. Bridges, ed., *Gifted Children: the Brentwood Experiment* (New York: Pitman, 1969).
2. Maurice F. Freehill, *Gifted Children, Their Psychology and Education* (New York: Macmillan, 1961).
3. Walter Barbe, "Reading Aspects," in Louis A. Fliegler, *Curriculum Planning for the Gifted* (Englewood Cliffs, N. J.: Prentice-Hall, 1961), p. 219.
4. Lewis M. Terman and others, *Genetic Studies of Genius,* v. 1–5 (Stanford, Calif.: Stanford Univ. Pr., 1925–59).
5. Ruth Strang and others, *Problems in the Improvement of Reading* (New York: McGraw-Hill, 1955), p. 361.
6. Bertha Friedman, "Brains Should Be an Asset," *Library Journal* 80:2623–25 (15 November 1955).
7. J. Stanley Marshall, "Science in the Elementary School," in Louis A. Fliegler, *Curriculum Planning for the Gifted* (Englewood Cliffs, N. J.: Prentice-Hall, 1961), p. 138.
8. Randolph Quirk, *The Use of English* (New York: St. Martins, 1964).
9. Daniel Keyes, *Flowers for Algernon* (New York: Harcourt, 1966).
10. William K. Durr, *The Gifted Student* (New York: Oxford Univ. Pr., 1964), p. 79.
11. Foster E. Grossnickle, "The Arithmetic Program," in Louis A. Fliegler, *Curriculum Planning for the Gifted* (Englewood Cliffs, N. J.: Prentice-Hall, 1961), p. 70.
12. Juster Norton, *The Phantom Tollbooth* (New York: Collins, 1962).
13. Walter M. Miller, *A Canticle for Liebowitz* (Philadelphia: Lippincott, 1960).
14. Durr, *The Gifted Student,* p. 127.

BIBLIOGRAPHY

French, Joseph L., ed. *Educating the Gifted: A Book of Readings.* 2nd ed. Chicago: Univ. of Chicago Pr., 1964.
Shields, James B. *The Gifted Child.* New York: Fernhill, 1968.
Torrance, E. Paul. *Gifted Children in the Classroom.* New York: Macmillan, 1965.

A Comparison of Three Reading Media for the Blind—Braille, Normal Recording, and Compressed Speech

DEAN W. TUTTLE

Purpose

This study attempted to compare reading by braille (B), reading by listening to normal recording (N),

---

Reprinted by permission from *Education of the Visually Handicapped* 4: 40–44 (May 1972).

and reading by listening to compressed speech (C) with respect to an index of learning efficiency (comprehension score per unit of time).

Statement of the Problem

Three of the alternatives to print reading available to the blind are braille, normal recordings and compressed speech. Each has its own advantages and disadvantages:

Braille: Generally accepted alternative to print . . . best tactual system . . . yet bulky and slow (104 words per minute average)

Normal Recordings: Reading by listening is another alternative (175 wpm) . . . lose advantages of spatial display

Compressed Speech: A third alternative becoming available . . . speeds up recordings without voice or pitch distortion (275 wpm)

When one considers that the average print reading rate for high school seniors is between 250 and 300 words per minute, there is an obvious need to find a medium which is more efficient than braille.

Another aspect to the problem under study is illustrated by the student who is verbal, who can communicate his thoughts and ideas with ease, but who cannot learn to use braille as a communication tool. Educators tend to feel obligated to spend many hours trying to teach him braille, rather than developing more fully another alternative mode of reading. The study sought to identify some students who were low in braille skills but high in auditory skills and, conversely, students who were high in braille skills but low in auditory skills. The relative efficiency of compressed speech could then be determined for each of these groups.

Summary of Related Literature

Some studies have compared reading by listening to normal recordng with reading by braille, suggesting that, though more is comprehended through the latter, the former is more efficient. Other studies have compared reading by listening to normal recording with reading by listening to compressed speech. As the word rate of compressed speech is increased, comprehension declines more rapidly than intelligibility. An optimum rate for students of average or above average ability appears to be 275 words per minute. However, the optimum rate for below average students seems to be 250 words per minute. There was no conclusive evidence regarding the effectiveness of a training program in the use of compressed speech.

The relative superiority of reading print to reading by listening is undetermined. With respect to compre-

hension, half of the research studies favor the visual mode while the other half favor the auditory mode. When controlling for amount and difficulty of material and age of subject, there is a moderate to low correlation between the two media. This suggests that some students read either print or braille better than they read by listening, while for others the reverse would be true.

Preparation of Materials

As reading by listening to compressed speech is a relatively new medium, compressed speech materials had to be prepared and distributed to each subject, to expose him to compressed speech. Five 20-minute reading selections were chosen representing a variety of interests and compressions. Fifty copies of each of these reading selections, with accompanying questions, were duplicated.

After reviewing currently available tests, some were found to be oriented to the college bound, some sampled only one type of reading, some were too long, etc. The test which most nearly met all of the necessary criteria was the *Reading Versatility Test* published by the Educational Development Laboratory.

The *Reading Versatility Test, Intermediate Level, Forms A, B, C,* and *D,* were all transcribed into each medium: braille, normal recording and compressed speech. Peninsula Braille Transcribing Group, San Mateo, California, brailled masters and reproduced 30 copies of each of the four forms, giving a total of 120 braille test pamphlets. The Perceptual Alternatives Laboratory, University of Louisville, produced the normal recording and compressed speech masters for each of the four forms. Thirty copies of each of the masters were reproduced, making a total of 120 tests in normal recording and 120 tests in compressed speech.

Sample

Braille readers, 14 through 21 years of age, who were attending schools in California were included in the sample. Students with additional handicaps were not excluded. Information regarding the age, grade, degree of vision, amount of braille instruction, reading habits and preference, and any additional handicaps was obtained for each subject.

Research Design and Methodology

After an introduction to reading by listening to compressed speech, each subject took three equivalent forms of the *Reading Versatility Test, Intermediate Level—* one in braille, another in normal recording and a third in compressed speech. Care was taken to distribute the effects of form and order. Each test included four prose reading selections and 24 multiple-choice questions. Students were permitted to skip or reread any of the reading selections whether B, N, or C. An index of learning efficiency was computed for each test by dividing the number of correct responses by the number of minutes spent reading the selections.

One-hundred-and-four subjects satisfactorily completed the testing procedures. Utilizing the medians of both braille comprehension scores and normal recording comprehension scores, four levels were identified:
I. high braille readers, high listeners (39 subjects);
II. high braille readers, low listeners (13 subjects);
III. low braille readers, high listeners (13 subjects); and IV. low braille readers, low listeners (39 subjects).

An analysis of variance procedure was used to analyze each of the contrasts B–N, N–C, and B–C, across the four levels and overall.

Results

The accompanying tables are among the most important upon which the conclusions were based.

Table 2 gives the average number of correct responses on the multiple-choice questions. The differences were tested for significance and the results are shown in table 3.

Confidence intervals were computed across the four levels and overall for each of the contrasts: B–N, N–C, and B–C. Comprehension scores of N and C did not differ significantly at any of the four levels. It is interesting to note that B–C was significant for Level I as well as Levels II and III. Yet, for over all subjects none of the three contrasts was significant.

Table 4 gives the average number of correct responses per minute of time spent on the reading task. Again, the differences were tested for significance and the results are shown in table 5.

For each of the contrasts, N–B, C–N, and C–B, confidence intervals have been computed across the four levels and over all levels. The natural logarithm of the index of learning efficiency was utilized for this analysis. The order of the variables in the contrasts has been reversed to present positive rather than negative numbers in table 5.

TABLE 1. NUMBER OF MINUTES SPENT ON THE READING TASK

LEVEL	BRAILLE	NORMAL RECORDING	COMPRESSED SPEECH
I	30.4	16.7	11.3
II	37.0	16.1	12.3
III	27.2	16.8	11.0
IV	32.8	17.3	11.2
Overall	31.8	16.9	11.3

TABLE 2. COMPREHENSION SCORES

LEVEL	BRAILLE	NORMAL RECORDING	COMPRESSED SPEECH
I	20.2	19.6	18.0
II	19.2	12.2	13.9
III	10.8	18.8	17.5
IV	11.4	10.5	11.5
Overall	15.6	15.2	15.0

TABLE 3. CONFIDENCE INTERVALS FOR COMPREHENSION SCORES

LEVEL	B–N	N–C	B–C
I	.54 ± 1.87	1.62 ± 1.84	2.15 ± 2.05*
II	6.92 ± 3.26*	−1.62 ± 3.17	5.31 ± 3.59*
III	−8.08 ± 3.26*	1.31 ± 3.17	−6.77 ± 3.59*
IV	.87 ± 1.87	−1.03 ± 1.84	− .15 ± 2.05
Overall	.38 ± 1.60	.18 ± 1.17	.57 ± 1.57

(Confidence intervals noted by asterisk are significant)

TABLE 4. INDEX OF LEARNING EFFICIENCY

LEVEL	BRAILLE	NORMAL RECORDING	COMPRESSED SPEECH
I	.83	1.19	1.65
II	.60	.76	1.18
III	.43	1.14	1.50
IV	.40	.62	1.05
Overall	.59	.92	1.36

TABLE 5. CONFIDENCE INTERVALS FOR INDEX OF LEARNING EFFICIENCY

LEVEL	B–N	N–C	B–C
I	.46 ± 0.33*	.30 ± 0.18*	.77 ± 0.33*
II	.26 ± 0.54	.42 ± 0.30*	.68 ± 0.57*
III	1.31 ± 0.54*	.32 ± 0.30*	1.63 ± 0.57*
IV	.50 ± 0.33*	.51 ± 0.18*	1.01 ± 0.33*
Overall	.56 ± 0.21*	.40 ± 0.12*	.95 ± 0.21*

(Confidence intervals noted by asterisk are significant)

Conclusions

1. For the total sample, there was no difference in comprehension among the three reading media.

2. For the total sample, reading by braille took almost twice as long as reading by listening to normal recording and almost three times as long as reading by listening to compressed speech.

3. For each of the four levels, reading by listening to compressed speech was more efficient than either reading by braille or reading by listening to normal recording.

4. For the total sample, reading by listening to compressed speech was more efficient than reading by listening to normal recording which, in turn, was more efficient than reading by braille.

Implications

This study focused on but two aspects of reading behavior: comprehension and time. The reading of graphs, maps, and other technical materials was not represented in the tests. The effects of reading by listening on the acquisition of allied skills such as spelling and punctuation were not examined.

However, this study has demonstrated that blind students do not all respond in the same way to reading by braille and reading by listening. There are some students who comprehend much more through one medium than the other. This implies that, for any given individual, textbooks and recreational materials must be made available in the medium which is most effective for him.

Since compressed speech is the most efficient of the three reading media under study, local, state, and national agencies must not hesitate to provide visually handicapped students with materials in compressed speech in order to help them meet ever-increasing reading demands. Furthermore, since reading by listening is an effective reading medium for the blind, it may well be an effective reading medium for the sighted who encounter difficulty reading print.

This study does not imply that braille is outmoded. Braille is still the most exact medium for reading and writing for the blind.

Selecting Picture Storybooks for Young Children with Learning Disabilities

JED P. LUCHOW

Picture storybooks are a valuable source of learning and pleasure with preschool and primary students. As a teacher of young learning disabled children, I became curious about which type of books had the greatest appeal to students. In spite of hyperactivity and distractibility in many of my students, certain picture books seemed to hold their interest and atten-

Reprinted from *Teaching Exceptional Children* 4: 161–64 (1972) by permission of The Council for Exceptional Children. Copyright 1972 by The Council for Exceptional Children.

tion far better than others. I wondered if there were common characteristics in the more popular books which both teachers and parents might use in the selection of picture storybooks for young children with learning disabilities.

In order to explore these common characteristics, I began a survey. Using the *Directory of Facilities for the Learning Disabled*, I sent questionnaires to over 100 special class teachers. The questionnaire requested that they list picture storybooks both "enjoyed" and "not enjoyed" by the children. Enjoyment of a book was determined by student behavior such as repeated requests for a book, voluntary use of the book by individual students, and attention during storytime. Nonenjoyment was to be noted for books which were rarely or never selected by the children. From the 44 returned questionnaires, I compiled a list of those books which were mentioned 5 or more times in one of the categories. The list came to 30 "enjoyed" books and 9 "not enjoyed" books.

The next step was to compare these books with a set of specific literary characteristics to see which factors occurred frequently and which did not. The following list of items was used to help identify various aspects of content and illustrations of the books. These factors were derived from Leland B. Jacobs of Teachers College, Columbia University. Dr. Jacobs has been involved with the study of children's literature for many years.

Content Factors of Picture Storybooks

The following factors represent broad characteristics common in children's literature.

C-1. Plot centers about one main sequence of events.
C-2. Outcome of events can be easily anticipated.
C-3. There is no midstory shift from realism to romance to fantasy.
C-4. Much direct conversation is used.
C-5. Detail development is limited to its place in the story, as opposed to its importance in life.
C-6. Colorful, tongue tickling words and phrases that can be easily memorized are used (example: *Green Eggs and Ham*).
C-7. Stories are not melodramatic or theatrical; story climaxes are simple.
C-8. There is one main character or a group operating with oneness.
C-9. Either boy or girl hero is present.
C-10. Plot has brevity.
C-11. Everyday experiences are described.
C-12. Imaginative play is used.
C-13. Talking animals are present.

Illustration Factors of Picture Storybooks

The factors describing characteristics of illustrations are more subjective than the content factors. Therefore, any statements about the illustrations of the various books are brief and inconclusive.

I-1. There is complete harmony of print and picture.
I-2. No discrepancies appear between text and content of illustrations.
I-3. The art captures the mood and tone of the story.
I-4. Illustrations avoid pastoral passivity or decorativeness for its own sake.
I-5. Various media are included—photography, charcoal, watercolor, stone lithographing, pen and ink drawings—but the medium is appropriate to the spirit of the story. For example, charcoal and pastoral colors *can* be appropriate if the story is light.
I-6. Amount of detail in illustrations is dependent on the demands of the text.
I-7. Illustrations may be black and white or color but are outlined with strong lines.
I-8. Picture is large, simple, and uncluttered.

The procedure for rating each of these factors in the 30 books chosen was uncomplicated. One point was recorded for each factor occurring in a particular book. Thus, if one factor were present in every book, it would receive a score of 30. Conversely, if one factor were present in none of the books, it would receive a score of 0. The range of actual scores was 0–28.

Characteristics of the Enjoyed Books

In respect to the 30 books on the "enjoyed" list, the most important positive factor was the underlying theme of "unity." In factors C-3, C-6, C-8, I-1, I-2, I-6, unity was expressed in the oneness of mood, plot, character, harmony between picture and story, or harmony between picture and detail. So often the problems of children with learning disabilities center around poor motor organization and poor organization of behavior. The children have trouble in sorting out details and structuring the world around them. Perhaps, they enjoy these stories which are organized with one main plot, one main character, and without elaborate illustrations because they organize a seemingly disorganized world in a rather pleasant way for this kind of child.

For example, *Are You My Mother?* is apparently enjoyed because it revolves around one character's pursuit of one goal until it is eventually found. *The Camel Who Took a Walk*, though lengthy, has a main character, repetition, and suspense. *Horton Hatches the Egg* with its theme of steadfastness also has one main character. *The Carrot Seed* is perhaps the best example of this unity and simplicity. Its ideas are:

Could It Happen?
Would It Happen?
It Happened!
The End.

A number of stories on the list have a slightly more complicated plot, but the oneness is still present, i.e., *Mike Mulligan and His Steam Shovel, The Story about Ping, Play with Me, The Story of Ferdinand,* and *The Little House.* In each case, although there are a number of minor incidents, the author never allows us to lose sight of the goal for one page, i.e., to dig a foundation in one day, to return to the safety of home, to get animals to play, to be allowed to roam free, and to return to the simple pleasures of the past, respectively. In all, the theme of each of these books is present on every page. The children know it, feel it, and sense it. Perhaps this is still another reason why these books are enjoyed.

Characteristics of Books Not Enjoyed

In evaluating the nine books which appeared on the list of books "not enjoyed," one factor seemed most significant—complexity. In each one of those books, either the plot was too complex, too long, had too many characters, or contained illustrations that were too cluttered. For example, in *Blueberries for Sal*, the switching between the bear episode and the people episode occurs too rapidly. With *In the Night Kitchen*, there is no story or character at all. *The Little Airplane* appears on this list because of the attempt to instruct rather than to tell a story.

Characteristics of the Illustrations

As far as illustrations are concerned, it seems that the children accept either those in color or black and white. It is important to add, however, that in all the illustrations of either variety, strong lines are prevalent. Strauss and Lehtinen (1947) observed that if a picture which the child is to color is outlined with heavy black crayon, the heavy line is a cue which enables the child to keep constant the relationship between the foreground of the picture and the background of the paper. Strauss also noted that color perspective and responsiveness to color remained intact in spite of the most severe disturbance to perceptual or general integration. Again, we see that illustrations must have some kind of organization, a primary need of these children.

Less Important Aspects of Picture Books

In examining those factors which do not seem to affect the popularity of picture storybooks among children with learning disabilities, we do not find such a unified causal theme as we did in the positive factors. It might be helpful, however, to note which factors in our survey appeared to be the least important factors in selecting appropriate books for a special classroom.

First, good picture storybooks for learning disabled children do not have to be centered around everyday experiences, imaginative play activities, or animal stories. Neither do they have to contain direct conversation or lengthy dialogue. This factor widens the horizon for selection since it negates the notion that concrete stories are more favorable for these children. These children enjoy the fancy of *Where the Wild Things Are* just the same as other preschoolers. They also seem to enjoy with equal enthusiasm other such fanciful stories as *The Cat in the Hat, Green Eggs and Ham*, and *To Think That I Saw It on Mulberry Street*.

Brevity, another one of the factors which is not significant in the selection, might be misleading. Although the learning disabled child is often hyperactive and easily distracted, when given lengthy books like *Mike Mulligan and His Steam Shovel, The Story of Ferdinand*, or *The Camel Who Took a Walk*, he may be found to be an unusually attentive listener.

Colorful, tongue tickling words are another less important aspect of a good picture storybook. In some cases, noting the confusion and perseveration of these children, one might especially want to avoid such phrases. Though the children may perseverate on lines like "Caps! Caps for sale. Fifty cents a cap!," these same lines can be used for language stimulation. Although books like *Hop on Pop* and *Fox in Socks* were not among those reported as "not enjoyed," I have found they add to the language confusion. The speech and sound patterns of the *Horton* books or *The Cat in the Hat* series are more rhythmical and, therefore, not confusing to the children.

Finally, as far as a hero, the children do not seem to have a preference for a special type—boy, girl, animal, or machine. The factor that is important is that there be only a main character or a group operating with oneness. It is not necessary to have specially designed picture books for learning disabled children. There is a rich resource of older, readily available books which can be selected according to the teacher's purpose and student's needs.

List of Enjoyed Picture Storybooks

Madeline, Ludwig Bemelmans (Viking Press, 1939).
Mike Mulligan and His Steam Shovel, Virginia Lee Burton (Houghton Mifflin Co., 1939).
The Little House, Virginia Lee Burton (Houghton Mifflin Co., 1942).

Are You My Mother?, P. D. Eastman (Random House, Inc.; 1960).
Play with Me, Marie Hall Ets (Viking Press, 1968).
Gilberto and the Wind, Marie Hall Ets (Viking Press, 1963).
The Story about Ping, Marjorie Flack (Viking Press, 1933).
Angus and the Ducks, Marjorie Flack (Doubleday and Co., 1939).
Millions of Cats, Wanda Gag (Coward-McCann, Inc., 1938).
Snowy Day, Ezra Jack Keats (Viking Press, 1962).
Whistle for Willie, Ezra Jack Keats (Viking Press, 1964).
The Man Who Didn't Wash His Dishes, Phyllis Krasilovsky (Doubleday and Co., 1950).
The Carrot Seed, Ruth Krauss (Harper and Row, 1945).
The Story of Ferdinand, Munro Leaf (Viking Press, 1938).
The Little Train, Lois Lenski (Henry Z. Walck, 1940).
Policeman Small, Lois Lenski (Henry Z. Walck, 1962).
Little Blue and Little Yellow, Leo Lionni (Astor-Honor, Inc., 1959).
Make Way for Ducklings, Robert McCloskey (Viking Press, 1941).
Bruno Munari's ABC, Bruno Munari (World, 1960).
The Little Engine That Could, Watty Piper (Platt and Munk Publishers, 1946).
Curious George, H. A. Rey (Houghton Mifflin Co., 1941).
Mike's House, Julia Sauer (E. M. Hale and Co., Inc., 1954).
Where the Wild Things Are, Maurice Sendak (Harper and Row, 1963).
And to Think That I Saw It on Mulberry Street, Dr. Seuss (E. M. Hale and Co., Inc., 1937).
Horton Hatches the Egg, Dr. Seuss (Random House, 1940).
The Cat in the Hat, Dr. Seuss (Random House, Inc., 1957).
Green Eggs and Ham, Dr. Seuss (Random House, Inc., 1960).
Caps for Sale, Esphyr Slobodkina (William R. Scott, Inc., 1947).
The Camel Who Took a Walk, Jack Tworkov (E. P. Dutton and Co., 1951).
Harry the Dirty Dog, Gene Zion (Harper and Row, 1956).

List of Less Enjoyed Picture Storybooks

Mister Penny, Marie Hall Ets (Viking Press, 1935).
Goggles, Ezra Jack Keats (Macmillan and Co., 1969).
The Little Airplane, Lois Lenski (Henry Z. Walck, 1938).

Blueberries for Sal, Robert McCloskey (Viking Press, 1948).

One Morning in Maine, Robert McCloskey (Viking Press, 1952).

Songs of the Swallows, Leo Polite (Charles Scribners Sons, Inc., 1949).

In the Night Kitchen, Maurice Sendak (Harper and Row, 1970).

The Biggest Bear, Lynd Ward (Houghton Mifflin Co., 1952).

Hide and Seek Day, Gene Zion (Harper and Row, 1954).

BIBLIOGRAPHY

Carlson, R. K. "Ten Values of Children's Literature." Paper Presented at International Reading Association Conference, Kansas City, Missouri, May 1969.

Larrick, Nancy. *A Teacher's Guide to Children's Books.* Columbus: Charles E. Merrill, 1960.

McCutchen, C. C. "Evaluating Young Children's Experiences with Literature," in L. B. Jacobs, ed., *Using Literature with Young Children,* pp. 58–63. New York: Teachers College Pr., 1965.

Schatz, E. E. "Evaluating Picture Books," *Elementary English* 44:870–74 (December 1967).

Strauss, A. A., and Lehtinen, L. E. *Psychopathology and Education of the Brain-Injured Child.* New York: Grune and Stratton, 1947.

Can Reading Affect Delinquency?

WILLIAM C. KVARACEUS

The issue of law, freedom to read, and morality, particularly as reflected in the threat of censorship, bubbles like an unpredictable geyser just below the surface of every American community. It can be released with the publication of any new best-seller or any fancy reprint of an old classic that treats sex as a biological fact or that looks into the darker corners of life. No matter how close to truth and beauty a literary work may reach, it always runs the risk of condemnation as a threat to morals and manners. In this fearful and protective mood, the community in which I labor (Boston) has in the past banned such literary works as Dreiser's *An American Tragedy,* Elinor Glyn's *Three Weeks,* Remarque's *All Quiet on the Western Front,* Sinclair Lewis' *Elmer Gantry,* Percy Marks' *The Plastic Age,* Hemingway's *The Sun Also Rises,* Caldwell's *God's Little Acre,* Lillian Smith's *Strange Fruit,* D. H. Lawrence's *Lady Chatterley's Lover,* Kathleen Winsor's

Reprinted from *ALA Bulletin,* June 1965, p. 516–22.

Forever Amber, and, most recently, John Cleland's *Memoirs of a Woman of Pleasure.* In this paper I will examine some factors that relate to the fear, implicit in censorship, that reading of such literary works will corrupt behavior.

The American citizen spends a good part of his nonworking hours in various kinds of reading. In a national survey of leisure-time activities of Americans fifteen years of age and over, Opinion Research Corporation of Princeton reported that "reading magazines" and "reading books" represented the fourth and fifth most popular activities "engaged in yesterday," according to their sample of respondents. These reading activities were overshadowed only by "watching of TV," "visiting with friends and relatives," and "working around the yard and garden."[1] What are the effects on behavior of this time investment on reading, if indeed such activity can be unscrambled from the many other forces that shape behavior? More particularly, is there in the reading of certain kinds of literary works—such as are frequently removed from the bookshelves—a subversive threat to the reader's moral growth and development?

The primitive habit of blaming books—classics or comics—for delinquency and crime represents a simpleminded approach to a many-sided and complex phenomenon. At the same time, to deny the importance of the rich library experience in the development of the educated man is to negate the personal-social-cultural effects of reading. There is a marked and obvious difference in the way of life of the educated (readers) and the uneducated (nonreaders), although it may prove impossible to trace direct cause and effect between reading a book, banned or approved, and a particular form of behavior such as stealing, mugging, or raping.

The outstanding characteristics of the leisure-time activity of the delinquent boy or girl are, first, an aimlessness seen in a random quest for something to do, and second, an almost complete lack of adult guidance or supervision. Few adults stop to buy or select a book and place it in the hands of a potential delinquent.

Controlled studies of delinquents show them in significant contrast to nondelinquents in reading skills and interests.[2] Merrill reported, for example, that 22 percent of her delinquents read nothing as against 11 percent of the nondelinquent controls.[3] Delinquents more frequently are nonreaders, their basic abilities in reading fall far below their nondelinquent counterparts, and they generally come from homes devoid of reading materials. As a result, retardation is unusually high, low school achievement and failing marks predominate, truancy becomes habitual, dislike for school and teacher is the rule rather than the exception, and early school leaving is often the delinquent's only solution to an unbearable and frustrating school situation. Books are not their best friends; they have become their worst enemies. A case may be drawn showing how nonreading sets a pupil out on the long road to delinquency. Removing books from the reading shelf to save delinquents is a vain and futile gesture, although it may satisfy the missionary zeal of the censor. In order to understand and cope with the freedom-to-read problem, we will need to become better acquainted with the censorious mind.

Preoccupation, Projection, and Perception: the Censorious Mind

The censorious minds in our society are supersensitive to what they deem salacious. They are fast to march in the name of prudence—if not prejudice. They condemn and suppress what tends to stir their sex impulses or what they imagine might stir the sex impulses of others or what they fear will lead to sexually impure and lustful thoughts. Embarrassed and repelled by the fact of human sexuality, they are intent on protecting others, especially the young, from the "unpleasant" and "dirty facts of life" in our social-economic system. Via suppression, like the Puritans and Victorians before them, the censorious mind is deeply and obsessively preoccupied with sex. In the hurried movement to protect others from any evil consequences of sex, the censor projects his own fantasies, fears, and guilt on those around him. At best he may tolerate the sex act, but only for the purpose of propagation; at worst he may disavow and condemn it. Thus the censor's values and needs strongly determine his perceptions.

Psychologists have reported in experiment that poor children imagine coins to be much bigger than rich children imagine them. The particular ways in which an individual—child or adult—perceives a situation, such as a passage in a novel, is a consequence of inherent psychological factors. Sex represents a greater concern and threat to the censorious mind because somehow it has been made more conscious of sex. Like the poor child with the distortion of the size of the coins, the censor views sex in exaggerated terms. One or two four-letter words expressed in the vernacular suffice to condemn a literary work.

To illustrate our point: Recently in that unhappy state of South Africa an official customs censor barred a paperback edition of Thomas Hardy's *The Return of the Native* as "undesirable literature." Obviously the censor had not read the story of the Englishman who finally makes his way back home on Egdon Heath. In reading the title and with his psychological set, he perceived the word "native" as something black and undesirable and hence as something to be condemned in the land of apartheid. It is on such fragile projections as this that censorship spins its shaky and sticky web.

Turning now to the reader, what factors should be considered before we let out on loan or before we remove from the juvenile shelves books such as *The Catcher in the Rye, Dictionary of American Slang, The Amboy Dukes,* or *The Group*? I will discuss five focal principles as they relate to this question:

1. *Principle of word and deed.* There is a wide gulf between knowing and doing or between intellectual insights and behavioral insights. Most young offenders know the text of the law and the legal consequences of car theft, but their knowledge does not always inhibit their stealing the unlocked car from a parking lot. In the same sense, most of my education students have read the basic psychology texts but frequently fail to apply mental health principles they have learned either to themselves or in their teaching situations, in spite of the fact they may pass our written examinations with high honors. While there is a slight and positive correlation between knowledge and behavior, it is true that the millions of readers who follow the assaultive and sexually aggressive antics of Spillane's Mike Hammer or Fleming's James Bond remain staid and law-abiding citizens. Both of these tough and virile men defend the law by breaking it, both kill, both seduce or are seduced by women—it is never quite clear who is the subject and who the direct object of the four-letter predicates, but it is always dangerous and exciting.

It has been argued, and not without good reason, that the vast army of readers of the standard murder mystery make better husbands and wives or fathers and mothers even though they have learned many novel and secret ways to commit murder. In fact, having carried out their baser misdeeds vicariously or in fantasy, they are perhaps safer to live with in the humdrum daily routine of kitchen, bedroom, and bath. Of course, if the reader begins to confuse reality with fantasy, he may soon end up in court or in hospital. We shall need to return to this possibility later. But with the younger readers, it may be more strategic to let them experience an illicit love affair in the fantasy of *Peyton Place* rather than in the back seat of a parked car in their home town. To restate our principle: The fact that a reader has acquired information or understanding as a guide to action is no guarantee that his attitudes and behavior will ipso facto be modified.

2. *Principle of differential effect.* Reactions to literary works are always highly individualistic. I am concerned here with something more than taste and judgment; my concern is with erotic response. Emotional engagement and psychological identification with characters in literature vary with the individual reader. Kinsey and his colleagues provide us with some insight concerning the range and intensity of stimulation found in literary materials.[4] His interviews with 5699 males and 3952 females indicate that 40 percent of men and 41 percent of

women acknowledged no erotic arousal. At the same time, 16 percent of the women readers and 21 percent of the men readers admitted "definite and frequent erotic response," whereas 44 percent of the females and 38 percent of the males were recorded as having "some erotic response." Accepting the Kinsey data at face value, we can conclude that reading literary materials evokes a measure or more of erotic response in more than half the adults.

The extent, duration, and intensity of erotic response while reading novels, essays, poetry, or other literary works will depend upon the general emotional content of the work, upon the specifically romantic materials that are included, upon the sexual vocabulary, and upon the description of the sexual encounter. But more than with the literary material itself, the nature and intensity of the response will depend upon the reader's own capacity, predisposition, or readiness to be aroused psychologically.

As Douglas Waples and others well state:

The reader's total background of training and experience determines what meanings he will assign to particular words and passages; wide variations in such meanings have been revealed in recent studies. And, finally, his previous knowledge and his previous attitudes influence his whole understanding of and response to the publication. How much of it he credits, what he accepts and rejects, the criticisms and the applications he makes—in short, his various responses to the publication are determined by the kind of person the reader is, i.e., by the nature of his predispositions.[5]

Predispositions within the child's personality and character are already pretty well established by the time he picks up his primer; they are even more rigidly set by the time he begins to thumb through the heavier adult literature found in the high school. Any study of the possible negative effects of reading should more profitably be turned toward exploration of the first five years of life. The importance of early childhood in shaping personality and establishing psychophysical set or predisposition cannot be overstressed. Psychoanalytic case studies have reaffirmed often enough that most standards of behavior are learned at a very early age and become so engrained in the individual's patterns of response that they persist long after the situation in which they were learned has been erased by time and forgotten. Since the lessons learned in the preschool years have such a powerful and lasting impact on later experiences, such as reading, it becomes clear that we must look into the early life space of the reader in order to unlock or unravel the reasons why some youngsters and adults become sensitive, allergic, or immune to certain kinds of reading content. Thus, when an adult is pushed over by a book, we will find a greater part of the answer closer to the crib than between the covers of a questionable novel.

It is true that unstable, confused, and emotionally disturbed children (and adults) who have difficulty in distinguishing clearly between the world of fantasy and the world of reality can be further disturbed and confused by an exciting book. For these individuals, teacher, librarian, and parent may need to build a special reading diet of more "neutralized" reading materials. Just as we keep sweets out of the reach of the young diabetic, we may also need to take similar precautions with certain vulnerable children. Unfortunately, with many of these readers, even if the paperbacks are carefully screened and selected, a TV show, a failing grade, or a chum's sneer may send them off.

I believe it was Emerson who said, "The good reader makes the good book." And the old adage suggests in our case that "bad readers make bad books." Recall, if you will, how Stephen Vincent Benet's Bible-reading captain made a "bad book" out of the Good Book as he trafficked in black bodies and souls with messianic justification.

3. *Principle of the book as a source of hard-to-get information.* The overemphasis on sex and the overproduction of sex signals in life, in literature, and in fantasy suggest that the subject remains a major problem for all of us; at least it is much with us late and soon. But this very overemphasis also carries a strong element of denial. Youngsters (and adults) begin to reason: "There is so much talk about it, it *can't* be real." The overproduction of sex materials and sex symbols in itself can be silencing or it can produce a plethora of Don Juan caricatures which are found in the pages of so much of our contemporary literature.

A thick curtain of silence surrounds sex in the American home and school. It is hard to get informed, although some high school and college students do develop skill in mating (even the degree of proficiency is greatly exaggerated) through the practicum of boy-girl relationships. They may know how, but they seldom know why. The result can be seen in young adults who are either uninformed or misinformed in the meaning and practice of sex behavior. The growing boy and girl have very few sources of information. Both the home and the school are either ill-equipped for or most uncomfortable with the task of satisfying curious and questioning minds. Hence almost all youngsters gain most of their information (and misinformation) from their peers in the back streets. Or they can acquire it through the trial and error of direct experience with the usual hazards. With the self-imposed silence of parent and teacher, the best source and perhaps the only source of information is in the literature. Yet it is these very sources that are closed off for the inquiring mind.

Hollingshead, in the study of *Elmtown's Youth,* describes how the felt need for sex information was met by the boys who had dropped out of school:

The boys avidly read salacious comic books sold by disreputable hangouts. These stores also commonly sell "sport," "screen," and "art" magazines so full of suggestive pictures and sex stories that they have been barred from the mails. On the racks of these stores, titles, such as *How to Attain Perpetual Potency, The Forty-Three Positions, The Young Man's Guide, The Maiden's Fulfillment, Love's Dream Manifest, What Every Woman Hopes, Get Your Man and Hold Him*, are prominently displayed along with legitimate screen, comic books, and popular magazines. The Public Library is not a hangout for any withdrawee.[6]

It is unfortunate that the school dropout cannot be lured into the library where he can make use of better sources of information than are available in a street-corner hangout.

Youth's need and readiness for sex information varies, but sex can become a boring topic as well as a risky one. Freud recognized this in one of his later papers:

. . . a cultural community is perfectly justified, psychologically, in starting by proscribing manifestations of the sexual life of children for there would be no prospect of curbing the sexual lusts of adults, if the ground had not been prepared for it in childhood. But such a community cannot in any way be justified in going to the length of actually *disavowing* such easily demonstrable, and, indeed, striking phenomena.[7]

Today the secrecy surrounding sex comes close to a denial of an important aspect of man's basic nature.

4. *Principle of therapy.* The preceding discussion has centered mainly on questions concerning the corruption of behavior through the reading of certain types of literature in which there has been a heavy exposure of man's sexuality. Now, reversing the question: Can a "good book" salvage a "bad boy"? Is there a role for a teacher or a librarian to play as bibliotherapist?

Historically one can always dig up a few examples of St. Paul-like personalities who have dramatically changed their course in life after reading an inspirational psalm, a moving passage of scripture, or even a line of purple prose. But lightning and lasting postreading conversions are few in number. They are seldom witnessed within the personal circle of friends, relatives, or clients.

Studies of the influence, for example, of biblical information on moral conduct are difficult to control and tend not to be conclusive, but they provide some data for discussion. An early study by Taylor and Powers reported higher correlation (r .50) between results on a Bible knowledge test and character ratings of teachers than were found with intelligence test scores (r .24).[8] In other words, teachers were more favorably impressed with the behavior of youngsters who had more biblical knowledge, and the difference was not attributable to differences in intelligence. However in a similar study, Hightower reported little or no relationship between biblical information and various phases of moral behavior.[9] Comparisons with teacher ratings of character and with cheating, lying, and unselfishness were disappointing or inconclusive. These are old studies, and it is significant that little research has been carried on in this area in the past several decades. Two reasons can be offered: First, it is difficult to isolate and to control all the relevant variables that influence moral behavior; and, second, the oversimplification of an hypothesis suggesting a direct relationship between the reading of certain literature and the complex dynamic of behavior —norm violating or norm conforming—offends the inquiring mind of the behavioral scientist. He no longer expects nor seeks to find simple or single explanations for delinquent behavior. Such research proposals for rehabilitation of delinquents, alcoholics, drug addicts, or neurotics would not receive serious consideration by the National Institute of Mental Health nor the private foundations.

The positive effects of continuous and concentrated reading of the "best and most serious literature" should be most in evidence in the behavior of the college graduate. After all, the major business of the college centers around book reading and the library. Yet studies at the college level indicate how difficult it is to obtain fundamental changes in personality and behavior. Jacob[10] and Sanford[11] in separate studies indicate that a majority of students graduate from college not much different from when they entered. They report that the intellectuals become more intellectual, bohemians become more bohemian, and conservatives become more conservative. This is not so much a change in personality or character as a reinforcement of existing behavior traits. Radical changes are noted only within exceptional personalities and in exceptional institutions.

Nevertheless, one can still anticipate the generally benign effects of the reading habit among the young and the adult. Filling free time with book-reading activity will always be classified under the category of "good use of leisure." It will always represent a wholesome mental health activity. But in this day of passive, social, and mass-programmed leisure-time pursuits, reading can play a very special function. The library can preserve through individualized reading the important elements of reflective leisure and independence that are so lacking in the daily life of the American citizen. The passive, commercial, and unthinking activities in which so many young people and adults engage, and which are tied to mass media over which they have no control, represent a greater threat to the general welfare than does the loud and annoying element of youth we label delinquent. It is here that the library may make its greatest contribution. So long as library stacks remain open, the inquiring citizen can exercise his personal choice of entertainment in selecting any book to read.

In doing so, he will also continue to exercise his mind, for reading is more than viewing.

5. *Principle of guidance.* Studies of institutionalized delinquents have always revealed them to be singularly lacking in cultural accomplishments and interests, although they show marked athletic prowess and strength. Few of them can play a musical instrument; they seldom reveal any hobbies such as stamp collecting or building model airplanes or automobiles; they devote little time to reading or writing activities. We have indicated earlier that in Merrill's study there were twice as many nonreaders in the delinquent sample as against the number within the nondelinquent controls.[12] This does not reflect any lack of innate aptitude or talent among the delinquent; but it does reaffirm the serious lack of interested adults who willingly take the time and trouble to introduce youngsters to the pleasures of collecting, playing a musical instrument, or reading a novel. Hence, when delinquents read a book or a magazine, it is generally to kill time while waiting for something else to do.

The delinquent and predelinquent are much in the need of direction and supervision of their reading. Guidance in reading for delinquents and for many other youngsters should include three kinds of assistance: (1) help in selection of reading materials; (2) help in developing and reinforcing their reading skills; and (3) help in discussion and assimilation of what has been read. The low reading skill accompanied by high reading interest level presents many problems in selection of appropriate books and magazines. Making material available with respect to these two criteria can do much to encourage and advance the reading habit. But what is even more frequently absent is the opportunity to discuss informally with another reader the significance and meaning of what has been read. A friendly dialogue between the reader and the parent, teacher, or librarian can do much to bridge the gap between word and deed, between what is read and what might be applied in meeting the problems of everyday living.

A Symptom More than a Cause

Finally, reading must be viewed more as a symptom than a cause of adjustment or maladjustment. Reading tends to reinforce what is already present and what has already been learned or experienced, frequently as far back as the early childhood years. Viewed in the chain of events that make up a young or old reader's daily life, reading will not change behavior so much as will direct experience and exposure. The sad and tortured lives that many youngsters live often sink beyond anything they might experience vicariously in the most questionable literature.

Numerous forces determine the extent and character of the effects of reading on behavior. The reader's background of experience, his predispositions and set, his emotional status, the confidence that he places in the author or the printed word all modify his reaction. Reading a specific book will seldom cause a "normal" or "average" child to go out and commit a similar act. However, with seriously disturbed and frustrated youth who no longer are able to distinguish between their world of reality and their world of fantasy, a steady and strong literary diet may develop receptivity for a type of response and may trigger behavior of a violent, sadistic, or aggressive nature. But this is the risk we must take in the preservation of freedom to read. And it is a small risk. (It is a minor consideration when compared to the risks taken in the general licensing of auto drivers whose weekly death toll amounts to a public slaughter.)

On the positive side, books will always play a very special role in everyday life, for they can help a child to live more fully in the world of reality and the world of the imagination. In this sense, books do make "the full man." Recognizing that there is and always will be a wide range in the quality of reading materials, from comics to classics, it may profit us to remember Cervantes' observation in *Don Quixote,* "There is no book so bad but something good may be found in it." Occasionally it may be worth the hunt to try and find the good.

NOTES

1. Motion Picture Association of America, *The Public Appraises Movies* (Princeton: Opinion Research, 1957).

2. William C. Kvaraceus, *Juvenile Delinquency and the School* (New York: Harcourt, 1945); *The Community and the Delinquent* (New York: Harcourt, 1954).

3. Maud A. Merrill, *Problems of Child Delinquency* (Boston: Houghton, 1947).

4. A. C. Kinsey and others, *Sexual Behavior in the Human Female* (Philadelphia: Saunders, 1953), pp. 669–72.

5. Douglas Waples and others, "Why They Read," in Wilber Schramm, ed., *The Process and Effects of Mass Communication* (Urbana, Ill.: Univ. of Illinois Pr., 1955), p. 57.

6. A. B. Hollingshead, *Elmtown's Youth* (New York: Wiley, 1949), p. 407.

7. Sigmund Freud, *Civilization and Its Discontents* (New York: Norton, 1961), p. 51.

8. H. R. Taylor and F. F. Powers, "Bible Study and Character," *Journal of Genetic Psychology* 35:294–302 (June 1928).

9. P. R. Hightower, *Biblical Information in Relation to Character Conduct* (Iowa City, Iowa: Univ. of Iowa Pr., Studies of Character, 3, no. 2, 1930).

10. P. E. Jacobs, *Changing Values in College* (New York: Harper, 1937).

11. Nevitt Sanford, *The American College* (New York: Wiley, 1962).

12. Merrill, *Problems.*

PART 3

Materials Utilization: Technology and Tactics

Among the vital and persisting concerns of the librarian are the obligations to inform colleagues and students about the scope and variety of materials available, to demonstrate how these relate to general curricular requirements as well as to specific academic problems and to facilitate access to these materials as they are desired. Users must be able to define what they require, locate what they have defined, and use what they have located. To expedite this process, librarians must provide ready entry to the collection in a multiplicity of ways.

The traditional organization of the library collection is unresponsive to the specialized demands of exceptional children. It is common practice to group books alphabetically or by subject matter; for some purposes, however, the content is of less significance than the book's format or level of difficulty. For exceptional children level of difficulty is of critical importance. This may be described as the comprehensibility of the textual matter and would include an evaluation of such elements as comfort level of reading (ratio of words known to words presented), sentence length, complexity of story line, relationship between content and experiential background of the reader, and other such factors. Occasionally, the critical overriding concerns are the congruence between the textual and pictorial material, relative ease of use in terms of internalization of the concepts, and absence of structural or ideational elements which interfere with utilization by the special child. For instance, the teacher may want an illustrated book to read to a class containing visually impaired and mentally retarded children. Whether the book is about a mouse or a Munchkin may be less important than the presence of a simple, strong story line combined with explicit figure-ground contrast in the pictures.

Similar considerations apply to the selection of media. The medium of choice for deaf children would be transparencies, not filmstrips, because the former mode of presentation enables the teacher to face her students in a lighted room so that speechreading is possible during presentation. In other instances, the disability automatically precludes the utilization of print materials. In some cases, when the librarian is aware of past negative attitudes toward reading or of experiences of failure with print or hardcover bound books, a decision to explore other options is clearly in order. Thus, unusual and selective demands are brought to bear on the ability of the librarian to retrieve, analyze, and present materials to the child with special needs.

It is quite clear that an insufficiency of commercially produced materials exists which would have the capability of responding to many of these needs. In the past, publishers had evidently concluded that the market was too small or the demand too weak to be able to profitably produce for this population.

Although this picture has improved slightly, the librarian will be frustrated by age-inappropriate material, publisher bias (noted in some high-interest/low-vocabulary books and multimedia kits), high costs per item, and severe limitations in scope of material as well as dysfunctionality for children with certain disabilities. Consequently, it becomes imperative for the specialist to enter into the production of materials which are prescriptive in application and design, thereby supplementing available resources.

Proper utilization of these media demands a sophisticated knowledge of the complexities of learning deficits. After the particular problem requiring amelioration has been identified, the media specialist must mentally scan the repertoire of emendatory possibilities, apply judgment as to the most potentially efficacious medium, and either make recommendations or provide direct service.

In addition to using one's self as a resource, the librarian should contemplate using the exceptional child as a producer of print or media products. Students who invest their own energies bring a heightened involvement and excitement to a task. Very often the process of material development may have multiple affective and cognitive benefits or consequences. When a retarded child produces a book or slide show which subsequently becomes part of the library collection, he or she has not only learned such intellectual tasks as concept development and sequencing, but has also learned to stick to a task and has discovered a satisfying personal as well as an academic relationship to instructional materials. A set towards receptivity to these now nonthreatening materials has been encouraged and an improved estimate of self-worth can be anticipated.

Authors with special technological expertise, and those with sensitivity and savvy about the motivational and cognitive development problems of the special child report in this chapter on the innovative ways in which they have produced, modified, or utilized instructional materials.

By definition, some exceptional children have limitations, distortions, or total barriers in one or more learning channels, e.g., visual or auditory, which consequently demand alternate modes of learning. McIntyre emphasizes the need to look beneath the label or the particular impairments to discover the intact aspects of the learning mechanisms of the child. The media specialist evaluates the child's learning strategies, designs or shapes responses which bypass deficits, and capitalizes upon those often well-differentiated, compensatory skills the exceptional student has exhibited. Auditory, visual, and haptic channels are examined for the intrinsic strengths or obstacles to understanding which they present to the handicapped. Preferences for responding in vocal, written, or gestural modes are also discussed. McIntyre suggests that final analysis of the preferred mode must be made after a careful consideration of all these factors. Unfortunately, he does not relate modes of response to handicap as specifically as one would wish. However his ideas for hands-on, in-service training for staff who will work with special children are instructive and should be read in tandem with Kelly's contribution.

Jackson explores some major breakthroughs which have come about in the education of the deaf as a result of technological progress. Of particular interest in this article is the combination of various media used to exploit many possible means of communication. Instead of relying on a single format, he asserts that the unique qualities of 8mm loops, slide-tape programs, overhead projection, dual screen presentations and remote control projectors all should be used to overcome the learning deficits of hearing impaired children. Although limited in detail, Jackson's descriptions are suggestive of some of the many areas in which librarians can apply advances in media technology to improve instruction.

Despite the data-based support for audiovisual instruction, there is a dearth of materials especially designed for the mentally retarded student and a relative absence of evaluation centers where material assessments made under rigorous, field-based research conditions can be analyzed and disseminated. Aserlind deplores the bleak consequences of this situation—namely, the underutilization of appropriate media in the instructional process or the borrowing and utilization of inadequate tools. He systematically defines some criteria which should be considered in material selection and use. Although some of those grievances which Aserlind cites are being gradually redressed, media specialists working with the retarded will need to come to terms with his basic remonstrance.

In a school with a student body widely heterogeneous in ability, Geeslin's idea of a difficulty-coded collection has potentially great utility. He advocates a library practice which is simple in concept but enormously useful for those teachers who value diversity and prescriptive instruction. His difficulty-coded collection enables the teacher or librarian to accurately correlate the demands of the learning situation with the abilities of the child. If reading level is known only by the librarian and the book itself is code-free, this makes possible more precise reading guidance without advertising to peers precisely where the book and the reader are located on the difficulty and consequently status hierarchy. Geeslin ignores, however, the considerable research which indicates a child may often read above his tested achievement level if the subject matter is of sufficiently compelling interest. He calls attention to the benefit of using multiple sources on the same topic so that each child can explore books on his or her own level and bring a meaningful contribution to the general class discussion.

A critical deficiency in media utilization is that it frequently ignores the need for viewer involvement. Pfau explains how specially designed films, filmstrips and video tapes have the potential for providing pupils with a response role so that intermix between learner and media is unavoidable. The prelingual deaf child makes especially heavy demands on media which must attempt to compensate for little or no language input; without substantive development in this area, instructional progress is virtually impossible. Thus, Pfau postulates a roster of language development needs as well as a brief model that illustrates a progressively

more abstract level of concepts based on a hierarchy of learning difficulty. Although specific materials from Project LIFE are evaluated, similar considerations can be applied to other materials.

Students with neurological impairment, emotional problems, and those with foreign language backgrounds jointly worked on television production, a rich experience which generated a harvest of improved learning and language skills. Cohen's article graphically describes the symbiotic relationship between achievement, involvement, and self-interest. The timing for initiation of media utilization was unusual: media usage preceded reading; it was not used simply for supplementary purposes. It is interesting to note that the teacher did not precensor themes and that reality testing by children of content limits revealed to them that any substantive topic seriously handled was acceptable as a project. The reader may be troubled by the report, which is never fully explained, of the differences between Cohen's first and second group in transfer of appropriate behaviors. Educators who wish to duplicate this project will need to insure the inclusion of the financial, administrative, and material adaptations which were so crucial for success in her program.

Knight lucidly explains how inexpensive, easily made, teacher-produced slides can contribute significantly to the acquisition of a basic reading vocabulary by children with limited vision. He claims that the increased manipulation of materials necessitated by visual deficits interferes with ease of comprehension. Large print may not be big enough for some children or may confine the size of the visual field to the point of incomprehensibility. The adaptability of Knight's technique is virtually unrestricted and gives almost limitless control over size and content of visual stimuli.

One day, checking a camera out of the media center/library will be as common as checking out a book. This tool, with its tremendous potential for instructional impact on deaf children, has often been ignored or rarely used. Its utilization increases autonomy, promotes self-direction, and impels the hearing impaired child to excavate verbal skills in interpreting photographs. Personalization of the stimuli with consequent high involvement and excitement clamps attention to the material and compels the students to bypass their gestural behaviors and to extend oral vocabulary. Many claims are made about the constructive influence photography has on self-image, sense of time, linguistic growth, etc., but the reader may be uncertain as to how these elements interrelate or in which ways they could be maximized. In this article, the camera (see also Cohen) is the key to startling educational growth: the medium is the message.

Chang and Johnson's highly specialized article on map reading for the blind has been included to graphically illustrate the challenge and uniqueness of demands which an exceptionality makes on the developers of media. A model is developed which exemplifies how the media specialist must design prescriptively by clarifying and simplifying the educational objective and then drawing on professional competencies for remediative solutions. The reader can clearly see the congruency between educational need and medium response. The authors aptly illustrate a cardinal rule for the professional working with the disabled: one must exploit skills in one area to compensate for limitations in another. Despite the deliberately narrow scope of the article, the alert media specialist can readily see other applications which would be useful for teachers of history, geology, astronomy, and disciplines where space and time dramatically influence movement and change.

One of the overwhelming problems of the handicapped is that too often they are ghettoized in the world of the similarly disabled. Twin-Vision books, described by Horn in a concise but informative article, provide the opportunity for the severely visually impaired to share literary and pictorial experiences with the sighted. This new format presents facing matched pages of standard print and braille, enabling sighted readers to read to the blind, or blind readers to read while the sighted listener follows along using the standard text.

Inefficient learning behavior is a prime deterrent to educational success for the blind. Braille reading or other informational input modes such as talking books demand excessive, often intolerable amounts of time. Leavitt specifies how tape recorders with variable speed capabilities handle the variety of demands which textbook assignments, chapter and lecture notes, fictional and recreational reading, term papers, and examinations make upon the blind student. Implicit in Leavitt's article is the requirement that media specialists understand the potentialities of specific pieces of hardware and manipulate them to achieve maximum efficiency. His comments must not be misconstrued as an exclusive endorsement for specific products. The librarian should be prepared to use the material Leavitt describes but must continue to monitor technological advances which might supplant or complement those recommended.

The MIVR system reported by Wyman offers several distinct advantages for the education of deaf children. The equipment has intrinsic appeal; each student must react to each stimulus; and there is immediate feedback for every student response. Although tremendously promising, there will probably be considerable restriction in widespread adoption of this program because of financial factors. More work needs to be done in providing low cost adaptations of such successful projects. The underlying message in Wyman's article is the heavy media needs of these special learners. If the deaf child is to function in the library program to the fullest possible extent, the librarian will need to be aware of such multimedia instructional combinations and translate them so that the library holdings provide a high visualization component and otherwise reflect their learning style.

In a perceptive essay, Kelly poses some critical but embarrassing questions to the users of media: Is communication heightened as a consequence of mediation? Whose needs are being satisfied by mediated instruction—the teacher's or the students'? Are there alternatives which are more instructionally productive but are either less status-conferring or less technologically impressive? Kelly insists that the focus of teacher behavior always be on user needs and that media usage must address itself primarily to the instructional ramifications of impairment. Teacher aspirations for status which are derived from identification with innovative or faddish behavior should be discouraged. While librarians must heed his warning, experimentation with new materials and procedures should continue because, out of such efforts, valid and more useful developments will emerge which will be increasingly more responsive to curricular and individual requirements.

Media Systems and the Handicapped Child

KENNETH MCINTYRE

A frequent first reaction of persons coming into contact with children who show a variety of handicapping conditions is to focus on the most obvious aspect of the child, his deviation from "normal" in some aspect. Sometimes this reaction remains for years but usually those who work with these children who are different begin to relate to the child first and to his handicap only as it interferes with the job of growing and learning. In discussing media use for the education of handicapped children with professionals who have not had a direct involvement with special education, we can expect a "first reaction" question of, "What medium is best for teaching a child with X handicap?" The exact wording may change, but the emphasis is usually on the handicap of the child—with his limitations—rather than on the characteristics of the media or the objectives of instruction.

A more fruitful approach involves considering the educational interaction between the student and the educational environment as a system and focusing on the characteristics of the various media of communication as they might be used. We must be concerned with the transmission of information to the child; with his communication back to the environment. The following rough taxonomy of input and output channels has been found to be useful in educational planning for handicapped children.

Input Modes

Auditory—Information might be transmitted to the child by the teacher's spoken word, by record or by a variety of magnetic tape modes. Obviously one does not choose an auditory input for children who are deaf, but electronically amplified speech is used with children whose hearing loss is moderate to severe. Less obviously, some children display some deficit in immediate auditory memory. For these children, the use of recorded

Reprinted by permission of Association for Educational Communications and Technology from *Audiovisual Instruction* 14:21–23 (Nov. 1969).

instructions which they may review frequently can prevent failures due to misunderstood directions and, possibly, strengthen the immediate memory. The use of auditory input media can also bypass a reading deficit when the immediate educational task does not require reading print. Many teachers of the mentally retarded have found that tape recorded instructions can effectively supplement standard texts and workbooks with poor or nonreaders.

Visual—Information is usually presented visually in both a print and a representational format. Where a child's ability to read print prevents his progress in other aspects of a program, steps should be taken to supplement or replace the print medium except for those tasks which have the learning of reading as their specific objective. The use of pictures, including films and filmstrips, projectuals and graphics, can help accomplish this. In addition, some children experience unusual difficulty in perception and interpretation of the visual elements in their world. Some special materials have been developed to overcome this perceptual problem and are used with a variety of pupils, including the retarded and those with specific learning disabilities.

Haptic—Presentation of information to children through touch and body position is somewhat more common in special than in regular education. Among children with multiple sensory impairments, this modality may be the only undamaged communication link. Among those with impaired learning ability, certain learnings may be mastered only through the use of several senses at once. The old techniques of Itard and Montessori are really preelectric multimedia approaches and are still found effective with a variety of learners today. Again, children in special classes may present subtle deficits in their ability to integrate information received through body position or tactile sensing. For these children, special activities and media have been developed and are in use.

Output Modes

If we assume that feedback to the educational planner is essential, then we must consider the modalities open to the learner in communicating with the environment. Too often our educational plans show concern with the activities of the teacher in presenting information to the student and too little concern with what the student does or can do as a result of the experience. This problem can become acute with severely handicapped children whose ability to communicate is hampered by speech or physical problems. For these children a significant part of their education is devoted to developing some usable output modes.

Vocal—The most available output mode is speech. Depending on spoken replies creates some problems since a listener is required and the time necessary to listen to children's responses is often too great to permit adequate feedback to the teacher, even in small classes. When work is highly individualized, as is often the case in special education, each learner's responses might be different and irrelevant to the rest of the class, precluding any great use of class discussion as a teaching technique. This problem can be partially overcome through the use of recorders and "language-lab" arrangements which depend on the learner to listen and compare his response with a model but allows the teacher to spot check the responses later.

Written—Writing or marking responses has become a major response mode in special just as in regular classes. This is the form favored by most individualized instructional media. Unfortunately, many special education pupils, including some of the more retarded, find writing particularly difficult and slow. Typing has been used with some success to increase the legibility and speed with which some handicapped children write. In cases of severe impairment of functioning of the hands and arms, striking the keys of an electric typewriter may be the only way a child will be able to write.

Gestural—Children can also communicate meaning through gesture, pantomime, and through making choices, sorting, pointing. When the medium permits recording of choices, as in some types of teaching machines, even severely physically handicapped children can progress through programs designed for general use.

Individualized Instruction Needs

Perhaps the most significant aspect of special education, as it relates to media choice, is the great need for individualized instruction. Some children in special classes need very slow-paced instruction with a great deal of review and over-learning. It is inefficient and uneconomical to provide this instruction in groups exclusively or to depend on the live teacher for what is really a mechanical instructional task. Other children in special classes are there simply because the usual methods of group instruction have failed. For these children, individual and frequently unique materials and methods must be developed and used. For other children with sensory impairments it is often necessary to translate instruction from one medium to another, sometimes into a medium not used at all by other children as in the case of braille books for the blind or signing and cued speech for the deaf. Often the adaptation of material, as well as the choice of media, occurs at the level of the individual teacher and pupil.

The task of helping teachers make, choose, and use a variety of appropriate media has been assisted in recent years by several national programs operated by the Bureau for the Education of the Handicapped of the U.S. Office of Education. The oldest in point of time began with the Captioned Films for the Deaf Project which established four Regional Media Centers for the Deaf. These centers, in addition to developing special media, have done an extensive job of placing equipment and media in classrooms and in training teachers to use and develop visual media and programmed approaches to the education of their children. More recently the Instructional Materials Center Network for Handicapped Children and Youth was established with the charge of getting information about the use of effective media to teachers of all types of handicapped children. This project, now entering its fourth year, has developed models of dissemination and teacher inservice education which are now being implemented by many of the state departments of special education. The most recent project in this area is the recently funded National Media Center for the Handicapped which will provide a model demonstration school as well as its other functions.

Training Special Class Teachers

One specific activity of one Instructional Materials Center for Special Education in this area may serve to illustrate some of the needs and a few of the approaches being employed. During the summer of 1969, the SEIMC at the University of Southern California, in conjunction with the California State Department of Education, planned and ran three short, three-day conferences for a total of 600 special education teachers and administrators. This institute was organized around three main themes: use of behavioral objectives in curriculum development, use of reinforcement contingencies and behavioral reinforcers in classroom management, and selection of appropriate media and methods based on the planned objectives. With this basic structure, part of the afternoon was devoted to media production workshops in five areas. The emphasis was on helping the participants successfully make and use at least two pieces of instuctional media for achieving their defined objectives.

Overhead transparencies—Participants were shown how to make transparencies with a Thermofax and how to add color with acetate pens and chart tape. Each participant made three to five transparencies using their own drawings and lettering, letters and art work from newspapers, or predeveloped masters.

Filmstrips—Participants were shown how to use Hudson's "U-Film" materials to make short filmstrips. Each particpant made one strip by first planning it, frame by frame, then writing or drawing on the strip material with a variety of pens, and finally splicing in frames from discarded or damaged strips and specially prepared single frames.

Audiotape—Both standard sized tape and battery-operated cassette recorders were available for use. A variety of uses for the tape medium were suggested and participants prepared a 15-minute tape incorporating one or more lessons for their students. In addition to the applications mentioned previously, participants used the portable recorders to collect environmental sounds for auditory discrimination and identification training and developed tapes with a gradually increasing level of background noise to increase the student's auditory figure-ground discrimination and attentiveness.

Audio cards—Using Language Master equipment, the possibilities for using audio cards as multimedia devices were demonstrated. The participants added sound to the cards by voice or from prerecorded material. Visual elements were added with pens, pictures from magazines, Polaroid pictures, and paints. Tactile stimulation was achieved by use of glue and glitter and flocking. Again the participants were encouraged to develop a set of cards, sequenced to perform a specific function.

Cameras—The use of photography in the classroom was approached by using Polaroid cameras so that there would be no delay in processing. Each participant planned a sequence of pictures which could be used to illustrate a concept, develop a visual discrimination skill or provide a stimulus for a language lesson. They then shot the sequence and placed the pictures, in order, in acetate folders, adding whatever lettering or other elements were necessary. As an additional example of the use of photography, each participant had been photographed during registration and the heads were cut out and mounted on a row of cartoon bodies with the persons' names added.

For all the media workshops, the objective was to help the participant become aware of some of the specific uses of a medium, to help him achieve success in making instructional material, and to introduce him to some of the available material in the medium considered. Our ultimate objective is to have the participants increase the amount and quality of media used in their classrooms through a combination of teacher-prepared and commercially available materials. Follow-up surveys and classroom observations during the academic year will indicate the extent to which the conference succeeded. At present, we know that the immediate goals were achieved to the extent that each conference participant left with at least two completed media projects and a feeling of success in entering the area of media production and use. The job of increasing appropriate media use for handicapped children can be done and has begun.

Educational Media in Teaching the Deaf Child

WILLIAM D. JACKSON

For a deaf child to learn to speak and to read speech on the lips and the expressions of others is a minor miracle—but a miracle that is happening every day in hundreds of classrooms for the deaf throughout the country.

The child who is born deaf or becomes deaf in his early years before the acquisition of language has hurdles to overcome that stagger the imagination. Information which we gain through the auditory process must come to the deaf person through another channel. Language, the indispensable tool of learning acquired with little effort by the hearing child, is acquired only after great effort and determination by deaf children assisted by dedicated teachers and parents.

Deafness is a communication handicap, and extensive research is currently being conducted in the field of medicine and related areas such as audiology, psychology, and acoustics. Several research centers in conjunction with established schools and classes for the deaf have devised new techniques for accelerating speech and language development, as a consequence of early diagnosis, testing, and follow-up services. Very young children are being fitted with new types of instruments as early as 18 months. Increased emphasis is also given to a variety of new media and instructional materials.

Such an approach to the education of the deaf child is a very recent undertaking when compared with formal education of hearing children. The first known public school for the deaf was founded in Paris in 1755, and it was not until 1817 that a permanent school for the deaf was established in the United States. The first public school class for the deaf was started in 1869 in Boston. Most schools and classes for the deaf in the United States were residential; but around the turn of the century, Chicago began integrating deaf children into classes for hearing children, and thus into the hearing world of their peer groups. Day class programs, public and private, now have spread throughout the country and number some 300 classes with more than

Reprinted by permission of Association for Educational Communications and Technology from *Audiovisual Instruction* 11:715–18 (Nov. 1966).

9,000 students. The total deaf and hard-of-hearing student population enrolled in all types of schools and programs in the United States has been estimated at more than 30,000.

A recent report to the Secretary of Health, Education, and Welfare by his advisory committee on the education of the deaf pointed up the need for a more systematic approach to the education of the deaf. Legislative support in Congress and by the President has provided funds and leadership for important new services and facilities which offer promise of alleviating old problems persistently encountered in the education of the deaf.

An awareness of the need for developing language and communications skills in deaf children has forced educators to focus much of their attention on speech, lipreading, and writing—particularly during the early years of the deaf child's formal learning period. Consequently, several educators of the deaf began to investigate the feasibility of using 8mm loop films in cartridge form as a means of teaching lipreading to young deaf children. Funds were available through Captioned Films for the Deaf and other departments in the U.S. Office of Education. Certain private schools and research organizations were also looking to technology and especially to the newer educational media for a "breakthrough" in visual communications which would speed up the education process for the deaf child.

Pilot School for the Deaf, a division of the Callier Hearing and Speech Center in Dallas, Texas, a private day school, employed a full-time audiovisual specialist in the spring of 1963 and began to develop an extensive media program. Pilot School had an enrollment of approximately 50 children and 10 classroom teachers, but very limited space and facilities. Research projects were also initiated with other institutions, notably the Illinois School. Six Technicolor 8mm projectors with rear-screen projection cabinets were obtained along with approximately 200 lipreading films, several hundred 2″ × 2″ color slides, and synchronized tape cartridges for auditory training. These units were designed for self-instruction with a minimum of supervision. Carrels and movable booths were designed to fit the individual needs of the children and teachers in a variety of situations. Addition of portable, 12′ × 24′ buildings, air-conditioned and carpeted, also led to development of a unique classroom arrangement.

The importance of visual communications for the deaf student cannot be overemphasized. However, lighting, screen placement, viewing angles, desk arrangement, room acoustics, ventilation, and numerous other factors are often neglected when designing classrooms for the deaf. The necessity of adapting equipment, techniques, and classroom management to spaces not originally intended as classrooms led to some other innovations at Pilot School and provoked other researchers to find out more about the role of educational media in teaching the deaf.

The basic system, evolved at Pilot School, incorporates the use of two 50″ × 50″ wall-mounted projection screens, a remote controlled filmstrip projector, overhead projector with acetate roll, and arrangements for some degree of room light control. The reasons are obvious. The deaf student must be able to see the teacher and the teacher must face the students at all times. Classes are usually small, 10 students or less. Remote controlled projectors with both forward and reverse allow the teacher or student to project visual materials on the screen to the teacher's left. The teaching station utilizing the overhead projector is located in the center of the room on a 17″ movable cart. The teacher is seated with an eight-foot chalkboard behind her and the second screen above and to her right. She then is in the most favorable position for the students to see her face and for her to maintain eye contact with them. Use of the acetate roll on the overhead projector allows the teacher to write vocabulary, instructions, information, language, and student responses, questions, etc. The acetate roll can be moved backward for review or as a reference to a previous hour or day. Individual acetate sheets or prepared transparencies can also be placed under the acetate roll with vocabulary, questions, or other information added as needed to clarify visual displays on the other screen, chalkboard, or on charts.

There are numerous other advantages of overhead projection in a classroom for the deaf. The light from the projector lights the teacher's face in such a way that lipreading is enhanced and fingerspelling is possible in a semidarkened room. There appears to be some research evidence which indicates the placement of light on a person's face when using an overhead projection on a 17″ stand helps to highlight tongue, lip, and teeth placement, enabling deaf students to recognize certain words more easily. Other techniques and innovations utilizing two screens, an overhead projector, and remote control projectors are being developed by teachers of the deaf in an effort to overcome the communications problem of a hearing handicap.

Another innovation has been the development of autoinstructional devices for the very young deaf child. Programmed slides and tapes for auditory training and 8mm film loops for speech and language are used with dependable and inexpensive hearing aids in conjunction with a loop system installed in the classroom. A variety of visual experiences not only reinforces language principles but also provides greater opportunities for creative teaching, enhances learning, and makes it interesting and worthwhile for the deaf student.

Equipment, materials, techniques, facilities, and administrative support must be readily available to the teacher and student, and, we hope, a real breakthrough will result.

The dependence of the deaf child upon visual communications is manifold, and a systematic approach is necessary. Such an approach, utilizing educational media and technology, can provide the long-awaited breakthrough in helping the deaf individual overcome the isolation and frustration of living in a hearing world, experiencing a communication revolution in which he is not a participant by virtue of his deafness.

Audiovisual Instruction for the Mentally Retarded

LEROY ASERLIND

Examination of virtually any topic leads almost inevitably to two results: exposure to and, hopefully, assimilation of new knowledge; and creation, establishment, or discovery of paradoxes inherent in that topic. This is true when the topic under examination concerns audiovisual instruction for the mentally retarded child.

What is the paradox? It is that the educable mental retardate is extremely dependent on many of the inherent elements of learning offered by audiovisual instruction. Perhaps no other single descriptive category of our population has had so much legislative, research, financial, and academic attention directed toward it in such a relatively short period of time; and yet despite the proximity of these elements there generally exists today a serious lack of good, field-assessed audiovisual material directed to the retarded learner.

Currently a tremendous amount of published information on mental retardation exists, an amount hardly conceivable six or seven years ago. Research has expanded knowledge of the etiology, psychology, and physiology and the educational, social, and occupational aspects of mental retardation. Not too many years ago, institutions for the retarded were looked upon as primarily terminal facilities for the more severely and profoundly retarded persons, whereas today entirely new concepts of institutional care and personnel characteristics are arising due to the changing and dynamic roles of institutions as research and total care facilities.

Textbooks which were entirely acceptable for university classes on mental retardation five years ago are no longer adequate in the average graduate class. Medical

Reprinted with permission of Association for Educational Communications and Technology from *Audiovisual Instruction* 11:727–30 (Nov. 1966).

texts of a decade ago are anachronistic in such areas as chromosomal and metabolic abnormalities.

The most recent surge of interest in mental retardation is largely due to legislative and personal interests evinced by the late President Kennedy at a time when the United States was academically, socially, and economically ready for it. Much of the effectiveness of this national attention might be related to preparation of the research climate through adoption of a definition and classification system.[1]

Why the Paradox?

Years of empirical educational experience, verified by laboratory research, indicates that the mental retardate is characterized by certain deficits in learning. In fact, it is these learning deficits that most generally tend to differentiate the educable retardate from the normal child within the usual school situation. These differences are felt to be of sufficient magnitude to warrant separate academic facilities, specially trained teachers, specially derived curricula, separate administrative units, and essentially modified methodological approaches to teaching. Why then is there not a surfeit of audiovisuals for the mental retardate? Why does this paradox exist? One can answer only by postulates based on observation, experience, discussion, and conjecture. These postulates might be that:

1. There is no concerted effort or demand on the part of special educators for the development of these materials; most teachers have grown accustomed to developing their own general materials. Acceptance of this lack of audiovisuals is often at the expense of the retarded pupils themselves.

2. Comparatively speaking, the area of special education represents a small market for the commercial producer of audiovisuals who has financial commitments based on a large-volume break-even point.

3. There have been no facilities specifically charged to evaluate and assess audiovisual materials to be used with the mentally retarded.

4. Persistent emphasis on basic research has been at the expense of applied research. Even so, there is a general failure to utilize basic research findings in mental retardation to the field of material development.

The answers postulated are not intended to be totally inclusive of the problem, nor are they designed to be mutually exclusive of one another. They are meant to be suggestive of later possible approaches to tempering the paradox of audiovisual education for the mentally retarded. Currently vast amounts of audiovisuals are being utilized in almost every classroom for the mentally retarded, and almost without exception these aids are designed for the child of normal and above normal intelligence. This is not to say that the materials are not effective, for they are; but their effectiveness is frequently limited by the deficits of the mentally retarded learner.

AV for Remediation and Development

Generally speaking, many retarded children might be characterized as having deficits in meaningful perception of stimuli, retention, attention, comprehension, assimilation and utilization of the abstract, as well as deficits in speed of learning. It is truthfully difficult to conceive of any medium of instruction, with the exception of actual experience or contrived synthetic situations, that has the potential effectiveness of audiovisuals. Yet one has only to search the existing body of literature on this specific aspect of instruction to be aware of, and concerned with, how little has actually been done.

The teacher of the retarded child must be concerned with both remediation and developmental aspects of education; hence an almost clinical approach is indicated. Peters, in writing of prescriptive teaching methods with the retarded, states:

Activities are gradually lengthened in duration in view of the child's increased attention span. Since lectures are not an appropriate teaching method, a lesson must be broken down into simple steps and each step taught separately and mastered before the next step. Then the sequence is repeated many times on succeeding days. It should be overlearned for retention and returned to from time to time for reinforcement.[2]

From the point of precision of objectives, repetition, and reinforcement, it would appear that sound motion pictures and filmstrips could most adequately meet these criteria. Peters writes further, "Learning for these children is so difficult and requires so much time that it is essential that time is not wasted on unnecessary content." Audiovisual material prepared for the normal child most frequently has unnecessary or even distracting content for the retarded child.

A very recent example of this latter point within the writer's own experience might be cited. An excellent series of filmstrips on basic number concepts, developed for the normal child, was in use in a class for the retarded. Conceptually the class was ready for the idea of simple subtraction. One frame in the filmstrip developing this concept showed a series of milk bottles on a shelf. One bottle was being knocked off by a kitten playing on the shelf—the idea, of course, being that subtraction is the process of reducing the total by a specified amount. This frame, only one of any number that could be discussed similarly, brought out mainly in the pupils the concept of milk bottles. Since none of the retarded children had ever seen a glass milk bottle before, the discussion first focused on this concept. Then the wrongness of the kitten's being on the shelf with the milk became the central focus of the discussion. Normal children would have had little trouble in assimilating and applying the visual stimuli to the concept of subtraction, while the retarded carried forth from the filmstrip concepts of milk in glass bottles and kittens on shelves. In short, the particular frame, though interesting and educational from several points of view, contributed little to the primary purpose of the situation. The problem is not inherent in the filmstrip, nor its theoretical conceptualization, which was excellent, but rather in the adaptation of material prepared for the normal to be used by the retarded.

Studies which specifically investigated utilization of audiovisual materials and methods with the mentally retarded have almost universally indicated good results. Neuhaus conducted a study designed to investigate audiovisual job training for the mentally retarded.[3] He utilized a population of 25 young adult retardates with IQ's between 60 and 80, achieving on a third- to fifth-grade level. The program used audiovisual materials to teach job skills needed in an electronic assembly plant, specifically those needed to assemble a television antenna. The equipment consisted of an automatic slide projector and 35 colored slides, accompanied by audio instructions for each slide. The speed of slide presentation was governed by individual acquisition rate.

At the end of the program, the trainees were unanimous in preferring the audiovisual method over the conventional lecture method. They praised the clarity and consistency of the instruction and repeatedly commented that the program allowed them to see exactly what was required in each step. It must be reiterated that the program was designed for this purpose and for this population. Principles of education for the retarded which guided the programmers, according to Neuhaus, were as follows:

1. Skills were broken down into as many independent job steps as possible.
2. Repetition of job steps was important.
3. Verbal instructions were easily understood.
4. Reinforcement was supplied, in this instance, by a training supervisor.

In a recent study Vergason investigated retention of sight vocabulary in retarded individuals, comparing traditional and autoinstructional methods.[4] The autoinstructional method used an automatic slide projector, with paired words and pictures appearing on the slides. The study showed good retention rates for both methods with subjects not differing on retention after one day, but with significant differences appearing at one, two, four and fourteen months in favor of autoinstruction. Whereas the specific intent of the study was to compare traditional versus autoinstructional methods, it also has implications for audiovisual instruction. Without belaboring the point, and in the author's words, "Systematic overlearning may have been responsible for the gain in retention." Methodologically, overlearning in a class for the educable mental retardate would seem to be most efficiently and advantageously brought about through audiovisual instruction.

No teacher has enough patience with or inborn resistance to the intellectual boredom that inevitably accrues within him from numerous repetitions of pedantic material. An audiovisual unit never expresses boredom, exhibits decay, or develops resistance to material it is asked to repeat over and over again.

Another definitive study of the efficacy of audiovisual instruction with mental retardates has been completed by Goldstein.[5] He predicated his study on "the ability of the film to produce situations which appear real and vital in every detail. . . ." This, he explains, is one explanation of why children of low ability and limited opportunity do well in their studies when films are properly selected and used. Upon reviewing this study in which the adolescent experimental subjects were taught food serving concepts through films, it again seems safe to conclude that learning by educable mental retardates is facilitated by the use of selected sound motion pictures. The author emphasizes several points:

1. The films contain concrete rather than abstract material.
2. Films are most profitable when used as summaries to a specific lesson.
3. The motion pictures must have synchronization of sound and action.
4. Narrative type pictures with oral descriptions and with too few pictorial sequences are not adequate for the retarded.

Goldstein suggests, based on his research, that increased emphasis on direct experiences for the retardate be coupled with more extensive use of audiovisual materials and lesser use of the traditional methods of instruction.

A broad conceptual extension of the work done previously by Neuhaus and by Goldstein is seen in a recently reported study by Leland, Edmonson, and Leach at Parsons State and the University of Kansas.[6] Their approach is valuable in that it represents an effort to help the mental retardate understand and learn social and occupational cues through use of audiovisual techniques. Essentially the program shows what people do in everyday situations. Through this program, the prevocational young adult retardate can live the role of a worker living on his own in a community. Through audiovisuals, the limited life of a low-paid employee is displayed, with particular emphasis on the social and employment settings, the basic behavior expectancies, and adaptive cues. The 10-week program consists mainly of a series of 440 slides, tape recordings, and lesson plans. To date,

the program has been shown to be effective with the young adult retardate in reducing confusion and establishing realistic expectancies for the individual.

It can be seen, in the above applications, that the preponderance of emphasis in research and in the development of audiovisuals expressly for the mentally retarded has been toward teaching specific vocational skills and shaping the preoccupational behavior of the 16- to 22-year-old.

AV for Institutional Care

An interesting and promising departure from this general trend of audiovisual instruction is being studied by James J. McCarthy at the University of Wisconsin, utilizing a population of moderately to severely retarded infants at Central Wisconsin Colony and Training School. Extensive use is being made of slides, both sound and silent color movie film, and tape recordings of music, human voices, and noise. The materials are created expressly to present institutionalized infants with auditory and visual stimulation not ordinarily provided under normal conditions of institutional care. The infants themselves can select, through the use of "paddle switches" placed in their cribs and playpens, the type of projected audible or visual stimulation they will receive. Though only in the first year of the study, the results are giving positive indications that specially prepared audiovisual materials may eventually be used as a primary adjunct of institutional care programs.

Special Education IMCs

And yet the paradox exists that even in the face of theoretical and empirical evidence which overwhelmingly indicates effectiveness and, in instances, superiority over traditional classroom methods of instruction, audiovisual instruction for the mentally retarded is not what it should be. A logical step in the overall resolution of this situation and one of the newer concepts in the educational schemata for the retarded child is the development of special education instructional materials centers.

The prototype for this particular type of center was established in 1964 at the University of Wisconsin under Title III, section 302, of PL 88–164. In addition to the usual library functions of lending, receiving, and cataloging books and materials, this new center concept calls for extensive commitment to the evaluation and assessment of existing materials. Also, through provisions of the original grant, the center is to assist whenever possible and feasible in the creation of new instructional materials and in the revision or adaptation of existing materials to meet the critical and special needs of the mentally retarded pupil.

Currently, in addition to the Wisconsin unit, there

is one other federally funded operative center at the University of Southern California. Additional regional centers have now been funded in various parts of the United States. At this initial stage of development, there are positive indications that these special education instructional materials centers will operate as individual units of a national network. This aspect of intercenter planning, cooperation, and information dissemination will greatly increase the evaluation and assessment function potentially available to the special class teacher and the local and state administrator when it comes to selecting and using audiovisual materials for their special classes. It will also facilitate communication between the commercial producer and the areas of critical need. These centers likely will conduct and generate research which can readily be translated into classroom application. They will eventually demonstrate a measurable impact on the field of audiovisual instruction for the mentally retarded.

Hope for the Future

In reviewing this field, several salient facts emerge. There is an ever-increasing abundance of excellent audiovisual instructional methods and materials available to the special class teacher. These materials, when developed for the child of normal and above normal intelligence, though often entertaining, quite frequently do not and cannot be effectively adapted to the particular academic needs of the mentally retarded child. They cannot be adapted due to his (a) particular learning disabilities, (b) restricted experiential and vocabulary background, (c) inability to deal with the abstract, (d) psychological disparity between chronological and mental ages, (e) relatively low levels of expectancy, and (f) frequently failure-induced low motivational levels.

Progress is being spurred by federal programs such as those made possible by PL 88–164 and PL 89–10. The results of these programs will directly and indirectly result in developing stronger programs of audiovisual instruction in all fields of special education. The creation of special education instructional materials centers is one direct manifestation; another is the increasing amount of material being developed for undereducated adults which can establish and strengthen trends for similar curricular growth with the intellectually handicapped child.[7]

To maintain this optimistic current direction, several points might be presented. One point would be the necessity of thinking of audiovisual instruction for the mentally retarded as structurally different from education of the normal child. This may mean utilizing audiovisuals as a training or developmental medium in such specific areas as perception, differentiation, attention, visual scanning, and retention, to name a few.

Another point would be the encouragement of applied research designed to enhance the effectiveness of audiovisuals in the classroom, both from a methodological and materials point of view. Implicit in this point is the development of more adequate and simplified methods of material assessment.

A final point lies in the establishment of stronger, more productive relationships between the special class teacher, special education materials center, and the commercial producers of audiovisual materials. Hopefully, this would effect the amalgam of the empirical, theoretical, and the practical necessary to take audiovisual education for our retarded children from paradox to paradigm.

NOTES

1. R. F. Heber, "A Manual on Classification and Terminology in Mental Retardation," *American Journal of Mental Deficiency*, Monograph Supplement, 1959.
2. L. J. Peters, *Prescriptive Teaching* (New York: McGraw-Hill, 1965), p. 115.
3. E. C. Neuhaus, "Audio-Visual Job Training for Mentally Retarded," *Rehabilitation Record* 5:32–35 (March-April 1964).
4. G. A. Vergason, "Retention in Educable Retarded Subjects for Two Methods of Instruction," *American Journal of Mental Deficiency* 70:683–88 (March 1966).
5. Edward Goldstein, *Selective Audio-Visual Instruction for Mentally Retarded Pupils* (Springfield, Ill.: Charles C. Thomas, 1954).
6. Barbara Edmonson, Henry Leland, and Ethel M. Leach, *Teaching Retarded Adolescents to Interpret Social Cues* (Paper presented at the American Association of Mental Deficiency Convention, Chicago, Ill., 1966).
7. William F. Brazziel, "The Revolution in Materials for Undereducated Adults," *Audiovisal Instruction* 11:254–56 (April 1966).

The "Graded Difficulty" Library

ROBERT H. GEESLIN

With the advent of so many "process approach" science programs, inquiry programs, and individualized "subject area" programs, teachers are finding it increasingly difficult to guide their students to proper material. All too often, the material of interest is so difficult that the student might as well not have found the book. There is no immediate solution to the problem, although many schools are trying first one attack then another.

Reprinted with permission of the International Reading Association from *Reading Teacher* 24, no. 7:644–46 (April 1971).

One solution, of course, is to improve the reading ability of the students to the point that the various texts used
present no problems. However, this is not always possible. No matter how well the average child reads, half
the students will read less well—and texts will be written
for the average (or better) reader.

Other approaches have been tried. Some schools use
films or tapes instead of texts. This only avoids the
problem without solving it, and this approach has the
drawback of expense, inflexibility, and the necessity for
all work to be done in class. Some teachers have tried
pure lecture as a solution. The students tune them out.
Others have tried discussions, but students who have no
information cannot easily discuss a topic. Others have
tried teaching content as the comprehension part of a
reading lesson. They are quite surprised to find the students learning neither the the content nor the reading
skills taught because of the difficulty of the text. Others
have adopted the "pure" inquiry approach and find
that the students often cannot bring enough information
to bear on a topic. The information may be quite out of
reach if the students do not read well enough to search
for it.

Matching Pupils and Materials

All of the above are admirable attempts to solve a
difficult problem. Yet, they all lack one essential ingredient, an ingredient that might make all of them successful. The approaches do not reflect a direct attempt to
reach the heart of the problem, the discrepancy between
difficulty of material and ability of students. If, in any
of the above, the student could be matched with material on his reading level, much more success would be
evidenced. Films and tapes would arouse interest and
teach as well, while out-of-class assignments would
add flexibility and additional opportunity for learning.

Discussion is a good teaching technique if the students have information about the topic—information
gained from reading material of appropriate difficulty.
The teaching of content as one part of a reading lesson
works well if the reading lesson is on the student's level
rather than from a standard text. The inquiry approach
also works well if the student can be given material on
his level in which to seek answers to his questions.

Since the content of topic areas is subject to change,
as the knowledge explosion has emphatically demonstrated, many schools are no longer devising curricu-
lums based upon "content." Instead, they are teaching the skills of study, questioning, and approach to
questions. With this as the basis of instruction, a multitude of problems are solved by matching materials and
reading abilities.

There are now becoming available a few sets of multilevel content area materials. However, one cannot expect the publishers to provide information on all topics
on a variety of difficulty levels, much less timely information on several levels. However, there is a solution, involving a school-wide or system-wide task.

The books available in the libraries (the public and
the school's or system's) may be "graded," that is, the
difficulty level of each may be determined and a master
list compiled of titles and difficulties. This is, of course,
a chore requiring hundreds or thousands of man-hours.
However, once the task is complete—using the aid of
civic groups, P.T.A., etc.—and the titles have been sorted
into topic areas, teachers have at their disposal one of
the most valuable of tools—information. At any time, a
student, a topic, and difficulty can all be matched. Such
a match will aid the teacher in providing growth in reading ability and growth in content area simultaneously.

This idea was acted upon at Madison Elementary
School in Madison, Florida. The personnel at the
R.E.A.D. Center, in cooperation with the librarian at the
elementary school, typed a master list of all the books
in the library. From this list catalogs were requested from
all publishing companies having books on the list, and
bibliographies that give readability levels were ordered.
The grade levels were then found for each book. Some
books, in fact many books, were out of print. Lists of
the out-of-print books were made and the respective
companies were asked for grade levels. In most cases,
the response from these companies was immediate and
informative. Of course, a readibility formula run on
each book would have provided a much closer estimate
of the difficulty of each book. This monumental task
still lies ahead.

A master graded book list was then compiled and
distributed to all teachers at the elementary school.
The amount of time involved was, of course, great. One
person spent most of her time during an entire school
year on this project. She was aided periodically by
another staff member. However, once this initial step
is taken, the list is easily kept up to date.

Using the List

In order to use such a list with greatest effectiveness,
the teacher may find that some instructional approaches
may have to be varied, although the list is functional in
any setting. The teacher who wishes to cover some topic
and assigns differential readings (according to ability/
difficulty) will find that the children have *different*
answers. To those teachers who wish to transmit certain
facts or concepts, this state of affairs is irking. They
find that different authors approach problems differently, that there is *no one "right"* answer. Unfortunately,
many teachers abandon individualized instruction because they demand *the* right answer and all right answers must be the same. Such teachers usually revert

to lecture, single-text approaches, or single concept films. On the other hand, teachers who wish to transmit skills of inquiry, critical thinking and flexibility will use discrepancies in "answers" (i.e., information gathered) as a springboard for questions (from the students) and further inquiry. The questions raised by students should, of course, lead not only to further inquiry into facts, but should also involve the assumptions of the writer, changes that are taking place in the field, changes that *should* (or should not) take place, and the restrictions language places upon the topic (i.e., categorizing information, perception of meaning attached to phenomena, etc.). This point is made because teachers influence the type of questions asked by students. Teacher influence evolves from their reactions, whether in a positive or negative manner. Teachers will find it easier to obtain the desired direction (questioning assumptions, questioning the informational influences imposed by the language, etc.) if they will attempt to limit themselves to no more than *one* declarative sentence per hour and no more than one closed-ended interrogative per hour. Open-ended questions lead to student participation, questioning, and inquiry. (See *Teaching as a Subversive Activity* by Postman and Weingarten, 1969, Delacorte Press.)

In summary, matching topic of inquiry, student ability, and material difficulty level can be accomplished using a listing of titles available, under topic areas, that gives difficulty levels. Such matches can yield more efficient achievement of goals, but have the "drawback" of leading to inconsistencies in "facts," which leads to questioning, critical, learning students.

Programmed Movies—A Supplemental Medium for Language Development

GLENN S. PFAU

The central problem facing educators is that of determining the most effective means of meeting specified needs. Traditionally, the classroom teacher was almost totally responsible for meeting these determined needs of her students. She was, in general, limited to her own talents, abilities, blackboard, bulletin board, field trips, and various types of printed matter. By contrast, the contemporary teacher has at her disposal a multiplicity of different media, each of which has inherent advantages and disadvantages.

Reprinted by permission from *The American Annals of the Deaf* 115:569–72 (Oct. 1970).

In the learning of any new task or subject matter, learning theorists concur that progression should be from the concrete to the abstract. The concept of "dog" might be arranged into an abstract-concrete hierarchy as follows:

7. Visual Linguistic Symbol (word "dog" in print)
6. Auditory Linguistic Symbol (word "dog" articulated)
5. Still Picture (photograph of dog)
4. Motion Pictures of Object (movie of dog in movement)
3. Replica (small model of dog)
2. Realistic Replica (life size model of dog)
1. Actual Object (live dog)

From the hierarchy, it can be noted that a still picture of a dog is more abstract than a motion picture sequence of a dog in movement. This difference is even more pronounced when one attempts to teach the meaning of action verbs. For example, the concept of "run" can be denoted in a more concrete manner through a realistic movie sequence than by a still picture. The concrete aspect is one of many advantages that characterize the motion medium.

Recent technological breakthroughs have provided means whereby the student can interact with the projected movie. The status of the child can be changed from a passive observer (of a movie sequence) to an active responder. The Project LIFE motion series elicits a measurable response by means of the Project teaching machine, the "Program Master." In this case, the machine serves as a master response-control unit when connected to the remote outlet of the Kodak Ektagraphic MSF-8 super 8mm projector. The movies which do not exceed six minutes in length, are programmed to stop at given response frames. Only when the child provides the correct response and obtains the green confirmation light, does the separate advance button become operative. Impulses from the advance button restart the film and it again continues until the next response frame is reached.

Motion Picture Considerations

Usually, the normally hearing infant finds himself immersed in an environment that abounds with oral communication, including much that is related to the nonverbal concepts he has developed. Thus, he acquires language through the thousands of repetitions of it that he hears while seeing familiar concepts illustrated or dramatized. While playing with him, his parents are usually talking about what he is doing or what they are doing. The child thereby learns to associate what he hears with what he sees. But the case of the deaf child is quite different. He must depend upon the single sense of vision for input of both the language and the accompanying illustration or dramatization. In addition, the necessity for him to be in a most favorable position to see language—whether on the lips, the printed page, or the fingers and/or hands—creates difficult problems for him. First, it retards the rate by which he can learn to associate his nonverbal concepts with the proper verbal labels in any language medium or media through which he is being taught; second, it reduces the number of repetitions he receives to a point far below essential requirements for effective language learning. Finally, there are the problems inherent in the English language itself, with its many structural irregularities, function words, multiple meanings, idiomatic expressions, nonphonetic spellings, and other features difficult to master.

In light of the above considerations, it seems apparent that the prelingually deaf child is in need of far more opportunities to interact in a meaningful way with his native language. Furth states that the deaf child needs "thousands of straightforward, unambiguous language contacts."[1] The child must be given thousands of opportunities to not only come in contact with language but to respond to it. Then, there must be some means of confirming the appropriateness of his response. That is, immediate feedback, or knowledge of results must be provided.

It would seem that the educational technologist can be of tremendous assistance to the teacher as she attempts to provide a learning environment which will bring the student into direct and meaningful association with his language. Both the media specialists and the teacher must remain cognizant of these factors:

1. The linguistic instructional system must keep pace with the child's expanding need for language. A child's inner language of ideas and interests can far outdistance his ability to integrate this into a visible language system. The step from prosaic language occurs all too slowly for want of more individual contact and one-to-one interaction in the school day. Supplemental educational materials to aid the teacher in providing a dynamic language system must in themselves be dynamic and action oriented. This would therefore indicate a need for media capable of becoming an extension of the teacher by forming a part of the learning environment.

2. Stemming from this problem is the realization that if a dynamic language is to be learned, the child must participate fully in the learning process. The teacher's presence in this learning process is invaluable, not only in providing a language curriculum format but also by evoking the sometimes overlooked ingredients of the child's own imitative responses and emotional involvement. Should a media system hope to supple-

ment the teacher, these considerations must be taken into account.[2]

3. At a time when mass media has enjoyed the success of effecting the receptivity and retention of learned behaviors on the general public, a few educational engineers have attempted to utilize these same techniques in an instructional process for specific populations of children. Taking into account the needs of the deaf child, the potential of motion pictures as a supplemental tool in education seems limitless. Yet, to insure a responsive media system, a structure must be developed which is based on the specific needs of the child and his classroom environment.

Project LIFE Motion Picture Series

The larger task of Project LIFE is the development of programmed filmstrips in the areas of language, thinking activities, and percepto-cognition. These materials are intended to assist the child with a language deficit to acquire a functional receptive language system. The 35mm filmstrips are built around child-level concepts within his anticipated interests and needs, and are organized into hierarchical units progressing from the very simple to the increasingly complex.

In order that the concepts presented in filmstrip form be fully internalized by the child, Project LIFE provides additional modes of reinforcement through specially designed story booklets, workbooks, and dictionaries. As previously indicated, another mode of reinforcement currently under development is the Motion Picture Series.

The Motion Picture Series provides receptive language learning of those words or language concepts which conceptually incorporate the dimensions of sequential time and motion. It uses live action, color, super 8mm single concept films, photographed in elementary classrooms for hearing impaired children in the Washington, D.C., and metropolitan area. The camera candidly captures the children as they actively express their language. The films are then edited, captioned, and programmed into a system of subject matter units which increase in complexity with each subsequent unit.

The Project LIFE Motion Picture Series proposes a division of its films into the following ten units or subject areas: Self, School, Home, Clothing, Nature, Farm, Community, Sports, Health, and Holidays. These subject areas are further divided into pivotal noun areas upon which action verbs, adverbs, abstract nouns, and adjectives are attached. They are then captioned and presented in programmed context in much the same manner as the LIFE language filmstrip series.

In addition to the series mentioned above, a group of films are being developed under the topical heading of "Emotions." The objectives in the emotions series go beyond programmed language but are designed to more fully develop visual literacy. Each subject matter area portrays an emotion(s) associated with that area, such as the feelings of respect and pride with the school unit, and the feeling of well being with the self unit. These words are not demonstrable by just a happy face, for example, but require a sequence of visible actions which, as a whole, comprise the particular emotion.

By utilizing the relationship established with the filmed students, the learning child can readily relate his own body actions in imitative responses to the graphically presented vocabulary. For example, in the films using "Arms" as a subject upon which adjectives, adverbs, action verbs, and other parts of speech are gradually attached, the adjectives presented in the first film are "strong" and "weak." The camera might move in for a close-up image of a boy's arm raised to make a muscle. The caption might read, "Some arms are strong." When another boy playfully displays weak arms, the camera might again close in for the critical visual effect and the new appropriate caption would appear simultaneously. Several children might demonstrate the same concept from appropriate viewing angles. The learner participates fully with the visual presentation by continually responding in a meaningful manner to both the visuals and the language.

Applications of Video Tape to Media Development

The development of meaningful and effective single concept movies can be a time consuming and expensive process. The employment of closed circuit television in the designing, planning, developmental, and evaluative stages can greatly reduce the cost and increase the probability of success. Project LIFE has begun to apply the video tape capabilities to the programmed motion picture series. It has been found to lend itself well to the development of scripts, script ideas and techniques of filming thought to be most suitable in a given situation. It allows for inexpensive experimentation in camera angles, camera techniques, and the like. Closed circuit TV can also be used by inexperienced personnel in determining the suitability of filming locations, acquaint teachers and students with film crews and overcome camera shyness, camera awareness, and/or camera phobia.

Regarding filming, the video camera can be valuable to "block out" camera positions or camera movement for optimal effects. It can help the script writer or programmer overcome apparent limitations or problems in many ways. For instance, the video tape preview allows determinations to be made as to the length and placement of sequences, identification of irrelevant content, special video effects that might be needed, and

the like. Also, it allows the director to be better prepared for the situation when the shooting of film begins.

A particular use that Project LIFE anticipates exploiting is in the area of captioning and caption techniques. The optimal method of presenting vocabulary has not been determined. Thus, a considerable amount of experimentation will be carried out by video taping the edited film in a variety of ways. Several different captioning techniques will be attempted, as well as variations in words, time, and reinforcement. In this way, the entire area of captions in programmed movies can be easily assessed.

Another valuable use of video tape is in the field evaluation of materials. It is impractical for the entire staff to be involved in field testing of media, but it is also essential that every staff member be cognizant of the children's reaction to, and interaction with, the material. The split screen, two camera techniques, is the least disrupting method of recording accurately all of the child's responses. It can be viewed by the staff for informative or evaluative purposes. Furthermore, it can acquaint inexperienced staff members with the learning and behavioral characteristics of deaf students.

The area of teacher training is another important facet of any media producing project that should not be overlooked. With any given media, there is one best method of presentation. This can be visually demonstrated by video taping different live classroom presentations.

Finally, a significant amount of time can be spent in developing a teacher's manual to be used in conjunction with new media or material. However, if it goes unread, or if the teacher fails to see how her classroom can be adapted to favorably present the materials, then the manual has failed. Conversely, by video taping similar classroom situations, the teacher can see how her classroom can be adapted and that the new method of presenting material is not impractical. Through this mode, effective techniques can be communicated to the classroom teacher regarding the relative worth of new media.

NOTES

1. H. G. Furth, "Research with the Deaf: Implications for Language and Cognition," *Psychological Bulletin* 62: 145–64 (September 1964).

2. Media should not be viewed as supplanting the role of the teacher in any way, but if it is well conceived, it can supplement and complement classroom instruction.

Geniuses at Work

JUDITH H. COHEN

At Sousa Junior High School in Port Washington, New York, we focus our remedial reading program at the seventh grade. One of my seventh grade classes was composed of nine boys and three girls. In September 1968, their performance on the Gates MacGinitie Form D survey showed composite vocabulary and comprehension scores ranging from 3.5 to 5.0. Further diagnosis revealed common deficiencies in word analysis skills and language development.

These students had many severe problems. Their individual folders revealed that many had been diagnosed in elementary school as having perceptual problems, neurological impairments, foreign language backgrounds, and emotional difficulties. Now in their teens, these students, after years of failure in education, rejected the need for formal learning. Moreover, they viewed school as a hostile and threatening environment. The students refused to admit that they were concerned about reading. Their behavior demonstrated little concern about succeeding in junior high school.

For these students conventional remedial techniques were not enough. These methods did not meet their individual needs and many of the students had been in "conventional" reading programs while in elementary school. As a group they pretended to be uninterested or at times even belligerent. Superficially they seemed totally uncritical of their deficiencies, and many of them, with low aspirations for success, had resigned themselves to being in poor achievement groups. The students had fallen into the vicious cycle of poor reading ability, poor learning ability, poor achievement and poor behavior. It seemed necessary to break this cycle somehow to improve their communication skills and their self-image. We had to convince them to try gaining recognition by academic achievement.

In the fall of 1968 our school was given the opportunity to borrow television equipment worth $15,000. I was told that this television system was designed to encourage students to become television producers themselves. Since many schools had found that closed circuit television is a potent device and invaluable instructional aid, I was interested in its application to remedial reading.

With the aid of our district's TV consultant, we established a TV studio. The students would be encouraged to develop their verbal skills and to improve

Reprinted with permission of the International Reading Association from *Journal of Reading* 13, no. 4: 275–80 (Jan. 1970).

their ability to communicate by using this medium in conjunction with our reading program.

The idea was introduced to the students through general discussions about television. This proved to be something about which all of them had opinions. "What programs did they like? What's wrong with television? How would THEY like to try producing television programs? How important was television in their lives?" The students were enthusiastic but skeptical about their ability to do something that seemed to require technical know-how. Gradually it was established that, although we didn't have very complicated equipment or the special knowledge needed to produce another *Mod Squad*, we could still enjoy the experience and learn in the process.

It soon became apparent that a wide range of language skills is needed to produce a television program: research (use of library, reading books and magazines), script preparation (writing skills), selection and preparation of graphics (word-picture relationships and organization skills), performance and production (verbalization and mechanical skills), evaluation (criticism and self-confrontation), and program acceptance (image building). Therefore we not only sought to incorporate reading and writing skills into a meaningful activity, but we sought to establish more positive behavior patterns and to build better self-images. The aim of the program was not to develop technical studio skills. In fact we emphasized the individual growth of the producers and deliberately deemphasized the equipment.

After several group orientation sessions which involved the TV consultant and the designer of the equipment, the students and I learned about the variety of ways in which materials could be shown on this television equipment. I divided the class of twelve into groups of three to five members. Each group was to produce cooperatively a video tape based on graphics, drawings or pictures, on whatever one subject interested them all. This first experience showed the students that producing a television tape had to be a cooperative venture and antisocial behavior would prevent the accomplishment of anything worthwhile. They also realized that no subject was taboo; drinking, drugs and crime would be highly acceptable topics provided that the students were willing to work within the process of production. Together we evolved these steps for the production of what came to be called miniprograms:

1. Pick a topic.
2. Do research.
3. Prepare graphics.
4. Write a script.
5. Practice reading the script.
6. Record a run through.
7. Evaluate the tape.
8. Make a final tape.

As soon as the students became technically comfortable with the equipment and familiar with the process of production, they were started on individual programs. Hobbies, adolescent interests, content area subjects, interesting pictures, news stories—all stimulated ideas for programs. What evolved was a highly individualized course designed to improve the communication skills of the students while catering to their variety of interest areas and skill deficiencies. The process of production allowed enough variety so that each student could find an area of specialization. Some of the boys seemed fascinated by the equipment; others enjoyed the creativity of making graphics; use of the tape recorder and typewriter motivated others toward script preparation. However, each student was required to know how to operate all of the equipment and to work independently so that the tape would be completely his.

Students progressed at their own rate. Some needed more encouragement and individual guidance than others. Often when information was needed, the student and I would go to the library together and search through the stacks to find just what we wanted. Sometimes, special material would be brought into the school when the library information was insufficient. Much of the material from the reading room gravitated to the TV room and found its place as readable reference material. When help or information was needed we would find a way to provide it. If script typing were needed, I would often do it. In many ways we helped the students break the "book barrier," and they soon came to realize that books were often the best sources of information and pictures. With a need to seek out information, students had a purpose for improving their reading skills. There was little need for the extrinsic motivators and the heart-to-heart talks about the importance of reading that often accompany remedial reading programs.

The students began to look upon their school and the entire school district as resources. If a topic had academic implications the students were directed to various faculty members who could help them out. The science department furnished many props, some of them live, which added vitality to reports on gerbils and rabbits. One boy did a tape on skin diving with equipment borrowed from his science teacher. A math teacher taught another student how to create intricate designs as the basis for a report on geometry. This involvement with the faculty had several effects. Primarily, these students who had never been academically motivated came to faculty members with a keen interest in subject matter. Many teachers, who had formerly viewed these students as troublesome or completely lacking in ability, reevaluated their opinions. Teachers began to realize that these students had special talents and were worthy of attention. Again, self-image for the student changed as teacher expectations changed. Many content area teachers suddenly developed an awareness of the plight of the student with a reading disability in reading-oriented content classes. Frequent conferences on the growth of individual students ensued, as well as discussion of materials and methods that would aid these students in their other classes. Some teachers allowed for flexible scheduling so that the student might be excused from his class to work in the TV room. The preparation of script and graphics went on not only in the TV room but in other classrooms and study halls.

The satisfaction of producing a tangible product, as well as the acquisition of a new set of skills required to work with television, did much to improve student self-image. One of my students is a Puerto Rican girl whose poor self-image was related to her shame about her origin. She was reticent about speaking English and would not talk about herself or her former experiences in Puerto Rico. Now, after having produced a Spanish/English program about Puerto Rico, she takes pride in her area of special knowledge as well as her usefulness to the school. The programs in English and Spanish will be used by the language teachers in their classes. Another student considered himself to be quite dull and unable to "get with it" in school. Because of his recognized expertise in handling the television equipment, he has become a resource to other students and teachers who wish to learn how to use the equipment. Another boy, who after years of speech therapy had made poor progress, suddenly decided that he wanted to improve his speech for a really professional television narration and embarked on a self-improvement program with noticeable results. A black student who was hostile towards the establishment was able to attain positive recognition for a tape on Black Beauty and African Inheritance that, while angry in tone, was artistically appealing. The tape was used to promote discussion in human relations classes and suddenly this young lady became a "star" to students who had never even noticed her before.

The work accomplished by the initial group of twelve students, in the short span of two months, far surpassed the quality of their work prior to the inception of the program. In February 1969 the course was expanded to include an interdepartmental approach involving other children with the same types of problems as in the initial group. The results were similar, although it did take some students longer to transfer the positive behavior and attitudes that developed in the TV situation to other learning experiences. Almost all of the students' retest scores on the Gates-MacGinitie have shown substantial growth. Perhaps more important is the fact that, for the first time, many of these youngsters voluntarily have become actively involved in the learning process.

While visitors were prohibited at first in view of the students' initial self-consciousness, visits by district administrators soon went unnoticed. The students came to realize that they were very special—not "special" in the sense that they can't or won't learn, but "special" in the sense of being capable of extraordinary work. They were being paid special attention because they were doing something quite out of the ordinary. One of our visitors was Mr. Raymond Graf, who is Supervisor of Educational Television in Albany. Mr. Graf corroborated many of our opinions about the course when he wrote us:

My recent visit to Port Washington to observe the "television process approach" in remedial reading was a genuine revelation. With a minimum of fanfare and complication, you have apparently brought to reality a theory of the use of television that had been broadly afield for the last several years. I think your contributions are both unique and extremely important. I want you and your Board of Education to know that you have our full support for extending the method to other schools and age groups in the district.

The Port Washington School System has taken Mr. Graf's advice and this year there will be six of these systems in operation—two in the two junior high schools and four in elementary schools. The attempt is to reach problem readers at an even earlier age—before frustrations have set in. The process is not mysterious nor is it excessive in cost. The cost of the system, redesigned by Telegrafix, Texts and Techniques of Port Washington to eliminate technical complexity and to add more electronic flexibility, will not exceed $5,000 installed and operating. Anticipating fifty students per system, or a district total of 300, the per student cost, including equipment and materials, will be $44 per student for the first year and then less than $10 per student for the second year and years to come.

This fall, for the first time in the history of our school, our eighth year students have demanded more work in reading. In continuity classes many of our students from last year will be working in what we now call the TV/reading elective. Our new group of seventh graders are now about to embark upon what we've seen to be a most exciting learning opportunity. How exciting it is to see students who view learning as a privilege! I now see former reluctant students approaching the learning situation with pride, interest and vigor. When asked by what name I should refer to them, my students quickly volunteered, "Call us Geniuses at Work." Let it suffice to say that self-image has changed dramatically. I must concur with one of my students who said, "I hope all kids with problems get this stuff [the television equipment]. They need it. It does a lot of things—good things. They deserve it, too!"

Teacher-Produced Slides Aid Reading for Low Vision Children

JOHN J. KNIGHT

The low vision child in the primary grades may rapidly fall behind his average seeing peers in the acquisition of a basic reading vocabulary because of the difficulties he encounters when working with visual information. He requires extra time to master mechanical reading motions considerably more complex than those a child with normal vision must develop. He also needs additional time to read a page of material even after he has acquired the necessary mechanical skills. This extra time may prevent him from learning new information at the daily rate of the rest of his class.

Problems with Reading Materials

One of the important reasons why a low vision child may have problems with reading is the manner in which the child, due to his visual limitations, must manipulate reading materials to see them. His reading material is usually very close to his eyes. For him, following a sentence requires an elaborate system of hand, arm, eye, head, and shoulder coordination, all necessary to keep the sentence and its contents moving past the eye at the critical distance required.

In addition to being burdened with the necessity of mastering reading movements that are more elaborate and time consuming than those utilized by children with normal vision, the low vision child may be required to use standard learning materials designed for use by a child with normal vision. In many cases these materials are unsuitable for the child with low vision. The primary textbook, in spite of its already large type, may need to be printed in an even larger size for him to perceive a recognizable image of each printed symbol.

As soon as he enters school the low vision child needs a special reading program designed to meet his needs. The program should attempt to present the child with new information each day in a form that will allow rapid comprehension, but one that does not depend entirely on extended linear scanning movements.

Basic Reading through Slides

A technique that will fit well into a standard reading program, and at the same time attend to the specific needs of the low vision child, is the use of a 35mm slide projector and teacher-produced 35mm slides. The child

Reprinted from *Teaching Exceptional Children* 3: 203–8 (1971) by permission of the Council for Exceptional Children. Copyright 1971 by The Council for Exceptional Children.

can use the projector to view the alphabet and a basic reading vocabulary during his school day. With the supplemental use of a basic reading vocabulary slide program, the low vision child can acquire a basic reading vocabulary at the same rate as the rest of his classmates and still be allowed to perfect his physical reading movements in the regular reading situation.

The slide technique helps the child by presenting words in almost any size the child may need in order to see most comfortably and accurately. The letters can be 1/4 inch high or 6 inches high—their size determined by the distance between the projector lens and the projection screen. The 35mm projector presentation also minimizes laborious and time consuming linear scanning movements. The child can focus his attention on the examination and interpretation of the reading material without being distracted by having to manipulate the material in order to see it. He can concentrate on the screen.

The student can use three surfaces to project and view these slides—a standard projection screen, a reflection box, or simply a clean, light colored wall. Of the three the reflection box is by far the best, because it allows the low vision child to move his head as close to the screen as is needed for him to see. His head will not block the projector's light beam because the projector casts an image into the reflection box from the side and not from the back of the child as with a movie screen. The image reflects off of a mirror and onto the back of a transparent screen. Therefore the front of the screen, which faces the student, resembles a television screen.

Reflection boxes are produced in various forms and can be purchased for use in the classroom. The size which is ideally suited for the classroom is 10″ × 9″ × 8″. The box can be purchased from various camera or department stores in a durable plastic for about $14.

The reflection box teamed with an automatic programmed slide projector becomes an automatic programmed teaching machine. The teacher can have as many as 80 slides in a slide series. He sets the timer on the projector for a specific display time for each slide, from 5 seconds to a full minute, and leaves the child to work on his lesson alone for the next 5 to 50 minutes.

The slide projector and reflection box can be used in coordination with a tape recorder. Verbal questions, answers, and explanations recorded on tape by the teacher can be synchronized with the presentation of the slides. In some areas, such as letter and word recognition, the student needs verbal reproduction of the sound of the letter.

Tapes—Complements to Slides

In working with low vision children at the primary level, for instance, letter recognition can be taught and practiced with a programmed slide unit. Any letter can be presented. During the presentation the student can repeat its sound or name or copy its shape on a teacher produced mimeographed lesson sheet that can accompany the tray of slides. A tape recorder can give instructions and supply answers.

For instance, the image of the letter "b" appears on the screen. The tape recorder begins, "Print this letter on your sheet of paper.- - - What is the name of this letter?- - - The name of this letter is 'b'.- - - Say it.- - - 'B'.- - - Say it again.- - - 'B'."

Words can be presented in the same manner. A word appears on the screen. The tape recorder begins, "What is this word?- - - This word is 'dog'.- - - Say it.- - - 'Dog'.- - - Say it again.- - - 'Dog'."

Names and objects can be easily associated through the use of slides. A photograph of a cat appears on the screen. The tape recorder begins, "What kind of animal is this? - - - It is a cat.- - - A cat.- - - Say it.- - - 'Cat'.- - - Say it again.- - - 'Cat'."

Teacher-produced 35mm programmed slide units may be used in other areas of development such as the early phases of mobility and safety training. Street and traffic signs can be identified by their shapes and colors as well as their printed message. Knowledge of this sort may be quite valuable to the low vision child who can identify globular shapes and masses of color but cannot define more intricate details such as printing on signs. A red octagon appears on the screen. The tape recorder begins, "What word is on a red sign shaped like this? - - - The word 'Stop'. - - - The word 'Stop'. - - - S-T-O-P. - - - 'Stop'."

Preparation of Slides

The uses of 35mm slides are as extensive as the teacher's imagination. They can be introduced into almost any curriculum area. The steps for preparation of such slides follow.

Most of the materials used to produce a 35mm slide program can be found within the school building. These materials are: a pair of scissors, a soft lead pencil, a ruler, a typewriter, a clothes iron, some 3M Company's number 127 projection transparencies infrared reproduction paper, a Thermofax secretary model reproduction machine, and several boxes of cardboard 35mm slide frames which can be purchased at camera counters for approximately $3 per 100.

First, using a soft lead pencil, rule a sheet of typing paper into 1½ inch squares. One word is typed in the center of each ruled square of the master. Each square will eventually be a slide and will contain a symbol of some sort when the master is complete.

The master will be used with a sheet of 3M Company's number 127 projection transparencies infrared reproduction paper. This economical reproduction paper is a clear sheet of plastic that will pick up the images from a master sheet. The 127 sheet is carefully placed on top of the master sheet, making sure that the edges are aligned and that there is no dirt between the two. The 127 sheet and the master are then inserted into a Thermofax secretary model infrared production machine. When they come out of the Thermofax machine, the two sheets are separated. The ruled squares and the symbols from the master will be imprinted on the 127 sheet which can be cut along the ruled lines into individual squares. Each of the squares will be mounted in a 35mm frame.

The 35mm frame is first folded and then reopened part way. The transparency square is carefully placed inside, making sure that the word is in the center of the open picture area. When the transparency is properly positioned, the slide frame is folded down over the square, sandwiching it within. Then the tip of a hot iron is pressed firmly around all four sides of the frame. The inside of the frame is treated with a glue that bonds with the application of heat and the iron firmly seals the transparency into its frame.

When all of the slides are completed, they are placed in a slide tray. The teacher can arrange and rearrange the slides for the best results for the individual student.

Conclusion

There are several prime advantages of the 35mm programmed slide unit. It is relatively inexpensive, costing approximately $3.50 per 100 completed slides. Automatic presentation of material by the projector frees the teacher to do other things in the classroom. Most important, it presents the low vision child with visual information that he is required to learn, yet in a size and brightness that more adequately meet his unique visual needs. The programmed slide unit is not a total solution to the low vision child's problems in the primary grades, but in many situations it may enable the child to move closer to a position where he can actually compete with his peers instead of spending his school years trying to catch up with them.

Teaching the Deaf with Photography

"Mark is one of those 7-year-olds with a ready grin and a shock of dark hair that constantly tumbles into his eyes.

Reprinted by permission of Association for Educational Communications and Technology from *Audiovisual Instruction* 14:47–49 (Nov. 1969).

"I remember one day last spring when he came into my office and put a snapshot of a little dog on my desk. I looked at it carefully and then told him what a fine picture it was.

" 'That's my dog Tinker,' Mark said proudly. 'I take him for walks and I play with him. He's my friend.'

"We smiled at each other; then Mark retrieved the photo and left. Although he didn't know it, Mark had just made a remarkable breakthrough. When you're seven years old and deaf, it's quite a feat to string together three sentences about any topic and then communicate your thoughts to someone else."

That is how Joseph R. Piccolino, energetic director of the Instructional Media Center at St. Mary's School for the Deaf in Buffalo, New York, describes the results of a unique program initiated at the school. Ever since the fall of 1968, he has been experimenting with the use of cameras, film, and snapshots as a means to help deaf youngsters communicate their perceptions of their environment and gain new language skills.

"The new term that's used today is visual literacy—literally, making visuals, or pictures, function as a language," Piccolino says. "Naturally, much of the teaching we do with deaf children is already geared to the visual mode."

"However, allowing the youngsters to create their own visuals through photography is an exciting new dimension. Suddenly, the students are working with visuals of their own making. They choose the subject matter and they press the shutter to capture their view of the world around them."

The visual literacy experiment began in November 1968 when, at Piccolino's suggestion, the school secured Kodak Instamatic cameras and film for 21 seven-, eight-, and nine-year-olds. These youngsters represented three classes of first and second graders at St. Mary's, where classes are small, averaging seven students each. Most deaf children, in fact, require four years to master the important basic material covered in first and second grades.

The school, established more than 100 years ago, currently enrolls 300 students, ranging in age from 21 months to 21 years, and maintains a professional staff of 75.

The three classroom teachers involved in the visual literacy experiment, each a specialist in deaf education, instructed the youngsters in the use of the Instamatic cameras, cartridge-pack film, and flashcubes.

"Then the students were turned loose to do 'their own thing'," comments Piccolino with a smile. "Each child had a camera and each one was allowed to keep it with him at all times—at school and at home. Neither the teachers nor I offered any framework for the pictures. It was a completely unstructured and continuing assignment."

What were the students' reactions?

"In a word, fantastic," according to Piccolino. "They couldn't wait to get their pictures back from the processor each time. And once the word was out that the snapshots had arrived, there was no way to satisfy them until the packets had been distributed and they had had a chance to examine their photos.

"In fact, I received a minor complaint from one of the teachers that the children wanted to spend so much time with their photos that she was having difficulty in channeling their interest into their other work."

The students took their cameras with them everywhere—to record field trips, their life at home, and activities in school. On one occasion the supervising principal at St. Mary's came into a classroom to reprimand one of the children—a disciplinary process that involves a lot of gestures to get the message across. Another child whipped out his camera and snapped a photo of the principal in mid-gesture!

What were the results of the visual literacy experiment?

While it is difficult to obtain accurate measurements of achievement in this area, Piccolino and the three teachers are enthusiastic about the changes they could observe in the youngsters.

First, the children were so "involved" with their own photos that they broke through their normal reticence about communication in order to share their experiences with the teacher and their classmates.

"We found a great increase in the willingness to use both written and verbal language," Piccolino comments. "The deaf students were confronted with material that was exciting to them, that represented themselves—and they were motivated to communicate."

In addition, the students' photos gave the instructor a fresh supply of resource materials for teaching language skills.

"Instead of a picture of a dog or a family in a textbook, the class was presented a photo of Jimmy's dog or Margaret's family at the dinner table," Piccolino says. "The interest quotient was built-in."

Another result was that the youngsters began to express themselves in more complete thoughts. Instead of merely using a word or phrase to identify a situation in a photo, they would speak two or three sentences.

"This is quite an achievement," Mr. Piccolino comments, "especially if you remember that deaf youngsters in the early elementary grades commonly are educationally behind their chronological age, because of the language deficiency inherent in their lack of hearing."

Another byproduct of the experiment was the observation that the youngsters began to use more varied language when they wrote and spoke about their photos.

"It was clear that they were communicating about people and animals and situations that they cared about," he says. "They began—some of them for the first time—to search for new words to express their feelings."

The teachers found, too, that the practice in sequencing photographs helped the children to develop a sense of time. Deaf youngsters at this age usually do not have a firm grasp of the sequence of events, of one thing happening before another.

Also, the children were able to transfer their newfound communication skills to other areas of the curriculum, in both verbal and written language. The youngsters discovered, for example, that a new word they had learned in describing their own photos could be used in a report on a science project. Likewise, the confidence they gained in talking and writing about their pictures carried over when they were called upon to discuss an arithmetic problem or to engage in social contact with other students.

Piccolino adds that many of the children seemed to gain a new and better self-image, as well. "They were taking pictures of their classmates and their own families, and they could see themselves and others as part of an interacting society. It was a thrill, for instance, when Mark could spot himself in a picture that Jerry had taken. The photos were a visual record of their personal experiences."

The teachers also noted increased abilities in memory and in creativity, perhaps as a result of the confidence the youngsters gained from their success in choosing and photographing their own pictures and then in recalling the event or situation in communicating about the photo.

The teachers themselves gained valuable insights into the problems facing some of the children as they studied the kinds of photos the students chose to take.

One shy little boy, for example, never photographed any other children—at home or at school. When the teacher investigated, she found that the deaf youngster felt he had no friends. Now, he is receiving extra help from the school's psychological staff.

Piccolino plans to continue the visual literacy program at St. Mary's.

"We are adding some refinements to our approach," he says. "For example, our teachers felt that they themselves would have benefited from more background work in the concepts of visual literacy and its application in the classroom before the project got under way."

There is also a place, the teachers say, for more structured assignments in producing visuals. They suggest that the unstructured picture-taking be combined with occasional specific tasks—for example, for each child to create a series of pictures that portrays a definite time sequence.

"One of the chief problems in deaf education is communication," says Piccolino. "Through the use of the students' own visuals and visual literacy, the school has found a means to help youngsters communicate through an avenue of perception where they are not handicapped—what they see.

"We have discovered that the youngsters' success in creating their own visuals can be transferred to other areas of language where they are handicapped. The children exhibit the natural desire to speak and write about their photos, and their high degree of motivation helps them overcome their reticence to attempt to master these new language skills.

"This may be the kind of breakthrough that will eventually shift the entire emphasis of the curriculum in deaf education—from the early elementary grades through high school."

Tactual Maps with Interchangeable Parts

CAROLYN CHANG
and
DANIEL E. JOHNSON

Distorted concepts of spatial relationships and facile verbalisms which hide a lack of direct experience can obstruct the blind child who is seeking to learn orientation and mobility skills. Frequently his contacts with his physical environment have not been integrated into accurate concepts of physical reality. Children blind from birth or early childhood have been found who believe that streets extend indefinitely, who do not have a useful concept of a "city block," who could not sense a gradual curve in a sidewalk, or who think that all intersections have the same shape.[1] Unlike the newly blinded adult who knows how the world of the traffic engineers and landscape architects looks and how it functions, the child who has never had vision must be taught how spatial phenomena are related to one another.

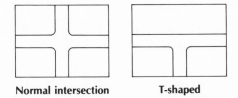

Normal intersection   **T-shaped**

In the Alameda County [Calif.] mobility demonstration project, tactual maps which condense and store a

Reprinted by permission from *The New Outlook* 62:122–24 (April 1968).

wealth of spatial data have been designed to help blind children organize and make sense out of the information they get from their canes and from their other senses. A map is not a substitute for the long cane any more than a wiring diagram is a substitute for a radio, but a map does help the blind person fit what his cane tells him into an organized, dependable framework of meaning. Presumably, a blinded adult could use a tactual map for many of the same purposes that he had for maps before he lost his sight; but before the congenitally blind student can use tactual maps in this way he first needs to use them to learn about topography itself. At first, the map is more of a model of what the world is like than it is a guide to get him some place. The model enables him by touch to condense into one perceptual closure the meaning of a whole "scene." By touching a model of a neighborhood he can encompass widely separated spots in one perception, but to move about in the actual neighborhood he will need his cane, his auditory acuity, and his other senses.

A tactual map for the blind to use during mobility instruction is a relatively new tool for teaching concepts of streets and intersections. Sherman[2] reports an almost total absence of city maps for the blind, and discusses the problems of presenting cartographic data tactually. Schiff[3] discusses tactual symbols and the problems of "conveying graphic diagrammatic information to blind persons." Gilson et al.[4] in 1965 described the uses of raised maps in the Alameda County School Department project to teach orientation and mobility to blind public school students.

As a result of her experiences as mobility instructor in the ESEA Title III Project # 1678, the senior author discovered the need for a rearrangeable type of tactual map which would be portable so that it could be used in field work. She developed this new idea into a prototype tactual chart or diagram with interchangeable, movable pieces. This chart serves many of the purposes of a tactual map as stated by Gilson et al. but instead of the laborious detail required to create permanent maps, the new approach makes it easy for the instructor to construct a single chart which is suitable for all of his students. With one set of portable materials, he can teach orientation concepts to different blind students by simulating in a tactual diagram the actual topographical problems facing each successive student.

Permanent tactual maps are bulky to carry and are time consuming to construct, but the flexible chart is portable and is adaptable to the instructional needs of the moment. The greater detail of the permanent tactual map sometimes distracts from the precise learning task at hand, but the chart allows the instructor to limit the presentation to the immediate learning task.

The amount and approximate cost of materials required to construct the prototype chart were as follows:

1. Valcro pile (retail value $5.00 for a piece 18″ × 24″);
2. Valcro hook (retail value $1.89 a yard for two yards of one inch tape);
3. Cardboard 1/16″ thick (50¢ per sheet for 2½ sheets 18″ × 24″);
4. Canvas board 3/8″ thick ($1.05 per sheet);
5. Glue, contact cement (98¢ per pint, of which half was used);
6. Tools (Exacto knife, paper cutter, ruler, compass, glue spreader).

The approximate cost of materials for one chart was $11.46, and the labor involved in actual construction was approximately four hours. Much time was spent in finding sources of materials and in trying alternatives which proved less satisfactory than those which are described here. The sample chart used a canvas board backing as noted in the materials, but a honeycombed drafting board of the same size would be more durable and still be lightweight.

To form the background of the chart, an 18″ × 24″ sheet of canvas board was covered with the pile section of a nylon material called Valcro, and the pile and canvas board were firmly bonded with contact cement. The result was similar to a felt or flannel board except that Valcro pile is able to hold more weight. The pieces for the chart are composed of cardboard polygons of different sizes and shapes needed to show different types of intersections and city blocks. Several rectangular pieces had two corners rounded representing the curb returns found at street corners. Pieces for islands, medial strips, and other types of differences in intersections were also made. The hook section of Valcro was attached with glue on the reverse side of these pieces so that they would adhere to the board with pile.

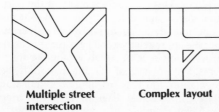

Multiple street intersection   **Complex layout**

By this simple process, a very flexible instructional tool was created. Unlike the rigid tactual map, this chart, because of its flexibility, can be used with many different students and not just the few for whom a complex map can be constructed. The chart and its pieces can be rearranged to illustrate a wide variety of field situations ranging from a specific intersection to general concepts about traffic flow and streets. It can clarify a single intersection that a student has trouble understanding; it can show a whole pattern of streets in an area; and it can show the relation of one street to others. The variety of situations which can be diagrammed with this board is limited only by the user's imagination. Additional pieces of different shapes can be made and used when necessary, and pins can be used to designate vertical objects such as fire plugs, light standards, and signs.

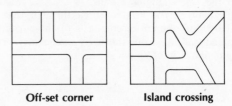

Off-set corner   **Island crossing**

The diagrams illustrate some of the common arrangements for which the chart is used.

As is true of all tools, there are both advantages and disadvantages in the use of this one. Some of the advantages of this type of map are:

1. Immediate construction of the problem. The area traveled can be diagrammed for tactual inspection right on the spot.

2. Ease of transporting the map. The flexible chart requires less space in the instructor's car than the heavy permanent maps and can be carried as the instructor walks with the student.

3. Time saved since actual maps require more painstaking construction.

4. Student communication with teacher. The teacher can test the student's knowledge of the different concepts by having the student construct his interpretation of the topography.

5. Adaptability. It can be refined and elaborated by each teacher to suit his own needs and ingenuity.

Some of the disadvantages are:

1. It is not permanent and it is not a map. It is schematic rather than precise in scale, direction, area, and in the relationships its parts bear to the actual ground.

2. As yet, it has been given only limited field trial.

3. The cost is rather high if each teacher must make his own, and much time is required to assemble the materials.

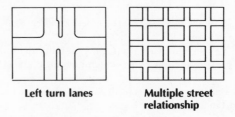

Left turn lanes   **Multiple street relationship**

A new tool, a tactual map or chart with interchangeable pieces, has been created for teachers of the blind. The chart can be used to teach general principles of the geography of foot travel, and it can be used to diagram actual specific situations. Because it is lightweight and portable, one set of materials can serve many students who are taught in different locations. The materials are relatively permanent, but can be used in infinite combinations and for many purposes in addition to orientation and mobility. With it the instructor can test the student's orientation and his grasp of concepts. The flexible chart challenges but does not restrict the instructor's ingenuity in developing his own modifications and uses. To the best of our knowledge, it is a genuine innovation in the field of education of the blind.

NOTES

1. Charles Gilson and others, "The Raised Map in Teaching Mobility," *The New Outlook for the Blind* 59:59–62 (February 1965).
2. John C. Sherman, "Needs and Resources in Maps for the Blind," *The New Outlook for the Blind* 59:130–34 (April 1965).
3. William Schiff, "Research on Raised Line Drawings," *The New Outlook for the Blind* 59:134–37 (April 1965).
4. Gilson, "The Raised Map."

To See and to Touch

WILLIAM A. HORN

A blind mother, whose little boy was too young to read, once expressed a wish to a friend. "I wish," she said, "that I could read to my son." The friend was Jean Dyon Norris, whose imagination, energy, and humanity could not let such a remark pass unheeded. The result was Twin Vision, a special publishing house for the blind that made that wish—and many similar wishes—come true.

Open a Twin Vision book at random and you will find that on one page its story appears in regular print, while on the opposite page the same story is told in the raised symbols of braille. Thus, the sighted can read to the blind or the blind can read to the sighted or, if they choose, they can read together. Hence, the name Twin Vision.

Using a special process, the publishing company also produces picture books in this same Twin Vision format. Under rights granted by cartoonist Charles Schulz,

Reprinted from *American Education*, Aug.–Sept. 1970, pp. 35–36.

it recently opened the world of "Peanuts" to sightless children and gives their parents a better chance to enter into the fun of their youngsters' new discoveries. Snoopy and the other lovable characters who surround that greatest of all nonheroes, Charlie Brown, now romp through the pages of two Twin Vision books, *Happiness Is a Warm Puppy* and *Love Is Walking Hand in Hand.* Five hundred copies of each have thus far been produced and, like all Twin Vision products, the books are distributed free to the blind in the United States, Canada, and 46 other countries.

The self-contained braille printing plant in Tarzana, California, is manned by 60 volunteers who give as much time as they can, when they can. Since its beginning in 1960, the plant has developed an impressive list of children's books in the Twin Vision editions. According to Mrs. Norris, who directs the operation, more than 100,000 copies from the childhood series, Little Golden Books, have been distributed. "Last year," she notes, "we produced almost 20,000 different items and we distributed 10,000 braille calendars. We also kept circulating through the mails a 5,000-volume Twin Vision lending library that is now in its third year."

Over the last three years Twin Vision has added great documents to its catalog beginning with the Constitution of the United States, the Declaration of Independence, and the first volume of *An Anthology of Great Documents.* The series has twice won the George Washington Honor Medal from the Freedoms Foundation, but there is no resting on laurels: the publishers are now starting to circulate copies of a new volume of Americana that contains patriotic songs, information about the various states, and an illustrated story of the Statue of Liberty.

Another Twin Vision service is the *Hot Line to Deaf-Blind,* a newsmagazine that keeps those who can neither see nor hear abreast of current happenings. "As it was, news became history before these people got to know about it," says Mrs. Norris.

Hot Line is edited by Rockey Spicer, a volunteer who is also public relations director for the U.S. Steel Company's Pacific Southwest district. Spicer made up special 24-page editions for such big news breaks as man's first landing on the moon and the assassination of Senator Robert Kennedy.

All funds for the Twin Vision project come from its parent organization, the American Brotherhood for the Blind, a nonprofit, nonsectarian, charitable, and educational foundation established in 1919. Mrs. Norris has many friends in the brotherhood, whose officers serve without pay and are themselves blind. From time to time Mrs. Norris would help them with a project, but it wasn't until the blind mother's plea in 1960 that she really got involved and began studying braille in order to transcribe children's books. Working from her home, she purchased the paper and materials and made the books by hand, even distributing them locally herself. She enlisted friends into the venture. Finally the demand became so great that the brotherhood felt they should consider expansion. They made a test mailing to regional schools for the blind and to State libraries to find out whether they would be interested in the books. The response was overwhelmingly favorable and the brotherhood purchased the equipment to publish the books in larger quantity.

One of the original volunteers, Jean Scott Neel, a housewife with two children, perfected the process that adds the pictures, which are simply raised so that they can be traced with the fingers. Mrs. Neel handmakes the molds like a piece of sculpture, and a thermoform braille duplicator transfers the design onto a plastic page.

Mrs. Neel has also written all the original books published by Twin Vision. One of them, *The Shape of Things—Birds*, explains how a bird looks and then describes the appearance and function of its different parts—the claw and the beak, for example. A raised drawing of each part described allows the blind person to feel the shape for himself. Mrs. Neel's books have all been researched with the help of blind readers and with the guidance of a volunteer psychology professor from a nearby university.

In addition to the 60 volunteers at the plant, there are 40 others working from their homes on more specialized assignments. The wife of a rabbi, for instance, is transcribing a child's story into Twin Vision in Hebrew for a library in Tel Aviv. Others are transcribing titles into French, German, Spanish, Italian, and Norwegian.

Since all volunteers must be qualified in braille transcription, the question arises, Where do all these trained people come from? Twin Vision takes care of that, too. The group set up its own braille school with a course that covers 22 weeks and recently graduated its fifth class. And, of course, like the students, the staff were all volunteers.

Time, Money, and Students with Visual Limitations

GLENN LEAVITT

Time is money, and time costs money. Many students with visual limitations find that their methods of study take up too much time and that their haphazard

Reprinted by permission from *The New Outlook* 65:271–75 (Oct. 1971).

attempts to improve their efficiency are often ineffective. Experience, however, has shown that an investment in certain high quality devices and their methodical use can result in better learning and the saving of *hours* of study time every day. When a sighted college student chooses to spend $500 on a skiing outfit or even $1500 on a car, few people feel that he is being extravagant. A visually limited college student, who will probably never buy a car or a skiing outfit, should, therefore, not hesitate to arrange for the use of equipment worth from $500 to $1500. Such an investment will not only greatly increase his learning efficiency, but it will afford him more time for a social life and for the other recreational activities that are so essential for balanced, healthy development.

The equipment and methods which are discussed in the following pages have proved to be quite effective for a typical visually handicapped student who is a slow braille reader and a rather inaccurate typist. More highly skilled students may find that some of these suggestions will not apply to them.

Virtually any student whose handicap interferes with his ability to read can receive a talking book machine on free loan from the Regional Library serving his geographical area. A variable speed adapter for a talking book machine, also available on free loan, enables the reader to increase the playback speed of a talking book record. Thus, a record which would normally take one hour to read can be read in as little as half an hour. The increased speed is more demanding of one's attention, but the result is that comprehension is generally better.

A taped book of 400 pages may require 12 to 15 hours of reading time when played at normal speed. Through the use of the Sony Model TC 105A tape recorder with variable speed adaptation, it is possible to reduce the reading time by as much as 50 percent and yet, in most cases, actually increase comprehension. Also included on this model is a button which allows the user to "mark" a tape that he is recording with a low frequency beep which is audible only at fast forward and reverse speeds. The TC 105A ($189) is available from the American Printing House for the Blind (1839 Frankfort Avenue, Louisville, Kentucky 40602). A student who is serious about learning efficiency should have two of these at his disposal.

The Sony Model TC 40 cassette tape recorder is slightly smaller and heavier than a 400-page textbook. It can be operated on batteries and has a built-in microphone—allowing one to record or play at the flip of a switch, with no set-up whatsoever. When recording, an alarm device sounds as the end of the tape is reached. It has a fast forward speed (cue) with the playback head engaged, which greatly eases the job of finding certain places within a tape. There are two reverse speeds. Any six-volt AC adapter (not more than $5) can be used to save battery power when an outlet is nearby. The machine fits easily into a briefcase or purse and is just as convenient to carry around all day as an inkprint book. It weighs only 1.7 pounds with batteries. Without such a device, most visually handicapped students must do all of their reading in their rooms, haul around heavy machines or bulky braille volumes, or read at the convenience of a sighted reader. With a TC 40 one can read at any time and in any place that a sighted reader would read an inkprint book. A lot can be done with just one TC 40, but two are much more than twice as efficient. The TC 40 costs about $98.

At present only Sony cassette tapes have the necessary foil to activate the end alarm in the TC 40. Cassettes that play for one hour on each side (C 120) are by far the most efficient. Any good quality, lubricated tape can be used on the TC 105A. Seven-inch reels are not recommended, however, because they cannot be left on the machine when the dust cover is closed. Since the cassettes are used repeatedly, five or six should be enough. On the other hand, material to be stored for the entire semester is kept on reels, and therefore it is best to have a separate three- or five-inch reel for each major aspect of each course, i.e., one for notes on sociology class sessions, one for notes on reading assignments in the sociology textbook, one for notes on the outside reading assigned for sociology, and one for notes for the sociology term paper. While recording or rerecording onto reels, the low frequency beep is used to indicate sections of the material for future reference. A simple code of beeps differentiating Monday's notes from Wednesday's notes, for instance, may also prove helpful.

Whenever the professor will allow it, his entire lecture should be recorded with the TC 40. Most instructors, who might object to systems requiring the stringing of plug and microphone wires around the room, will not mind this inconspicuous little device. Even though the complete class session is on tape, braille notes of the questions and observations which come to mind during the hour should not be neglected. Every student, whether visually handicapped or not, should spend some time reviewing the notes on a class session before going to the next meeting of that class. The individual must decide whether there was enough content in the lecture to warrant replaying the whole tape during the review. If not, the tape may be used to record something else and nothing will have been lost.

If, however, the recorded material is important to supplement one's memory and braille notes, it should then be recorded onto a reel by means of a patchcord strung between the TC 40 and a TC 105A. (If the reel will take an hour or more of recording time, then this process will involve no more time than it takes to turn on the two machines and turn them off an hour later.) With the taped class session on one of the TV 105As and a blank tape on the other, the tape can be played at the fastest comprehendable speed and a "digest" of the important points recorded onto the blank tape, using the "instant stop" switch between comments. This should not take much more than half an hour, after which additional thoughts from the braille notes may be recorded. Thus, an hour's class will be condensed to not more than five minutes on a tape reserved for notes for that particular class. The complete class session tapes or the braille notes are not saved as rereading them is much too inefficient. Throughout the semester, a supply of basic information is built up on one tape and is easily reviewed at examination time.

Students are often asked to read only one chapter of a book which is held on reserve in the library or an article of five or 10 pages in a journal. If the material is available for more than two weeks before it is due, it can be sent to Educational Tape Recording for the Blind (9911 South Wood Street, Chicago, Illinois 60643). For $10 a year they will record any material sent to them. Short pieces can usually be done within two weeks. If the ETRB service cannot be used, arrangements should be made for a local volunteer or paid reader to record it. In any case, a quality recording is important. Tapings without bibliographical information, table of contents, page numbers, and clear enunciation waste the time and effort of both the student and the reader. Reading with a "live" reader is recommended only as a last resort. The physical act of meeting together is time-consuming, and one of those involved is bound to be tired or inattentive.

Notes from the reading should be made just as with the rerecording of class sessions: playing the tape at the fastest comprehendable speed on one 105A and recording a condensation of the important points onto a tape on the second machine. If there are more than five minutes of notes on an hour's reading, it is probably not a very good job of "digesting" the material into notes. A low frequency beep should be placed between the notes on different items. Complete recordings should not be saved, only the digest notes for use at examination time.

If advance notice about a required textbook is received more than a month before the beginning of the semester, two copies of the book can be sent to Recording for the Blind (215 East 58th Street, New York, New York 10022) or one copy to ETRB. Although they are much slower, RFB produces much more efficient tapes. The material comes on five-inch reels with about one hour of recording per track, which makes for convenient rerecording onto C 120 cassettes. ETRB tapes are on seven-inch reels which means that a half-read tape cannot be left on the 105A with the dust cover closed; and, more importantly, there is a bothersome time overlap between one side of these tapes and one side of a cassette, making rerecording somewhat less convenient.

If there is no advance notice of a textbook, a *quality* recording should be done by a local volunteer or paid reader. Notes on reading assignments in the text should be made in the same manner as suggested for short reading assignments. However, it is probably wise for the student to keep the recording of the entire textbook on hand until the end of the semester. Then, unless some section of the text must be reread, only about half an hour's worth of notes on the text need to be reviewed at examination time.

Assigned literary readings seldom require the exacting attention that a textbook does and much of the reading can therefore be done with the aid of a TC 40 at times and in places where it would not be convenient to take notes while reading. A taped copy of a novel can be procured by one of the methods already mentioned. It should then be rerecorded onto cassettes. If a student can get into the habit of carrying a TC 40 with him during the day, there will be many opportunities to read for 10 or 15 minutes at a time; and before long, a novel of considerable length will have been read completely. A few minutes in the evening spent recording observations on the day's reading may prove valuable. As with other types of material, a separate tape should be kept for notes on literary readings assigned for any one course.

Many visually handicapped students are slow braille readers. This means that using braille will not only waste time but also reduce comprehension. If a needed book is only available in braille, "digest" notes should be taped as the book is read.

For recreational reading, talking book magazines, for example, can be speeded up with the variable speed adapter on the talking book machine and rerecorded onto cassettes by means of a patchcord just as is done with novels. For instance, one side of a talking book recording of *Newsweek,* when speeded up, will fit on one cassette. Still the material cannot be skimmed, although the TC 40 can be carried during the day and each section of the magazine given only as much attention as it deserves.

Much of the strictly mechanical part of preparing a term paper (bibliography, looking for books, proofreading) should be turned over to a paid reader who can carry out assigned tasks without the constant presence of the student. When pertinent materials are found, they should be taped. A live reader is more efficient than tape only when what is needed is a few paragraphs or pages which must be sought out of a long work; or when it is getting late in the semester and no source of fast quality taping can be located. "Digest" notes on these readings should be made. An outline of the term paper can then be sketched in braille after listening to these notes. This outline is referred to while the final form of the paper is dictated to a paid or volunteer reader who can type it up later.

The student should take care to use a method of taking tests which does not interfere with his ability to express clearly and completely in the time allotted for the test what he has learned during the semester. Since most students seem to be slow and inaccurate typists, it is probably best to dictate the answers to a paid or volunteer reader, if the professor will allow it.

Although all that has been said above may seem rather complicated and expensive, an application of these ideas should substantially simplify the task of learning effectively from college assignments. In applying these suggestions to a student's particular situation and to the evaluation of his need for new equipment, the following basic points made in this presentation should be considered: (1) Everything is read at the fastest comprehendable speed; (2) A small, portable machine is useful for recording lectures and for reading during available bits of time throughout the day; (3) Ideas from what is read are condensed and recorded onto separate reels for each major aspect of each subject (low frequency beeps are used to identify sections or dates on tapes); (4) Notes, rather than the original works, are used for review; (5) Face-to-face reading is kept to a minimum; (6) Braille reading is also kept to a minimum; and (7) Paid or volunteer readers are used to do as much "mechanical" work as possible.

Progress Report on the Visual Response System

RAYMOND WYMAN

The Visual Response System was invented about 18 months ago in order to provide a class of eight deaf children with the ability to communicate individual responses to their teacher by means of individual overhead projectors grouped in a V format. Preliminary experimentation with ordinary overhead projectors was encouraging enough to prompt a report at the 1969 Symposium. Experienced educators of the deaf saw enough merit in the unique system to encourage the author to proceed with additional experiments.

During the ensuing year, constant experimentation has been conducted at the American School for the Deaf

Reprinted by permission from *The American Annals of the Deaf* 114:838–40 (Nov. 1969).

in West Hartford, and for brief periods at Clarke, Austine, Crotched Mountain, Governor Baxter and Sterck Schools.

A special overhead projector model designated 80 MIVR has been developed by the Buhl Projector Company with help from the General Electric Lamp Department and the author. It has a 150 watt low voltage lamp that provides adequate lumens for the images that are only about three feet across. The fan is operated by a thermostat only after it becomes hot, which is infrequent in usual use. The eight student machines require only 1200 watts or ten amperes and they ordinarily make no noise (figs. 1 and 2).

Two journal articles describing the system and its use have been prepared and published. "A Visual Response System for Small-Group Interaction" was published by *Audiovisual Instruction* in September 1968, and "A Visual Response System for Teacher-Group Interaction

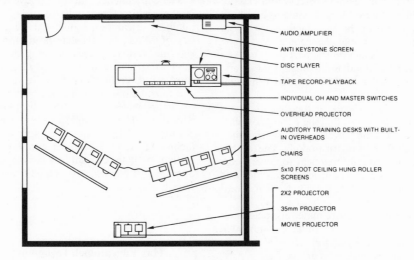

Fig. 1.   MIVR system set up in a small classroom or seminar room.

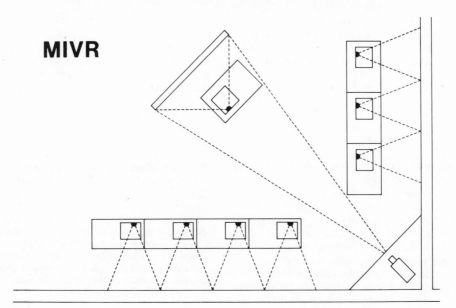

Fig. 2.   MIVR set up in a corner of a large classroom with the two walls used as screens.

in the Education of Deaf Children'' was published by *The Volta Review* in March 1969. Diagrams of typical room installations are included in the articles.

Three complete systems have been purchased with funds provided by Media Services and Captioned Films of USOE to the Northeast Regional Media Center for the Deaf. They have been transported and demonstrated by the author and Joseph Panko.

Although the system was designed for deaf children, it has also been used with seeming success in a class of mentally retarded children. A new system has been promised on a loan basis by the manufacturer for tryout in ghetto, bilingual, and normal classrooms.

There seems to be a feeling on the part of those who have taught with it or seen it demonstrated, that several very important contributions can be made to the education of the deaf.

Children seem to like to work at the machines and maintain attention over unusually long periods of time. Every student must respond every time by pointing, writing, etc., so that there is no turn-taking. The teacher provides constant human reinforcement for every correct or acceptable response. The teacher identifies and corrects every error within a few seconds of its commission.

Although teachers must prepare materials in advance to use with the system, many of them have commented on the absolute lack of correcting to be done after class. All correcting is done as the errors are made.

The system has been used with success by deaf teachers. One veteran teacher commented that he was now having a real dialogue with his students.

The system has been used with success by inexperienced personnel who were otherwise understood with difficulty by the students, and who found it very difficult to understand the students. It may be that aides can conduct review or drill with the system on material taught by a teacher.

Programmed learning materials that are ordinarily used by individual students can be put on overhead transparencies and projected by the teacher's projector for response on the eight student projectors. Of course the advantage of individual rates is lost, but the tremendous advantage of human reinforcement and encouragement is gained. It may be that many Project LIFE materials could be used in this way.

The 200 language transparencies produced by NERMCD last year have been particularly useful with this system. (These transparencies were distributed to all schools by Media Services and Captioned Films.) Various ruled and numbered or lettered response sheets are used by the student so that the teacher will know where to look for the answers during the brief scanning period.

Although eight students were assumed to be the proper number to be involved, several trials have been conducted with up to 12 students at overheads simultaneously. It is too early to tell if this number is feasible, but if it were, another revolution might be in the making.

Only a little experimentation has been done with materials for response presented by tapes, discs, audio cards, slides, filmstrips, motion pictures or television. These would seem to provide a variety of stimuli for visual response.

The experiments indicated above are, of course, not in the realm of research. In order to remedy this, a qualified researcher, a doctoral student at the University of Massachusetts, has been employed to conduct rigorous research. This is being done in the area of sentence structure in the primary building at the American School. Preliminary data are very exciting.

It must be pointed out that no claim is made that this system provides more than a part of the deaf child's education. The tremendously important speaking skill is only aided by helping to improve written language facility. If larger numbers can be drilled with this system, or if fewer qualified personnel are required to operate it, it might free qualified teachers for individual speech instruction.

Has Educational Technology Misplaced the Deaf Learner?

RONALD R. KELLY

The total spectrum of educational media offers vast potential for education of the deaf, but unfortunately, successful implementation has been elusive during the past decade. Various reasons have been put forth as to why the potential of educational media has not been realized in education: teacher indifference; administrative problems; inadequate equipment; poor programs; inaccessibility; lack of training; and inappropriate use of media specialists.[1] A prominent educator has suggested that those who are responsible for curricular and technological innovations are partly to blame:

Persons away from the classroom, busy devising and seeking to introduce a host of innovations, make several kinds of errors. Some fail to recognize the long distance between the conception of an idea in one person and the translation of it into practice by another. They are impatient and unable to understand why teachers cannot move

Reprinted by permission from *The American Annals of the Deaf* 117:427–30 (Aug. 1972).

into action as soon as they learn of the innovation. Others, lacking respect for the experience teachers have had with pupils at a particular school level, fail to invite the good advice teachers could give them on improving the innovation before costly mistakes have been made. A third group, with little confidence in teachers, makes up packages of "teacherproof" materials as a way of implementing an innovation.[2]

These reasons may be valid and probably contribute in part to the inability of educators of the deaf to harness the full potential of educational media. However, in order to understand this problem, another dimension must be considered—a dimension that is central to the role of educational media in the learning process.

Several years ago, Robert E. Stepp, Director of the Midwest Regional Media Center for the Deaf, raised a question: "Should instructional materials be designed for teacher or learner use?"[3] This simple question focuses on the very essence of educational media. It is important because *we often assume that when educational media are used by the teacher, they are being used for the benefit of the students.* But are they? Do teachers use educational media in order to improve their own teaching image, while erroneously assuming that it will automatically benefit the learners?

This problem came to light as a result of the author's experiences in both a Special Educational Instructional Materials Center (SEIMC) and a Regional Media Center for the Deaf (RMC). Teachers come to the instructional materials centers in search of ways to improve their instruction. Invariably they ask one of several questions: (1) "What materials do you have to help me improve my teaching?"; (2) "Can you show me how to produce instructional materials and operate the equipment? I want to use media in my teaching."; or (3) "Do you have anything I can use with my class of special children?" These questions suggest that the teachers who come to the instructional materials center are sincerely concerned about improving instruction, but notice the emphasis on the teacher and *not* the students. Subsequent visits to these teachers' classrooms further confirmed the suspicion that teachers tend to perceive and improve the "teaching-learning process" from their own perspective rather than from the students' point of view.

Other experiences in several summer media institutes for teachers of the deaf have reinforced this view. Since 1966, the Midwest Regional Media Center for the Deaf at the University of Nebraska (this is one of four Regional Media Centers for the Deaf funded by Media Services and Captioned Films, Bureau of Education for the Handicapped, USOE) has conducted a six week Summer Media Institute for Teachers of the Deaf offering six hours of graduate credit. In this program, teachers learn to plan, produce, and apply instructional technology to education of the deaf. The sessions are organized so that the participants actually design and produce their own instructional materials (overhead transparencies, 2×2 slides, Super 8mm movies and videotape programs, etc.). Each summer institute is concluded with demonstrations of instructional media designed by the participants.

For the most part, these demonstrations of teacher-produced educational media have been extremely impressive. In fact, it is remarkable that complex media skills can be acquired and also implemented in a six-week institute. However, a disturbing situation has occurred in the demonstration critiques during the past several institutes. Both staff members and participants have made comments about some of the demonstrations to the effect that "You certainly have an excellent mediated presentation, *but* I'm not sure deaf children would comprehend."

Statements of this nature would not be important if the particular units referred to were badly planned and produced. However, these statements applied to some very exciting educational media that were well planned and organized. Needless to say, such comments evoke some rather disturbing thoughts. Are the teachers merely acquiring media skills that enable them to put on a more "showy" presentation, but which do not necessarily contribute to the learning of deaf students? Is it possible to "systematically" plan, produce, and utilize educational media and still fail to reach the hearing impaired learner? Obviously, the answer is yes. The question that must be considered, then, is whether it is possible to get teachers to *focus on the students* while they are increasing their own media skills. *Perhaps technologists and teachers are victims of their own involvement.*

All educational technologists engaged in teacher education and in-service programs need to deal with these questions. They must take definite steps to assure that teachers focus on their students while acquiring new media skills. However, in order to do this, the educational technologists conducting the media institutes and workshops must themselves be able to focus on two groups of students: the teachers who are the immediate learners; and their students who are the intended beneficiaries of educational media. All too often "technologists" and "media specialists" are so enthralled with their "media machines" they seem to misplace the learners—both the teachers and their students.

In regard to teachers of the deaf, several techniques might be used in media institutes and workshops to help them focus on their students while acquiring teacher-oriented media skills. At the 1971 Summer Media Institute for Teachers of the Deaf, conducted by the Midwest Regional Media Center for the Deaf, an attempt was made to do this. During the demonstrations of teacher-produced instructional media (discussed previously), eight hearing teachers were randomly selected to have their hearing blocked out in an attempt to simulate deafness. This was accomplished by feeding "white noise" into headsets worn by each of them. Their objective was to analyze each demonstration unit to see if the media communicated the intended information to people who could not rely on their hearing.

There were six different mediated teaching demonstrations developed by teams of from four to six members. Each team of teachers submitted the following planning information to the staff:

1. The concept(s) and content they planned to teach.
2. Specific information and behavior they wanted the students to learn.
3. Criteria for acceptable student performance.
4. The media that was selected to provide the learning experiences.

After each demonstration, the eight "headset" observers were asked to do two things:

1. Describe the objectives of the mediated teaching demonstration, listing the concepts and content they learned.
2. Describe their reactions and "feelings" of having to participate in a learning experience with impeded hearing.

For comparison purposes, staff members and participants without the headsets were also required to describe the objectives of each demonstration and list the concepts they learned.

Every participant and staff member had an opportunity to view at least one demonstration with headsets. In addition, the deaf participants were required to view at least two demonstrations without the aid of an interpreter. Thus, everyone had to rely on *visual media only*, at least once, in order to understand the purpose and concepts of the instructional media demonstrations.

It was hoped that this type of observation technique would provide certain types of feedback. Basically, we wanted to analyze whether the participating "students" understood the purpose of the demonstration as intended by the teachers who developed the materials. And if so, did the "headset" observers learn as much from the media demonstration as the hearing group. In short, did the media communicate effectively with students who could not rely on their hearing?

Although rudimentary in design, this experience was invaluable. It enabled the teachers to analyze their own instructional media from a viewpoint closer to that of hearing impaired students. For example, some of their comments were:

I felt the necessity to keep my eyes on the teacher *constantly*, which was a strain, and I felt out of all the classroom participation which went on behind me.

It will help me make sure my students fully understand what I am trying to teach.

I experienced an insecure feeling because I could not understand what was required of me.

Now I know a little more what my kids live with.

Furthermore, this experience "forced" self-questioning as to why they designed and used the media in a particular way. Most important, the teachers seemed to be discussing media *in terms of communication* rather than as a supplementary teaching aid.

Another possible technique to help educational technologists and teachers focus on the learners is to include deaf students in the media program. Hearing impaired students and their teachers should work together to learn media skills in order to communicate more effectively in the learning process. Media institutes and workshops have traditionally been the teachers' domain and because of this, have tended to emphasize the teachers' interaction with technology. It is now time to integrate the deaf students into the media programs.

A third technique that might be used is an internalized accountability check on the part of the teacher. For example, in planning a mediated instructional unit every teacher of the deaf should ask himself:

1. Why do I think this medium will help the students learn?
2. In what ways can the students interact with this medium?
3. If this medium were not used, what alternatives exist for student interaction with this topic or concept?

Some teachers will probably discover they are using educational media due to personal likes and interests. Others may discover they use media because they live in a technological society and it is in vogue. There will even be those who find out that their media use does indeed focus on their students' learning.

Conclusion

Regardless of the techniques involved, there definitely need to be new perspectives toward media utilization in education of the deaf. If educational media are used only to aid, improve, and polish existing teaching methods for the hearing impaired, then success will be limited. However, if educational media are conceived as communication and interaction tools to develop new learning experiences for the deaf, then the potential of media might be within our grasp. A key determiner in this developmental process will be the ability of the teachers and technologists to focus on the students.

Students, teachers, and media must be seen in a new light. In dealing with this problem, educators and technologists should ". . . not search for solutions, but for new ways to view the problem."[4] As long as educational technologists and media specialists persist in merely supplementing existing educational practices with media, then Dr. Silverman's analysis will gain adherents:

Ours is a time of "rising expectations" nurtured by "great advances in technology" with its inevitable idolatry of evangelistic technologists and its comforting faith in equating change with improvement, newness with validity, gimmickry with innovation, and public relations with evaluation.[5]

Educational technologists and media specialists are directly responsible for determining the direction and depth of technology in the learning process. Unless they are able to help teachers focus on their students while designing and using media, then the deaf learner will surely be misplaced—and educational media will merely remain a technological titillation for teachers.

NOTES

1. *A Report to the President and the Congress of the United States by the Commission on Instructional Technology* (Washington, D.C.: The Commission, March 1970), pp. 79–84.

2. Alice M. Miel, "Developing Strategies of Planned Curricular Innovation: A Re-View with Implications for Instructional Leadership," in Marcella R. Lawler, *Strategies for Planned Curricular Innovation* (Columbia Teachers College Pr., 1970), p. 163.

3. Robert E. Stepp, "Educational Media and Deaf Education: The Emerging Literature," *Volta Review* 70:366 (September 1968).

4. Eugene Raudsepp, "Forcing Ideas with Synectics . . . A Creative Approach to Problem Solving," *Machine Design* 41:135 (16 October 1969).

5. Richard S. Silverman, "Some Thoughts on Curriculum Improvement," *Volta Review* 70:372 (September 1968).

PART 4

Program: Delivering the Instructional Message

The school library must play a dynamic role in the delivery of the instructional message. This facility is not a place wherein books are merely stored and circulated, but the coordinating hub in which materials, curriculum, and children's academic and personal needs converge. The program is the means by which this convergence occurs.

The school library program consists of those activities directed by the librarian which develop reference skills, promote reading, provide enrichment, and supplement the curriculum. Students are taught to be independent library users and are introduced to significant and exciting authors, particular books of note, and the spectrum of literary genres. Provision is made for enrichment in the content areas, channels are created for the pursuit of special interests, and materials and programs for remediation are designed. Activities such as storytelling, dramatizing with puppets, creative writing, and role playing engender enthusiasms and understanding. Obviously, the aesthetic and exhilarating experiences which literature can provide should permeate the entire literary experience.

For the special child, additions and adaptations to the program are imperative. The delivery of service to the exceptional child provides the hookup between the setting, the equipment, the prescriptive materials, and the recipient's cognitive and affective development. The indispensable compo-

nents of a successful program are: careful planning, sophisticated knowledge of sources and materials, awareness of the instructional potentialities of a variety of print and nonprint media, sensitivity to the requisites of the special child, knowledge of previously successful strategies combined with a willingness to experiment with unconventional and eclectic approaches, ability to target in on procedures which benefit special children, energy and endurance to persist when confronted with obstacles or resistance, and coordination with other concerned faculty.

Librarians must be willing to reexamine their own modes of delivery of service to ascertain whether their orientation, style, personal preferences, or other idiosyncratic behaviors are appropriate to suit the exceptional child's requirements. Often they are not. The librarian cannot function as an elitist or exclusionary agent. The library must be conceptualized as a zero-reject model, accepting and welcoming all the diverse segments of the school population. The program must be modified to accommodate the needs of each child rather than insisting that each child conform to the demands of a preconceived protocol, and this objective must be accomplished without impinging on the reasonable demands of other users.

In a wide-ranging article, Mullen and Peterson explain how a large urban library system has adapted to meet the extraordinary needs of all catagories of exceptional children. Programming within a single school or a relatively small system presents fewer problems. The very size of the student population in the major cities of this country compounds the difficulties of providing effective service, yet the imperative for doing so is not diminished. The authors describe how sufficient flexibility was maintained to provide library service despite the dissimilarities in classroom structure. Libraries responded to the needs of heterogeneously or homogeneously organized classes as well as to individual students. Programs had to be consistent with school policy, yet responsive to the highly specific needs of each child. The novice library administrator should not be misled into believing that such a variety and complexity of services is readily obtained or that cooperation between librarians and other faculty members is easily achieved. The success of such an endeavor requires much collaborative planning for program development, implementation, and evaluation by special educators and librarians.

A stimulating library program should be axiomatic for gifted children, a group whose requirements are often overlooked on the assumption that they are self-directed and capable of satisfying their needs without guidance. The classroom is, of necessity, restricted in the quantity, variety, and breadth of materials and facilities it can provide; the materials center, while providing these in abundance, will be inadequate unless the program generates activities for bringing the child and the resources together.

Although librarians frequently are exhorted to develop creative, challenging opportunities for gifted children, there is not much in the way of specific guidance as to what should be done or how to do it. Periodically, the community cries out that we are wasting our most precious resource, our academically talented students, and demands are made to "do something." Librarians are more than willing, but they need to know what that "something" is. The succeeding articles suggest practical and effective programs for these students.

Bigaj maintains that gifted readers comprise one of the least served groups in the public schools. He asserts that their needs are often discounted or glossed over. Subsequent to the identification of their ability, highly individualized programs must be formulated. Librarians are often unaware of the ability of these high achievers and thus are unable to bring their considerable knowledge to bear on the problem. Bigaj suggests the establishment of a critical reading lab, the use of appropriate reference books, the initiation of opportunities to evaluate the library experience, and makes other recommendations calculated to capitalize upon the highly able reader's talents. Except for the drab example of creative writing which is not really germane to our topic, Bigaj constructively illustrates how the librarian's tools and skills enlarge the gifted reader's world.

Baskin and Harris develop the concept of the library as a learning laboratory for gifted children. Specific activities are included which encourage divergent thinking, experimentation, intellectual growth, and creative, imaginative responses to literature. Diversity in reading behaviors, greater involvement in library experiences, increase in varieties of reaction modes, curriculum-related enrichment activities, and bibliophilic expressions are priority goals advocated by these authors. This article is derived from pragmatic sources rather than theoretical ones. Its applicability is not strictly limited to the high-achieving child but, with adaptations, could be used with other exceptional groupings or with some children in regular classrooms. Those activities which allow for imaginative, open-ended or varied reactions can be used with a spectrum of ability groupings. Their special virtue with gifted children is that they are nonrestrictive and permit the child free play of talents while providing high levels of stimulation and motivation. Tactics for improving cooperative arrangements between the librarian and the teacher of the gifted are also included.

Batchelor, exploring this theme further, examines the central role which books and reading play in the life of the gifted child who must be educated in the skills and encouraged in the desire to engage in a lifetime of self-directed learning. Although media and direct personal experience provide much information, still the printed word is the critical format through which most ideas are exchanged, explored, and analyzed. Thus, the gifted child's facility in using the library will influence her/his ability to mature scholastically. The art and science of reading guidance for the highly able require genuine enthusiasm for reading and good rapport with the reader. The librarian should work toward increasing analytical reading abilities, promoting the enjoyment of difficult reading matter, and maximizing receptivity toward new concepts or beliefs. Batchelor advocates that discussion and exchange of ideas about books be stressed and quality of interpretation be recognized as more significant than quantity read. This author's philosophy will be unpopular with those who respond to the problems of the highly able with neglect, permissiveness, or acceptance of minimal effort.

Storytelling is so firmly entrenched as an accepted library practice that the reasons for its popularity are often unquestioned and frequently undervalued. Yet there are few activities that achieve so many academic aims through so enjoyable an experience. Storytelling teaches new vocabulary, stretches attention span, introduces cultural events, norms and values, provides a socializing experience, develops attitudes, and can be the stimulus for language practice, dramatic interpretations, artistic expression, creative writing, and research projects. Clearly then, it is essential that storytelling be included in programming for the exceptional child.

Storytelling for the sensorily impaired presents very special problems to the librarian. Brown delineates those components of a story which make it appropriate and exciting for the blind child. The usual planning and delivery considerations which apply in a storytelling situation with sighted children are not always germane for the visually impaired. Obviously, facial expressions and gestures are of no value while voice quality, inflection, and variation all work to increase the possibility of pleasure and comprehension by the listeners. The blind child may react in a different manner than sighted peers, and librarians unused to working with these children will have to moderate their expectations. Storytelling with deaf children is an even more complex problem due to the paucity of their language background and dependence on visual cues. Huston identifies the five sections of a story: introduction, buildup, action, reaction, and climax and explains how each must be handled in developing a successful storytelling experience for middle school level deaf children. Very precise and detailed instructions are specified in the treatment of each section and the explanation of how each contributes to the deaf child's understanding is demonstrated. Huston cautions that while stories can serve many instructional purposes, the key requirement is that they be enjoyable. Librarians who have never worked with deaf or blind children will appreciate this blueprint for their first storytelling experience. The situations described in these two articles occur in disability-segregated settings. The librarian will have to adapt these suggestions when a handicapped child is a member of a class of sighted or hearing children.

Baskin and Harris have provided guidance for the librarian in planning and implementing a storytelling experience for the young retarded child. The rationale for selecting stories, techniques for behavior management, and procedures for involving the listeners are presented. Emphasis is on expected results and many suggestions for overcoming various deficits in the children's capabilities are proposed. Although only two dozen books are critically discussed, the reader will be able to extract some important guidelines for standards of rejection or acceptance of books and techniques for their effective use.

The learning disabled child often displays such irritating bibliophobic behavior that he or she virtually demands to be ostracized from the library, a setting with thousands of reminders of his or her deficiency. Morgan summarizes the steps which led eight children, described as having learning, social, or emotional disorders accompanied by reading retardation, from being antipathetic to books to clamoring for opportunities to become librarian-surrogates. His treatment strategy emerged from a thorough knowledge of their specific needs, capacities, and fears. He describes how the children exchanged failure and avoidance behavior for roles which enhanced their status and responsibility and ultimately led to quantitative and qualitative improvement in library behavior. The practical procedures described are valuable in settings containing small groups of children; large special populations with similar demands will diminish the likelihood that the quality of such personalized services can be maintained.

Dempsey describes a reclamation project with five male adolescents who were reading two to six grade levels below their chronological age peers. These boys had successfully staved off confronting their deficiencies by such techniques as passivity, insubordination, and avoidance of activities in which their inadequacies might be disclosed. Dempsey, working with other faculty, took an active role as a remediator in Library Reading, a course supplementing the regular reading class. Brief descriptions of the academic behavior of the participants, problems in book selection, and the evolution of this program are chronicled. Post-tests revealed a notable increase in achievement. Other librarians, interested more in action than rhetoric, will find this article helpful. Although the conditions of cooperative faculty planning, released time, staff dedication, and other program components described by Dempsey approach the ideal and are atypical of many library situations, this article clearly shows that such programs can work and are well worth the effort. Implementation of a similar high quality program will require considerable initiative and ingenuity on the part of the librarian.

"The Furious Children and the Library" is a three-part account of some of the seminal work of Fritz Redl and his colleagues in developing a program characterized by creative responsiveness to seriously emotionally disturbed youngsters. In the introduction, Noshpitz mentions the contributions the library makes as a socializing agent. Hannigan explains that the library must encompass nonaca-

demic functions including reality orientation, limit-setting, and personal success experiences. In the second section, Glaser and Vernick highlight the benefits obtained by orienting children to the structure of the library so that they can operate within the restrictions it imposes. The authors also suggest that the library function must be redefined to accommodate the special requisites of these children without losing sight of its role as a source of information and enjoyment. The procedures by which this library satisfied these children's curiosity as well as their considerable emotional needs are graphically spelled out. In the final section, Maeda and Redl assert that the library has a normalizing function for maladjusted children in providing a realistic, but benign model, a refuge, and a status-producing and reality-testing environment. Children awaiting assignment to and returning from treatment centers, as well as those not sufficiently disturbed to require institutionalization, will comprise some of the population with whom school librarians must come to terms; and this series offers direct assistance for them. As Redl indicates, the library program can have both a restorative and salubrious impact on the functioning of the easily combustible child. Many librarians may be startled to discover that the library was the setting in which improved behavior first was manifested. The therapists indicated (see also Morgan) that housekeeping and library skills were an antecedent to reading readiness for these children, a finding in contrast to common practice. In light of the impact the program had on "library-obnoxious" children (Redl's phrase), we share the authors' lament that an extensive research and service proposal was not mounted at this treatment center. Dr. Redl was one of the pioneers in promoting the therapeutic use of books with disturbed adolescent youngsters; his study remains a classic in the field.

Special Education and the School Librarian

FRANCES A. MULLEN
and
MIRIAM PETERSON

Handicapped students, like normal young people, need educational opportunities that will enable them to achieve optimum growth and development in keeping with their own unique natures and individual capacities. The school librarian has an important role in providing library service and guidance to serve both the curricular and the personal needs and interests of these students. Although the general objectives of library service are the same for both the normal and the handicapped students, library facilities, equipment, organizational patterns, materials, and services are provided and adapted according to the needs of the particular types of handicaps.

Library Facilities and Equipment

In the special schools for the crippled children the buildings are provided with special features such as ramps and therapy rooms to accommodate the students. Likewise, library equipment and its arrangement must be appropriate to the needs of the handicapped. In the Spalding High School library, wheelchair tables, dictionary and atlas stands, globes, and museum cases are on wheels so that they can be easily moved or brought to the students who are unable to go to them. The card catalog is low enough in height to be readily used by students in wheelchairs or in walkers as well as by those in a standing position. Round tables are provided to accommodate three students in wheelchairs. Aisles are wide to permit the passage of students in wheelchairs or on crutches. For ready access materials are shelved neither too high nor too low. In schools that serve the blind the shelving must be ample to house the braille volumes that take so much more space than printed books. Filmstrip viewers, radios, and record players must also be placed according to the needs of the handicapped. In the Spalding Elementary School library the reading tables do not accommodate children in large wheelchairs, and for them various types of book rests and book holders are provided.

Library Materials for the Handicapped

The same general criteria as applied in the selection of books for regular students are applicable for the handicapped. Like normal children their reading patterns are highly individual, and their general interests in

Reprinted from *Illinois Libraries*, May 1965.

books are for the most part similar to those of regular students of comparable age and grade level. As a rule they are not particularly interested in books about the handicapped. There are, of course, those with psychological problems for whom materials of therapeutic value are provided. Such materials must be factual, as for example the *Roy Campanella Story*[1] by Milton Shapiro and *The Trembling Years*[2] by Elsie Oakes Barber, which deals with the emotional recovery of a polio victim, both books used at the high school level.

In conjunction with the general principles of good book selection are some factors to be taken into consideration regarding the needs of particular types of handicapped students. The size of the book must be appropriate for the student who is to make use of it. Students on crutches, in a walker, in a body cast, with cerebral palsy, or with muscular dystrophy are unable to handle anthologies, trilogies, or oversized books. Printed materials for the partially seeing must be suitable in format—type-point, spacing, ink, and paper, to enable them to be read with ease. The educable mentally handicapped need easy-to-read materials having a simple sentence structure, an easy vocabulary, plenty of action, ample illustrations, and high interest level. For the trainable mentally handicapped, the illustrations must be simple and uncluttered and the stories within the growth level and experiences of the children.

Among the types of resources provided for the handicapped are braille books, braille globes, and talking books for the blind. The *World Book* available in braille is a great asset in providing reference material for the blind. The radio brings educational programs to the blind, and alphabet and phrase boards are aids to the deaf nonspeakers in making known their library needs. Filmstrips are in demand by many types of handicapped groups. The orthopedically handicapped students at Spalding High School are attracted to the paperbacks in bright washable bindings. Boys can slip them into their pockets and girls into their pocketbooks. These books are sturdy and can withstand physical wear and tear that accompanies handling by students with poor physical coordination.

The Role of the Librarian in Developing a Program of Services

In serving handicapped students the librarian renders far greater individual guidance and personal service than are usual for normal students. Some children need assistance in taking books from the shelves, in signing their names on book cards or slips, in turning pages, and in removing and placing books in their briefcases.

Because handicapped students seldom are able to get to the public library, the school library becomes their chief and in many cases only source of library materials.

Therefore, librarians in these schools endeavor to circulate for home use a wide range of materials—books, magazines, pictures, maps, and pamphlets. Classroom lists and assignments are carefully checked for the availability of materials; mimeographed lists of new materials are distributed to students and teachers; and collections of materials related to curriculum units of study are sent to classrooms. The school library also services hospitalized and homebound students and their teachers. Materials are sent to the various hospitals by the librarians via the school bus.

At the elementary school level, handicapped children are scheduled to the library according to their class groups. In schools for the orthopedically handicapped, students are members of classes composed of children with similar handicaps. This is also true for the educable mentally handicapped and for the social adjustment students. Many regular schools have special divisions of blind, partially seeing, deaf oral, and hard-of-hearing students. These children are often programmed to regular classes and come to the library with classes of normal students. The librarian must be alert to the personal needs of students so programmed. In addition to scheduled periods a reference table is always set aside in the libraries to provide opportunity for individual students to pursue reference assignments throughout the day.

Instruction in library skills is provided for the handicapped the same as for regular students. Of necessity such instruction for the physically handicapped must be on an individual basis. Many students despite severe physical limitations learn to locate materials, to take books from the shelves, to use the card catalog, and to use reference books. Simple library skills are taught to the educable mentally handicapped, and in some instances they use these skills in rendering service as library aides.

Much is done by the librarians to vitalize library experiences for handicapped students. In the primary grades storytelling and reading aloud from the array of splendid picture books to discover the joys of reading and to build literary backgrounds are emphasized. At the Medill Primary School a reading aloud by the librarian of *The Alligator's Toothache*[3] by Marguerite Dorian to a class of educable mentally handicapped students led to a series of rewarding experiences. The students became acquainted with the sequence of events in the story and discussed the characters. Stick puppets were made, songs were composed, characterizations were developed, and the story was presented through puppetry to the entire school in cooperation with the classroom teacher. The project resulted in many worthwhile outcomes. Growth in oral expression and creativity developed as students behind the puppet stage lost their inhibitions while speaking through characterizations. The project afforded an opportunity for coopera-

tion and for working together harmoniously. Students experienced the meaning of success and accomplishment, and developed a better self-image as they explored the potential of their own creativity. There followed closer identification of these students with the school as a whole. Not all storytelling or reading aloud on the part of the librarian takes on such proportions, but an occasional project in cooperation with other teachers motivates interest and brings valuable outgrowth.

At the Mosely Social Adjustment School, the librarian employs audiovisual materials widely to stimulate interest in reading and in the use of the library. For example a multimedia approach in the story of *Tom Sawyer* included use of the printed book, an audio book recording, a filmstrip, dramatizations of various scenes by the students, and tape recordings of the students' own narration of the story. With these students, interest in poetry that is filled with action or humor and that has a clear story is sparked through an audiovisual approach. Tape recordings have been made of both individual and choral readings.

The librarian at the Bell School participated in a team teaching program which included a primary group of hard-of-hearing children. A brief book report sheet was developed by the teacher and the librarian cooperatively for use by the pupils when they completed the reading of a book. They derived pleasure and delight in exploring many types of easy and picture books. The pupils developed a wider acquaintance with books at an earlier age than was formerly the case.

Handicapped students enjoy participating in field trips and in excursions. Generally they are unable to make regular visits to the public library. In order that they may learn something about the breadth of public library resources, orthopedically handicapped students in a high school English class, working on a bibliographic unit, are taken to the main building of the Chicago Public Library. For some, this is their first visit to the public library and it becomes an exciting experience to learn about the library's extensive resources and services.

A particularly rewarding trip is the annual visit to the Miracle of Books Fair for Boys and Girls held at the Chicago Museum of Science and Industry. Although many handicapped children visit the Fair with regular class groups, the Monday morning following the close of the Fair is set aside for students from schools for the orthopedically handicapped. They arrive with crutches and wheelchairs and are eager to see and examine the many types of books so attractively displayed, and to enjoy the dramatic presentation of a literary sketch performed by a professional cast during the previous week and repeated especially for them.

The school library plays a significant role in the educational opportunities provided for the maximum growth and development of handicapped students. It is essential for the full depth and breadth of curriculum experiences. Young people who cannot participate in many of the games, play activities, and sports enjoyed by normal children may enjoy vicariously these experiences through books. That they should discover the pleasures and riches inherent in the use of library resources, and that doors should be opened to them for a lifetime of good reading are tremendously important.

NOTES

1. Milton Shapiro, *The Roy Campanella Story* (New York: Messner, 1958).
2. Elsie Oakes Barber, *The Trembling Years* (New York: Macmillan, 1959).
3. Marguerite Dorian, *The Alligator's Toothache* (New York: Lothrop, 1962).

A Reading Program for Gifted Children in the Primary Grades

JAMES J. BIGAJ

Educators today face an all-important challenge in providing for the reading needs of gifted students in the elementary grades. The nation as a whole tends to lose most when pupil capability is high and his reading achievement low.

In the *Harvard Reading Report*, Austin et al. indicates that while some educators seemed aware of the need to do something about superior readers, there was little evidence that much of any consequence was being done.[1] Her conclusion was based on the interviews the investigators conducted in which respondents from twenty-nine of fifty-one school systems indicated that bright readers in the classrooms received the *least* instructional emphasis. In only one instance did the replies from a school system say that instructional emphasis for the talented was greater than for any other range of pupils. Based on these and other findings, all teachers, administrators, reading consultants, and other members of the school staff must obviously be concerned with the need for some action to be taken early in the elementary grades to effectively identify and challenge the reading potential of gifted pupils through proper motivation, methods, and materials.

Reprinted with permission of James J. Bigaj and the International Reading Association from pp. 144–48 of *Reading and Realism:* Proceedings of the 13th Annual Convention, ed. by J. Allen Figurel (Newark, Del.: IRA, 1969).

Identification of Gifted Pupils

In developing a reading program for gifted pupils, it is important that one identify these children through a variety of methods.

In some school systems, the identification of gifted children does not create a problem for the classroom teacher since they have already been examined using formal and informal measures and placed in special schools and classes.

In the primary grades, much information can be obtained through teacher observation, cumulative records, standardized individual and group tests of mental ability, and other informal tests and procedures, such as the results of memory games and contests.

Through informal observation primary grade teachers can determine the bright child who possesses a large speaking vocabulary, retains much of what he sees and hears without a great deal of drill, and performs difficult mental tasks, such as being able to reason things out, generalize, solve problems with ease, and recognize relationships. Young gifted pupils also often possess a wide range of interests and are very curious and respond quickly in class. They are often very original in their thinking and can often do work one to two years above that of their classmates. They often have a high capacity for listening to oral directions and are able to note details within the stories they tell, in the reports they give, and in the pictures they paint. It is important to note that the child who exhibits only one of the above characteristics would not likely be considered a bright pupil as opposed to one who possesses many of the above characteristics.

Standardized group tests of mental ability should also be used as a supplement to teacher observation in the identification process. Whenever possible, a potentially bright pupil should be given an individual intelligence test, such as the Revised Stanford-Binet, Form L-M (Houghton Mifflin) or the Wechsler Intelligence Scale for Children (Psychological Corporation).

One might also consider certain reading readiness tests such as the new Gates-MacGinitie Readiness Skills Tests (Bureau of Publications, Teachers College, Columbia University) when attempting to obtain an estimate of general intelligence since research has indicated a high correlation between intelligence and reading readiness test performance.

Very often standardized achievement test scores from such tests as the SRA Achievement Series (Science Research Associates) of the California Achievement Tests (California Test Bureau) may provide a clue to potential giftedness at the primary level. These tests may reveal consistent scores in several areas such as reading, math, or science that may be two or more grades beyond the subject's present level. These achievement tests may also be used to discover certain academic disabilities in bright children and point the way for remedial work or special emphasis in teaching. If the score in reading on an achievement battery is low, a more diagnostic reading test might be given to further pinpoint the gifted underachiever's strengths and weaknesses in reading. Potential gifted underachievers can also be identified through systematic observation of the physical, social, and psychological factors which may cause or contribute to underachievement in reading. A comparison of the bright pupil's listening ability and reading ability as determined either formally or informally may give some insight as to whether the pupil is reading up to his capacity if standardized reading and intelligence test scores are considered invalid or unavailable.

During the process of identification it is important to remember that the gifted pupil should be selected *only* on the basis of all available data, not merely on an IQ score obtained from a group test of intelligence.

Essential Principles of Instruction

In attempting to provide a stimulating and challenging reading program for gifted readers at the primary level, it may be essential to consider the following principles since these children's reading needs do vary somewhat from other average or slow learning pupils:

1. Emphasis must be placed on individualizing instruction for the gifted pupil. Differentiation of instruction is the hallmark of an effective reading program for this learner. The practice of lockstep instruction is deadly for any student and particularly so for the gifted student.

2. The gifted pupil is often more capable of self-directed learning. He may want to go ahead under his own steam in reading if he is provided with some very simple directions and adequate materials. He often does not require the step-by-step instruction other students need.

3. The gifted pupil at the primary level also needs flexible reading assignments. The pupil who is forced to conform to general reading assignments for the entire class may become bored and disinterested. If this situation continues over extended periods of time, the gifted child's boredom may become habitual.

4. The gifted pupil may not need an intensive and extensive readiness program at any level as average and slow-learning pupils may require. The readiness program must be adapted to the bright child and his needs at that time and not to the class in general.

5. The gifted pupil also needs guidance in critical and creative reading skills since his powers to do logical and critical thinking may easily become much greater than the average student's.

6. Since the gifted reader often can think, generalize, and solve problems at a higher level than other children can, he must be challenged constantly if learning is to take place and interest maintained. Emphasis on drill in reading should be avoided. The gifted child may need less participation in class-wide drills, in workbooks, or in readers that have very limited value and appeal.

7. Since the gifted child at the primary level can gain a great deal of self-fulfillment through reading, instruction should not only assist him in developing information-gathering skills but also in becoming a confident happy individual by enlarging his pleasure in reading.

8. The gifted pupil should not be penalized by expecting him to complete huge assignments merely because of his potential. More of the same is not what is needed. An important consideration in all the reading he is required to do should be quality and not quantity.

9. The gifted pupil frequently has a longer attention span than the average learner. Therefore, one may be able to teach him for longer periods of time. He often does not require as many repetitions when mechanical or other reading skills are presented as other children in the classroom may need.

10. For the gifted pupil emphasis during reading instruction should be placed more on inductive rather than deductive instruction. Reading instruction should aim at comprehension of broad principles rather than the accumulation of detailed facts for these students.

11. The gifted pupil often displays more diversified reading interests than do other pupils. Teachers, therefore, should build on these interests during reading instruction.

Bearing these basic principles of instruction in mind, reading should become more interesting and challenging for these pupils in the primary grades.

Instructional Materials and Methods

As indicated in the preceding section, instructional materials as well as techniques must be individualized for these pupils. A wide variety of thought-provoking materials are necessary ingredients in a well-designed primary reading program for gifted students. As he gains in reading skill during the beginning stages of reading instruction, an ever increasing range of reading material must be made available. It is important that the classroom library and the central library have current reading material for gifted pupils.

It is very important that materials be selected on various levels of difficulty to challenge the most advanced readers in the classroom. A few copies of a number of different kinds of skill books for developing word recognition skills and other materials dealing with critical reading skills should be available for those gifted children who need this development. These materials might be separated according to exercises, classified, and filed under different headings for use by bright pupils. By developing a kind of "critical reading lab "of this kind, bright pupils can be challenged in their ability to do logical and critical thinking. Enrichment programs, such as the *Sights and Sounds Program* (Random House), train beginning readers in reading and listening through a wide variety of books, accompanying tape recordings, and listening posts. *The Carousel Books* (L. W. Singer) offer gifted readers a completely individualized program that stresses literary appreciation and critical evaluation which should provide the challenge they seek. Each box in the Carousel program contains for each book a set of discussion cards which list key words and questions that can be used for teacher-pupil conferences. The *Owl Series* (Holt, Rinehart and Winston) should also supplement and extend the bright child's learning in science, math, literature, and social studies. All these materials should certainly broaden the scope of many existing reading programs and provide the necessary enrichment for the gifted at the primary level.

Many bright pupils at this level also enjoy the challenge of locating words, learning the country of origin, and ascertaining meanings. With the gifted pupil's deeper interest in the historical development of language, books like Epstein's *First Book of Words* (Franklin Watts, Inc.) and the Lairds' *Tree of Language* (World Publishing Co.) should have appeal in the upper primary grades. Lower primary bright youngsters would enjoy Krauss' *A Hole Is to Dig* (Harper) and *Pop-Up Sound Alikes* (Random House). Another book telling what words are and what they can mean to lower primary youngsters is Rands' *Sparkle and Spin: A Book About Words* (Harcourt, Brace and World). Bright pupils should be given an opportunity to explore the meaning of foreign words which are sometimes listed at the back of basal readers and other trade books. Further individualized vocabulary study can be done by using newspapers, magazines, pupil-selected books, and content area materials.

The "experience" approach is another valuable technique to use with bright underachieving pupils in developing vocabulary. By capitalizing on their varied interests, teachers can develop experience stories. The bright underachiever will evidence enthusiasm and enjoyment if he has a part in the preparation of his instructional materials as his vocabulary increases.

Since gifted pupils can be challenged to do more logical and critical thinking in the early grades, a balanced program should also provide instruction and materials which will allow for further development of these abilities. For example, pupils might compare two different new articles on a subject. Other gifted children might compare various biographies and fictionalized stories about famous individuals.

In the primary grades teachers, secretly adding some untrue statements, can give an oral account of a story that the children have read. As soon as bright pupils hear something that is not true, they can clap or raise their hands and supply the correct answer or tell on what basis they know the statement to be false.

Provisions for critical reaction of books read should also be a part of the primary program. In preparing an oral or written report, bright pupils should be encouraged to include a few evaluative comments or opinions on the merits or demerits of a particular book. Book evaluation could be based on criteria which the child may have established himself or in conjunction with his peers.

Several specific lessons should be included on teaching such study skills as outlining, summarizing, using a table of contents, index, and glossaries. These lessons are especially valuable for bright pupils who want to work independently on some problem or project.

Bright youngsters in the primary grades also need an opportunity to balance their reading interests since many tend to concentrate too much reading in a single area. This tendency sometimes appears in an area such as science and other informational type reading. With this in mind, it is certainly desirable to have a wide variety of books accessible to stimulate these bright children to read in other areas. Geboe found that a program of folklore reading was very effective for superior readers in the third grade.[2] In her report, folklore was confined to the reading of fairy tales, fables, and myths.

Informal book talks by other classmates should encourage others to read these books and expand interests. Attractive book displays and colorful exhibits of book jackets, which are changed regularly, help to broaden interests.

Time must also be provided for the sharing of books. This activity can be done most effectively at the primary level through radio and television plays, puppet shows, flannel board stories, tape recorded stories and reports, dioramas and fairy tale dramatization.

Children's literature also offers a wealth of stories which will stimulate the creative writing ability of these students. The teacher may want to read part of a book, stop at an exciting point, and have pupils write their own endings. Other story starters, such as, "If I hibernated . . . ," "If I were a teacher . . . ," "If I invented . . . ," "If I discovered . . . ," "If I followed a bumble bee . . . ." should spark the creative imaginations of many gifted youngsters.

With the ideas presented in this paper, it is hoped that teachers, reading consultants, and administrators will be in a better position to recognize and aid bright underachievers reading below grade level, those reading at their present grade level, and those reading two or more years beyond their grade placement. This nation's future depends on how teachers have met the challenges of the bright pupils today.

NOTES

1. Mary Austin and Coleman Morrison, *The First R: The Harvard Report on Reading in the Elementary Schools* (New York: Macmillan, 1964).

2. Juanita Geboe, "Folklore for Superior Readers in the Third Grade," *Elementary English* 37:93–97 (February 1960).

Gifted Children and the Elementary School Librarian—Theory into Practice

BARBARA H. BASKIN
and
KAREN H. HARRIS

Identification of the Gifted Child

Among the many teaching tasks facing them, librarians must include the challenge of stimulating and maximizing opportunities for growth of gifted children in their schools. Identifying the gifted child is not, however, as easy as it might appear. Semantic confusion, differences in socioeconomic conditions, and varying policies in schools combine to confound a universal definition of this unique child. In addition, where giftedness coexists with physical, sensory, or emotional problems which tend to mask ability and consequently result in understimulation, the problem of identification is further exacerbated. Uneven development of abilities and interests in the child may also be a confusing factor. Nevertheless, the highly able child evidences a constellation of demonstrably different behaviors which, when present in large measure, provides a basis for a description of giftedness.

The gifted child is different from age peers in ways which require a broad spectrum of responses from the librarian. These children are able to deal with abstract concepts earlier than age mates, formulate critical judgments, make inferences, and perceive unusual relationships. Their rate of reading and learning is more rapid than their peers and their sense of humor and irony are usually more fully developed.

The Librarian and Gifted Children

Highly intelligent children have traditionally been frequent and consistent users of library services. In the past, they have usually been offered the following services at the elementary school level: librarians have guided them in obtaining more and better books in response to their interests and avocations, and fre-quently have permitted them greater access to the resources of the library in order to accommodate their sometimes avid and rapid reading habits; when requested, the librarian has provided more difficult books in the kits provided for classroom teachers; and often the librarian has encouraged these children, as more sophisticated library users, to become members of the library staff.

The creative, activist librarian has often felt particularly frustrated in trying to provide an adequate number of options which would encourage gifted children to develop their potential. The librarian's objective is not merely to provide the time, space, and materials for high-ability children to make more elaborate or longer reports, but rather to expand and accelerate the development of the children's skills and generate opportunities so that they can imaginatively respond to the materials presently available. Because of their superior intellect, these children need to be aware of the diverse ways problems may be approached. Their efforts to criticize, improve, innovate, take short cuts, review, restructure, or otherwise respond creatively or unconventionally should not only be permitted, but also specifically planned for and encouraged.

The library should offer gifted children a multitude of opportunities to maximize their capacity for self-directed learning. Initially they must be introduced to a sizable quantity and wide variety of tools and materials which have the potential of generating intellectually stimulating experiences. Children should be familiar with the resources of the library and their use so that they may research in depth those interests stimulated by the curriculum as well as those they already have.

The library is obliged to aid these children in the accomplishment of their intellectual tasks as well as in their social and emotional growth. They, like all children, need to possess and expand their feelings of self worth, to achieve emotional stability and security, and to enjoy rewarding social relationships. The literature program of the library can help in these critical areas. The library needs to play a major role in the acculturizing and humanizing process. Children must become familiar with their own cultural heritage, while also learning that it is not the only heritage, that others of equal worth and validity can be meaningful to them. As a result of well thought-out exposure to the variety of materials available in the library, children can enjoy the satisfactions and be aware of the acclaim which emerges from creative and divergent activity, at least in literary endeavors.

The Library as a Learning Laboratory

Just as the library acts as the hub of the school both educationally and geographically (since many of the new schools place the media center at the physical core), so the librarian acts as the nurturing source for many programs and innovations within the school. The library can provide a learning environment in which children have a multiplicity of opportunities to grow and practice their capacity for self-direction and exploration. An added dimension to the concept of the library as a resource room is that of a laboratory in which children are able to transpose and express what they have learned into a personalized and creative experience. Children must find a way to take the printed or recorded word and make it personally meaningful. In their search for information, gifted children can choose among diverse perspectives and literary styles. They can pursue personal or academic interests which the classroom has neither the time nor the resources to encompass. They can compare and contrast the interpretations of an event among a wide range of materials available on the same topic.

Benefits to the children are extensive. Libraries offer children the opportunity to exercise their potential for leadership. Children can extend their fund of information. They can work and create, using a variety of media. Moreover, by participating in an exciting and satisfying library program, they are able to achieve more understanding of self as well as expand their horizons.

Suggested Activities for Gifted Children

The following activities are intended to promote more intensive and extensive use of the library resources. Many of them incorporate novel ways of responding to the library experience and contain a built-in expectation and acceptance of original or creative reponses. Implicit in these activities is an encouragement of bibliophilic behavior—an involvement with both the technical and creative process in the production of books and media.

Many of these suggestions are as workable in one curricular area as another. The technique remains a constant; the content differs. Much of the best material is not confined to specific curricular areas; it overlaps several disciplines and is useful in amplifying the child's understanding of the interrelationships of disparate fields of knowledge.

Assessment and Promotion of Breadth. In order to promote diversity in reading, the librarian needs to know what the children are currently reading, which literary content areas and genres have not been encountered, and which library skills have yet to be mastered. The library program can include or adapt the following procedures:

1. Ask to have a section of the school-wide pupil inventory reserved for pupil interests and avocations. These may provide clues for selection of print and audio-visual material.

2. Set up a literary "riddle board" outside the library which is changed weekly, giving clues to a character in children's literature. Give children an opportunity to guess who the character is. Provide one sparse clue Monday, another more complete clue Tuesday, etc., and on Friday publish the answer. Add the specific book jacket and others by the same author to the board.

3. Encourage good readers in the very early grades to bypass the easy-to-read books with controlled vocabulary in favor of books like *What Makes the Sun Shine* (Asimov) which has an advanced vocabulary but would be more stimulating to the gifted student.

4. Maintain an up-to-date news kiosk on local news of specific interest to children. This might include sports events, concerts, movies, new museum exhibits, etc. Include books and media which provide in-depth background information.

5. Prepare lists and displays of books related to special events or special programs featured on television. The recent *Little House on the Prairie* series offers an ideal opportunity for promotion of the Wilder books as well as related historical fiction, biographies, and nonfiction. Season schedules are readily obtainable on request.

6. Help children set up a display table with a variety of biographies they have already read on it. With string, tie to each book samples of objects relating to book content, e.g., a stylus and slate to a book on Helen Keller, a plastic apple to a book on Newton, etc.

7. Develop a file for scripts and introduce them as a literary form. Encourage children to adapt stories with considerable dialogue into script format. Show them how to act out or interpret the story using the reader's theater technique. Suitable stories include *Thidwick the Big-Hearted Moose* (Seuss) and *The Reluctant Dragon* (Grahame). *The Reader's Theatre Handbook* provides excellent guidance for the librarian unfamiliar with this technique.

8. Introduce the children to the diary as a literary form. Encourage them to write a diary as if they were Gulliver or with Captain Nemo 20,000 leagues under the sea.

9. Organize a collection of adult books that would have particular appeal to children, e.g., *Born Free* (Adamson), *Kon Tiki* (Heyerdahl).

10. Promote those books of high quality but uncommon appeal which nonetheless have the capacity to provide profound literary experiences for some children, e.g., *At the Back of the North Wind* (MacDonald), *The Little Prince* (Saint-Exupéry), the *Green Knowe* books (Boston), etc.

11. Set up a film program for the school presenting folk tales or legends to awaken interest in the companion stories. *Anansi the Spider, The Stonecutter,* and *The Loon's Necklace* are typical of the high quality films of this type currently available. Encourage the children to compare and contrast how the themes are handled in the different genres.

Intensification of Participation in Library Experiences.
It is important that students be able to participate in the
book-promoting plans of the library. Providing opportunities and encouragement for reflection and discussion of what has been read is essential. As students
become more deeply involved in the total library program and the librarian is able to deepen his/her understanding of the students and of how their literary experiences are developing, a more accurate assessment can
be made of the kinds of books which have particular
appeal for individual students.

1. Arrange for older children to act as "big brothers"
or "big sisters" to introduce new school children to the
library and to be available for literary or informational
consultation.

2. Organize a troop of readers who will work in the
primary grades reading stories they select to the younger
children. (This is especially effective if children can be
sex-paired.) Reluctant readers are impressed when they
find that books and libraries are important to the older
students in the school.

3. Have volunteers temporarily attach a paper star
on books they've enjoyed and recommend. Such books
could be designated "Featured Book of the Month for
this Shelf."

4. Add a note to the backs of books: "If you liked
this book, you might also like——, and——, and
——." This device is useful for both fiction and nonfiction, leading the child to expand interests in a particular topic or to pursue more challenging related books.
Encourage readers to add their own suggestions.

5. Prepare an ungraded list of recommended books,
arranged in order of increasing difficulty, to be included
in the preholiday newsletter to parents suggesting books
which would make pleasurable gifts. Have annotations
written by able students.

6. Help groups of children prepare a reading list for
each grade of suggested summer reading based on their
own favorites.

7. Work with the language arts teachers in facilitating
the preparation and illustration of mini book reviews
for the school newspaper, library news showcase, or
library bulletin board. Negative book reviews by children are as important as laudatory ones and often stimulate much peer interest. Contrasting reviews might also
be posted.

8. Establish a panel of upper grade students to review
books and recommend purchases. All of the students
should read, trade, and discuss books prior to recommendation.

Expansion of Response Opportunities. Children need
to express their understanding of what they have read.
If it has been pleasurable, they will want to share that
experience with others, exchange ideas, refine their own
impressions, and even have a platform from which to
discuss their reactions. On occasion, a literary expe-

rience can be used as a springboard for inventive responses that go far beyond the original literary source.
Opportunities for the students to write are particularly
important. Not only do these experiences in critical
analysis provide outlets for self-expression, they also
are a potent stimulus to further reading.

1. Guide children into divergent modes of response
to the conventional book report assignment. Have pupils use alternate attacks such as: (*a*) retell the most
moving, funniest, most surprising, etc., aspect of a
story; (*b*) develop a character extension such as a diary
or journal a character might have kept or conversation
he/she could have had if alive today; or (*c*) create imaginary letters which could be sent from one book character to another on a specific topic common to both characters. One example would be the mouse Amos in *Ben
and Me* (Lawson) and the cat in *Benjamin West and His
Cat Grimalkin* (Henry and Dennis) about life with their
respective masters. Another might be the Dutch children in *Wheel on the School* (DeJong) writing to Kate in
The Good Master (Seredy) about their daily lives.

2. Use a felt board and figures to illustrate a folk tale
for very young children. Tell the story first, then have
the children retell the story using the felt figures as visual cues. Then let them act out the story with such
prompting as needed.

3. Introduce children to plays or stories that "play"
well. Help them make simple puppets to dramatize their
stories and develop sequels.

4. Examine illustrations of books on similar topics
and have children extrapolate as to what feeling tone
those illustrations generate and what the consequent
implications for interpretation of the text are. For example, Virginia Burton's illustration of *Song of Robin
Hood* (Malcolmson) could be compared with those of
The Merry Adventures of Robin Hood (Pyle); *Millions
of Cats* (Gag) could be compared with *The Cat in the
Hat* (Seuss).

5. Use the technique shown in the film *Rag Tapestry*
to make a class interpretation of ethnic folk heroes or
myths or legends. For a more complete explanation of
the process, consult the book *Rag Tapestries and Wool
Mosiacs* by Ann Wiseman.

6. Help children compare the "why" stories of various peoples after reading widely in folk literature. Stories of why we have seasons, why we have day and
night, have counterparts in the tales of many ethnic
groups. Alternately, encourage the children to write
their own mythological interpretations of such cosmic
events as the Milky Way or the Northern Lights.

7. Have children read various versions of the same
folktale and discuss similarities and differences, e.g.,
The Stonecutter as compared to *The Fisherman and His
Wife*, or *Anansi* and *The Five Chinese Brothers*.

8. In promoting sensitization toward poetry, use the
film *Autumn: Frost Country* in which Robert Frost

reads one of his poems at the beginning and one at the end. The center provides a musical background while the visual portion shows scenes of the Vermont countryside in fall. Encourage children to select or write their own poems to accompany the center portion, to try to match the mood of the poems to the visual images and music. This film offers a rare opportunity to discuss mood in terms of pictures, music, and poetry.

9. Tape record a choral reading of poems chosen by the children. Help children select a musical background for the reading and retape over recorded music. Encourage them to do others on their own.

10. Provide opportunities for younger children to act out poetry in pantomime.

11. After children have read several books by a number of authors, tape fragment samples of those writers and ask listeners to identify the authors. Choose writers whose style is sufficiently distinctive, e.g., Kipling, Pyle, Wilder, Cleary. Discuss clues which helped to identify the authors. This can form the basis for a discussion of the components of style, which techniques certain authors prefer, why some children find a particular style appealing, annoying, funny, boring, etc.

12. Read a story which lends itself to playacting. Stop at a crisis point and let several groups independently develop and act out a possible conclusion. Encourage analysis of the interpretations by the audience.

13. Have children read complete, abridged, and condensed book versions of the same story and have the group elect a leader to discuss the differences.

14. Guide children in comparing book and film or television versions of the same story: how they were similar, how different, and how the children reacted to each. Holling's book *Paddle-to-the-Sea* is available in an excellent film using the same title and produced by the National Film Board of Canada. The film follows the story very closely and would be good to contrast with a film which took great liberties with the original version.

15. Sponsor a creative writing magazine with different motifs for each issue, e.g., limericks, fables, etc.

16. Introduce children to Haiku through such books as *In a Spring Garden* (Lewis) or *Cricket Song* (Behn). Encourage the students to write their own poems and make slides or transparencies to provide an accompanying visual image.

17. After children have read wildly imaginative stories like *How Baseball Began in Brooklyn* (LeGrand) or *Just So Stories* (Kipling), have them write similar stories on imaginary origins of natural or social phenomena.

18. Use films such as the *Magic Moments* series (Encyclopaedia Britannica) as story starters and let the children write their own conclusions.

Provision of Curriculum Support. The library must function for the gifted child in ways that specifically support the curriculum. The following suggestions are illustrative of library activities that supplement academic programs.

1. Help children research and publish a newspaper with modern format, i.e., editorials, advertisements, news stories, letters to the editor, etc., but with content of another time and place. A newspaper from ancient Rome, the Middle Ages, the founding of the American colonies, etc., presents marvelous research opportunities. An annotated list of sources of information for the project could serve as the basis of a student-prepared bibliography covering that particular period.

2. Assist students in researching foreign sources of common English words and locating their origins on a large world map.

3. Work with teachers in the establishment of a debate club with assignments related to historical study. When students are studying ancient Greece, a simulated debate could take place between a citizen from Athens and one from Sparta. Assistance could be given to the club in obtaining research materials and planning for monthly projects.

4. Make available materials about table games played in foreign countries. Help pupils construct similar games—possibly displayed against a world map.

5. Introduce children to books about folk dancing. Help them translate the written instructions into physical action. (This is a reading skill often neglected.) This activity should be cooperatively planned with the music and physical education departments.

6. Introduce children to a variety of reference sources. Aid them in preparing minilessons (five minutes) on the use and content of each source and how it would be useful to their fellow students in future data searches, e.g., gazetteers, biographical indexes, etc.

Bibliophilic Activities for Gifted Children. The following activities are related to printing and the creation of books. An involvement with books as objects—aesthetic, informational, and functional—encourages reading and an esteem for books.

1. Invite children to write individual letters to their favorite authors. Mail a copy of a book for autographing and display the letter and the signed book when it is returned.

2. Invite authors or illustrators to visit your school to talk about their work. The children should prepare questions in advance and should act as interviewers.

3. Contact local bookstores to see if they have upcoming activities planned relating to children's books or authors. Arrange a visit.

4. Introduce the topic of making books. As part of this procedure, use the film, *Story of a Book*, which outlines all the steps taken by Holling in the creation of his book, *Pagoo*.

5. Visit the rare book room of a local public or university library. Ask the librarian to discuss incunabula or interesting books in the collection.

6. Discuss methods of incorporating advances in bookmaking techniques as part of the social studies curriculum. For example, reports on the ancient world could be written in scroll form. Reports on the Middle Ages might begin each paragraph with an illuminated initial letter—many examples can be obtained, in the absence of a real model, from the *Medieval Alphabet Coloring Book*.

7. Prepare a collection of old text books or old children's magazines. Encourage the children to compare them with modern ones in terms of layout, text, illustrations, etc.

8. Organize used book fairs. Children can set up tables and students will have an opportunity to learn how to browse in a simulated book store. Books may be sold for a nickel or dime or exchanged for tokens received for each library book already read.

Librarian's Role with Classroom Teachers of Gifted Children. The librarian has an important obligation to the teachers of these children. Classroom-based colleagues must be sought out and made aware of how the facilities of the library can enrich and supplement the curriculum and thereby provide opportunities for the intellectual growth of each child.

1. Initiate two-way communication procedures. In addition to informing the staff about new acquisitions, ask to be involved in changes in curriculum or in the planning of special programs so that variations in level of reading materials or instructional media can be obtained in advance of these events.

2. Prepare annotated descriptions of instructional materials already in the school library which have high potential for enrichment purposes and which point out cross-curricular applications and feature unusual relationships.

3. Examine reading texts to determine whether there has been an inclusion of excerpts from children's literature. In library kits sent to the classroom, include copies of cited books in original form for advanced readers.

4. Prepare suggestions for teachers on novel techniques which can be used in lieu of the standard book reports.

5. Promote and encourage the perception of interrelationships between curricular areas through films such as *Age of the Buffalo* (art, social studies, ecology), *Discovering the Music of Latin America* (music, art, social studies), and *Aaron Copland—Open Prairie* (music and art).

6. Promote the use of nonnarrated films, e.g., *Corral, Pigs, Rainshower, Leaf* and others which stimulate both verbal and emotional responses and which sensitize children to mood and tone.

7. Use films with literary bases such as *Discovering American Folk Music* or *The Stonecutter* to explore the changes which take place in literary forms when they are modified by cultural forces.

8. Obtain books (perhaps on loan from the junior high school library) on topics studied by elementary level children for use by advanced readers so that they may have challenging material but may participate with the rest of their class in the standard curriculum.

9. Obtain test scores for children from the psychologist, reading consultant, or other person operating in that capacity who could apprise you of the exceptional child's functional reading level. Plan a program of reading guidance based on this as well as on an assessment of the child's interests.

These lists of activities are intended to be suggestive rather than exhaustive. They will need to be adapted to the unique requirements and concerns of children with exceptional intellectual talents. These should, however, provide a jumping-off point for the librarian and suggest some ideas which are unorthodox and pleasurable and have been used with gifted children to extend and deepen their involvement with the library.

BIBLIOGRAPHY

Books

Adamson, Joy. *Born Free: A Lioness of Two Worlds.* New York: Pantheon, 1960.

Appiah, Peggy. *Anansi the Spider: Tales from an Ashanti Village.* New York: Pantheon, 1966.

Asimov, Isaac. *What Makes the Sun Shine?* Boston: Little, 1971.

Behn, Harry, ed. *Cricket Song.* New York: Harcourt, 1964.

Bishop, Claire. *The Five Chinese Brothers.* New York: Coward, 1938.

Boston, Lucy M. *Children of Greene Knowe.* New York: Harcourt, 1967.

———. *Enemy at Greene Knowe.* New York: Harcourt, 1964.

———. *River at Greene Knowe.* New York: Harcourt, 1959.

———. *Stranger at Greene Knowe.* New York: Harcourt, 1961.

———. *Treasure at Green Knowe.* New York: Harcourt, 1958.

Coger, Leslie I., and White, Melvin R. *The Reader's Theatre Handbook.* rev. ed. Chicago: Scott, Foresman, 1973.

de Saint-Exupéry, Antoine. *The Little Prince.* New York: Harcourt, 1943.

DeJong, Meindert. *Wheel on the School.* New York: Harper, 1954.

Gag, Wanda. *Millions of Cats.* New York: Coward, 1938.

Grahame, Kenneth. *The Reluctant Dragon.* New York: Holiday, 1953.

Grimm, Jacob, and Grimm, Wilhelm. *The Fisherman and His Wife.* Chicago: Follett, 1970.

Henry, Marguerite, and Dennis, Wesley. *Benjamin West and His Cat Grimalkin.* Indianapolis: Bobbs-Merrill, 1947.

Heyerdahl, Thor. *Kon Tiki.* Chicago: Rand McNally, 1950.

Holling, Holling C. *Paddle-to-the-Sea.* Boston: Houghton, 1941.

———. *Pagoo.* Boston: Houghton, 1957.

Kipling, Rudyard. *Just So Stories*. New York: Doubleday, 1946.

LeGrand, Henderson. *How Baseball Began in Brooklyn*. Nashville: Abingdon, 1958.

Lewis, Richard, ed. *In a Spring Garden*. New York: Dial, 1965.

McDonald, George. *At the Back of the North Wind*. New York: Crowell, 1962.

Malcolmson, Anne. *Song of Robin Hood*. Boston: Houghton, 1947.

A Medieval Alphabet Coloring Book. New York: Bellerophon Books (n.d.).

Pyle, Howard. *The Merry Adventures of Robin Hood*. New York: Scribners, 1946.

Seredy, Kate. *The Good Master*. New York: Viking, 1935.

Seuss, Dr. *The Cat in the Hat*. New York: Random, 1957.

—— *Thidwick, the Big-Hearted Moose*. New York: Random, 1948.

Titus, Eve. *The Two Stonecutters*. New York: Doubleday, 1967.

Wiseman, Ann. *Rag Tapestry and Wool Mosaics*. New York: Van Nostrand, 1969.

16mm Films

Age of the Buffalo. National Film Board of Canada.
Anansi the Spider. Gerald McDermott.
Autumn: Frost Country. Holt, Rinehart & Winston.
Copland—Open Prairie. Musilog.
Corral. National Film Board of Canada.
Discovering American Folk Music. Film Associates.
Discovering the Music of Latin America. Film Associates.
Leaf. Holt, Rinehart & Winston.
The Loon's Necklace. Encyclopaedia Britannica.
Paddle-to-the-Sea. National Film Board of Canada.
Pigs. Churchill.
Rag Tapestry. Julien Bryan.
Rainshower. Churchill.
The Stonecutter. Julien Bryan.
Story of a Book. Churchill.

Setting a Reading Climate for the Gifted

LILLIAN BATCHELOR

At the same time that education for the gifted is being debated, our entire American educational system is under fire. We are all aware of the many criticisms leveled at schools by Rickover, by Conant, and others who label the curriculum inadequate or expensive of teacher and student effort. Rickover and Conant, for instance, agree in one respect—that our talented stu-

Reprinted from *Library Journal*, Jan. 15, 1961. Published by R. R. Bowker Co. (a Xerox company). Copyright © 1961 by R. R. Bowker Co.

dents are underestimated and underworked. They advocate more assiduous study, more content coverage more speedily, and more specialized methods and materials for the gifted.

Another critic, the noted anthropologist Margaret Mead, does not direct her remarks specifically to the gifted, but rather to our whole concept of education. Her approach is an iconoclastic one since she is convinced drastic steps are required to make the radical changes she proposes. She points out that *vertical transmission* of knowledge from adult to child, and from past to present, is no longer sufficient. We are moving, she says, toward a whole new dimension of learning, of *lateral transmission*, wherein knowledge is passed on immediately regarding new discoveries, inventions, creations, or manufactures. Education must assume the new function of "rapid and self-conscious adaptation to a changing world," she states.[1] A premium is put on the speed and ease with which ideas are communicated, a fact which must influence the choice of educational materials and methods.

The rate at which knowledge is increasing is truly phenomenal. Adults are often unable to comprehend its full import but must condition themselves to accept it. Our gifted, however, *are* capable of coping with this explosion of knowledge and communication—if they are educated with this concept in mind. As Dr. Mead says, only a short interval may elapse "before something which was taken for granted must be unlearned or transformed to fit new knowledge or practice."[2]

Under conditions like these no student can expect to complete his education at a given time, least of all the superior ones. Learning must be seen as a continuous, never-ending process—and the learner has to be zealous in its pursuit.

Dr. Mead is not the only one who recommends drastic reorganization, although she might move more vigorously to put such recommendations into effect. Educators concur in principle at least that modern education must be a more flexible and open-ended process, for how is it possible to foresee what will happen even in the near future? What we are saying, over and over again, is that students must acquire certain basic skills, then be trained and guided in efficient methods of learning so that they can continue with *self*-education, as independently as possible. School and society must somehow inculcate a respect and a desire for knowledge. Both must be pledged to this goal just as a scientist is dedicated to the pursuit of truth wherever he finds it.

I recall a recent talk by Stephen Corey, in which he expressed the idea another way. "We must," he said, "devise a new test of intelligence—one which will measure willingness and ability to meet and adapt to change." And he indicated that such a test should be applied to teachers, too—with which I'd agree—and to librarians!

Whether we have such a test or not, it is plain that our educational theories and practices need overhauling to keep pace with the times. But what, you will ask, do these stirrings in education mean for gifted children?

Simply this: they must learn more, faster, and better, because there is so much to absorb, and so little time to do it. They must acquire more efficient methods of studying and learning, of selecting and digesting significant information. They must be trained in critical thinking, in interpreting and weighing facts, in making generalizations and drawing conclusions, and just as importantly, in seeing relationships. Stuart Chase says there is a need to "see relationships between different fields of knowledge; the interdisciplinary approach takes on a new urgency in this atomic age."[3] The gifted can not neglect the humanities or science, for both are essential to creative leadership. They should see that ideas are power but that ideas must be kept in motion to be fully exploited.

The importance of self-education and of independent study are cited by many educators. In *Images of the Future*, by J. Lloyd Trump for instance, we find the recommendation that the "talented should spend 40 percent of their time in study activities with emphasis on creativity, depth, and development of independent learning abilities and habits."[4]

The Role of Reading

The role of reading becomes plainer as we continue for, obviously, there is no other single tool of learning that is as effective, flexible, or accessible as the printed word, which is not to deprecate at all the value of direct, personal experience or of other media like the film, TV, or radio. Printed materials are available on every subject under the sun and periodicals bring information up to date. Books can be utilized as personal convenience dictates, can be studied and referred to as frequently as desired, and can be reproduced widely at very small cost (as in the case of the paperbacks). As a means of independent study, reading is certainly unrivalled, so wide is the choice and availability of suitable materials.

No, there is no doubt that reading is important at every stage of learning, from childhood up, and at every level of expertness. Reading is the *sine qua non* of the gifted child's intellectual development, even though he has many other rich experiences as well. No other media can possibly offer the same wide variety and coverage; his reading must be both extensive and intensive.

If reading is to be the powerful instrument of individualizing instruction that we want it to be, it must be a satisfying experience, one which gifted students anticipate and enjoy while they work at it, too. It must be more than an idle pastime. Students should turn to reading for recreation and escape, true, but should also put their superior mental abilities to work on it. In every case we must emphasize what happens in the mind of the reader, how he assimilates and applies what he learns and how critical his reactions are. We do not want him to blot up ideas, but to weigh and evaluate them. This skill goes beyond the mere recognition of words; it is a unique and creative experience, requiring ability and training.

Reading does more than inform; it also exerts a strong emotional influence as well and affects attitudes and understandings tremendously, although it is difficult to measure the exact degree. This emotional impact can not be overlooked, for building the right attitudes is important for future leaders. No child, no matter how bright or fortunate, can possibly have first hand contacts with all the peoples of the world, but he can learn about them vicariously through reading. This is a substitute, but it need not be a poor or ineffective one if proper guidance is given and if the reader learns to think for himself.

Robert Frost once wrote that "the whole reason for going to school is to get the impression fixed for life that there is a book side to everything." We agree with Frost for we have seen the fascinating and illuminating exchange which occurs when writer and reader meet via the printed word.

We can expect gifted children to excel in reading—and with some exceptions, they do. They learn to read early, do it well, like it, often lose themselves completely in it, and read more than average children.

But quantity of reading is not the most significant factor. It is quality and most of all the effect on the reader. The gifted need guidance in learning that the quality of interpretation is far more important than the quantity of material read.

Reading is a uniquely personal experience to which book and reader contribute. The reader must do a great deal for himself by bringing his own background and intelligence to bear on what he reads. The result is never passive, except when trash is involved. The process should be a dynamic and catalytic one; if it is not, the reader loses—often irrevocably.

We have long recognized many types of reading for many purposes—for pleasure, information, understanding, guidance, and inspiration. Materials vary for each type of reading, but in every case one thing must occur—an intelligent and personal response to what the author has to say. This is the result we must demand at every step of the way. Thus far we have not conveyed this concept of reading to our young readers—at least, not adequately.

You may be interested to know what bright children

think of reading. Recently a group, questioned on this point, stated that they wanted: (1) books, time, and a place to read, (2) opportunity to share with others what they learned, (3) guidance, but not censorship, (4) help in speed, comprehension, and adapting to different types of reading, (5) stimulation from reading that holds their interest, rather than the boredom of rereading material they understood the first time, (6) reading for information as well as sheer pleasure.

These are interesting answers which you will agree also imply a justifiable criticism of the way teachers treat the reading of highly intelligent students.

The Art and Science of Reading Guidance

To give effective reading guidance is not a simple thing. There are both an art and science to it. We employ all the data available on reading skills and interests as scientifically as possible, then must go beyond this data to enter wide, uncharted areas where we must play it by ear, relying on our sensitivity to the reader, and on our instinct as to the right book, time, and place. There are no set patterns or formulas, and no one can tell accurately what the correct steps are, which is why I have called reading guidance an art. Just as one artist works in his own characteristic style, so does each librarian or teacher guide in his own special way. It is a highly individualized matter—this reading guidance, and we can never lose sight of the fact. We can study and observe others at work, but may find that their methods do not succeed for us. We guide as a solo performance, according to our own personality and tastes. Nevertheless, there are two prerequisites for anyone who attempts to guide: genuine enthusiasm for reading and good rapport with the would-be-reader.

We are assuming no one will attempt to guide without a thorough knowledge of books and of the children with whom he works.

Accepting our goal as freedom to choose reading, with guidance, we work along such lines as: (1) helping the gifted to learn to choose suitable materials for themselves by using many selection aids such as lists, reviews, and library catalogs; (2) assisting and encouraging them to achieve variety and balance in their reading; (3) providing for extensive and intensive reading, while recognizing that the two will sometimes conflict; and (4) striving ceaselessly to develop perceptive responses, intellectually and emotionally, to whatever is read, to stress critical thinking and changed behavior as the most desirable outcomes in reading.

Reading Is Not a Virtue in Itself

Gifted children should come to realize that reading is not a virtue in itself, that it is only as good as the use to which they put it. They must understand that reading is indispensable to progress in all fields of knowledge, that it is a tool as well as a pleasure. And they should not be ashamed to utilize this tool even if their peers disapprove or ridicule it.

To provoke and compel thoughtful personal responses to reading is of greater consequence than selection of a specific title, for, unless the reader sees and feels, unless something happens to him as the result of reading, what is the purpose of reading at all? Merely a waste of time and energy, and one might just as well play ball or exercise in some way that will at least benefit one physically! If I seem obsessed with this idea, it is because I have been appalled at the lack of honest personal response to reading. Teachers and librarians mean well, we are sure, but all too often stress content, or merely list "books read," or extract synopses, or description of characters—with small regard for thoughtful, critical comment.

Revamp the Book Report

This kind of treatment of reading must change. The "required book report" must be revamped. It stultifies and destroys the very thing we hope to nurture!

New approaches are being made. For instance, McSwain tells us that children show great progress in critical thinking when they read with questions like these in mind: (1) Why am I reading this? (2) Who wrote this book, and why did he write it? (3) Do I understand what the author is trying to say? (4) Do I think about what I have read before accepting it? (5) Should I check its accuracy by reading other sources? (*Do* I read other sources?) (6) Am I aware of the parts omitted by the author when he wrote the book? (7) Am I accurate when talking with other persons about what I read?[5]

In one instance a fourth grade teacher who was reading Paul Bunyan stories with her group asked why the story was manifestly impossible. The responses were interesting, penetrating and original. Critical judgment was being called for—and the children liked it.

Another teacher tried to develop the ability to make inferences by using what she calls the detective approach. A story is read up to a certain point. Then the books are closed and the children discuss probable endings. The story is then completed, and the author's conclusion seen. The class learns who made the best guesses, what the reasons were behind them, and why some were off the track entirely. There is no doubt this simple but different device aroused interest in reading as a creative process—and provided an adventuresome experience for young readers.

The art of reading must be intimately related to the art of thinking—of thinking well, clearly, fully, critically. Reading in this manner is the mark of the mature reader.

The stress put on recreational reading may cause some children to look upon reading as being only for pleasure and enjoyment. We do not mean to detract from reading as a recreation, for every child should enjoy this pleasure and satisfaction. But on the other hand, children, especially the bright ones, should not shy away from serious reading because it entails hard work. A recent poll of American readers showed that not more than 10 percent of adults voluntarily sought challenging, serious material. We cannot let the reading of our gifted children deteriorate this way. They need mental effort which stretches minds and imaginations, even though it seems distasteful at times. "Hard" reading can produce healthy mental fatigue, which is beneficial, and strongly to be recommended for those who have the intellectual capacity for it.

We have concentrated thus far on critical reading, but reading for the purpose of modifying attitudes and changing behavior is also important. There is reason to believe that such changes can be brought about even though we have not yet found a method to measure their exact influences. We assume that the reader identifies himself with the characters, and so becomes more sympathetic and understanding. If the experience is a deep, meaningful, and frequent one, attitudes are gradually affected. But it is also possible for the reader to get a different meaning from what the author intended or his reaction may be immature. Or he may see nothing at all in what the author has to say. The whole area of the reader's response calls for research. Now we are making "educated guesses" about the extent to which attitudes and behavior can actually be transformed.

There are many tricks of the trade, some of which are highly successful in providing motivation and stimulation in reading. No matter what device we use, our aim should be to give free rein to the gifted child's compulsion to read, to encourage the habit of reading for intellectual delight, and to urge him to read for the values he can derive for himself. We should capitalize at every point on his current interests, which we know to be many and varied in the gifted, to spur him to further study development. We must expect (and permit) the gifted to think and react and criticize, which means we must accept their honest comments even though they differ from ours. The authoritarian approach must be avoided at all costs with these young people lest we stifle creativity and discourage the habit of independent thinking. Our attitude in the home or classroom must be permissive and understanding if the reading guidance we strive to provide is to amount to anything.

Reading guidance is accomplished not so much by spectacular devices as by integrating reading at every possible point with school and everyday life.

It has been said that a wise adult waits until a child is ready to be introduced to a book. But this does not mean that guidance has to be entirely opportunistic; a clever guide helps a child to get ready and contrives to present multiple opportunities for developing readiness.

Guidance Is a Long-Term Project

To achieve any degree of success, guidance must be looked upon as a long-term, cooperatively planned program which begins in preschool days and continues throughout life. The parent's role is a vital one, so is the teacher's and librarian's. When the skills and resources of key people are directed toward improving reading, an outstanding program will result.

Reading is essentially a solitary occupation, peculiarly adapted to meet the unique personal needs of an individual. Paradoxically, it is also a remarkably effective means of communication between readers. The dynamics of a group discussion (even a two-way one) generate new insights and ideas and enable readers to become better acquainted. As we learn to share reflections on reading more and more, we become more articulate in expressing our personal reactions. We grasp the fact, too, that the combined power of minds mutually exploring is practically unlimited. This is the big dividend of the "Great Books" discussions, and students who learn to share reading can profit in the same way. Sharing may take the form of reading aloud one incident, or a description, or merely a phrase that is striking, pungent, or memorable.

The need for specific training in the use of books and libraries must be emphasized. We cannot take it for granted that the gifted have the requisite skills to use such tools. Their knowledge is often too superficial. We must provide organized instruction first and then provide opportunities for directed research.

Certain points should be considered in setting up a good reading guidance program, such as:

1. Keep immediately accessible an attractive and well balanced collection that is suited in content, form, and readability to the gifted student.

2. Help each individual to find reading content that he cannot resist. By starting with current interest and taste, try gradually to bring him to higher achievement and more discriminating taste. We know now that Johnny *will* read what he wants to read. It is our duty to start him off with the material that interests him.

3. Encourage interpretation of what is read through dramatics or symbolism. Do not stress the written response exclusively. Use all possible media of communication. Whenever feasible, relate what is read to other learning experiences, such as trips, or TV and radio programs, magazine articles, etc. Use each to complement the other.

4. Share the delight of words by reading aloud to children and young people. Help them to enjoy oral reading and to develop skill in it.

5. Consult the school's cumulative reading records, and insist that students keep informal records for themselves of their independent reading. Such records serve as an excellent means of self-evaluation of variety and depth of reading.

6. Encourage students to build personal libraries. Paperbacks offer a wealth of good, inexpensive materials with which to begin.

7. Provide the opportunity, time, and place for independent reading sometime during the school day. An informal reading corner in the library can be especially attractive—and much appreciated.

8. Set up committees, seminars, or honor groups to work together to identify a problem and study it intensively with guidance, as needed, from teachers and librarians.

9. Utilize extra-classroom resources—individuals, organizations, instructions—to supplement the school's facilities. (Again we say the self-contained classroom is an anachronism and a contradiction for no single room can possibly include the variety of materials required for gifted students.)

10. Draw on exhibits in book stores, National Library Week or Book Week celebrations, book fairs, etc., to make children aware of the resources of attractive and stimulating reading materials.

11. Develop reading lists on subjects which concern students, including dating, personality problems, etc. Make these lists widely available to students and adults to be used as they please.

New Look in Book Reports

Now, a few comments on the new look in book reports. The time honored custom of extracting one written book report per one book read with almost mathematical precision is an iniquitous one. I am convinced this practice kills the very thing we are trying to cultivate—a love of reading and a habit of reading voluntarily throughout life. We should use only those evaluation procedures that aid the child to assess his reading accomplishments concretely, and the conventional book report is certainly not an adequate instrument. Illustrated notebooks should give way to illuminating talks that display originality and initiative. In most cases, discussion is preferable. We need more novel and unorthodox "book reports," not reportorial ones. In the case of nonfiction, where young readers know so much about a field, résumés might be accepted. However, a discussion of cause and effect or implications for everyday life, or speculations on future steps in the field, or a debate on the author's point of view—any of these would be of greater value to the student than the stereotyped, noncommital "report."

A teacher who really wants to do a good job of reading guidance must prepare and solicit searching questions about the material read, and the questions should go beyond a mere synopsis or trivial comment. A teacher must be daring and ingenious in order to open up ways for students to think aloud about their reading, and also feel free to develop their thoughts orally without fear of ridicule or criticism. Small discussion groups are ideal for this purpose. In some instances where a child is an expert on a subject, the discussion may resolve into a face-to-face exchange with an adult expert.

All educational change is, in reality, a form of social change, and, as such, can only be brought about by modifications in the behavior of people, and in their institutions. Since they involve the beliefs and mores of a group, such mutations proceed slowly.

But each one of us has the power to do something on a small scale, even though the change seems infinitesimal. Each of us can be an innovator. What it takes is courage, conviction, willingness to do an extra bit of work, and patience to move slowly and experimentally. Action research has opened up exciting possibilities for those of us who like to experiment on the job. Anyone can initiate change and improvement. Indeed it is the only way in which we can establish a good program directed toward achieving balance, depth, and maturity in reading. This is the kind of program commensurate with the gifted students' talents.

NOTES

1. Margaret Mead, "A Redefinition of Education," *NEA Journal* 48, no. 7:16 (October 1959).

2. Ibid.

3. Stuart Chase, *Some Things Worth Knowing* (New York: Harper, 1958), p. 10.

4. J. Lloyd Trump, *Images of the Future* (Urbana, Ill.: Commission on the Experimental Utilization of the Staff in Secondary Schools, 1959), p. 38.

5. E. T. McSwain, "Problems of Interpretation When Evaluating What Is Critically Read," Chicago Annual Conference on Reading (1951), pp. 139–43.

Storytelling and the Blind Child

JEAN D. BROWN

Storytelling, mankind's oldest form of entertainment, still survives in this modern world because of those few adults, teachers, and librarians dedicated to the teaching and training of today's children.

In a recent survey conducted by the Carnegie Library

Reprinted by permission from *The New Outlook* 66:356–60 (Dec. 1972).

of Pittsburgh, Regional Library for the Blind and Physically Handicapped, on storytelling to visually and physically disabled children, 160 questionnaires were mailed to librarians, teachers, and specialists who work with such children, in order to explore their thoughts on the use of storytelling as a tool for aiding a child's mental development. Seventy-two questionnaires (45 percent) were returned, all responding unequivocally that storytelling is indeed an effective aid when properly utilized.

Many of us have sat in our chairs, or on the edges of them, listening and watching a parent, teacher, or friend recite a story. We eagerly watched the facial expressions, the eyes, brow, and forehead, which reflected and projected inner emotions as the teller set the tone of the story or described a character or incident. Perhaps we saw the teller motion with his hands and arms and use other body gestures to depict size, shape, or even relay emotions through mime as the tale was spun. We must admit that we not only listened, we also watched!

When telling stories to blind children a veteran storyteller soon realizes that his voice is the only instrument upon which he can rely to convey moods and tones and to describe actions and incidents as they unfold. He realizes that his narration must not only appeal to the aural sense, but also to the other senses— touch, taste, smell, and general awareness.

The teller, facing blind children for the first time, should thoroughly prepare himself not to receive the satisfying responses one expects when appearing before sighted children. Blind children have response characteristics all their own, some of which are quite uninhibited. After about two programs, one will adjust to their listening characteristics.

To look into the faces of a blind audience while storytelling may not always provide clues as to whether the child is actually enjoying the story, although in actuality he may be thoroughly engrossed by the tale. My first encounter with such an audience made me feel ill at ease. Even though I was well prepared, I was conditioned to the responses of a sighted audience, with the usual facial expressions, the bright flashing eyes, and alert faces and bodies turned in my direction while listening to every word. Instead, some blind children were facing me, but some were not; most, however, seemed to be completely relaxed. Those not facing me sat sideways with their ears directed toward me listening intently to the story. Some wore slight smiles (depending upon story incidents), and some, to my surprise, spoke aloud urging the hero to run or to beware of impending dangers. As a person I began to feel dehumanized. I felt as if I were a radio, or a tape recording. Then a child asked, "What is a wolf?" I did as no machine could ever do, I stopped the story, answered her quickly, and continued on until another child ques-

tioned me about the meaning of a word; again I stopped and answered concisely. As the tale progressed and became more exciting their breathing became very heavy with anticipation.

After the story ended, the children were eager, on their own accord, to discuss incidents and ask more questions. This discussion period gave me the satisfaction of knowing that my storytelling was successful and enjoyable. To those who may feel hesitant about storytelling to blind children, therefore, I would like to offer a few fundamental suggestions.

1. Learning about your audience beforehand is extremely important for story program preparation. Find out the average chronological and mental ages of the group. Inquire about home and school interests. Inquire about forthcoming units in the curriculum and about scheduled field trips. Ascertain average attention span. All such information can be supplied by the teacher. Thus prepared, the next step is to develop a theme or themes and to select books accordingly.

2. In the primary grades the curriculum generally deals with such areas as basic concepts, moral concepts, holidays, weather, seasons, foreign countries, animals, rural life, city life, etc. After the theme is chosen from an appropriate area, the next step is the selection of suitable books that will allow for its full development. For example, books on the theme of rain might include *Umbrella* (Yashima), *The Quarreling Book* (Zolotow), or *Noah's Ark* (Palazzo).

Many guides and lists of stories are available at public libraries and children's librarians can also suggest good stories. The stories selected should be checked to see if they maintain their impact and meaning without the aid of illustrations.

Look for good descriptive narrations and strong explicit details. If a story relies solely upon its illustrative content, it should not be considered unless the teller feels strongly that the book has merit, and that he can ad-lib and verbalize the illustrations accurately and without interfering with or spoiling the author's style and tone.

Many storytellers enjoy telling the old favorites (the Three Little Pigs, the Tortoise and the Hare, and countless others) that are good, exciting, fun stories which deal with moral concepts. This storyteller has been questioned numerous times by adults, of course, about "all that blood and violence in folk tales." A growing child cannot be shielded from all the evils that have been and are being perpetuated, exposed as they are to violence daily via television and newspapers. After they are taught to read, they are then taught the histories of many countries, and all of these have been written in violence and tragedy. When they advance to higher learning they are introduced to classic literature, and this too is filled with tragedy and heartbreak. Folk tales give children the chance to explore powerful emotions—anticipation, fear, relief, excitement, jubilation. I feel that folklore should be considered a functional introduction to the future literature that children and adults are expected to read in order to become "well read" persons. It can help soften the impact. It also presents an excellent example of what fantasy truly is, as compared to realism.

3. Read the material to be presented several times aloud and commit it to memory. One should not, however, memorize stories verbatim unless they are by Andersen, Kipling, etc. Outline the key incidents and review them constantly. Then practice reciting the story aloud. If a tape recorder is available, use it by all means; listening to your playback recording will aid you in self-criticism and the correction of faults. All of this preparation is essential for success, for if the storyteller is interrupted, the thread of the story can be picked up and continued without wasting precious time.

Timing stories is also a good practice, especially when dealing with a handicapped audience. Flexibility may have to be exercised in order to shorten a story for special circumstances, e.g., a shortened class period, a child who must be excused from class, etc.

4. While an agreeable sounding voice is desirable for all storytellers, it is especially needed for those working with the blind. The storyteller must rely solely upon his voice to convey all of the story. The teller should never feel inhibited when it comes to making voice changes or imitating the calls of domesticated or wild animals and birds. The children also enjoy hearing a change of voice for different characters represented in a given story when done effectively. Make use of inflectionary and modulatory voice tones to keep from sounding monotonous. The teller should keep in mind that blind children have access to talking books and other recorded media. They are used to good storytellers, so preparation should be thorough. They are also able to detect a storyteller's own interest in presenting the tale from the voice itself. If you are tired or bored with the story, the children will readily pick this up and react accordingly.

5. While blind children, like sighted ones, enjoy participation in a story session, use of this technique depends upon the individual storyteller, the selected story, and whether or not participation is desired. To some extent it should be encouraged, for it can become great fun for both the listener and the teller. During a telling of the Three Little Pigs, for instance, the children nearly blew me out of my chair during the "huff . . . puff" scene. They had no misconception as to where I was seated.

Realia (real life objects) may be used to enhance a program. These aids, when properly presented, can take the place of illustrations. Stuffed animal and bird exhibits may be borrowed on free loan from the educational departments of most museums for a period of one to two weeks. In some rural areas, the local taxidermist may be cooperative about loaning exhibits. 3M microfragrance labels pasted on cards and passed to each child to scratch and sniff will appeal to the olfactory senses and could be used for such stories as Hansel and Gretel.

To recapitulate, remember when selecting stories that it is wise to remain within the blind child's experiential realm. These children frequently have no concept of size, shape, or texture. Some teachers maintain that they are never fully assured as to whether or not a child has perceived correct dimensions. Therefore, preparation of story themes in advance (and after consultation with teachers to insure the particular concept involved has been previously taught or explained) will save valuable time by eliminating many questions and will make the story more effective.

Adults need to constantly remember that this old world is new to children, and what experienced adults may take for granted may not be within the realm of the child, especially a blind child, e.g., a trip to a farm or circus. Stories and books are highly valuable aids for they help fill in the gaps of a child's learning experience. Storytellers play the important role of catalyst in bringing books and children together.

Some Stories Enjoyed by Blind Children

Ali Baba and the Forty Thieves.
Angelo the Naughty One, by Helen Garrett.
Bremen Town Musicians.
Capt'n Dow and the Hole in the Doughnut, by Henderson LeGrande.
Cinderella.
Circus Baby, by Maud Petersham.
Country Bunny and the Little Gold Shoes, by Marjorie Flack.
The Five Chinese Brothers, by C. H. Bishop.
The Five Hundred Hats of Bartholomew Cubbins, by T. S. Geisel (Dr. Seuss).
Fredrick, by Leo Lionni.
The Friendly Beast, by Laura Baker.
Hansel and Gretel.
Jack and the Three Sillies, by Richard Chase.
John Henry: An American Legend, by E. J. Keats.
The King, the Mice and the Cheese, by Nancy Gurney.
Little Engine That Could, by Watty Piper.
Little Red Riding Hood.
Mike Mulligan and His Steam Shovel, by V. L. Burton.
Mike's House, by Julia Sauer.
Millions of Cats, by Wanda Gag.
Mollie Whuppie.
The Monkey and the Crocodile, by Paul Galdone.

Night Before Christmas, by C. C. Moore.
Noah's Ark, by Tony Palazzo.
Old Woman and Her Pig.
One Eye, Two Eyes, and Three Eyes.
Prince Bertram the Bad, by Robert Lobel.
Shoemaker and the Elves.
Slip, Slop, Gobble!
Stolen Turnips.
Toads and Diamonds.
Three Billy Goats Gruff.
Umbrella, by Taro Yashima.
Wait for William, by Marjorie Flack.
When the Root Children Wake Up, by Helen D. Fish.
Where's Prancer? by Syd Hoff.
Wolf and the Seven Kids.

BIBLIOGRAPHY

"The Art of Storytelling and the Storytellers," in *Compton's Encyclopedia and Fact Index* 21:460–82. Chicago: Compton, 1970.

Bryant, Sara C. *How to Tell Stories to Children.* Highland Park, N. J.: Gryphon-Gale, 1971.

Cathon, Laura E., and others. *Stories to Tell Children.* 7th ed., rev. Pittsburgh: Carnegie Library, 1960.

Education of the Blind Child: A Guide for Teachers (Publication no. 522). Los Angeles: Los Angeles City School Districts, 1951.

Fulker, Wilber H., and Fulker, Mary. *Techniques with Tangibles: A Manual for Teaching the Blind.* Springfield, Ill.: Thomas, 1968.

Halliday, Carol. *The Visually Impaired Child: Growth, Learning, Development; Infancy to School Age.* Louisville, Ky.: Instructional Materials Reference Center for Visually Handicapped Children, 1970.

Hardendorff, Jeanne B. *Stories to Tell.* 5th rev. ed. Baltimore: Enoch Pratt Free Library, 1965.

Sawyer, Ruth. *The Way of the Storyteller.* rev. ed. New York: Viking, 1962.

Shedlock, Marie L. *The Art of the Story-Teller.* New York: Dover, n.d.

Steinmetz, Eulalie. "Storytelling versus Recordings," *The Horn Book Magazine* 24:163–72 (May-June 1948).

Storytelling

PATRICK HUSTON

Many teachers of deaf children 9 to 13 years old find it difficult to tell stories that are exciting, yet easily

Reprinted by permission from *The Volta Review,* 74, no. 2:100–4 (Feb. 1972). Copyright © The Alexander Graham Bell Association for the Deaf, Washington, D.C., 1972.

understood. Sometimes the story fails because it is not told primarily for the enjoyment of the children. Usually, however, the story fails because its structure has inherent weaknesses. A story for deaf children has to move in very clearly defined steps. Each step must be understood before the children are led to the next. Each new step must be understood in relation to the previous step, and so on.

What follows is a detailed approach to the structuring of stories for middle school deaf children. The structure involves five basic steps: (1) *introduction,* (2) *buildup,* (3) *action,* (4) *reaction,* and (5) *climax.*

Introduction to the Story

The introduction is important for two major reasons: (1) it sets the scene; and (2) it gives the deaf children a chance to adjust to the storyteller's face and particular lip patterns. For these reasons, it is imperative that all "stumbling blocks" be removed from this section of any story. Vocabulary and sentence structure must be completely familiar to the children.

To set the scene, it is wise to start with the words, "Today, I will tell you a story."

Many teachers of the deaf never prepare their classes for what is to follow in a set lesson. The children are often mystified as to whether the lesson will be a formal language lesson, whether it will be written, whether it will be good fun or hard work. It is little wonder that signs of restiveness appear even before a potentially exciting and successful story is under way.

Once the children know that the lesson which follows is to be a story, they are, in a sense, prepared for a certain set of circumstances that will provide a fair degree of enjoyment. For this reason, it is helpful at this point to further enlighten the children as to what the story will be about. For example:

> *The story is about a little girl.*
> *The girl's name is Mandy.*
> *Mandy has long blonde hair.*
> *She has blue eyes.*
> *Mandy is 10 years old.*
> *She lives with her mother and father in a*
> *little white house.*
> *The house is near a forest.*

At this stage it may also be helpful to produce a picture of Mandy so that the children may have the opportunity to see that they have, in fact, understood the storyteller, and that their inner picture of a little girl with blonde hair and blue eyes is correct.

No difficult language should be used at any time in the introductory section of a story. Most deaf children are very much at home with a working vocabulary concerning colors and parts of the body such as hair and eyes. For this reason, it is good policy to include rather sundry details, if only to give the children the opportunity to settle into a story session.

Thus it is that, by the end of the introduction, the children are secure in the knowledge that: (1) there is to be a story; (2) the story will be about (in this case) a little girl who is blue-eyed and 10 years old; and (3) most importantly, the children themselves can lipread and understand the storyteller.

Buildup of the Story

It is at this stage that the story proper can begin. There are all sorts of adventures little blonde, blue-eyed girls may have, but for middle school deaf children, success can usually be guaranteed if the adventures involve such things as lost dogs, ghosts, giants, cruel wolves, etc.

In this particular example, Mandy is to meet a giant. It is necessary in the buildup section, therefore, to work clearly toward the projected encounter.

This can be done by preparing the children for what may soon happen in the story (Stage 3 for the storyteller). It is necessary for the children to relate very closely to the heroine and to the situation itself. The buildup in this case must, then, be a step-by-step introduction to a situation where danger is an intrinsic factor. For example:

One day Mandy went for a walk.
Her mother said, "Do not go near the forest.
A giant lives in the forest.
Keep away from the forest.
The forest is dangerous."

This type of buildup clearly emphasizes a dangerous situation. It now remains to project the heroine into this situation. For example:

But, Mandy was foolish!
She walked into the forest to look at some birds.
The forest was dark and cold.
The wind was blowing.
Mandy was rather frightened.

Obviously, something is about to happen. A little girl is in a cold, dark forest. Her mother has repeatedly told her to keep away from this forest. It is a dangerous forest. A giant lives there.

Without using any difficult vocabulary or sentence structure, the storyteller has led the children to *anticipate* some dark deed. This is the time for action.

Action Introduced

It is very important that this anticipated action live up to expectations. Storytellers in classrooms for deaf children often lose their audiences at this stage simply because the action does not catch the imagination.

In other words, it is not frightening (or, in some cases, funny) enough.

To help capture the children's imagination, it is wise to use, once again, short, simple sentences and familiar description. For example:

Suddenly Mandy screamed, "Aaaaggghhh!"
A huge giant grabbed her. "Ho! Ho! Ho! Ho!"
The giant had horrible red eyes.
He had long yellow teeth.
He had enormous hands.
His hair was black and dirty.
The giant laughed. "Ho! Ho! Ho! Ho!
You must come with me!"

Reaction Follows

To every action there is usually some reaction. This is a time in a story sequence where a good deal of direct speech may be used to positive advantage. It will help the children relate to the heroine's dilemma, and will also help them to predict an *outcome* for this particular set of circumstances (Stage 5 for the storyteller). Take, for example, a helpless heroine, extremely frightened—as revealed by direct speech. Some form of outside help may be anticipated. (This will mean, in Mandy's case, possibly a woodchopper, faithful dog, or brave older brother.)

Mandy screamed again, "Aaaggghhh!
Let me go! Let me go!"
The giant said, "No, I want you to look after me."
"Oh, no! No! Please let me go. Please."
"No. You must come to my cave.
You must sweep the floor.
You must cook my dinner every day."
"Oh, no! Please let me go!
I want to go home!
I want my mother."
"No, you must come with me."

Obviously, something has to happen now to end the story satisfactorily for the children. (It is essential that, initially, the children be led to typical conclusions for these typical story situations.)

Climax to the Story

Deaf children usually find it difficult to know just when a story is drawing to a close. For this reason, it is a good idea to conclude the story on a very definite note. For example, the lost boy is found, the princess is saved, the robber is caught, or, in this particular case, the giant is killed. There must be no room in the children's minds for doubt. For example:

Suddenly, a man came.
The man had a big axe.
The man was Mandy's father.

"Oh, help me, Father, help me!"
Mandy's father ran to the giant.
"Let Mandy go, you horrible giant!" he shouted.
The giant roared, "No! She must come with me."
Mandy's father hit the giant with his axe.
The giant fell down dead.
"Oh, thank you, Father! Thank you.
I will not walk in the forest again."

Stories Are to Be Enjoyed

Stories can be used as a springboard for many activities in a classroom for deaf children, and it is legitimate for the teacher to use stories in this way. It must always be remembered, however, that stories should be told primarily for enjoyment. If the story can be used as a vehicle for extension studies and still be enjoyed for its own sake, the studies are justified. If the story is greeted with glum faces, the teacher should discontinue any extension work and concentrate on telling a story that will easily catch and retain the children's imagination and will be enjoyed purely and simply as a story.

Stories *can* and *should* be fun for pupils and teacher alike.

Storytelling for the Young Mentally Retarded Child

BARBARA H. BASKIN
and
KAREN H. HARRIS

All children, including the mentally retarded, delight in participating in a storytelling experience. Storytelling should be utilized, not only for its recognized recreational value, but for its intrinsic capability to achieve valid educational objectives. Such an undertaking should not be approached casually, included as a time filler or solely to provide a change of pace. The storyteller should have specific purposes in mind and a clear idea of how this particular experience will work toward the attainment of his or her goals.

Careful consideration of the learning characteristics of retarded children must be made in the context of the demands the storytelling experience imposes. The retarded child's attention span tends to be limited. Therefore, at the outset it will be best to avoid long stories. By keeping the occasion relatively brief, the child will be better able to sustain interest for the duration of the story. One of the storyteller's objectives is to increase attention span, and to this end he or she will

Reprinted by permission from *Journal of Developmental Disabilities* 1, no. 3 (1975).

gradually prolong the experience to expand with the children's developing tolerance for longer sessions.

The storyteller at first may choose stories which call for a response. In *Which Horse Is William?*[1] the child can select the correct response for each picture. In *Davy's Day*[2] each little event—breakfast, nap-time, outdoor play—can be related to equivalent moments in the listeners' day and the book can become the basis for a dialogue, rather than a passive listening experience.

The retarded child tends to be concrete-bound and form literal interpretations. Abstractions and metaphorical language are confusing. When Lionni writes in *Swimmy*, "strange fish, pulled by an invisible thread . . . a forest of seaweeds growing from sugar-candy rocks" the child is apt to interpret this quite literally and "an eel whose tail was too far away to remember" presents a confusing mixture of time and space.[3] The storyteller, conscious of the conflict between the language limitations of the listener and the need to make the interaction between story and child a language-expanding experience, should examine the vocabulary of the book both for the level of difficulty and for the frequency with which obsolete or obscure words, obtuse meanings, localisms, or unusual idiomatic expressions are used. Books with many foreign words or phrases should be bypassed; the child has sufficient difficulty mastering his own language. When the storyteller feels that the inclusion of a rarely used word is justified, it should be retained, but followed by some synonym or brief explanation. "Porridge" is exactly the right word for what bears have for breakfast in fairy tales but will need some interpretation to be intelligible.

The ability of the retarded child to make associations and respond to stimuli in books is often limited. These children frequently have had narrow experience bases or restricted educational backgrounds. The storyteller must be prepared to provide foundational information using pictures, posters, models or toys to illustrate unfamiliar components of the story. A castle, a jungle, or a beaver may be just words without any concrete referents in the listener's mind. It is important to extend the child's world, but assumption of knowledge common to age peers must not be made for this group.

Clearly these children will share many of the same interests as their chronological peers and these interests should be exploited in story selection. Tales about animals, family life, and children of their own age can be expected to have appeal. Books should be considered which feature those problems, fears, or concerns of the child about which he may feel deeply but may lack the verbal skills, bravery or emotional security to discuss. *Will I Have a Friend?*,[4] *The New Teacher*,[5] and *What Mary Jo Shared*[6] are examples of mundane, school-

STORYTELLING FOR THE MENTALLY RETARDED 115

related issues which address themselves to topics that frequently have been areas of worry or failure for the retarded child.

Stories with exotic locales will often present difficulties. Generally, tales with familiar settings will be easier to understand. Since these children frequently have difficulty in integrating knowledge about their own immediate environment, the problem of relating to a fictional child in a French boarding school, or vicariously traveling by dogteam across a frozen tundra, or poling through Venetian canals in a gondola loads unneeded burdens on the ability of the child to comprehend his or her world.

Additional story elements to be considered are directness, lack of subtlety, absence of excessive peripheral components, inclusion of a definite climax and closure. Comprehensibility of ideas clearly is a paramount consideration. In *The Many Lives of Chio and Goro*[7] the characters are repeatedly reincarnated. The entire concept as well as the ability to separate and maintain character identities in the story is predictably beyond the abilities of our target group. When there is a contradiction between what a character says and what he actually means, the child may become confused. In *Whose Mouse Are You?*[8] the young mouse character makes up stories about his family which are untrue because of the insecurity he feels upon the arrival of his infant brother. It is unlikely that the child will understand the subtle, fantasy nature of the mouse's story—and hence the point of the book. Similarly, he may miss the irony in the Japanese folk tale "The Stonecutter," wherein the stonecutter, who aspires to be all-powerful, is finally transformed into a mountain which in turn is threatened by a lowly stonecutter.

Some books should be chosen for their role-modeling potential since story themes can serve didactic purposes. Stories stressing kindness, friendship, honesty, or perseverance can assist in the development of an appropriate value system or provide a nonthreatening basis for discussion. In many instances, at the conclusion of an exchange of ideas and impressions, the storyteller may have to tie in specifically the abstract aspects of the story with present situations since many children may have difficulty making the transfer from the concept in the story to their own behavior. *Two Is a Team*,[9] *Peter's Chair*,[10] and *A Bargain for Frances*[11] dealing with cooperation, jealousy, and friendship are excellent for these purposes.

Retarded children have diminished ability to make associations or to generalize. Their predictive and interpretive talents are poor. The amusement in a book like *The Adventures of Paddy Pork*[12] lies in the child's skill in making deductions and anticipating what might happen next. It is unlikely that many retarded children would be able to fully share in the fun. Moreover, these children often lack sensitivity to the incidental aspects or components of pictures or stories. The occasional amusing literary devices of authors are lost on them. When these are pivotal elements in the book, substitutions should definitely be considered.

If pictures are shown as a story is read, the probability of comprehension is increased. In contrast with the use of pictures with average or above average children to develop a visual aesthetic sense or to extend knowledge about a related creative form, illustrations in books for educable retarded children should be judged primarily on their ability to interpret or amplify the text, i.e., how well they reduce ambiguity or further clarify the verbal message. One outstanding illustrator, Arthur Rackham, often selected incidents from a story which gave play to his talent and imagination, but which were peripheral to the plot. For a child with limitations, looking at such pictures in tandem with hearing the story could be confusing in terms of understanding the significance of events as well as the critical thematic elements.

Ideally, illustrations should be representational and precise rather than impressionistic. Objects should not be shown where they are viewed from a perspective which is rare or unexpected, where the outlines are vague or distorted or where key identifying cues are missing or obscure. The illustrations in *Charley, Charlotte and the Golden Canary*,[13] as in almost all of Keeping's books, confound both expectation and perception. Characters and objects are not clearly defined, figures blend into the background, and the use of color is highly unrealistic. The pictures in *London Bridge Is Falling Down*[14] are too detailed and fulsome for a retarded child to readily absorb. In *The Adventures of Paddy Pork* the pictures are very busy and several of the animals are difficult to identify—one looks like a cross between a bear and an oppossum. In *Little Bear*[15] the hero wishes for a big red car, and is pictured seated behind the wheel of a black one—an unnecessarily confusing situation. In one illustration in *Stevie*[16] a character is shown from neck to ankles, her head and feet missing. The retarded child may find this distracting, even a little disturbing.

The storyteller should not be dismayed if retarded children do not react to amusing or funny stories as other children might; their responses are highly dependent on which literary devices the writer employs. If the author uses several levels of meaning, introduces bizarre events or counterposes unlikely circumstances to achieve humorous effect, the result may be too complex or insufficiently obvious for the listener to grasp. That is, the child may not be aware that the elements in the story are ludicrous, unusual, or amusing when juxtaposed and thus may miss the point. They may or may not understand *Amelia Bedelia*,[17] in which all humor depends on the main character's literal rather than idiomatic interpretation of that which is said to her. If an amusing story is desired, then one such as *Curious George,*[18] *Harry the Dirty Dog,*[19] or *Caps for Sale,*[20] where the humor is obvious and direct should be chosen. If, however, a story is unusually good, the children may enjoy and profit from its other qualities, even if its humor is only partially perceived.

The need for specificity is great. Mood pieces like *The Fog Is Secret*[21] or *The Little Island,*[22] or stories like *The Camel Who Took a Walk,*[23] in which the point of the story is that nothing happened, are often unsettling.

The intellectually limited child's ability to comprehend rapid changes in characterization or mood or to keep pace with complex themes is weak; he or she is considerably slower in reaction time, a critical variable in monitoring the movement of a story. Conversely, repetition, the association with something familiar, persistence of factors which create specific expectations are desirable story traits. Cumulative folk tales are a good choice for retarded children. Their characteristic repetitive qualities develop the idea of anticipation. They present a pattern and a rhythm to which the child becomes attuned. Henny Penny goes from creature to creature being asked the same question and giving the same response. Each character's name is a double rhymed word which is a diminutive form of the kind of animal he is. This pattern which undergirds the story line assists the child in following the progression of events. In another example, the Gingerbread Boy runs away from each character chanting the same taunting lines. The repetition sets up situations of sequential expectations and fulfillment. The pace is serene enough and the plot sufficiently redundant that the child's slower response rate is accommodated.

When beginning the storytelling experience, the teacher/librarian should establish a climate of expectancy and attentiveness as free from auditory and visual distractions as possible. The storyteller should maintain close to horizontal sight lines with the audience, noting that all children can readily view pictures or supplementary items, that those children who require visual or proximity support are appropriately placed and that children are comfortable and have adequate space in which to participate in the experience. Warm-up discussion should be brief and highly stimulating. The introduction should anticipate vocabulary problems, motivate the listener, set the scene, introduce characters and relate some aspect of the story to the children's lives. To introduce *The Plant Sitter,*[24] the idea of a baby sitter might be discussed, followed by some references to plants growing in the library or the children's homeroom. It is a good practice to pose some questions so that the children will have something to listen for.

If it is apparent that the group is too physically restless to sit still for a story and needs an activity interlude, then it is sometimes advisable to begin with a recorded participation exercise wherein everyone moves around the room before returning to the listening group. Such records as Ella Jenkins' *Play Your Instruments and Make a Pretty Sound,*[25] are deservedly popular with children and their teachers. This could be followed by finger plays, pantomime, or other physical activities which are related to the story content and focus on the storyteller in her central role.

The storyteller needs to have read the material in advance to detect possible vocabulary problems and to prepare substitutes or synonyms for potentially troublesome words or phrases so that the story can proceed smoothly. If the teller detects problems in comprehension of the story, clarification should be made immediately. If the problem appears to be that events are moving too quickly, the speaker might rephrase the contents or elicit comments from the listeners about the illustrations which would amplify the meaning.

The storyteller must make continuous assessments of the audience during the session to determine the impact of the experience on the children. If just a few seem to be distracted, the teller might pose some low-key questions to pull them back or use unobtrusive eye or touch contact. If the story simply has little interest and attention markedly decreases, the experience should be concluded in as short order as logically possible.

The vocal role of both teller and listener are important. The speaker should talk clearly, audibly, and with animation. The tone of voice greatly assists in comprehension of the mood of the story underlining such elements as surprise, excitement, caution or whatever is appropriate. The teller may need to give facial, vocal, or gestural cues so that the child will know when to get ready to join in if there is a refrain.

Occasionally, the teacher/librarian may want to use media to help tell the story. Large pictures, realia, felt or flannel boards, puppets of all types, slides and transparencies are especially useful. It is best to avoid the opaque projector since it requires a very dark room and the storyteller is positioned in back of the children instead of in their line of sight.

The telling of a story should not be viewed as an isolated event, fragmented from the rest of the educational experience. Therefore, it should usually have some form of follow-up to ascertain whether the children have understood and enjoyed the experience, including a determination of whether concept closure has taken place. This period should be cognitively reinforcing and provide opportunities for the child to interact with the speaker and group freely. A retelling of the story in a variety of ways is an effective device for judging understanding. Dramatization, drawing pictures and sequencing them as the story is told, retelling the story in their own words are possible means to this end. On some occasions, the storyteller may judge summary activities superfluous.

An evaluation needs to be made after each storytelling session to see if the predetermined goals were accomplished. Pupil readiness, interest, attention span, comprehension, and retention should all be assessed so that preparedness to move to longer stories, more complex plots, and other such factors can be decided. Movement to higher levels should be contingent on the capability of the listeners but should be an inexorable and steady aspect of the literature program.

Storytelling assists in the educational growth of the retarded child. The story immerses the child in the richness and pleasure of the language. In contrast to the often isolated curricular activities the child has, this experience allows participation in a pleasurable group endeavor where his or her perceptual and performance inadequacies are camouflaged to some degree. Since an experiential repertoire is often scanty or uneven, literature provides an enjoyable means to extend and deepen knowledge. It can make less perplexing the relationship between problems, behavior, and resolution. It can stimulate the child to want to read so that his or her enjoyment can be extended in a book-related situation.

Although storytelling clearly has an aesthetic and social aspect for the retarded child, the emphasis here has been on the intellectual impact which this activity could have. The devastating effect of slow patterns of learning can be partially compensated for by a massive commitment of all members of the school faculty to join in the support of the retarded child's growth. The library's treasurehouse of books must be made available to this group. The irresistible power of a story to pull listeners into a situation which compels their attention and opens them up to affective and cognitive learning is vital to the retarded child and must not be ignored.

NOTES

1. Karla Kuskin, *Which Horse Is William?* (New York: Harper, 1959).
2. Lois Lenski, *Davy's Day* (New York: Walck, 1948).
3. Leo Lionni, *Swimmy* (New York: Pantheon, 1963).
4. Miriam Cohen, *Will I Have a Friend?* (New York: Macmillan, 1967).
5. Miriam Cohen, *The New Teacher* (New York: Macmillan, 1972).
6. Janice Udry, *What Mary Jo Shared* (Chicago: Albert Whitman, 1966).
7. Betty Jean Lifton, *The Many Lives of Chio and Goro* (New York: Norton, 1968).
8. Robert Kraus, *Whose Mouse Are You?* (New York: Macmillan, 1970).
9. Jerrold Beim, *Two Is a Team* (New York: Harcourt, 1945).
10. Ezra Jack Keats, *Peter's Chair* (New York: Harper, 1967).
11. Russell Hoban, *A Bargain for Frances* (New York: Harper, 1970).
12. John Goodall, *The Adventures of Paddy Pork* (New York: Harcourt, 1968).
13. Charles Keeping, *Charley, Charlotte and the Golden Canary* (New York: Watts, 1967).
14. Peter Spier, *London Bridge Is Falling Down* (New York: Doubleday, 1967).
15. E. H. Minarik, *Little Bear* (New York: Harper, 1969).
16. John Steptoe, *Stevie* (New York: Harper, 1956).
17. Peggy Parish, *Amelia Bedelia* (New York: Harper, 1963).
18. H. A. Rey, *Curious George* (Boston: Houghton, 1941).
19. Gene Zion, *Harry the Dirty Dog* (New York: Harper, 1956).
20. Esphyr Slobodkina, *Caps for Sale* (New York: W. R. Scott, 1947).
21. Theresa Smith, *The Fog Is Secret* (Englewood Cliffs, N.J.: Prentice-Hall, 1966).
22. Leonard Weisgard, *The Little Island* (New York: Doubleday, 1946).
23. Jack Tworkov, *The Camel Who Took a Walk* (New York: Dutton, 1951).
24. Gene Zion, *The Plant Sitter* (New York: Harper, 1959).
25. Ella Jenkins, *Play Your Instruments and Make a Pretty Sound* (Folkways 12″ LP).

The School Library and Children with Learning and Behavior Problems

KEN MORGAN

Through the cooperative efforts of the departments of Special Education, Elementary Education and the Edith Bowen Lab School Administration at Utah State University, and the Logan City and Cache County School Districts, a Learning Adjustment class at the intermediate level was established four years ago on the Utah State University campus. In the past, children have been referred to this class for emotional and social problems and learning disabilities. Forms of emotional problems have varied from complete withdrawal and severe school phobia, to expressions of high verbal and physical aggressiveness. Children referred with social problems have usually shown inadequacies in previous social experiences when placed in situations where they must interact with peers and adults. Children with learning disabilities usually experience feelings of intellectual inadequacy which inhibit their ability to read, do mathe-

Reprinted by permission from *Utah Libraries* 13:20-24 (Spring 1970).

matical computations, spell, etc. Such a child may have formed a mental block in one area, or in several areas of academic study which makes it difficult or impossible for him to learn.

The Intermediate Learning Adjustment program is one of development or reconstruction of patterns of learning, remediation work in subject matter, the development of emotional patterns more conducive to good learning through play therapy, reality therapy, behavior modification, and, most important of all, provision of many and varied opportunities for successful experiences in learning.

Eight children were enrolled in the Learning Adjustment class when the term began last fall. The group comprised five boys and three girls, ranging from nine to eleven years of age. Grade placement varied three years, from grades four to six.

The academic problems found most commonly among these children were reading difficulties. Difficulties in reading varied from child to child. Some were retarded in their reading by as little as six months, while others were unable to read at all. They were, on the average, two and one half years behind their actual grade placement in reading. (Levels of retardation were determined through the Gates Reading Test and the Metropolitan Achievement Test.) Six of the eight children enrolled had shown underachievement in all academic areas due to their inability to read at their grade-level placement.

When the school program was initiated in the fall, it was found that the children involved had undoubtedly developed some very negative attitudes toward school, reading, books, and library facilities in general. (Not to be overlooked is the fact that the library facility used in their program was the Anne Carroll Moore Library at the Edith Bowen Laboratory School, one of the finest elementary school libraries in the Intermountain area.)

During their initial involvement with the Moore Library, the children expressed the following:

1. They had no desire to become involved in library activities.
2. Once inside the library they wanted to play tag, talk to other children, look out the windows at other children involved in out-of-door activities, or just simply to sit.

Only one child expressed an interest in a specific area of reading. The others had no knowledge as to the type of books they might have an interest in. In general they knew nothing about the different categories of books or how they were shelved. They did not understand the function of the card catalog or how it could be utilized in helping to find a book by matching the number on the book's binding with that on the card. Only one child indicated any interest at all in library activities. The others wanted simply to stay away.

One day, by chance, the librarian who is also interested in these children was short of help. She was in need of a child to watch the desk and stamp library cards while she was reading to some younger children. Therefore, the L.A. class was asked as a group if someone would watch the desk for a few minutes. One child, a girl who would normally be in the sixth grade, volunteered.

After assisting the librarian, and upon returning to the classroom, this child made the comment, "Boy, was that fun! Can I help again, tomorrow?"

The instructor informed the librarian of this turn of events; she in turn immediately arranged a time for this girl to assist in the library the following day, and for several days thereafter. Each session in the library was limited to a half hour.

Very soon this pupil was not only assisting with "watching the desk" and checking out books, but with some assistance from the librarian, she soon learned to find books through the card catalog, file away book cards on books checked out, and assist the smaller children with finding titles on the shelves.

The climax for this child came one day when she asked to be allowed to read a story to kindergarten children during their library "listening time." A photo was taken of her reading to this group of children. This photo and an article explaining the activity appeared in the local newspaper.

During the period of this girl's activity in the library, other children in the Learning Adjustment class were watching with envy tinged by fear of becoming involved in such a venture. However, another child, a boy who would normally have been in the fourth grade and [who had been] diagnosed as having severe school phobia and an active ulcer, asked if he might "just watch the desk for a few minutes."

With the same technique as applied to the first, this boy was soon on his way to full involvement in the library. In quick succession, others followed in his footsteps until all eight children were involved.

Getting these children involved meant doing the following:

1. Getting each child interested.
2. Expelling his fears about "helping."
3. Keeping everything very simple in the beginning, with increasing complexity offered as time passed and the child felt more competent.
4. Encouraging them to voluntarily try the different operations of the library.
5. Willingness of parent, school director, and instructor to have time set aside for the child's involvement in the library.
6. Full cooperation of the staff in working out programming and planning.
7. Deep interest of every member of the staff in each child in the program.

8. Willingness of all staff members to overlook the "testing" behavior of some of the children and small mistakes a child may make. The philosophy here has been to let the child learn from his mistakes.

9. Common feeling among the faculty that these children can become more competent readers through library experiences, that they can develop such a feeling toward the library that they desire to investigate further the books and other materials available.

Four of the eight children involved in this project were thought to be reading so poorly that they could not apply any reading skills independently to any project or subject. They had no concern for any form of reading; they could see neither value nor enjoyment in it. They shunned books completely.

Within a six-month period each child was capable of assisting in the library. They can, through the card catalog, find books according to the Dewey Decimal System, they can check books in and out, file and find book cards alphabetically, shelve books with few errors, and assist others in searching out books.

They are choosing stories for reading to the various grades during the library story hour, using good judgment in determining material suitable to the ages of their listening audiences.

These children scramble for the opportunity to help in the library. To assist the librarian or to read stories to other children is considered an opportunity of high importance and responsibility. They enjoy searching out books shelved in the library. The slower readers now make realistic choices. One may choose a *Cowboy Sam* book, while another may seek out Dr. Suess. The more able readers might choose one of Beverly Cleary's books about Henry Huggins, or a mystery or adventure novel. Above all, they are inquiring into and reading books themselves, books that not only teachers and parents did not think they could read, but that they themselves had been afraid to try.

The reading progress, the emotional stability, the increased friendliness and communication between the children in the Learning Adjustment Program and the children in the regular grades, and the improved feeling of self-worth that has developed within these children, has been observed by the school director, the librarian, the Learning Adjustment teacher, and other faculty members.

However, simply to discuss such changes and improvements with others does not communicate a complete and accurate impression of what has taken place. University students enrolled in Special Education are usually not involved long enough to see at first hand the progress that evolves over a period of time. Proof of this is found in many of the reports and written observations graduate and undergraduate students have submitted to University faculty members. To see the progress that takes place in these children, one must be involved for periods of from three to nine months, or longer. Therefore it has seemed that filming of day to day experiences would be an answer in measuring and communicating results of the program. Through use of films, majors in Special Education and in Elementary Education could acquire knowledge in ways of developing units of study involving the use of the library, behavior control, attitudes of and understanding of interpersonal relationships of children. Librarians could possibly gain insights into new utilizations of the library and the development of better lines of communication between the librarian and teachers.

At this early date, with very little filming and videotaping completed, requests for viewing of the program when it is completed have been submitted by faculty members in Special Education, Elementary Education, and "Project Upward Bound." More such requests can be expected from departments of Psychology, Child Development, Library Sciences, and the Extension Services of Utah State University. Unfortunately, due to lack of funds, this videotaping project has had to be temporarily delayed.

Elementary schools are going to have more and more children of the type with which this paper concerns itself. Emotional problems of children will not decrease in the near future—neither will the various educational problems of children we conveniently place under the blanket term of "Learning Disabilities." University students who will one day be involved in working with children need as many and as varied experiences with children as time will permit. It is time that programs in education, and especially those in Special Education, begin documenting programs and experiences through use of techniques which make it possible for those involved in the education of children to see at first hand the internal workings of educational methods of today and the experimental educational models of the future.

A Junior High School Program for Retarded Readers

ANGELINE DEMPSEY

The work described here is an outgrowth of a discussion with the school counselors about students who do poor work in school because of not being able to read. In my work with these students in the library, I have noticed their poor work habits, their resistance to books and reading, and the number of their emotional

Reprinted from *School Libraries,* Spring 1967, pp. 9–15.

and discipline problems. Leveling by ability had placed these students in the four level group.

It is the practice in this particular school system to group students by their achievement and ability as shown by standardized tests, into four groups: Level I includes the best students and those in foreign language programs; Level II, the good students; Level III, the average students; and, Level IV, the poor students. This does not necessarily mean that the students in Level IV are those with low IQs, but rather that many of them are nonachievers. Many students are placed in this group because they cannot read, and therefore are unable to do the work required of them. In Levels I to III, the attitudes mentioned are not apparent. Here the students are eager readers, anxious to explore on their own, and like nothing better than to have time to read and to use the many facilities available to them.

In checking, I found that teachers were as frustrated as the students because they had to teach material which the students could not comprehend, and because they had textbooks which the students could not read. In fact, much of the material had to be read to these children.

Many students in Level IV, before reaching junior high school, had been referred to the guidance counselor because of their poor work in class, to the reading consultant who tested them and made recommendations, and then sent back to the same classroom situation. The child, reacting to this, began to protect himself from failure in whatever manner was individually possible and effective. He refused to perform and was insubordinate or withdrawn when faced with exposure of ignorance. In this way he avoided failure and preserved his self respect even though he incurred the teachers' displeasure. By junior high, he still could not read, and in many cases had become a discipline problem. Could something be done for them now?

The guidance counselor asked if several of us would be willing to give extra time for a pilot study with a small group of these students, and in the second semester the following program was begun with five boys who needed help because they were completely lost in the regular classroom situation. Two were reading at a second grade level; two at third to fourth grade level; and one at fifth grade level. With the exception of one boy, these were not discipline problems, although continued failures could very well make them so. A special program, including English, reading, library reading, counseling, industrial arts and mathematics, was scheduled for these boys. The following characteristics were used to identify students for the pilot program:

1. Students who had not participated in education as such.

2. Students who had very few success experiences.

3. As shown by tests and conferences with teachers,

students who could not read with comprehension most materials beyond the third or fourth grade level.

4. Students who were frustrated by these experiences and had no socially acceptable method of expressing their frustration.

5. Students who had experienced little or no improvement in reading since third grade.

6. Students who had been retained at least one grade in elementary school.

7. Students who *did* have interests which could be stimulated and developed.

8. Students who were able to communicate orally and to write in an elementary fashion.

9. Students who could relate to a warm, encouraging teaching relationship.

10. Students who were capable of improving their academic skills to a certain extent.

The purpose of the pilot program was (1) to provide an adequate learning environment in a nonstructured, small group situation; (2) to provide learning experiences commensurate with the students' abilities, with appropriate materials and direction to assure success; (3) to improve reading ability through remedial and directed reading; (4) to modify and enhance the individual's self-concept through counseling; (5) to encourage self-expression in a small group relationship; and (6) to develop a *liking* for reading by having books read to the students and by encouraging them to read interesting books on their reading level in a situation which would not be embarrassing to them.

No specific curriculum demands were to be made of these students. Grades would be arbitrary and individual progress, however slight, would be stressed constantly. Subject matter would be determined by the teacher according to the individual needs and potential of each student. Success experiences would be emphasized and frustration would be avoided as much as possible.

Profiles of the boys selected for the program:

Tim. IQ 80 Age 14 Reading level—2nd grade. Tim is a transfer from a private school in which, according to his record, he has had reading difficulties throughout the grades. He was retained in kindergarten and again in third grade. At fourth grade, he was reading at a second grade level.

In the seventh grade, Tim was brought to the attention of Pupil Services of the school because he was having so much difficulty with regular school work. There seemed to be no satisfactory place for Tim in the private school, and the parents were approached regarding Tim's attendance in public school. The father was very concerned and seemed to be most anxious that Tim graduate from high school. The father, a successful businessman, had had the same difficulties that Tim was experiencing, and was therefore very sympathetic toward his son.

Tim is a very likable, polite and well-mannered boy, and liked by his teachers, but he is a loner and has not been able to make friends. His work habits and motivation are considerably above the others in his group, and he is aware that inability to read is the cause of his trouble.

Everett. IQ 100 Age 14 Reading level—1st–2nd grade. Everett comes from a culturally deprived family of thirteen; he has five older brothers, two older sisters, two younger sisters and one younger brother. The family moved about quite often before coming to this city.

Everett began having reading problems in the first grade. Since tests placed him in the average range of intelligence, it was suspected that his reading difficulties stemmed partly from the deprived home conditions. He was retained in the third grade, and by the fourth grade seemed to have lost whatever reading ability he had achieved.

When Everett was again tested in the seventh grade, he had dropped 14 points on the verbal scale and 22 points on the performance scale (WISC Test). He is still using second grade reading skills. Everett's native intelligence is still average; but since he does not have the necessary communication skills, the learning process has, in effect, halted.

The psychologist in his report says, "Special planning augmented by individual help is the only method by which Everett will progress. Everett should not be subjected to, and graded on, our present curriculum."

John. IQ 90 Age 13 Reading level—4th grade. In the second grade, John was referred to Child Study because of his poor work. He was reading in a pre-primer; his social development was extremely immature; but, he was pleasant and eager and very delighted with elementary successes. Because of his immaturity, John was retained in the second grade after considerable thought had been given to the effect this might have on his falling behind his twin brother. John also seemed to have a visual problem. In the sixth grade he was again referred to the school psychologist because of his poor level of achievement. Tests indicated that John was a slow learner, but that he could achieve much more than he had so far. How much his visual problem affected his work is not known, but he did seem to have difficulty in seeing words correctly on a printed page.

Gerald. IQ 89 Age 13 Reading level—3rd grade. Gerald is a very pleasant boy who gets along well with others. He has good work habits and a deep desire to do well in school. His reading scores show that he has some difficulty in this area. At third grade he was about a year below the median for his class, but at seventh grade he is still reading at a third grade level. He had attended a summer reading program in the third grade, but other than this he has been given no special help.

This is unfortunate because Gerald really wants to do well.

Maurice. IQ 90 Age 13 Reading level—5th grade. Maurice has been a discipline problem both in the elementary and junior high school. He has been sent repeatedly from classes because of his disturbing behavior. Baby talk, facial grimaces, loud noises, unusual attire (a ribbon in his hair) are devices used by Maurice to draw attention. When the parents were called in for a conference, they admitted that they were unable to cope with Maurice; and they showed little concern about him. On several occasions, Maurice has disappeared from home for several days. Although Maurice did not seem to fit in with the other four boys, he was selected for this program because we felt that he might be helped by the closer association with his teachers, the special attention, and the security that we could give him. Maurice was also referred to the school psychologist.

The following generalizations can be made about the group: (1) these boys are low-average to average in intelligence; (2) they have done poorly in school because of not being able to read; (3) they have been referred to the school reading consultant and to the school psychologist; (4) no intensive special help outside the regular classroom has been given; (5) all were transferred to junior high school without any problems being solved; (6) most of the reading skills acquired up to this time had been lost; (7) none, except Maurice, was a discipline problem and each one, except Everett, came from average or above average income homes; and (8) they seemed to have happy, well-adjusted family relationships.

During the course of the program, the most significant change was in the personality of the boys. When I met them, they were shy and not very talkative. To create an informal, friendly atmosphere, we sat together around a table and the first week was spent in talking about the things the boys were interested in. We discussed what they liked and didn't like, their hobbies and what they did at home and after school. These boys had been loners, with few friends and few opportunities to express themselves. Soon they were doing the talking and I was doing the listening. They had their dreams and their hopes, some of which were very unrealistic (a characteristic of many slow learners). Gerald wanted to be an astronomer or scientist; Tim, a nurseryman; Everett, a sculptor; John, to work for his father. Maurice was the only one who did not seem to fit in with this group. He continued to draw attention with his baby talk, animal noises, and facial contortions. When the guidance counselor suggested that it might be better to take him out of the group, he asked to be allowed to remain. He had his relapses, but as the weeks passed these became fewer. He began to accept help, to assume some responsibility and to help the other boys with their reading. After

Easter vacation, he returned to school with a haircut, and the ribbon which he had worn in his hair for a month, and which we had disregarded, had also disappeared.

Like most boys this age, these were interested in cars, adventure and mysteries. We found good browsing books and magazines at first. The magazine *Hot Rod* was a favorite. As Everett and I were checking the shelves for books on cars, he asked about *Dragging and Driving,* and there was longing in his voice when he said, "I wish I could read that." Although he could not read the books, Gerald enjoyed the charts and maps in astronomy books and *Sky and Telescope* was one of his favorite magazines.

After the boys felt at ease, we selected easy books for them to read. This was the most difficult task because the boys were reading at a first to fourth grade level. Books for these teen-agers should have strong immediate appeal with themes of adventure, danger, sports, cars, dating, and mystery. Also good are plots dealing with the need to belong to a group, the need to be accepted by peers, the need to succeed at something, the need to feel the individual is important, and the need to feel satisfied about the status of parents. It is difficult to find books with easy-reading style and vocabulary; with characters that are adolescents or adults; and, dealing with the above mentioned themes. We tried *Cowboy Sam* and *Dan Frontier* books, easy mysteries and the Dolch books. The boys read them but there was not enough plot to hold their interest, and they were embarrassed to have books with pictures on the covers, although they were not ready to admit that they couldn't read anything more difficult.

One day I told the boys a fable to illustrate a point and was surprised to have Everett volunteer to tell one. I got a copy of *Aesop's Fables* and read several. Everett then asked to read one to me. At the end of the period, he stayed to finish another one. The other boys became interested and each one read several fables. That was the beginning! They no longer pretended nor felt ashamed when they read to me or asked for help. After this it was easier to find materials because the boys were willing to try, and they could admit that a book was too hard; they accepted the easy books although they were not as mature in their themes as the boys would have liked them to be. Books which the boys enjoyed were the *Morgan Bay Mysteries* and the *Jim Forest* books by John and Nancy Rambeau, and the *Deep Sea Adventure* series by Berres. Everett enjoyed the *Flip* stories and *Hundreds and Hundreds of Pancakes.* The reading consultant continued to work with the boys on basic reading skills, and as they gained more confidence in their ability, they began to read more and to feel more secure. John read *Trouble After School*; Maurice, *Old Yeller*; and Gerald, *Capture at Sea.* This was quite an accomplishment since

these boys had not read books previously for enjoyment. Their span of attention increased and they enjoyed listening to books read to them. Sometimes recordings such as Poe's stories were used.

A fifty minute class period is a long time for this type of student, and therefore a variety of activities was planned. Part of the period was devoted to silent reading, and part to listening. Browsing and the use of magazines was encouraged. Buzz sessions and much praise were an important part of the program. Gerald helped check out books for the first graders; Tim learned to alphabetize circulation cards; and Maurice helped John with his reading. The English teacher also used a variety of activities: oral discussion of a short article from a newspaper or magazine, or a short written assignment on any subject of interest. In all classes, praise and encouragement were stressed.

At report card time, the boys were very happy because they had received mostly A's and B's. In this program we were able to give these marks for the progress these boys made without having to justify them according to the standards of a regular class. All of the teachers involved in the program agreed that the time and effort spent was worthwhile and that the boys did benefit to some degree.

Maurice started at 5.0 on the Gates Oral Reading Test. At the end of the period, he tested 7.0. He was not a success in his attitude toward reading. His was an involved problem with emotional aspects predominant. However, he did take pride in leadership of the group and responded well to group situations where he could dominate, but reacted very poorly to any individual work.

Tim started at 2.3 on the Gates Oral Reading Test and finished at the end of the semester at 3.2. He became at ease in group situations, when material was suitable to his ability level and showed a gain in reading comprehension. He showed improvement in word analysis and with encouragement, he would try words that normally he would avoid. Throughout the program, he indicated enjoyment and appreciation.

Everett progressed from 2.4 to 3.0 on the Gates Oral Reading Test. His problem was complicated by a long history of antipathy toward school. The only time he tried to work in school was in the third grade, and for the remainder of grade school was a passive nonresister. During the pilot program he went from being very withdrawn to somewhat aggressive in behavior in his total school associations. As he said, "Now I hit back when someone hits me." Everett's long history of failure made him apt to quit at the smallest frustration in reading, and although he had adequate mastery of consonant and vowel sounds, he did not readily transfer this knowledge when he was confronted with an unfamiliar word. He was pleased and surprised at his own abilities when he was held to independent word attack. His vocabulary was very limited; but anything he could read he could comprehend, and he seemed to retain the information quite well.

From 3.0 on the Gates Oral Reading Test, Gerald went to 5.0. He was visibly pleased with his success and always cooperated well. He had good word attack skills; his errors tended to be mistakes of one or two letters in a given word. He relied heavily on configuration clues and his comprehension was erratic, but his attention span and motivation were excellent. His concept development and vocabulary were uneven, and he was relatively unaware of some "common knowledges," but understood some rather esoteric ideas. Throughout the program he was very dependable, but he operated slowly. He indicated a willingness to work on his own during the summer on free reading of easy books for practice.

John started at 3.5 on the Gates Oral Reading Test and ended at 5.3. John was better on words in isolation, indicating more strength in word analysis skills than in comprehension. His fluent oral reading was deceptive. Further work with John should be couched in the study skills area. His work habits were seriously hampered by his satellite relationship with Maurice. He was potentially the best of the group in working on his own, in terms of relatively small need for supervision and support. He was reinforced by his successes to an extent that the other boys were not.

At the end of the semester the boys were asked to write how they felt about the program. The following are their statements as they were written:

Everett. I am glad sumeone took tim to help me get better grades (Everett had help in spelling eight of the words).

John. When i first came to this school i was geting fs in almost every subject then when i got into this class i have goting B, C in almost every subject.

Gerald. I thind this grop was wetwile I lernd a lot and I inproved my grades a grat dill. I inproved on my read and English, Soc. St., math a grat dill in this grop this year.

Tim. I have injoyed this year in Cherokee more than enly year in school. The Teathers in Cherokee have been verry helpfull in Helpping me in school work. I was not getting grades at all before I come to this school.

Maurice. I thought that I was real dumb until I got into the special group the 2 secemester and I think I learned quite a lot durin the second part of the year by comporasind cards with the first report card with the secound one.

Low mental ability per se is seldom a cause of reading difficulty; the difficulty is caused by requiring greater achievement than should be expected of slow learners. With the best teacher efforts to meet individual needs, there still will be many children who will get lost in the early stages of reading instruction. We can be sure that most of these children do not outgrow their reading problems.

Are we offering too little, too late?

BIBLIOGRAPHY

Bamman, Hans, and others. *Reading in the Secondary School.* New York: Longmans, 1961.

Bond, G. L., and Tinker, M. A. *Reading Difficulties, Their Diagnosis and Correction.* New York: Appleton, 1957.

Bullock, Harrison. *Helping the Non-Reading Pupil in the Secondary School.* New York: Teachers College Pr., 1956.

Carriker, William R. *Selected Books for Retarded Readers: Annotated, High Interest, Modified Vocabulary.* Lincoln, Neb.: State Dept. of Education, 1957.

Gray, Lillian. *Teaching Children to Read.* New York: Ronald, 1963.

Heagy, Dorothy, and Amato, Anthony. "Everyone Can Learn to Enjoy Reading," *Elementary English* 35:464–68 (November 1958).

Hester, Kathleen B. *Teaching Every Child to Read.* New York: Harper, 1964.

Hunt, Jacob T. "Easy and Interesting Fiction for the Handicapped Reader," *High School Journal* 39:378–85 (April 1956).

——. "Easy Non-Fictional Material for the Handicapped Reader," *High School Journal* 39:322–32 (March 1959).

Jewett, Anne. *Improving Reading in the Junior High School.* Bulletin No. 10, U.S. Dept. of HEW. Washington, D.C.: Govt. Print. Off., 1958.

Lundeen, Alma, and Prendergrass, Margaret. "Books for Retarded Readers," *Illinois Libraries* 43:271–87 (April 1961).

Roswell, Florence, and Chall, Jeanne. *Selected Materials for Children with Reading Disabilities.* New York: City College Educational Clinic, 1959.

Ruth, Sister Mary. "A List of Books for Retarded Readers at First, Second and Low Third Grade Level," *Elementary English* 38:79–86 (February 1961).

Strang, Ruth, and others. *Gateways to Readable Books.* New York: Wilson, 1958.

The Furious Children and the Library

A Problem in Mosaic Work

JOSEPH NOSHPITZ, M.D.

Creating a residential treatment unit is in many ways similar to constructing a mosaic. One has first to develop the many bits and parts, the little colored

Reprinted from *Top of the News,* Mar. 1960, pp. 12–15, May 1960, pp. 24–30, and Oct. 1960, pp. 48–63.

stones, the elements that will go together to form the finished work; and then one must organize these, blend them, balance them one against the other, and build them into the overall pattern which is a finished treatment design. Such a problem in mosaic work faced Dr. Fritz Redl when he undertook to create a residential setting for emotionally disturbed children at the Clinical Center of the National Institutes of Health.

The project began in 1953 when Dr. Redl came to Bethesda to initiate a long-range program for the study of hyper-aggressive youngsters. Patients were considered for this project when they had demonstrated severe disturbance in school, in the home, and in the neighborhood; in short, when they were showing aggressive behavior in every sphere of their lives. The children who were selected for this program have been variously dubbed "angry," "wolf children," "furious," and many another similar cognomen, all of which attempt to catch in a single colorful phrase the uncontrollable, impulsive, invasive, and incorrigible character of these youngsters. After the staff had gone through some preliminary training experiences, six boys were eventually admitted to become the subjects of intensive and protracted study. These boys were between eight and eleven years old at the time of admission. They were housed on a closed ward within the huge hospital building that dominates the grounds of the National Institutes of Health just outside of Bethesda, Maryland. The lives of these children were organized in great detail, with intense concentration on the possible psychological meanings of the many events and experiences that befell them, with a careful and conscious attempt to turn each of these experiences into a therapeutic vector. Thus, whether it was mealtime or ball game, quiet hour or excursion, disciplinary talking to or a picnic, the eye of the many trained people who worked with these youngsters was always on the therapeutic goals. Ever parallel to the more conscious and immediately available attention that the staff paid to the activities ran a secondary stream of thought asking: What does this mean? What will the long-range effect of that be? Is it too much? Is it too little? Is it the right kind of thing that should be happening here and now? And so forth.

Among other elements and bits that were fitted into the youngsters' lives were many events that might crudely be grouped under the term *socialization*. Ultimately the program was trying to make healthier people and better citizens out of these boys, and, by implication, to get them to use all of the potentials in their own character and personality make-up toward this end. It is with these values in mind that the following material should be read, for the library was one element in the mosaic, and an important one, as you will see, and the authors are some of the people who worked with the youngsters to help make it a therapeutic experience.

What the staff did with this particular treatment modality and what befell the boys is set forth in unvarnished detail in the ensuing pages; what lessons this story may have for educators, librarians, and the adult world in general in its contact with children time alone will teach us.

As the Librarian Sees It

MARGARET C. HANNIGAN

To the library staff, the boys were only six of four hundred patients who received service from the patients' library. They were an important six, however, and soon became our friends. For almost four years they visited the library once or twice a week. During this time we learned much about their background and personalities; we observed changes in them and rejoiced when they went on from us to public and school libraries. Nevertheless, we could give them only a fraction of our time, and in that respect our relationship with them parallels that between librarians and young people everywhere. It is with this in mind that I review our experience.

The boys and the library grew up together. When we first met them in the fall of 1954, they were little boys and our collection was meager and not completely catalogued. We were busily ordering new books and, naturally enough, the boys regarded many of these acquisitions as "just for them." We fostered their interest by showing them new materials as they arrived and explaining the processes required in order to prepare books for the shelves. We also demonstrated the reading aids provided for use by the physically handicapped and allowed them to operate each machine a few times to see how it worked.

We feel that the library held a unique position in the lives of the boys and in relation to the project in which they were participating. It was the first, and for some time the only, "trip" they made to other departments of the Clinical Center, and thus, from the beginning, it probably represented the world outside the hospital. The library is a pleasant, inviting room with an atmosphere of cordiality and freedom that cannot always be provided in other areas of the Center. Because the visit to the library was a privilege, the boys were on their best behavior when they came to see us and the many unhappy incidents which marred their lives and about which we heard so much seldom occurred on our premises. Only one or two boys, accompanied by a teacher or counselor, came to the library at a time. This eliminated much of the competitive sibling struggle and the associated behavior problems characteristic of the group; each of the youngsters had a chance to pursue his interests without fear of ridicule and an opportunity to feel that he was important in his own right to someone outside the ward and the schoolroom. Their visits were of two types; from the first, they came to the library weekly as part of their school program. In addition to selecting material they needed for class, they could choose books to read or have read to them on the ward. Later, a trip to the library to select recreational reading became a "free choice" part of the ward program, as well.

In addition to making the library a friendly, attractive place where the boys and their requests were treated with respect, we consciously tried to give them experiences they would not have on the ward. For instance, they met Gray Ladies and patient-workers on the staff as well as other patients and visitors who happened to be in the library. We tried to make them aware of the need to share materials with patients throughout the hospital. We felt rewarded when, in time, two boys brought their therapists to the library and introduced them to us, and when one offered to lend us his precious copy of *Air Force, a Pictorial History of American Airpower* which he had received as a gift, so that other patients could enjoy it.

Of course the main purpose of a library visit is to borrow books and magazines and to look up information. We were businesslike about this, giving serious attention to the boys' requests, keeping records of their interests, and making every possible effort to acquire or borrow anything that was needed. Four of the six boys had serious reading difficulties at first, but nonetheless learned to use the card catalog and to locate material on the shelves even before they developed skill in reading. With the teachers' help, the boys learned to state their requests with clarity and to examine books intelligently in order to locate the information they were seeking.

Several times we displayed the boys' work on the library bulletin board, and once we had an exhibit of their project on explorers. They seemed proud to have their work shown off, and would stop to call attention to it and to admire it when they passed the door. I mention this because the same boys found it almost impossible, at this time, to accept success on the ward or in the schoolroom and often destroyed what they had made rather than allow someone to see it. The library apparently was an "uncontaminated" place where they could safely enjoy their laurels.

If we had realized that one of the boys' main sources of difficulty lay in coping with restrictions, we might have been hesitant about setting limits and enforcing simple library rules. As it was, the library staff was not trained especially for work with disturbed children, so we adopted an intuitive common sense approach in our dealings with them. We were matter-of-fact about stating and trying to enforce our regulations and acted as if we took it for granted that they would be observed. As it developed, this was exactly what the clinical staff wanted us to do; we were representatives of external reality for the boys and would serve as a proving ground for their ability to pull themselves together to meet limit setting of this sort. We always explained the reasons for rules to the youngsters, and when we needed to set certain places apart as "off limits," we let the boys explore these work and storage areas before making them off limits.

Our experience with six "furious" boys, then, would indicate that the library is a place in which disturbed children can feel secure and are able both to accept certain controls and to experience gratifications that are not always possible in other situations.

The Library as a Tool in Reeducation

FLORENCE GLASER

Our youngsters were off the street, the "furious ones" who had been brought to the National Institute of Mental Health because of acts against society, and it seemed crazy to some of the hospital staff to contemplate taking them to the library. But I was their teacher; books and a library were part of teaching; and so, as a matter of course, I took our delinquent gang of six to the small, personalized library provided for the hospital's patients.

It turned out that the worriers had some basis for their concern; certainly, neither the school staff nor the library staff was prepared for what happened. Each of the six boys found something of interest in this library. One found the pneumatic tube station and started to monkey with its paraphernalia. One was attracted by the date stamps on the library desk and began marking everything within reach. One found boxes of materials at the end of the stacks—still unpacked in this very new library—and ripe for his unpackaging. One discovered a shelf of comics and stashed away a shirtful. One "escaped" through the door and into one of the many halls of this tremendous, then only partially inhabited, new hospital and had to be brought back.

It took some time to get over the "I told-you-so's" from institutionally more experienced staff members. Indeed, it took at least two years of planning and careful supervision for the library to become more than just one more arena for the wild impulsiveness of these boys —to make it a place for successful and meaningful experiences, a place for quiet understanding and refuge.

It was quickly obvious that things could not work out for the librarians, for the teachers, or for the kids if all the youngsters came at once. Trips were therefore planned for two boys at a time, accompanied by a teacher. Limits were worked out for the library by the teacher and the librarians, who then acted to enforce them. As spelled out to the boys, the limits said:

1. You must be quiet and thoughtful of other patients here.
2. You can't play with gadgets without specific permission, although you may ask to use the stamper, or see how the machine works for readers who can't hold a book.
3. You may take out whatever books are required for school assignments, but you may take out only two books to have on the ward.
4. You may take out only two comic books, but they must be left with a ward counselor, or deposited outside the schoolroom.
5. Running away from the adult on the way to or from the library, or other disapproved acts, deprives you of the privilege of a library trip for as long as the teacher thinks advisable.

Such rules as these built up a specialness to this trip off the locked ward, and as the library was one of the few places in this huge building where the children were welcome, and where it was expected they could conform, it became a more and more desirable place.

Interest in the books in the library came later.

Library Became a "Choice" Spot. At first, the regular weekly trips to the library were scheduled as part of the program rather than left to the choice of the individual child. (On the other hand, if a child refused to go, no effort was made to compel him.) As time went on, however, these trips became so popular that they were included among the activities children could choose on two afternoons a week, such as trips to the mouse lab, the carpenter shop, and the glass blower. A child considered himself "gypped" if he didn't get to go to the library at least once a week; and often children requested the library as their first choice on both "choice afternoons." Eventually, several of the boys were allowed to go alone, i.e., unaccompanied by an adult, when a special book was needed or when there were books to be returned.

The ability to conform to socially required behavior patterns manifested itself in these brief visits to the library quite a while before acceptable behavior became a general pattern for these boys. At the time it helped both the children and the teachers to know that there were sparks of potential for adjustment within these otherwise grossly maladjusted boys.

A library is for books—and I have talked only of library behavior. As I said before, the books came later—and slowly. In spite of the concerted efforts of an understanding, patient librarian and determined teachers to touch on the right interests and reading levels of these boys, for a long time it seemed hopeless to try to bring reading into their lives. Some couldn't read and others wouldn't. Some of the staff conjectured, "to read is to learn, to learn is to grow up, and to grow up is too much of a threat."

We tried to use direct action. Some of the boys went to the library only to get new comic books; under the duress of our condition of "no book—no comic book," they would grab any book without even looking at it. One boy would read only the *Hardy Boys*, and we had to extend the comic book rule to include this series.

Interests Were Contagious. However, we found that indirect approaches worked better. We had white mice, brown mice, pinto mice, and black mice in the schoolroom, given to the boys by indulgent workers in the mouse lab. Care of these mice first led two boys to reference books. Later, turtles became the focus of all living for one boy. Contagion of all kinds was easy among six boys who ate, slept, played, and went to school together with no outside stimulation. All six were soon slaves to turtles of every kind. The library then became a source of "terribly" needed information about the care of turtles. Frogs and fish were caught on ward fishing trips, and these increased the boys' curiosity to "find out" from books what no one could tell them. So the first interest in books was to satisfy real curiosity about the animals which had become important to them.

Along with this went one boy's interest in electricity, which for him served more as a device for gaining prestige than as a genuine interest. When he was younger, his older brothers had played tricks on him with electrical gadgets, and out of this he had acquired some practical knowledge. But his knowledge soon turned out to have many gaps, whereupon he was led to books on experiments with electricity. Again contagion turned the interests of the others, too, toward experiments and, in time, to the books describing them, from "How to melt a crayon" to "How to build a rocket."

School-directed projects and film strips in the classroom, and the unlooked for assistance of TV on the ward led the boys into a fascination with dinosaurs, Davy Crockett, Paul Bunyan, Robin Hood, knights in armor, army tanks, guns and insignia, to name just a few. These topics in turn easily led to books for reading, being read to, looking at, and copying from. And the library was the source for satisfying the fascination.

One of our youngsters had severe difficulties in reading. Even after two years of work, he could still read only in a preprimer in the classroom. Nonetheless, by dint of the tolerance and patience of the librarian, he learned how to use the card catalog, and he could find anything on the shelves by himself. He became the school's self-appointed librarian, kept track of books that were due, and was efficient in getting them back to the library. When this boy moved from the hospital school to a public school, he became the librarian for his class there and won recognition for a good job.

They Learned to Share. The fact that the library was small made it easier for the children to make use of it. Physically, it was cozy, something of a refuge. Choices were limited, a helpful state of affairs for boys to whom a broad range of choice was disorganizing. The boys gradually learned to share a good book among themselves; later, they came to appreciate that other patients in the hospital might be waiting for a particular book, and therefore made a point of returning it as soon as they could. Before they left they had even learned to exhibit school projects in the library for the enjoyment of others and to loan their own personal books and comic books to the library so that other patients might use them. For such "antisocial" children this was a significant accomplishment indeed.

Use of the Library in a Psychiatric Setting

JOEL VERNICK

The planning of a daily activity program on a children's psychiatric ward makes it necessary to consider such elements as the use of games, sports, outside trips, arts and crafts, shop, etc., in terms of their treatment potential as well as from the point of view of the degree of enjoyment and gratification they provide. These are media through which the children would express their symptoms in relation to impulsivity control, learn new skills in their relationships with peers and adults, increase their physical skills through participation in the activity itself, and also test out their newly developed, reorganized, or improved skills. From the participation of the children in the daily program, the staff would be in a position to gather information which would make for a better understanding of the individual and group patterns of behavior, data which, in turn, can lead to more adequate and appropriate techniques for dealing with behavior as well as to more productive program planning.

During the beginning phase of the boys' hospitalization, their numerous behavior and relationship problems made it necessary to plan for activities which involved a minimum of contact with adults and children outside the ward setting. However, later on, when it was felt that such experiences were indicated, the library became one of the sources to be utilized for treatment and research. This went on at many levels. Thus, it was felt that while using the library the children would have the opportunity to meet other patients, both adults and children, with whom they might interact. This could be on a very informal basis—a few words exchanged, some general conversation, or no interaction at all. They would not be thrust into a situation which would make too many demands upon them to relate to others. Moreover, the library could offer them a setting in which, at their own slow pace, they might establish and maintain a relationship with the librarians, adults with some authority who were not "contaminated" by the disturbing events in the daily life on the ward.

Autonomous Experience. Among other facets of the library experience which were considered of potential value was the high degree of autonomy offered the child in this setting. A brief period of observing children in a library will quickly make one aware of the significance of this as they wander about the room viewing and handling many books and magazines with much gratification. With our youngsters this usually terminated in a decision to check out certain books. The library also offers the child an opportunity to learn the use of materials and procedures which increase his capacity to function more adequately and independently. Last but not least, the library is a place where the child can go to "get away" from the pressures of his daily life.

In order that the children might obtain maximum benefit from use of the library, it was necessary for the ward and library staffs to evolve specific techniques and procedures for managing them while they were there. During the beginning phase of their treatment, one of these consisted in offering the library as a free choice activity, one which they could accept or reject. To judge by the minimum of refusals, it was immediately evident that the library had assumed no small area of interest for them.

Another technique utilized was to schedule only one boy, or at the most two boys, for each trip. This enabled the ward and library staff to offer each child the maximum of individual attention with the library procedures and in selecting books. If at all possible, the ward person would let the child and librarian work together, thus supporting the opportunity for the child to become involved in a positive experience with an "outside adult." It was necessary to plan in this way so that the child might feel that if his own controls were in danger of breaking down there would be an adult from the ward who could and would be able to help him settle down. During this phase it was not uncommon for a child to start dashing about the room, misusing library equipment, etc., and when efforts of staff to help him gain control were not successful, it was necessary to remove the child from the room. Usually the ward person would then take over, since he was familiar with the child, his behavior, and handing techniques indicated. This use of the ward person was also necessary since we wished the library staff to preserve its positive, "uncontaminated" role, and not become involved in such matters.

During this period we also limited to two the number of books the children might check out. This placed less pressure upon the child to make decisions about which books he would check out; decision-making was one of the areas which aroused much confusion and anxiety. The limit of two books was also necessary since staff recognized that the care and return of the books would be largely up to them, for the children, as yet, were not able to assume such responsibility.

Avoided "Over-Exposure." We also spaced the library

periods so that the children would not get an "over-exposure" to the setting which could limit its effectiveness for the purposes already mentioned. However, sufficient flexibility was maintained to allow for unscheduled trips when requested. As the boys were more able to participate in the planning of their weekly activity program, and as they acquired an increasing proficiency in the use of the library, improved ability to read, and increased attention span in pursuing subjects of interest, we were able to use the library as a more flexible segment of the ward program. We also were able to do away with the limitation on the number of books which they could withdraw.

Ultimately, when the ward was no longer a locked ward, during their free time the boys could go to the library unaccompanied. With this degree of flexibility, the library developed another function; in effect, it became a place of refuge. In earlier periods, when a child had difficulty with his peers or adults, a temper tantrum would be the usual outcome. As the youngsters began to develop techniques with which to cope evermore realistically with their problems with peers and adults, several of them learned to utilize the library as a place they could go to "cool off," instead of venting their feelings in a tantrum. This was an important step in their struggle between the infantile mode of living, with its uncontrolled behavior, and more healthy and realistic methods of coming to grips with their daily problems.

During a later phase of the children's hospitalization, their positive relationship to the library and its staff was utilized in yet another area. They became interested in money, and working, and requested part-time work for pay. At this point, it was not possible for us to arrange for payment for their work, but we offered them the opportunity to help out in various parts of the hospital. This they accepted. The matter was discussed with the librarian and a plan was set up for one of the boys to help out in the library once a week. This job involved the sorting of magazines according to months and years. Superficially, this might appear to be an extremely simple task for a ten-year-old; in fact, it was a rather demanding job for this boy whose interest span, even in the games and other activities he liked very much, was of short duration. It was necessary for a person from the ward to remain "on the job" with him to help carry through the instructions of the librarian, to help him stack the magazines, and to be on hand to help bring the job to an end when it was evident that he was rapidly reaching his saturation point. After several weeks, the boy decided that he did not wish to return to his job. Even though his tolerance for the demands of his job was of short duration, it was an important step in this phase of his treatment. This was a time when several of the boys were feeling the need to test out their in-creasing capacity to delay impulsive gratification and to substitute newfound skills and positive relationships to peers and adults on the ward and "in the outside world" as well. Their readiness to permit themselves to succeed at some given task, and to accept the appropriate praise from adults for their efforts, was of no minor significance in their progress.

Importance of Large Room. The physical plant of the patient library was also a factor in the success of our program. It was contained in one room, the size of three patient rooms. Why was size important? For our impulse-ridden children, the spatial stimuli often aroused their need to act out their impulses. A large room "invites" mobility, and even in a public library it is not uncommon for the librarian to have to caution children not to dash around. Usually, of course, this limit is accepted. Our children were far more ready than normal children to respond to the lure offered by space; thus, a rather small but well stocked library was conducive to establishing a good relationship with the staff, general acceptance of limits, and proper use of materials and equipment.

While I have been discussing the use of the library in a specific psychiatric setting, I believe it is possible to extend similar thinking and strategy to children in the community who use the public library. Librarians are often called upon to deal with children who have difficulty in adjusting to limits. The usual suggestions and warnings about "not making too much noise," "no running around," etc., often are not successful, and as a result the child might be asked to leave the library. Another frequently identified "type" is the child who spends a great deal of time in the library. While he is no management problem for the library staff, his extensive isolation from "the outside world" is symptomatic.

The library, as a refuge from the pressures of the "outside world," is utilized to varying degrees according to the needs of the individual and may serve an important purpose for a given child. We have long since recognized the importance of the teacher in the life of children; perhaps it would behoove us to take a closer look at the role played by the library and librarian. Just as has been done in the classroom, we might now turn toward the development of techniques and strategy that might be utilized by the librarian to recognize, to understand better, and to help the "problem" children enjoy a more productive experience in contacts with her.

Link between Hospital and Community

EDITH M. MAEDA

Attending a library was not a brand new experience for our children. Prior to their hospitalization, each child had had access to a school or public library. The patients' library, however, had the advantage of providing a setting for them within the hospital that was at once familiar and yet free from involvement in their immediate treatment procedures. They grew to know their library well and to adjust to it in a relatively healthy way.

This familiarity remained a factor in the later steps out into the community. While they boys were still living on a closed ward, the librarian and the school teachers arranged a trip to the public library in the community. Now the children had the opportunity once again to explore a piece of external social reality and their own capacities to adjust to it, but this time a familiar setting which offered built-in limits and controls. In many ways, the public library was similar to our own National Institutes of Health library, but it was housed in a much larger structure. This larger space allowed more freedom for movement, a situation which had often enough created problems for these children; here, however, they were able to call on past experiences for support, and they managed it well.

After several years of closed ward care, the children moved to an open setting on National Institutes of Health grounds. They lived in a homelike cottage, attended public schools, and the public library became a part of their immediate orbit. It was for them a place they could go to by choice. Each child applied for a library card, the possession of which became an important link to the community after their two and one-half to three years on a closed ward. Since our own National Institutes of Health library was closer, even after they transferred to the cottage, the boys often found it convenient to go there for reading material. However, when special subjects, such as sports, became prominent in their school adjustment, several of the boys asked to pursue this subject in the public library.

The help that the library provided in the transition from a closed to an open setting, and the role it then played in the public school adjustment of these boys was very material. By allowing the youngsters to retreat in some instances, it permitted them the chance to make a healthy choice, a choice they had to make in order to exercise some control over the impulsivity which was their main behavioral problem. It is interesting to note that two of our most impulse-ridden children found the library a haven of special value.

For example:

Tony, the most infantile in the group, requested many hours in the library, both from the school staff and from the ward personnel. Superficially, it would seem that he was using the library as a means of running away from difficult problems that might arise for him in the classroom and on the ward. Actually, this was a tactic he had learned as a constructive activity to help him organize himself. The structure of the library and its immediate availability gave him the containment he needed; from there he could go on to learn other skills. He was considered the "baby" and the "scapegoat" by the other youngsters in the program, and he inevitably acted these roles when he was with them. It was at our National Institutes of Health library that Tony applied himself long enough to learn the card catalog system, a bit of mastery which assumed the proportions of a real discovery for him, and allowed him to make a big step in independence, one that otherwise had little room to take place while he was closely involved with his peer group.

The use of the library continued to be important for Tony during the critical phase of his adjustment to the public school system. Shortly after his enrollment in school, he was selected as class librarian, a situation providing this insecure "baby" with a built-in role that carried respect and was known to and accepted by his classmates. This made the classroom situation more safe for Tony. Predictably, however, in his less structured recess contacts, where he was exposed to a larger group of free-milling youngsters, he had more difficulty and on several occasions got into "fights" when kids teased him. This in turn resulted in his confinement to the classroom during recess periods, for there he did so much better.

This illustration points up the influence of group role on one individual. Whether Tony was being the respected class librarian or the teased schoolyard scapegoat, he was still responding to group demands. However, with the opportunity to practice techniques which made him acceptable and which in turn gave him confidence in at least one important situation, he could concentrate on expanding his area of competence in the hope of some day becoming an acceptable member of the group in more areas as well. In this instance, the library offered a vital link from the hospital to the community.

On the other hand, another child who "fought" hard and furiously, as if he felt that he had to test each new and meaningful contact, also used the library or a book as a retreat. But in his case this pattern, which was clearly recognized by the staff, could be pointed up to him as a springboard from which to discuss his real problems.

For example:

Frank had been having difficulty in school all day. He had not been able to settle down to his work and had spent the time trying to annoy others in the class. He had been removed from the classroom at one point and had remained in the hall for a short while with a counselor. When school was over and the afternoon program on the ward commenced, Frank continued his efforts to annoy others in the group. At one point a kick ball game was suggested. When the two captains were chosen, both made it clear they did not want Frank on their teams. He was rather unhappy about this rejection by the group. The counselor made an attempt to "help" the captains choose Frank, but to no avail. He stood by sullenly as the game started and after a few moments he requested a trip to the library.

His technique to get out of difficult situations was recognized by the adults who used this as an "in" in opening up with him a discussion of the reasons he felt he had to "hide" behind a book. This latter point offered a natural beginning for many life space interviews on the ward. It gave the adults a grip on a problem which Frank would have to face realistically in order to get along in the school and the community.

These were disturbed children who needed help in filling the "gaps" between home, hospital, school, and community. Special places had special meanings and particular jobs to do, and the library was exploited to its fullest to provide the links to the community to which these children would eventually return.

What We Can Do for Them Right Now

FRITZ REDL

After all that has been said in these columns by my coworkers—Dr. Noshpitz, Miss Hannigan, Mrs. Glaser, Joel Vernick, and Miss Maeda—the main thing I could add is a deep regret that we didn't have sense enough to insist on a chance for a much more thoroughly organized and more solidly supported research project on the full range of the book-and-library experience of our children, from the day we started out—all the way through. As it stands now, all we can do is hope that others may take our warning to heart after reading about our trials and tribulations and build a full-fledged research—*and* service—design along the library line into any residential therapy project they may have the opportunity to undertake.

Two questions, though, seem to me especially urgent, and in need of being pulled into the limelight right now: (1) Just what is it that the "library experience" can contribute to the overall therapy design for the hyper-aggressive and ego-disturbed child? (2) What does it take to bring it all about?

To tackle question number two, namely, just what it takes on "our side"—the librarian and the rest of the treatment staff—beyond the hints already contained in my coworkers' stories as they appeared in this sequence, would fascinate me no end, but it seems to me an issue so important and so involved that I cannot hope to manage even part of it in this short space. Since question number one, about the actual "clinical value" of our children's library experiences, has already been amply illustrated by my colleagues, I might try to remain less loquacious while simply summarizing the highlights they have been trying to convey.

It seems to me that on any tentative—and of course most incomplete—list of "this much we know right now," the following items would appear as essential "chances" the library has in its therapeutic role for the "Children Who Hate":

A Piece of "Outside World," Safely Smuggled into the Children's Lives. With child patients like ours, it is absolutely essential that one create a "closed" framework for their lives. While rich in program and activity opportunities, affectional supplies, and loaded with wise clinical and educational handing, a "closed ward" still remains—and purposely so—shut off from the rest of the world. For some of these children such a state of affairs needs to continue for months, or even years. It must be obvious what price we may be paying for keeping them in such "clinically airtight" life space for such a long stretch. So, naturally, as improvements set in, we are eager to find ways in which to puncture this clinical tightness so as to let the outside world in—and our kids out—without too heavy a price in terms of therapeutic risks.

It is the library of a hospital or treatment center of this sort which seems to have the best chance to become this "first door into the outside world" for many child patients. In the case of our youngsters, this was quite visibly so. At a time when more or less "normal" interactions with other people—even on our guarded trips and excursions outside the hospital—were quite impossible or rare, it was our National Institutes of Health library where we could provide such a chance. There they met "adults" who were not perceived by them as part of their more narrow "home base treatment team" at first, such as librarians—in their role as such—or other patients of many varieties, not psychiatric patients only. There they met other children who had been hospitalized for different reasons and with whom they could not yet have been able to manage any reasonable play life on their own ward. The fact that our National Institutes of Health library was, geographically, still part of our larger life frame, yet kept free from the too "treatment oriented" excitement of daily ward life, made the uniqueness of this experience possible.

Exposure to High-Structure and High-Status Patterns, Yet Tax-free from Otherwise Battle-loaded Demands. Of course our children were exposed to books, to situations where they would be required to remain still and sit quietly (for a change and for a while), and to a wider variety of limitations of their behavioral desires, in many other places in their ward and school life with us, too. Only our school, in order to have any chance at all, already had to lower its "status" assumption as well as loosen its structural pattern, to accommodate the severe disturbedness of the children's pathological needs. The same holds true for their daily program on the ward. In short, ward program and school, during this phase of their treatment, had stopped being representative for them as a world where "books and learning" are revered for their own sake, and these situations had become for them much more a battleground for the daily struggle between educational challenge and pathological defiance, with all the fireworks this entails.

What I am trying to point at is the fact that, while all this was, necessarily, going on, it was the *library* which could remain a *high status and high structure* situation in its own right—not "just" there for the therapy of our child patients with a purpose and a value system of its own well maintained and clearly "oozing" out of its book-studded walls. Yet, this specific library didn't just "ooze" its values at innocent customers. While offering all the "kudos" that come from being a proud consumer in such a highfalutin' joint, this specific library could afford to smile tolerantly on a considerable range of inappropriate behavior and usage, without having to challenge it too much. Thus, the experience for our child patients would read something like this: "Look at us, here we are, in this fancy place with all them books and stuff around, and moving around in this like any regular guy or even grownups. Even the adults who bring us here change a little bit when they enter this joint. And yet, while there are lots of books and it is quite obvious these gals would like us to read them, they still don't really mind too much if we don't. They like us enough to have us around even if we don't do much more with their stuff than play with it, or put these books in and out without really reading anything. They only let our counselors bounce us back to the ward if it gets too rough, and even then they seem sorry to see us go. . . ."

In short, our children had a chance to *visualize themselves as people sane enough* to go to a library with a real library air in it, not just "one of those things the therapists make up for us to destroy to begin with," without at the same time being taken up too seriously on the degree to which they could live up to such a role. And all this in a phase of their treatment where such an experience of even allowing themselves to be seen by themselves as normal and sane would be quite unthinkable in the rest of their lives. To provide for them—though only for short durations at a time—this opportunity of experiencing themselves in a much more "worthwhile role" than they would be able to live up to for long is one of the trickiest clinical maneuvers known in residential therapy. For us, it was our library that helped us come close to it, when we could hardly produce it as yet anywhere else.

Taste-Preparation for Postsituational Use. Some of the books our kids would finger during their library visits remained nothing but the manipulative discharge-prop of the moment. Yet, sometimes they would begin to drag books with them. True, at first with not much serious intent, and certainly with no intention of "reading them." However, these books were lying around in their playrooms, their bedrooms, on their bunks. And sometimes they didn't remain just "any books." They were books "their librarians had allowed them to take out." They still had the smell of that generous gesture with them, and that aftertaste of an experience of "trust"—never mind all the other smells to which they had been exposed in the meantime.

Occasionally, some of this would pay off. In idle or empty, and angry or sad moments, some of these books would suddenly remind them of the "feeling tone" of that library visit the other day. An accumulation of such events would finally get them to change some of these books from the "play gadgets we had wheedled out of those adults," which they had become, back into books. Anyway, it seems to me—though I have no decently recorded "evidence" to prove all this—that this factor might also explain why most of their borrowed library books received so much better treatment from our kids than we had any reason to expect. Also, during their visits in the library, they could pick up an image of the "model" of a "person as a reader," without being prematurely forced into that role. I think that the acquisition of this image, through their library experience, had something to do with their ability to find and accept themselves in such a role earlier than we would otherwise have hoped.

Emergence of the Concept of the "Benign Guardian" of Societal Treasures. The way our kids would naturally look at life, *anybody who guarded anything*—from a museum statue to the gadgets in a gift shop to the paints the teacher might keep locked up when not in use—would be seen by them in either of two ways only. He would be viewed by them as a stupid, pompous ass—"who does he think he is anyway?"—who doesn't like kids to finger his prized hoard and deserves to be outwitted by ruse. Or he would appear to them as a hostile, kid-devouring ogre who hates people in general, kids in particular, and has only one aim in life, namely to "protect his precious stuff from being enjoyed by anybody else, the dirty SOB."

In our life with the children on the ward and in the therapy hours and even in school, we had to avoid this image in a wide berth, relinquish our "guardian" role as much as we could afford, just so as to make ourselves understandable as benign facilitators rather than preventors of enjoyment or the use of tools. By the very necessity of doing that, though, we had also surrendered—or at least blurred—our image as "guardians" in their eyes. In the library, however, we could manage to maintain both: The reality-role as a "guardian" of toys and tools, and the perception of our benign attitude toward their consumption and toward the enjoyment of what we were guardians of.

Such an achievement is possible only if librarian and child-caring adult (counselor, nurse, attendant, teacher, psychiatrist—whoever would be with them on their library visits as part of their "ward personnel") would function as a well-orchestrated team. Thus, as you have seen from the stories of my coworkers, we took great care to protect the librarian from interventions in child behavior which would have been too damaging to the children's perception of her "benign role." We—those of us who lived with them all the time—could afford more easily to draw upon us their temporary wrath of interruption-hostility or whatever other child anger is produced in the unavoidable melee of behavioral interference. For we could "live down" in the rest of the hours of a given day whatever hostile feelings a bouncing or other intervention incident might have drawn upon our heads. It was through this carefully planned "division of labor" that we were able to help the librarians remain in the role of "friendly enabler of fun with books." Their role, whenever things did get out of hand, would thus remain limited to that of the person who only points out where the limits are, while we loaded ourselves with the task of enforcing them. However—this is only half the story. For, in order for this "role protection" to work, it was also essential that our own intervention in the children's behavior, no matter how drastic, remain totally benign and nonpunitive. Had we, for instance, punished the children for library misbehavior, however wisely or deservedly, the anger for this experience would still have fallen on the librarian's head as the one whose fault it really was that they got punished by us. Since our interventions, including that of bodily removal from an excited scene, were always of the nature of "marginal situational restraint," with all the cautions that such policy demands on clinical grounds, and since even such situations were usually picked up for later discussion in a "Life Space Interview,"[1] any contamination of their perception of the benign intent of the librarian through all this was avoided. The wonderful spectacle of at least one "uncontaminated" and correct perception of an adult's benign role in their lives, namely the librarian's emerging in their messy minds, was well worth the temporary loss of relationships that we had to take upon ourselves through such strategy. I, personally, have no doubt that the wonderful team arrangement between our "life space staff" and the "librarians" in our project made it possible for those children to elevate their perception of the benign guardian role of the librarian to the level of a model which later helped to decontaminate even other "guardian" roles from pathological distortions, in their subsequent return to the community.

Refuge from Unbearable Stress. I was worried at first, when I noticed how much emphasis our librarians, as well as the rest of my staff, put in their articles in this sequence, on the benefit our kids derived from using our library as a "refuge and haven" from the stress of life, as a welcome niche for "escape." What worried me a bit was not the issue as such, but the danger that this type of statement might be misread as meaning that the library experience for a sick child might primarily be viewed as "just an escape if things get too tough" on the ward, and nothing more. So I would like to hasten to add to my colleagues' descriptions the following argument as a defense for what they portrayed:

First of all, if we call our children's use of the library, or of books and reading in general, occasionally a "defense" or an "escape," we do not mean to imply that this is all there is to it, or that this is one of the major "goals" in the library experience to begin with. We do, however, imply that in the treatment of children as severely disturbed as ours, even a gain as little and "low down" as this one may become, clinically, of very great importance indeed. So if librarians might worry that the most important values their medium has to contribute seem to be blurred through these statements about "escape," I would like to remind them that even a long detour is very much worth while if it eventually leads a kid closer to accepting the more important goals we may have in store. In short, what I am trying to say is this: No matter how devoted and proud you are of the value of the treasure you are trying to insert into people's lives, never mind if you see it temporarily "abused" for ulterior motives or "wasted" on "subordinate subgoals." Those who can't stand to see their religious symbol abused or ridiculed, or even misused at times, had better stay in their home-town church. They certainly wouldn't do much good as missionaries with a tough heathen tribe. You have to be willing to have your best books somewhat abused, your valuable atmosphere of reading and contemplation "wasted" occasionally, on something as trivial as "escape from the stress of the day," if you hope at all to find a pathway into your child patient's soul for your more lofty goals.

Second, though, I also want to stick up for the clinical value and therapeutic realism that lie in the use of anything—even a library—for really effective temporary relief and escape, whenever pressures from within or without become too much to bear. It is our experience that there are many moments in the process of growing up and therapy where the ability to find an escape that works without doing clinical damage is not only something to be "indulged in," but is an essential condition for the continued treatment process as such. far as our kids are concerned, what was wrong with them was *not only* that they were escaping many of the issues of real life they should have faced, but that they were quite unequipped and unable to find constructive escapes for those pressures which they were not ready to face at a given time, anyway. In fact, if I had the time and space to do it in, I would like to show you in detail how much the treatment success with this type of child depends on the skill of teaching them *how to escape constructively, instead of meeting a stress situation in a sick way.* In short—for the stretch of therapy which we are talking about now, we needed, as one of the important offerings which a good library can supply, its ability of being perceived, by the child, as an uncontaminated haven from unbearable strain. The fact that, after this therapeutic phase has been gone through, other functions become more important in their lives, is a story in its own right, but does not deduct from the clinical value of the "refuge service" to the child, who often needs a nice and psychologically clean haven from the inner and outer stress of reorientation to a new life.

What holds for many people in their ordinary lives is certainly true for life in a psychiatric ward, especially a closed one: There is no hiding place down there. The hiding places the kids have brought with them are no good and can only support and prolong their sickness. Life without a hiding place, even in the best "therapeutic milieu" is more than any child patient can take. To find "hiding places" which we can clinically afford and which are therapeutically clean and yet perceived as effective by the child, is probably one of the most urgent—and as yet sorely neglected—challenges in all residential treatment strategy.

In conclusion, as librarians, as well as in your role as therapists, you may now be angry with me for closing my list of "library benefits for the hospitalized child" right here, instead of going further down the line and arriving at more lofty, more "library-conscious," and also therapeutically fancier points. However, do not mind too much to have to stop so soon. For, I have no doubt that the librarians among you are all aware of the "deeper" levels of what a library and its books, and the people who mediate between them and the patients, have to contribute to the overall therapeutic task. It is the "little things" that become paramount in the survival with patients who have library-obnoxious symptoms and are ridden by a book-alien type of pathology to begin with, that we have neglected far too long. Also, I have a hunch that any one of the points we have listed in this sequence might strike a familiar chord in all those librarians who do not deal with a hospital population of "furious children" undergoing residential therapy, but who are trying to be of help to the normally library-consuming child population in open community life. For what we saw emerge, in condensed and often grotesquely distorted form, with the children in our ward, might well turn up as an occasional problem here and there in library life with the "normal child," especially during their periods of developmental change or environmental stress. We might hope that the strategies and techniques we had to evolve to help our kids make the grade as future library citizens might be a thought stimulant for the more community-imbedded librarian, too.

NOTE

1. "The Life Space Interview Workshop 1957," *The American Journal of Orthopsychiatry* 29:1–26 (January 1959).

PART 5

Conflict Resolution through Literature

Reading guidance and bibliotherapy should not be thought of as distinct entities, but as related behaviors on the spectrum of literature intervention. The significance of the two approaches lies in the power of literature, which, when carefully used, can clarify issues and show how problems might be solved. Historically, literature has been the vehicle through which men and women gained insights into the human effects of political, social, religious, and psychological conduct. Thus, books have long provided potent channels for emotional release or catharsis. With a vast repository of literary works available, a multitude of opportunities and options for developing a therapeutic milieu are open to the librarian.

Librarians have frequently identified some of the personal, developmental, and social situations faced by children and youth, found their counterparts in literature, and tried to help students develop models or insights into dealing with their problems. For example, sibling rivalry, feelings of loneliness, a sense of loss or desertion are all conditions mirrored in children's literature. Through exposure to selected stories, poems, and media, followed by role-playing activities or discussions, students' problems are analyzed, alternate modes of response are evaluated, and behavioral decisions are made. Thus, patterns for restructuring, as well

as emotional relief, can be found through a directed interaction with literature.

Bibliotherapy, though similar in principle to reading guidance, is much more focused. This technique addresses itself to individuals who manifest dysfunctional behavior and attempts to help them solve their problems. In an institutional setting, bibliotherapy is frequently directed by a psychotherapist and the librarian is a vital team member whose professional contributions are part of a coordinated treatment plan.

In a noninstitutional setting, the librarian still needs to perceive of one facet of that role as therapeutic, often coordinating her/his efforts with those of the classroom teacher and the counseling staff in expanding opportunities for need satisfaction. The librarian's knowledge of reading guidance and bibliotherapeutic techniques can effectively serve the entire school population. However, when the librarian is called on to respond to the adjustment problems often associated with exceptionality, these approaches become critical.

Handicapped children, like their age mates, have the usual stresses of growing up to cope with. In some instances, those conflicts are exacerbated by a multitude of factors which may emerge from the disability, and eventuate, in effect, in a second handicap. Ironically, the means of discharging

135

frustration are often closed off, the choice of responses are frequently inappropriate and consequently result in further difficulties. Social skills are sometimes underdeveloped because of uneveness in experiential background, lack of exposure to appropriate models, insufficient opportunity to perceive social cues and subsequently internalize modes of desirable behavior.

From the empirical and theoretical accounts which follow, the librarian planning to respond to the needs of the troubled child will find insight into the process of need satisfaction through literature.

Shrodes lays a foundation for the comprehension of the classical literary experience wherein the individual filters what he/she reads and invests it with personalized meaning. She views the act of reading as a profound life experience, an involvement with art and aesthetics at a deep emotional level. This symbiotic union is the basis for the possibility of the bibliotherapeutic process. Her assertion that the writer endows experience with meaning but does not impose judgment is open to question, however. Often the organization, stress, style, dialogue, or other elements of the endeavor are highly persuasive and influence by indirection, at least, the belief system of the reader. In other cases, the very ambiguity of the writing permits facile projection by the troubled reader. The power of the literary symbol is clearly demonstrated and yet on various personality types the effects are not necessarily beneficial. Literature acts as a catalyst for modifying defenses and thus becomes a potent force for influencing behavior in stressful situations. This author emphasizes the importance of fully understanding both the material and the needs of the reader, for the same literary stimulus will generate varied responses in different viewers dependent upon their psychological requirements. Thus, she implies the importance of a high level of expertise on the part of the bibliotherapist. Shrodes believes that literature does not create or initiate reprehensible behaviors, but, in its power to trigger latent feelings, brings to an accessible level emotions to which a competent therapist can respond (also see Kvaraceus).

Children must confront many tension-generating and traumatic events during their developmental years. Cianciolo contends that books can provide psychological relief in two critical ways: children can solve problems they are currently grappling with through vicariously experiencing similar problems in literature; and children can also develop coping competencies through reading which anticipates future sources of conflict. This is of prime importance to the handicapped who have few if any peer or adult models and often have limited social experience on which to build response strategies to stress. Characteristics of books which have promise of being bibliotherapeutic and reports on research in the field are included. Cianciolo cautions that books must have literary value to be effective and that librarians need to skillfully match books with readers. Further research is clearly necessary, particularly on the validity of her intriguing recommendations for preventative bibliotherapy.

Sattley contends that gifted children are frequently encouraged to read books which are beyond their experiential, maturational, or emotional level. She asserts that they will miss the pleasures and values of those excellent books which address themselves to the problems faced by chronological peers. Bypassing these literary experiences, she feels, has the effect of cutting them off from age-related concerns shared by their contemporaries and depriving them of the patterns they need for growth and self-understanding in the noncognitive areas. By drawing attention to the psychological and emotional needs of high-achieving children, the author reminds us of the necessity of responding to the whole child. She vetoes catapulting children into literary experiences for which they are presumably unready. How does the librarian resolve the conflict between the cognitive needs of gifted children which Beswick promulgates and their affective needs as described by Sattley?

Vidler, in a tantalizingly brief article, describes the values to the emotionally disturbed youngster of puppet therapy with a fairy-tale cast. The simplicity of character development, the highly visual, easily identifiable prototypes, and the impact of the medium itself combine to provide a powerful therapeutic tool for these children. The article suggests to the psychoeducationally oriented librarian how his/her skills can be utilized in moving from the print format to an action-based puppet theater experience, a mode especially desirable for the conduct-disturbed, low achieving reader. The brevity of this article places a burden on librarians to further explore this technique on their own.

In Sutherland's personal narrative, the reader observes a general psychological problem of the severely handicapped. Despite the strongest support and understanding, intangible barriers will be erected. Sutherland's article indicates that the exceptional youngster must not be placed in any situation that encourages psychological isolation, for this allows the handicapped to conclude that theirs is a tragic and solitary destiny. For Sutherland, literature was the means of minimizing her feelings of difference, of becoming convinced of the universality of her interests and aspirations. The title of her article is startling. It does, however, effectively shock librarians into squarely facing the significance of their role in the life of the severely disabled. The author compels the librarian to see beyond the obvious disability to the core human needs of these readers and to treat them with respect. Sutherland also insists that the impairments of severely disabled readers must not be sentimentalized, but urges that the existential human factor be elevated to prime consideration.

Another way to approach bibliotherapy is to consider not only the developmental needs but also those basic and persisting needs that are common to all. One can compile lists of books with possible therapeutic potential and attempt to classify general needs so that a prescriptive match can be obtained. Hutcherson's paper identifies these needs as emotional security, material security, spiritual security, and peer acceptance. Her particular contribution is in describing how individual titles can be used in compensating for particular lacks in these areas. Further, she avers that one of the major values of bibliotherapy with the young is that it provides an arena within which they can react to experiences without jeopardy or personal risk. Although some of the disabilities she includes in the section on physical handicaps are relatively trivial, the content and classification of the other material should assist librarians evaluating their own organization and utilization procedures in this field.

Hannigan provides a clear-cut role analysis of the bibliotherapist and forecasts expanded future task responsibilities. She presents both the rationale for the process as well as numerous examples of specific application of the therapeutic effort. Although her remarks were derived from the specialized setting of the hospital, the insights, the suggestions for bibliotherapeutic activities, the requirements such as accuracy in recordkeeping are all applicable to the school setting. She charges that the obligation to utilize bibliotherapy should be assumed by those librarians trained and skilled in this art and its application should be a standard professional intervention practice in the schools.

The Dynamics of Reading: Implications for Bibliotherapy

CAROLINE SHRODES

Through the centuries the philosopher, the critic, and the artist have attributed to the imaginative writer not only intuitive understanding of man's motives and

Reprinted from *ETC* 18, no. 1: 21–33 (1961) by permission of the International Society for General Semantics.

his nature but also power to influence his thinking, to move his heart, and even to alter his behavior. In the *Charmides* Plato admonishes that "If the head and body are to be well, you must begin by curing the soul . . . And the cure . . . has to be effected by the use of certain charms, and these charms are fair words . . . ." However, he also feared the affective power of art. In rejecting the poet from his *Republic* he attests to his importance. He believed that art excites and stirs man's emotions, destroys the rational, and generates evil. Aristotle, on the other hand, believed that the presence of evil in art is of the essence of tragedy, whose end is the catharsis of pity and fear. More recently psychiatrists and psychologists have acknowledged that the novelist and playwright have plumbed the deep reaches of man's nature and often anticipated the discoveries of science. Recent studies in bibliotherapy, drawing upon the insights of both artist and scientist, suggest that there is an interaction between the personality of the reader and imaginative literature which may be utilized to engage his emotions and free them for conscious and productive use.[1] Bibliotherapy is made possible by the "shock of recognition" the reader experiences when he beholds himself, or those close to him, in a story or some other piece of literature. So successfully does the skilled writer create an illusion of reality that, as Freud says, "he is able to guide the current of our emotions, dam it up in one direction and make it flow in another," or, in another context, "words and magic were in the beginning one and the same thing."[2]

Reading, like all other human behavior, is a function of the total personality. When we read fiction, poetry, or drama, we perceive selectively in accordance with our needs, goals, defenses, and values. Parallel in substance and function to the primary phases of psychotherapy, the vicarious experience induced by reading includes identification, projection, and introjection; transference of emotion from early experience to current symbols of it; catharsis; and insight. However, the reader will abstract from the work of art only what he is able to perceive and organize; what he experiences and feels will determine the nature of his perceptions and the meaning he attaches to them. He may make an identification that will enhance his self-regard; he may project onto a character feelings that have been repressed. He may introject meaning that will satisfy his needs and reject implications that are threatening to his ego.

Bibliotherapy, like deep therapy, can be effective in interrupting this circular process. In a work of art the writer has organized the chaotic fragments of human experience, endowing them with meaning but not imposing judgment. In its direct and concrete representation of experience which differs only in degree from that of the reader, fiction or drama may induce the reader to re-live his own experience. Since he cannot remain neutral in the presence of human beings in action, he will express feelings of anger and contempt, sympathy and understanding. In its portrayal of the extensional world, imaginative literature provides an external frame of reference which permits the reader to view his experience freshly from the perspective of the detached observer. Being at once phantasy and reality, it permits the reader to be both participant and spectator. As participant in the action of a novel he will move about in a symbolic world which is inaccessible to him in life. As spectator,

he will bring to bear upon the fictional situation his predispositions, the circumstances of his life, his unique perspective, and in adding them up in relation to what is given, he may be compelled to reevaluate his own experience.

However, the affective power of literature may induce a semantic reaction in the reader in which he confuses the symbol with what is symbolized. If he fails to distinguish between the organized sequence of experience portrayed by the writer with the unorganized events of his own life, he will react to the work of art in the same repetitive pattern with which he responds to his own experience. Thus it is not strange that for some readers identification may precipitate a destructive acting out of impulses; for others it may reinforce the reader's defense system; and for still others it may serve as a catalyst to free emotions from their unconscious roots. Some images will be intercepted by the reader and will work into life; other images will be projected by the reader and work back into art. As we illustrate the various symbolic responses to imaginative literature, we shall try to account for this apparent paradox.

The identification that we make with characters or situations portrayed in fiction or on the stage or screen is a universal one. Even without the help of advertisers and commercial motives Davy Crockett's name and the coonskin cap would be familiar to children throughout the land. Having found their hero, they sang his song, created new songs, and wore his cap even in temperatures above one hundred. After Mary Martin's performance in Peter Pan, the Associated Press described a six year old's reaction: "Peter Pan came right up to me and threw some pixie dust on my leg, *right here*." Accordingly, Larry worked his way to the upper deck of his bunk and took off, landing abruptly on the floor and suffering a knot on his head. More serious was the case cited by Wertham of a young boy who succumbed to the delusion that he was Superman and could jump off a cliff with impunity. The disastrous act culminated in his death.

Another youth identified with Superman with tragic results. Marya Mannes movingly describes his background and that of the other New York delinquents who sadistically tortured and killed an old man. The leader, characterized as a highly intelligent, sick, and potentially dangerous person, failed to respond to abortive attempts at psychiatric treatment. Miss Mannes cites Dr. Wertham, who talked with him at length after his incarceration. An avid reader of horror-comic books, he acknowledged that some of the more refined methods of torture came from these sources. Without doubt they nourished the hate and frustration his life experience had generated and precipitated the symbolic reenactment of these latent impulses. Images of torture do not fall into a vacuum. In this instance they must have entered a tension system ready to explode. We can hypothesize that there were no past experiences of love and compassion strong enough to compete successfully against the impulse to destroy, that there were no salutary symbols available to provide an alternative strategy for action. For the sick personality who has no self to accept or respect, who acts in disregard of law, reality, or ethics, the horror-comic book may act as a precipitant to self-destruction or homicide.

Response to symbolic experience may also culminate in self-destruction. In the account of the last hours of James V. Forrestal, we learn that in his bedroom was an anthology opened to selections from Sophocles and Euripides. He had begun copying the Chorus from Ajax, which relates the agonies of Ajax, who lost his mind after becoming famous for valor in time of war. The lines copied portray the legendary Greek hero as being "comfortless, nameless, hopeless, save in the dark aspects of the yawning grave." However, he did not copy the lines immediately following: "When reason's day sets rayless, joyless, quenched in cold decay, better to die and sleep the never waking sleep than linger on and dare to live when the soul's life is gone." Nor did he copy the lines on the opposite page from Euripides' *Chorus from Alcestis:* "The dead thou wilt not awaken from all their weeping again." The conviction is inescapable that Forrestal identified with the war hero, and that he selectively chose the passages that reflected his own anguished feelings. The fact that the uncopied lines reflect in the first instance the choice of death over life, and in the second the promise of relief from stress, suggests that they may have provided, in Burke's phrase, a strategy for encompassing a situation. We do not have sufficient facts to say that the reading of these passages might have precipitated his suicide. However, it provides a dramatic illustration of the process of identification and its possible relation to subsequent behavior. The symbols inherent in literature will not induce in a reader an affective response that is not already latent in him. With another reader and another equilibrium of forces, the mere reading of the lines might have produced a substitutive release and the symbolic experience might have sufficed as a relief from tension. This illustration provides a salutary reminder that in the practice of bibliotherapy "interpretations" of experience should not be given beyond the capacity of the person to receive them; that although the wisdom of the psyche may protect the reader from introjecting ideas which are threatening to it, one must exert extreme caution in recommending materials without full knowledge of the reader's ego strength.

Intermediate between these extreme cases in which the symbolic response takes the form of a destructive acting out of impulses, and those we shall cite later in which it leads to catharsis and insight, is the phenomenon of the book burners. These are the anxious ones, dominated by their unconscious impulses, for whom literature constitutes a powerful threat to their image of themselves. Their reponse to symbols takes the form of an interchange of energy in which the reader displaces his own emotions and view of life onto the characters or situations depicted by the writer. Instead of working into life, the images work back into art. In his own psychic wisdom the book censor, threatened by the mirror image literature may provide of his own impulses, needs, or desires, will repudiate them by projecting them onto the work of art. An extreme instance of this kind of response is not without its grim humor. It was directed at *The Rabbit's Wedding*, a tale designed for children from the ages of three to seven, which depicts the wedding of black and white rabbits in a moonlit ceremony. A senator from Alabama decreed that the book should be burned; a Florida columnist described it as "the most amazing evidence of brain washing I've run across recently"; a director of the Alabama State Public Library Service Division withdrew it from general circulation. The hapless author commented: "I was completely unaware that animals with white fur . . . were considered blood relations of white human beings. I was only aware that a white horse next to a black horse looks very picturesque . . . ." The unconscious projections of the censors served as a means of exorcizing from their minds the threat of integration and of containing the hate, anxiety, and fear it aroused.

For some a semantic reaction is evoked by a four letter word; for others it may be precipitated by a passage dealing with the natural functions of the body, by criticism of the social or economic order, or by a vision of world government. As William March interposes in *The Bad Seed,* "the eye finds what the mind is seeking." Walter Lippman, long before the current avalanche of perception studies, elaborated this concept in *Public Opinion.* He described stereotypes as "the pictures in our heads" and analyzed their influences on perception:

For the most part we do not first see, and then define, we define first and then see. In the great blooming, buzzing confusion of the outer world, we pick out what our culture has already defined for us, and we tend to experience that which we have picked out in the form stereotyped for us by our culture.[3]

The dynamic processes evoked by reading bear out the truth of this hypothesis. Not only does the eye find what the mind is seeking; the mind finds what the heart is seeking.

The readers (or audience) of *Death of a Salesman* whose lives are involved with selling offer further confirmation of the theory that we perceive selectively in accordance with our needs and goals. In a magazine that gives tips to salesmen a righteously indignant editor protests its filming. He regards it as a "grossly unfair and very harmful caricature of the American selling profession"; he views Willy Loman as a "tawdry character who would have been a failure in any field. . . ." Seeing in this play a threat to free enterprise and the American standard of living, the editor wrote to the president of Columbia Pictures in the hope the picture might be stopped, or, if not suppressed, that it repudiate the implication that selling does not constitute the very heart of our American way of life. (In another issue of *Opportunity* a contributor told its readers that the reason that Willy Loman was a failure was that he didn't love his product. A man attending the play was overheard during the intermission saying to his companion, "That territory always *was* a bitch!")

Whether the tirades of the book burners ostensibly proceed from a desire to protect the public from obscenity, pornography, and scatology or to safeguard nationalism and free enterprise, the phenomenon of censorship logically derives from the same basic source. The censor's projection allays his anxiety and fear. Charges of obscenity represent an unconscious reaction against his own unidentified emotions and reflect his automatic effort to contain and bridle his own errant impulses. The "evil" he finds contained in a book is the "evil" he would thrust outward; the fear or hate he expends on a character is the fear or hate he cannot endure in himself; the sickness he sees in literature is a symbolic reflection of his own obsessive sickness. If the self is unknown to the self, it is full of projections; it is synthetic and vulnerable to disintegration. Since the book burner is driven to preserve his synthetic self and fortify it, it is unlikely that his attitudes will be modified by vicarious experience. The images in his mind will work back into art.

We have illustrated the symbolic response which reflects a destructive acting out of impulses or a projecting outward of threatening feelings. We shall now turn to responses to vicarious experience in which energy is sufficiently free for positive identifications and adequately controlled for verbal discharge of aggression.

Since for no two persons can there be an equivalence of symbols, it is not surprising that college students, on being asked how they felt about its troubled protagonist, would vary in their responses to a novel as emotionally charged as *Catcher in the Rye*. However, in one upper division class of sophisticated students almost every woman identified with Holden. One stated that she had gone through the same experiences that he had suffered. When the instructor, visibly surprised, suggested that he had thought the novel described archetypically *male* experiences, the women insisted that Holden

was typical of all adolescents, irrespective of sex. One notable exception was the woman who made a strong negative identification with Holden on the basis of merely hearing the class discussion.

In a freshman class, a tall motorcycler in his early twenties who had driven trucks across country since he was sixteen, attacked the novel as immoral and the hero as delinquent:

. . . since the book has left me with only a feeling of nausea, my personal opinion is that the person responsible for this farce, the author, must be one of two persons: a person whose inner self comes out when he sits down at a typewriter and goes wild with words. Then finishing, he leaves to become a peaceful and civil person. Or that he is a rotten and corrupt individual who is so filled with this type of filth that he had to pour it somewhere. The only pitiful part is that he put it into a book instead of a garbage can.

A South American student did not care for *Catcher in the Rye* because there was sex but no love in it. A freshman girl expressed her ambivalence by admitting that the book gives an excellent picture of what can happen to a youngster who had not received proper guidance and understanding. ". . . it is especially important that we know what is wrong, in order that we may select what is right." Another girl protested that she and Holden had nothing in common. "I sympathize and pity him, but I feel that all his actions were unjustified because he lacked one factor which I value very highly, effort."

Some of the freshmen were able to make positive identifications. A woman who had three years of analysis (unsuccessful, according to her) had this to say:

To me this is an extremely perplexing novel. Although Salinger purports to describe the gradual mental breakdown of an extremely neurotic youth and his eventual arrival at the analyst's couch, most of the time the boy seems more "normal" than the people around him. At least he is more *human*, more alive.

Since each student brings to the vicarious experience his own needs, aspirations, neural traces, modes of adaptation, and values, it is inevitable that each will respond with varying degrees of acceptance or rejection. However, all of the students give evidence of having made an identification, however varied the nature and intensity of their feelings.

This variation in symbolic response to literature is less notable than the inconsistency to be found in the responses of the same person to the same book. The explanation is to be found in the ambivalence within the personality. A student, whose symbolic response to imaginative literature was correlated with autobiographical and clinical data, displayed significant contradictions in her reaction to the same work. After reading *The Great God Brown*, Elsa first identified with Dion, the artist-idealist: "Dion is a sensitive, honest individual who started out to be himself but allowed the forces of society to mold him into their pattern. He was human enough to weaken under the pressure." She liked him as a person and pitied him because he could not withstand his loneliness as "he kept digging behind the mask." She gratuitously added that she too has a mask to wear "which more than once repelled a friendship and thwarted opportunity"; that conformity to family and society need not result in a complete loss of identity. After these objective, perceptive comments on Dion she shifted to moral judgments: his cowardice, his need for group acceptance, his running away from conflicts, his selfishness, and possessiveness. This dramatic change in her view of Dion aroused Elsa's own incredulity, and she asked the experimenter, "Why do you suppose I did that? Am I angry at myself, maybe, and not Dion at all? Am I impulsive and emotional and then change after I begin to think?" On being encouraged to answer the question for herself, she subsequently had this to say:

I've been thinking of that strange contradiction of myself in those reports. I think I must escape into a book. I identify with the characters. And then I analyze, and when I analyze *I* am not present. It's a different part of me—separated. I think this matter of personal conformity explains it. I'm sympathetic with a person forced into conformity. I see their side but then I join the throng and feel they should conform more. There was a glaring difference in my reactions to Dion. I wrote the first yellow sheets right after reading the book. Then I had to study for an ex and I didn't write the others until three days later, and then I wrote red in the face and angry with him. I guess I am the one who changed, not Dion. Is my strong belief in the independence of the individual merely lip service? Maybe I'm hypocritical. First I am terribly sympathetic to Dion and then contemptuous. I got impatient with him and saw his weaknesses. It's just like with my roommate. I am highly opinionated and my sudden shifts in attitude toward her appear to be sincere. People I dislike I try to find what makes them the way they are. First I feel pity and then I am obnoxious. Sure, I'm right, I act impetuously, and then I think and then justify and rationalize to make me feel I was right. Until I wrote out these things and saw how they disagreed with each other, I didn't realize I did the same thing with my roommate and other people too. There is a consistent inconsistency in everything I do and in all my relationships. I guess I'm afraid to let the rein on my emotions go. Probably because I've been humiliated too often.

Elsa's response reflects the interaction between her own life pattern and her vicarious experience. It takes the form of a projection of her own needs, anxieties, and hate onto Dion. In her confusion of the symbol with reality, her own anxiety and guilt are translated into anger toward him. In her early responses to other pieces of literature, Elsa did not note her own projections; at the culmination of the experiment, she became conscious not only of her conflicting responses but of her ambivalence in life situations. For the first time she saw the relationship between her concept of herself and her symbolic response.

In some cases an identification is sufficiently strong to take the reader back in time and place to his own childhood. One student, a middle aged teacher, thought at first that *Sons and Lovers* was beautiful:

I spent more time in thinking about it than in the actual reading. It aroused many memories of my early life. They came to me in the middle of the night, in the streetcar. Memories of my mother, of her death, of her punishment of me, of my brother's scorn of me.

Later she commented on not being able to bear reading it and offered this explanation:

I never loved my mother. That is a dreadful thing to say, a dreadful thing to live through. I was happier when I was away from her. When I came home I was apt to be cross, sensitive, and unpleasant. My mother's spells of blues depressed me. Also she dominated me. I was ashamed of my attitudes toward her so I never admitted it. . . .

I was entirely too docile all my life, even submissive. That's why I hated the book even while I thought it was beautiful. It made me see how many years of misery I caused myself. I didn't like to admit I was so submissive. Also I didn't like to see my mother as she really was. Since her death I have idolized her. But now I know she wasn't mean like the mother in the book, nor spying and hypocritical. But she was efficient, too busy, ambitious, and brought up to believe in children's explicit obedience. I should wipe from my mind both the picture of a perfect mother and the lingering resentment toward her.

The sympathy engendered for Paul was sufficiently strong to dissolve her own guilt and to uproot her hitherto repressed feelings. She was able, for the first time, to recognize the hostility she had felt toward her mother. Furthermore, in giving expression to her emotions as well as her reason, she was able to view her relationship with her mother in a new perspective and to differentiate between Paul's mother and her own mother. In so doing she was freed from the ambivalence that had tormented her and was emotionally ready to make the healthy resolution: "I should wipe from my mind both the picture of a perfect mother and the lingering resentment toward her."

Literature may serve as a catalyst to bring defenses to consciousness and to modify them in the person who is free enough to flow into the identification but sufficiently controlled to distinguish between the character and the self and between the situations in the book and in his life. In the period of "willing suspension of disbelief," he can view the past in the perspective of the present; he can evaluate the present in the perspective of the past; he can envision the future in the perspective of both past and present.

We have sought to illuminate the interrelationship

between the personality of the reader and the nature of his vicarious experience; to demonstrate how this response evokes the same semantic reactions that take place whenever man has not made contact with his own unconscious. Hence it may precipitate a dangerous acting out of destructive impulses; it may take the form of a projection of fears and anxieties upon the characters the artist has created and reflect the sickness of the reader. On the other hand, it may provide a new frame of reference which permits the reader to understand and to alter reality. When this happens, the energy inherent in art has served as a catalyst to set his energy free; the work of art has been transformed by his energy.

NOTES

1. Caroline Shrodes, "Bibliotherapy: A Theoretical and Clinical Experimental Study" (Ph.D. dissertation, Univ. of California, Berkeley, 1949).
2. Sigmund Freud, *Collected Papers* (London: International Psycho-Analytical Press, 1924). 4v.
3. Walter Lippman, *Public Opinion* (New York: Macmillan, 1957), p. 81.

Children's Literature Can Affect Coping Behavior

PATRICIA JEAN CIANCIOLO

Regardless of when children grow up they have numerous problems to cope with in the process; they must learn to identify, and then take directly into account and do something about the presence of such barriers as alienation, cultural pluralism and pressures. The gratification children get from their areas of security helps them handle anxieties that face them, helps them through the ups and downs of development.[1] For each child there exist different states of temporary tensions, different degrees of attraction or repulsion between specific subjects, people or situations.[2]

Some of the normal, expectable sources of stress for children growing up stem from the things that are done to them or happen to them, others arise within them. Such things as operations, childhood diseases, the uprooting from friends and a familiar neighborhood, war anxieties, separations from parents and tensions between parents constitute things that happen or are done to the child. Some of the problems that may arise chiefly within the child constitute the following—discrepancies between the child's abilities and his goals, instabili-

ties related to defects in the physical or psychological equipment of the child or feelings of being different from brothers and sisters or other children who may seem to receive more attention, love, or approval.[3]

Interaction between the Reader and Literature

The story and pictures of a book might be the source of psychological relief from the various pressures and concerns cited above. In general, a teacher or counselor may use bibliotherapy, a process of dynamic interaction between the personality of the reader and literature, in one of two ways.[4] First, he may attempt to solve a child's actual and existing emotional problems and pressures by bringing him a similar experience vicariously through books. Through recognition of a problem and its solution in literature the individual gains new insights into his own problem and presumably is then able to take a step toward solving it. Second, the teacher or counselor may use literature for preventive bibliotherapy. This technique involves the theory that a child is able to make a satisfactory adjustment when a problem eventually arises in his own life because he met one similar to that which was depicted in the literature that he read in the past. This latter defined technique is analogous to that of an inoculation to prevent the contagious disease. "A little vicarious injection of experience with a problem in a book is to prevent a hard case of this same kind of experience in the young reader's development."[5]

More specifically, bibliotherapy can help the individual in a variety of ways. The process may be used to help the reader (1) to acquire information and knowledge about the psychology and physiology of human behavior, (2) to live up to the injunction "know thyself," (3) to become extraverted and find interest in something outside himself, (4) to effect a controlled relief of unconscious difficulties, (5) to use the opportunity for identification and compensation, and (6) to clarify difficulties and to acquire insight into his own behavior.

The process by which the reading of a book affects a child should not be oversimplified, for the child is not quite so plastic a creature that he is easily changed by what he reads. Furthermore, the numerous variations and the factor of unexpectedness which is characteristic of human relationships prevents the categorizing of children as specific psychological types. The therapeutic effect that results from the process of dynamic interaction between the personality of the reader and literature is usually theorized in terms of *identification, catharsis,* and *insight. Identification,* or the act of affiliating some real or fictional character in literature with oneself or associates, is an almost universal experience of young readers. The *cathartic effect* occurs as the reader achieves identification with the character who works through his problem and releases his emotional tension. The book's solving of the emotional situation provides a purge for the emotions of the reader. When the reader realizes his identification with the book character he is able to see the motivation of his own behavior more clearly. Purged of some of his own emotional tension, the way is cleared to make a more intellectual approach to his problem. Thus, there is an integration of intellectual perception and emotional drive and the final component of the process of bibliotherapy, namely, *insight,* is achieved.

To a limited degree, bibliotherapy is an activity that lies within the province of every teacher working with children who are not seriously maladjusted and in need of clinical treatment. Since one recognized objective of the elementary school program is to contribute to the provision of the basic needs of the learner, it appears logical that teachers would make use of this technique. Studies have shown that through experiences in which literature is involved children can be helped to solve the developmental problems which they face.

Selecting and Using Books to Affect Coping Behavior

In advocating the use of bibliotherapy the writer does not mean to imply that there should be a return to the didactic literature that characterized the fiction of a century ago. Books that are to be used to change an attitude or aid in understanding other people should exemplify good literature. The characters of the books should be lifelike and complete—yet individual entities. Regional, racial, religious, or nationality groups should be pictured in an atmosphere which is accurate, showing the traditions and customs and the origination of each. Fiction, biography, drama, and poetry can effectively contribute to the social education of the readers.

Learning activities in which trade books are used to foster cosmopolitan sensitivity and growth in human understanding may be used in integrated activities of social studies units and they may be used with individuals in personal reading activities. The teacher or librarian desiring to offer learning experiences for the purpose of socializing the child should be diplomatic in offering him these books. Too, using books in this manner often calls for a discussion or other interpretative activity to follow-up the reading itself. If there is not an opportunity for cooperative sharing of a book, at least the readers should be encouraged to mull over, interpret, compare, and contrast the situations depicted.

It was reported that teachers have discovered during action research in their classrooms that discussion has a cumulative effect on the building of concepts and the extending of sensitivity; these discussions should have a sequence of questions or considerations. Heaton and Lewis provided steps for the sequence and stated that these steps had important psychological implications. There should be a retelling of what occurred in the story itself and the incidents, feelings, and relationships that are relevant to human relationships should be highlighted. There should occur a probing into what happened in feeling, in shift of relationship and change of behavior in order to make more vivid the identification with the feelings of the book characters. There should occur a stimulation to identify similar incidents relative to the experience of the students or from other stories in order to lend validity to the concept that literature can extend experience. The reader should be provided an opportunity to explore the consequences of certain behaviors or feelings, thus he can recapitulate what happened in a specific situation as a result of some specific behavior or consequences. There should be an opportunity to arrive at a conclusion or generalization about the consequences of certain behaviors or feelings in order to determine whether or not certain situations, behaviors, or feelings encourage improved human relationships and happiness. The reader is also encouraged to determine the desirability or helpfulness of several alternatives.[6]

The very nature of some of the problems and pressures of the children and about which the books pertain makes a direct approach to the children difficult; older children are less likely to confide their problems as freely as younger children. This approach calls for a teacher who is patient and friendly and does not pry. She must be informed about the numerous activities and devices that help the readers to identify themselves with the characters in the books.

Kircher was one of the first to study carefully the effectiveness of trade books as an intrinsic aid in treating the child with a social or an emotional problem. The author reported that the children with whom she worked insisted on making their own selection of books; they often refused any book the therapist offered. She described some of the techniques a teacher might use to guide a child into selecting a book that had potential in helping the reader understand himself or others better.[7]

Except for the Kircher study there have been literally few solid studies about activities in which books are used in this manner. There have been a few master's studies done in connection with graduate work in library science; a few action research projects that have been conducted by classroom teachers were reported in the professional periodicals.

The Fischer study resulted in a bibliography of available literature that was deemed useful in the solution of emotional problems.[8] Suggestions as to how teachers and librarians might use each of the books were also presented. The titles were classified in relation to the major emotional problems faced by children today and an approximate reading level was assigned to each book. The bibliography was sufficiently extensive in terms of number and classification to permit self-selection by children interested in reading about these problems. Fischer's bibliography would make an excellent supplement to the one developed by Kircher some 11 years earlier.

Biair analyzed recommended books for children in terms of one criterion; namely, the teacher or librarian, sensitive to the distributed behavior characteristics of the preadolescent developmental stage, should use realistic literature in fiction form so that the child can vicariously meet others who share his unexpressed problems and gain an insight into how these problems might be solved. The factors that determined suitability of the books that were included as appropriate reading material for nine-, ten-, and eleven-year-old children were similar to those presented by Kircher and the other authors who have written about this kind of activity with books. They include the following: The books should be written on the child's independent reading level. The author should recognize characteristics of the children that are in keeping with research and he should deal with problems in a manner that can be supported by research. The problem faced by the book character should be brought out as a main issue and it should be presented without moralizing. The book should be about the modern child or it should be so universal in appeal that the difference in time or locale is of little importance.[9]

There are several other studies, the findings of which serve to throw some light on the effects of learning activities in which trade books were involved for the purpose of influencing behavioral change. Comer read stories from carefully selected books to determine whether or not literature would help children to get to problems that needed discussing. This study involved group procedures and involved reading about problems common to many of the children in the class. The chief selection aid for appropriate titles was *Reading Ladders for Human Relations*, an extensive bibliography of trade books that can be used in learning activities, designed to influence changed behavior.[10]

Boone carried out a program on extending children's experience through literature under the theme of "Family Living—the Responsibilities of the Members to Each Other and the Individual Member to Himself."[11] *Reading Ladders* was used to select books for this study, also. Some elaboration, discussions, and summaries of the book content were made in order to stimulate interest in the various titles. Discussions followed the reading of the books and the children were encouraged to relate these situations to their personal experiences.

Role-playing techniques were used as were essays on open-ended questions. Children were also asked to write stories about pictures which depicted various human relations situations. Some change in behavior was noticed. This change was slow but continuous; the children developed a sensitive reading interest.

Timm reported that in her bibliotherapy program she made use of story hours; dramatizations with puppets; book displays; discussions about books, authors and illustrators; and guided "free" reading. The realistic and psychological novels that were involved in these learning activities were about economic problems, social relationships of individuals, family conflicts, and development of personality and character. Timm stated that the chief value of using books of this kind with the types of activities she chose was that the child could find a frankness in them that he was not likely to get from his family and acquaintances.[12]

In an important study, the staff of the Materials Center of the University of Chicago sought to determine whether or not the reading of certain books and identification with characters can have a deep-seated effect on the child. Fifty of the most popular books of fiction were selected for use in this study; 25 of the books were written for the later childhood age group and 25 were for the early adolescent age group. The books were selected because they seemed to reflect the current patterns of social experiences, interpersonal relations, and problems of childhood and youth. In studying the effects of books on youth, three techniques were employed, namely, the focused interview, a story projective technique, and a sociometric technique. With each technique the reader was expected to reveal his identification with or rejection of the characters in the book together with the negative or positive qualities that he attributed to these characters. The directions of the findings were reported in *Youth, Communications and Libraries* and are as follows:[13] The effects of the developmental values in a book are of a contributory sort; they will not produce dynamic changes but they do contribute to these changes. The vicarious experiences gleaned from reading are part of an overall pattern of forces, but to be effective the experiences or the values in the books must be appropriate to the developmental level of the reader. Children from different socioeconomic levels and cultural groups responded to different values. Responses varied from individual to individual also, and depended on the needs and receptivity of each child.

The implications of these findings are numerous, but there are two that are most significant and should be kept in mind by teachers who are using books in learning activities designed to change social and emotional behavior. One, children's literature has a place in changing behavior but the books should be carefully chosen for content and style. Two, reading of the books should be accompanied by follow-up activities if a significant amount of change is to occur. The statement below defines more clearly aspects of this implication:

The identification of developmental values in children's literature is an adult process in which children rarely play a conscious part either in their selection of what they read or in their postreading discussions. Children are reading because of interest factors and not "to be developed." The elements that contribute to a good story and to the book as a creative literary piece still remain among the major factors in our appraisal of books for children. Without them the developmental values of books would exist in a vacuum completely removed from the "child world" in which we wish to have them play their part.[14]

This statement would lend support to the emphasis on follow-up activities for this kind of reading. This same emphasis was apparent in the reports by Heaton and Lewis and Fischer. Because the primary objective of these activities is to develop a sensitivity to human relations, the trade books that were used with these activities were chosen primarily for their pertinent content. By and large, however, the selection of books that the writers listed in their reports did not appear to be inferior didactic literature. Indeed some had titles of very excellent books. Nonetheless, if the teacher or librarian becomes too preoccupied with selecting books in relation to the topic and ignores the literary quality, her ultimate goal of changing behavior through the use of trade books is unlikely to materialize. It was the investigator's experience when reviewing books for the latest edition of *Reading Ladders for Human Relations* that many of the books that were read for possible listing in this annotated selection aid could not be used.[15] Although the topics of the books were appropriate for one of the other "Ladder Themes" it was decided that little or nothing would be accomplished by reading them because of the inferior literary quality.

Books That Affect Coping Behavior

The investigator has identified a sampling of recent publications in the field of children's literature that might be used to affect coping behavior. These books could be used to enable the reader to recognize his own problems and pressures, find possible solutions for them; if not a solution then a realistic, wholesome view of these problems. These books might also be the source of understanding the behavior of others.

BIBLIOGRAPHY

Abaunza, Virginia. *Sundays from Two to Six*. Indianapolis: Bobbs-Merrill, 1956 (divorce), 13–16 years.

Apsler, Alfred. *Northwest Pioneer*. New York: Farrar, 1960 (minority religious group—Jewish), 9–13 years.

Armer, Alberta. *Screwball*. Cleveland, Ohio: World, 1963 (family relationships, mobility), 9–14 years.

Arora, Shirley. *What Then, Raman?* Chicago: Follett, 1960 (value of ed., family relationships, responsibility, conflict between cultures), 10–14 years.

Benedict, Steve. *The Little House on Wheels*. TellWell, 1953 (mobility), 6–8 years.

Biesterveld, Betty. *Run, Reddy, Run*. New York: Nelson, 1962 (mobility), 9–13 years.

Brenner, Barbara. *Barto Takes the Subway*. New York: Knopf, 1961 (language barrier, mobility), 6–8 years.

Brooks, Gwendolyn. *Bronzeville Boys and Girls*. New York: Harper, 1956 (poetry—all aspects of growing up), 7–12 years.

Buck, Pearl S. *The Beech Tree*. New York: Day, 1955 (family relationships, death, conflict between generations), 9–13 years.

Buckley, Helen. *Grandfather and I*. New York: Lothrop, 1959 (differences between generations), 5–8 years.

——. *Grandmother and I*. New York: Lothrop, 1961 (differences between generations), 5–8 years.

——. *My Sister and I*. New York: Lothrop, 1964 (family relationships), 5–8 years.

Bulla, Clyde Robert. *Indian Hill*. New York: Crowell, 1963 (conflict between cultures and generations, modern American Indian), 10–14 years.

Butterworth, Oliver. *The Trouble with Jenny's Ear*. Boston: Atlantic, Little, 1960 (family relationships), 8–12 years.

Calhoun, Mary. *Honestly, Katie John!* New York: Harper, 1963 (sex role), 8–14 years.

Carroll, Ruth and Latrabe Carroll. *Tough Enough and Sassy*. New York: Walck, 1958 (family relationships, economic security), 7–9 years.

Clark, Billy. *River Boy*. New York: Putnam, 1958 (commitment to change), 9–13 years.

Clayton, Barbara. *Tomboy*. New York: Funk & Wagnalls, 1961 (sex role), 13–16 years.

Cleary, Beverly. *Beezus and Ramona*. New York: Morrow, 1955 (family relationships), 8–12 years.

Cloutier, Helen. *The Many Names of Lee Lu*. Chicago: Albert Whitman, 1960 (minority race—Chinese, need to belong), 6–8 years.

Davis, Clyde B. *The Newcomer*. Philadelphia: Lippincott, 1954 (mobility, minority race—Negro), 15–18 years.

DeJong, Meindert. *The House of Sixty Fathers*. New York: Harper, 1956 (wartime pressures and separation from family), 10–13 years.

DeLeeuw, Adele. *The Barred Road*. New York: Macmillan, 1954 (minority race—Negro), 10–16 years.

Duncan, Lois. *The Littlest One in the Family*. New York: Dodd, 1960 (family relationships), 4–8 years.

Enright, Elizabeth. *The Saturday's*. New York: Harcourt, 1941 (family relationships, one parent), 9–12 years.

Estes, Eleanor. *The Hundred Dresses*. New York: Harcourt, 1944 (minority nationality—Polish, need to belong, economic security), 9–11 years.

——. *A Little Oven*. New York: Harcourt, 1955 (family relationships), 5–8 years.

Felt, Sue. *Hello-Goodbye*. New York: Doubleday, 1960 (mobility—need to belong), 6–8 years.

Fletcher, David. *The King's Goblet*. New York: Pantheon, 1962 (peer pressure, set of values), 13–16 years.

Foster, Genevieve. *Teddy Roosevelt*. New York: Scribner, 1954 (peer relationships, fears, physical problems), 9–11 years.

Friedman, Frieda. *The Janitor's Girl*. New York: Morrow, 1956 (family relationships, social status), 9–12 years.

Garthwaite, Marion. *Shaken Days*. New York: Messner, 1952 (orphaned), 9–13 years.

Gates, Doris. *Blue Willow*. New York: Viking, 1941 (mobility), 10–16 years.

Gebhardt, Hertha von. *The Girl from No Where*. New York: Criterion, 1959 (separation from parent, need to belong), 9–12 years.

Godden, Rumer G. *The Fairy Doll*. New York: Viking, 1956 (family relationships), 7–10 years.

Govan, Christine. *Willow Landing*. Cleveland: World, 1961 (sex role), 13–16 years.

Graham, Lorenz. *South Town*. Chicago: Follett, 1958 (desegregation, family relationships), 12–16 years.

Gruenberg, Sidonie M. *The Wonderful Story of How You Were Born*. New York: Doubleday, 1957 (sex education), 6–12 years.

Haywood, Carolyn. *Here's a Penny*. New York: Harcourt, 1944 (adoption), 7–9 years.

Hoban, Russell. *Bedtime for Francis*. New York: Harper, 1960 (family relationships), 6–8 years.

———. *A Baby Sister for Francis*. New York: Harper, 1964 (family relationships), 6–8 years.

Juline, Ruth Bishop. *A Place for Johnny Bill*. Philadelphia: Westminster, 1961 (mobility), 9–13 years.

Justus, May. *New Boy in School*. New York: Hastings, 1963 (integration of minority racial group—Negro), 8–14 years.

Knight, Ruth A. *First the Lightning*. New York: Doubleday, 1955 (peer pressure, set of values), 13–16 years.

Krumgold, Joseph. *Onion John*. New York: Crowell, 1959 (commitment to change), 12–16 years.

Latham, Jean L. *Carry on Mr. Bowditch*. Boston: Houghton, 1955 (value of education, sense of responsibility), 11–14 years.

Lattimore, Eleanor F. *Molly in the Middle*. New York: Morrow, 1956 (family relationships), 7–9 years.

L'Engle, Madeline. *Meet the Austins*. New York: Vanguard, 1959 (family relationships), 11–14 years.

Lenski, Lois. *Judy's Journey*. Philadelphia: Lippincott, 1947 (economic security—mobility), 9–11 years.

———. *Shoo Fly Girl*. Philadelphia: Lippincott, 1963 (minority religious group: Amish), 8–12 years.

———. *Strawberry Girl*. Philadelphia: Lippincott, 1945 (family relationships and responsibility, economic security), 9–11 years.

Lewiton, Mina. *Candita's Choice*. New York: Harper, 1959 (language barriers), 9–13 years.

Lindgren, Astrid. *The Children on Troublemaker Street*. New York: Macmillan, 1964 (sibling relationships, swearing), 7–11 years.

Lionni, Leo. *Little Blue and Little Yellow*. New York: Obolensky, 1959 (feeling of rejection), 4–6 years.

Martin, Patricia M. *The Pointed Brush*. New York: Lothrop, 1959 (minority racial group—Chinese, value of education), 5–8 years.

McCloskey, Robert. *One Morning in Maine*. New York: Viking, 1952 (family relationships), 5–7 years.

Means, Florence C. *The Moved Outers*. Boston: Houghton, 1945 (minority race—Japanese), 13–16 years.

Neville, Emily. *It's like This, Cat!* New York: Harper, 1963 (family and peer relationships), 9–14 years.

Olson, Gene. *Tin Goose*. Philadelphia: Westminister, 1962 (conflict between generations), 13–16 years.

Raftery, Gerald. *Twenty-dollar Horse*. New York: Messner, 1955 (minority race—Negro), 9–13 years.

Randall, Blossom. *Fun for Chris*. Chicago: Albert Whitman, 1956 (racial differences), 4–7 years.

Rutgers, vander Loeff, A. *Oregon at Last*. New York: Morrow, 1962 (sibling relationships, responsibility), 10–16 years.

Schlein, Miriam. *Laurie's New Brother*. New York: Abelard-Schuman, 1961 (family relationships), 6–8 years.

Selz, Irma. *Katy Be Good*. New York: Lothrop, 1962 (minority, religious group—Amish), 5–8 years.

———. *Wonderful Nice*. New York: Lothrop, 1960 (minority religious group—Amish), 5–8 years.

Seredy, Kate. *A Tree for Peter*. New York: Viking, 1941 (economic security), 9–12 years.

Sherburne, Zoa. *Jennifer*. New York: Morrow, 1959 (alcoholism), 13–17 years.

———. *Stranger in the House*. New York: Morrow, 1963 (mental illness), 13–17 years.

Shotwell, Louisa R. *Roosevelt Grady*. Cleveland: World, 1963 (mobility), 9–12 years.

Sorensen, Virginia. *Plain Girl*. New York: Harcourt, 1955 (minority religious group—Mennonite), 9–11 years.

———. *Miracles on Maple Hill*. New York: Harcourt, 1956 (family relationships, emotional disturbance), 10–12 years.

Steele, William O. *The Perilous Road*. New York: Harcourt, 1959 (conflict in political values, family relationships), 10–13 years.

Sterling, Dorothy. *Mary Jane*. New York: Doubleday, 1959 (desegregation), 10–14 years.

Stinetorf, Louise A. *Musa, the Shoemaker*. Philadelphia: Lippincott, 1959 (physical handicap), 9–12 years.

Stolz, Mary. *Belling the Tiger*. New York: Harper, 1961 (leadership of group activites), 8–10 years.

Stuart, Jesse. *The Beatinest Boy*. New York: McGraw-Hill, 1953 (relationships between generations, orphaned), 9–11 years.

Summers, James L. *Off the Beam*. Philadelphia: Westminster, 1955 (gang pressures, development of sense of values), 13–16 years.

Udry, Janice M. *Let's Be Enemies*. New York: Harper, 1961 (peer relationships), 4–6 years.

Vance, Marguerite. *Windows for Rosemary*. New York: Dutton, 1956 (physical handicap), 9–11 years.

Waltrip, Lela and Rufus Waltrip. *The Quiet Boy*. New York: Longmans, 1961 (conflict of generations and culture patterns, value of education, modern American Indian), 9–14 years.

———. *White Harvest*. New York: Longmans, 1960 (mobility), 9–13 years.

Wier, Ester. *The Loner*. New York: McKay, 1963 (mobility, need for love and acceptance), 12–16 years.

Wojciechowska, Maia. *Shadow of a Bull.* New York: Atheneum, 1964 (overcoming fears, selecting a vocation), 11–14 years.

Wooley, Catherine. *A Room for Cathy.* New York: Morrow, 1956 (family life, economic security), 9–12 years.

Yashima, Taro. *Crow Boy.* New York: Viking, 1955 (introverted, talented boy), 6–8 years.

———. *The Golden Footprints.* Cleveland: World, 1960 (family relationships, meaning of freedom), 8–11 years.

Zolotow, Charlotte. *Big Brother.* New York: Harper, 1960 (family relationships), 4–6 years.

NOTES

1. Lois B. Murphy, *Personality in Young Children.* 2v. (New York: Basic Books, 1956).

2. Ibid.

3. Lois B. Murphy, "Learning How Children Cope with Problems," *Children* 4:132–33 (July-August 1957).

4. David H. Russell and Caroline Schrodes, "Contributions of Research in Bibliotherapy of the Language Arts Program," *School Review* 58:338–42 (September 1950).

5. Robert L. Darling, "Mental Hygiene and Books: Bibliotherapy as Used with Children and Adolescents," in Charles L. Trinkner, ed., *Better Libraries Make Better Schools* (Hamden, Conn.: Shoe String, 1962), p. 293.

6. Margaret M. Heaton and Helen B. Lewis, *Reading Ladders for Human Relations.* 3rd ed., rev. (Washington, D.C.: American Council on Education, 1955).

7. Clara J. Kircher, *Character Formation Through Books: A Bibliography.* 2d ed., rev. (Washington, D.C.: The Catholic University of America Press, 1945).

8. Laurel J. Fischer, "Emotional Needs of Children as a Basis for Reading Guidance" (Master's thesis, Kent State University, 1956).

9. Virginia B. Biair, "Directed Reading through the Library for Improving the Social Adjustment of Older Children" (Master's thesis, Texas State College for Women, 1951).

10. Dorothea Comer, "Using Literature to Extend Children's Experiences," *Elementary English* 36:28–34 (January 1959).

11. Robert Boone, "Using Literature to Extend Children's Experiences," *Elementary English* 36:314–18 (May 1959).

12. Charlotte P. Timm, "Reading Guidance," *Wilson Library Bulletin* 34:146–48 (October 1959).

13. Alice Brooks, "Developmental Values in Books," in Frances Henne, ed., *Youth, Communications and Libraries* (Chicago: American Library Association, 1949), pp. 49–61.

14. Ibid., pp. 60–61.

15. Muriel Crosby, ed., *Reading Ladders for Human Relations,* 4th ed. (Washington, D.C.: American Council on Education, 1963).

Reading Guidance for the Gifted Child

HELEN R. SATTLEY

The gifted fourth or eighth grader may be reading on a level five to seven grades beyond his grade level. Do we then satisfy his reading needs by providing him—indeed, by urging upon him—books that are of interest to those five, seven, and more years older than he?

In some cases, yes, but in many other cases, if we are considering the whole child, we follow the more difficult path. We provide him—and guide him to it—a broader fare that keeps his interest challenged but is more in tune with his own social, physical, and intellectual growth. Although "the gifted" are usually considered more advanced than the average in these three areas, each gifted child is not necessarily socially and physically advanced beyond his classmates, and even the child with great intellectual potential has to go through a certain amount of actual living and experience before he attains the maturity of outlook and judgment of a child five or seven or so years older than he.

I recently visited a school and found on a bulletin board a book review of *Exodus* by a fifth grader. The review ended by commenting upon how interesting the book was and urging others—presumably, other fifth graders—to read the book. From the public libraries come inquiries about class assignments which send seventh and eighth graders to these libraries for Hemingway's *The Sun Also Rises,* books by Dreiser and Faulkner, plays by O'Neill.

To those of us who try to keep up with the world of children's and young people's books, such reading and such assignments are a sad commentary on the lack of knowledge among parents and teachers of the wonderful world of books existing today which are meaningful, challenging, and important to young people. During the past few years, about 1500 new children's books have been published each year. To be sure, many are potboilers and need not be considered at all. But among these books are those which will live for generations and which are often written more artistically than some of the old tried-and-true titles that are remembered by adults through the nostalgic haze associated with their childhood and the first excitement of discovering the magic of books.

If we are to open up the book world—and the world, itself—to children, we are going to have to know what books belong to today's children, and we are going to have to recognize the beauty, the worth, the appropriateness of them. To make assignments to children—even to high school students—of materials assigned to us in our own college courses, or of those from the best-

Reprinted from *Top of the News,* Mar. 1961, pp. 18–21.

seller lists which appeal to us as adults, is to deprive children of much of the excitement of the printed word today, and to miss some of the most subtle principles of reading guidance.

For even with the classics, the ones which still live for young people and which have meaning for them are those which touch upon some problem or theme which is close to them, or contain some character with whom they can relate. Thus, through something they share with the author, they can work out with him the solution, or struggle against the one he has given. Through the character that comes close to them, they can suffer or exalt and thus live out, perhaps more intensely than they dare to live in real life, their own emotions. The overtones may be absorbed, too, and that is a parent's or a teacher's hope, but the boy or girl will only take away from the book what he is ready for.

I well remember the teacher who brought me the book review of a seventh grade girl with the query, "Shouldn't this book about a drunkard be taken off the shelves?" The book referred to was Snedeker's delightful *Downright Dency,* the story of a Quaker girl on Nantucket Island in the days of sailing ships. Dency's only "sin" was stealing into the attic to read from the forbidden *Arabian Nights.* Upon going through the story again, I found a minor character whom Dency befriended at times, a pitiful and drunken sailor, but the seventh grader's whole book review revolved around this character. Why? I am quite sure, because of some experience in her own life, he came quite close to her.

Reading guidance recognizes the whole child, his reading level, and his ability, if it is meaningful. And, on the other hand, what a child is reading often indicates a great deal about the child. In some cases, it also indicates a great deal about the child's parents and the parents' aspirations for the child.

One girl who was not meeting her sixth grade classroom responsibilities although her teachers all knew she had the ability to do so, spent much of her free time reading and rereading *Gone with the Wind.* She had little in common with her classmates, whom she pretended to look down upon, but really was a very lonely little girl. Her teacher and I thought we would try to get her interested in some of the stories that the older girls in her class were reading. In this way she might have something in common with them because she needed to meet them on some level, and the stories were about teenagers and the activities close to them. She really seemed to respond to our suggestions, but within a few days I was visited by her mother, who wanted to know why we were giving her daughter "baby books." The mother said the girl read all her parents' book-club books, that she didn't like immature books, that her friends were high school young people and that, fortunately, she had little in common with children her

own age. No guidance the school could give could avail against the purpose of this mother for her daughter.

More often, however, the child who is being hurried along into adult books too soon for his own interests is not being hurried for his mother's social reasons, but is being urged on by parents or teachers who feel the reading of such books is a goal that must be attained. These books, read at an early age, are a "barometer" of his ability.

The reading of the individual books is not what should concern us, if these books are the tried-and-true books usually used as such barometers (lush historical novels and sensational best-sellers are another thing entirely). Of course, if *Moby Dick* is never picked up again by the boy grown to manhood, a great deal has been lost by his too early reading. But the greater concern is what has been done to the boy's or girl's interest in boys' and girls' books. Have they skipped these entirely?

I would not be concerned about the fourth grade boy who just had to read *Thunderhead* after he had finished *My Friend Flicka,* since his mother laughingly said, "He was reading *Mr. Popper's Penguins* at the same time and loving it." Mr. Popper, Mary Poppins, Dr. Dolittle, and, yes, Freddy, the Detective, all belong to fourth graders, or fifth graders, or third graders. They are a part of their social, as well as literary, life.

I would be concerned about the sixth grader who had missed all of the Laura Ingalls Wilder books and all of the De Angeli books because she had had an early obsession with Dickens that had crowded out all "lesser" books. She would be missing some of the most beautifully written stories on American life that are in print today.

And I would be concerned if a seventh grade social studies teacher felt *Dear-Bought Land* or *Rifles for Watie* not important enough to include in American history reading for his gifted students. *Rifles for Watie* is a boys' book about the Civil War, as exciting and thought-provoking for boy and adult as many Civil War stories on the best-seller lists and with more realistic characters than those romanticized heroes of James Fenimore Cooper. (It won the Newbery prize in 1958.) *Dear-Bought Land* brings the disasters of Jamestown realistically close.

And if our gifted students continue to miss—because we are not aware of the books' existence and importance—*Call It Courage, Wheel on the School, The Good Master, Thirty-One Brothers and Sisters, Daughter of the Mountains, Star of India, Crystal Mountain,* and all of the other stories which bring the children of other lands, their lives and their burdens, close to us through books of true literary style, then we should all be concerned. We have, here at hand, some of the bridges to an understanding of nations. Our gifted students can turn these reading experiences into vital learning activities. Through the wise guidance of gifted teachers, they can bring a vitality to their classroom work which is not possible unless these doors to the world of books are opened to them.

To broaden and deepen boys' and girls' experiences through reading; to fit the book to the child, not the child to the book; to recognize that every age has its masterpieces, and to set the masterpieces of the present and of the past into reasonable perspective; to challenge but not push; to be wise and patient enough to wait for the child's own pattern of growth to unfold—are these not principles of reading guidance for any child?

Use Puppets to Reach the Emotionally Disturbed

VIRGINIA VIDLER

Two years ago a team of Buffalo, New York, social workers and a professional puppeteer developed a brand-new program to help emotionally disturbed preadolescent youngsters. They found that puppet theater therapy (the use of fairy-tale characters to symbolize human emotional experiences) could help children come to grips with their feelings in real-life situations.

As part of an audience and by interacting with the puppets and each other, children safely experience events and emotions they will not or cannot otherwise acknowledge. This interaction gives children new insights into their problems and helps them to develop a sense of responsibility for their own actions. (Along with this responsibility comes a new generosity in understanding the feelings of others.)

Puppet theater also provides the freedom for children to express their feelings in a structured and nonthreatening atmosphere. Youngsters witness a whole gamut of emotions—a witch may represent cunning; a king, nobility; a princess, gentleness.

An intensive program, puppet therapy lasts ten weeks with a one-hour session weekly. Every performance is developed to create a particular structured experience. During one session, for instance, children confront whatever puppet they choose at the end of the performance. "Why do you feel that way?" a child might ask a villainous puppet. Then all the children can talk together about the response, and perhaps find some

Reprinted from *Instructor*, copyright © May 1972, by The Instructor Publications, Inc., used by permission.

commonality with their own feelings. Sue, an unconfident but very perceptive child, became upset when other youngsters called the witch wicked. Sue suggested that the witch might be helped if children didn't *think* of her as wicked.

Another time, children participate in a psychodrama, "freeze." A play from a previous session is reenacted, but this time a child can stop the action at any point by calling "freeze." The child then determines what he wants a particular puppet to do—often changing the direction of the play.

During "fantasy argument" a puppet asks children to imagine there are two puppets living within them. Then children take turns staging their arguments. This particular design emphasizes the internal argument within each child (and how to resolve such conflicts) and stimulates group interaction.

"Doubling" is probably the most complex design developed for the puppet therapy program. The therapist encourages each child to feel as he thinks one of the characters feel. Simultaneously, the child is asked to identify his own emotions at that particular moment. After the performance, the child defends his actions (as the character in the play) and responds as he thinks the puppet would. Sometimes the child doubling for a puppet joins the character on stage to hold hands while discussing their common feelings.

To supplement and reinforce the therapy program, the parents of participating youngsters have formed their own group. While meeting informally with the therapist, parents can discuss mutual concerns, provide feedback, and often search for solutions.

Puppet therapy isn't the grand cure-all for all emotional problems, but it has helped many youngsters take major steps toward dealing successfully with their environment.

Ten-year-old Bobby kept to himself most of the time; trusted others with extreme caution. But during one session he asked the Green Spirit, a fairy godmother character, "What kind of spirit do *I* have?" The Green Spirit told Bobby of his loyalty to friends and his willingness to help—genuinely true and positive traits. Bobby's new self-confidence became evident.

Cindy, fiercely self-critical, spoke to the princess who ventured into the forest alone. This, Cindy thought, was horribly dangerous. But the princess spoke gently of the many chances and challenges inherent in life and the need to accept them. Cindy's response was one of enlightenment. The next week she entered a race at school—and won.

Parents, school administrators, caseworkers, and the children themselves have all commented on noticeable behavior changes. Some teachers reported that puppet therapy has created some of the greatest changes that have yet been achieved with a particular child. And parents say their children are happier—a major aim in reaching these youngsters.

On the Need of the Severely Handicapped to Feel That They Are Human

PRUDENCE A. SUTHERLAND

The title of this article may shock or even enrage many nonhandicapped persons, who would feel that I am brutally overstating the issue. They may think that the severely handicapped person spends too much time meditating on the fact that he is different from those around him, thereby creating barriers against the rest of society. Yet the feelings of being different from everyone else are obvious, deeply conditioned, and ingrained in such a person, and therefore form one of his major concerns. Because he tries to suppress his anxiety at feelings of alienation, he develops rationalizations and sometimes guilt about the very act of introspection and ensuing self-doubts. But sooner or later his rationalizations and guilt will erupt in a prolonged emotional explosion which is likely to impair his mental health and affect his interpersonal relationships.

Since there is nothing to gain and much to lose from attempts to deny or avoid the problem of being different, let us meet it head on, explore the depth of this sense of isolation, clarify its ramifications, and, finally, take a look at the manner in which I, for one, overcame my feelings of gross difference and lost sense of personal worth. I shall first recount my personal experience with being different and then draw some conclusions which I hope may shed some light on, and ease the life of, other severely handicapped persons.

Well-Adjusted Parents Help

I was fortunate to have parents who adjusted exceptionally well to having a severely handicapped daughter; I know this both from first-hand observation and from what professionals in the field of rehabilitation have told me. My mother saw and accepted that, to put it bluntly, my body was practically useless, but she saw too that I was intelligent. She therefore raised me to value the things of the mind above all else and impressed upon me the idea that I was mentally just the same as my brothers and sister. I was encouraged to read, to take joy in nature, and to make happy, bright conversation with the other members of my family. I

Reprinted by permission from *Journal of Rehabilitation* 34, no. 5:28–30 (Sept.-Oct. 1968).

firmly believe that my mother's approach was the best that can be taken in such a situation. To build on and perfect what is not impaired, and to play down the importance of what is irrevocably damaged, is, I believe, the height of facing human reality.

Despite excellent psychological support and a happy childhood, there was still a touch of uneasiness, the vaguest foreboding shadow, to which I paid little attention when I was very young. I would sometimes wonder why I did not have any friends or if I would ever go to school. My parents were quite frank in discussing my disability and related handicaps with me— it was for them a source of amused pride that I knew all the biomedical terminology connected with it. My questions were fairly predictable; however, I had many more intimate doubts and unasked questions as to whether I experienced the same physiological sensations as other people (specifically, those experiences involved with bladder and bowel functions). As this was not a socially acceptable subject, and because I had an overwhelming urge to conform to the experiences and customs of those around me, I never asked anyone about this, and so did not relieve my doubts or anxiety.

Imaginary Friends, and Real

As I grew older and went to high school, the vague foreboding became more of a tangible wall. There was now an immense and very real problem of how to make friends and hold them. It is easy for a young child who wanders around in a kiddy-car to be happy by himself in a world of fantasy; but there comes a time when the reality of his social nature forces itself upon him, and imaginary friends are no longer satisfying.

The difficulty in socialization for severely handicapped persons seems to stem from the fact that the majority of people are so taken aback by the sight of the effects of the handicap that it is impossible for them to get to know the person who exists beneath all this disability—who is, so to speak, hidden behind the radically altered facade. Of course, this reaction comes in varying degrees, but the problem of relating is made more intense when people are embarrassed to ask a person with a speech defect to repeat uncomprehended words. Others are so overcome with pity, shock, or fear that they cannot even bear to relate to, much less associate with, a handicapped person.

Then there is a small minority of people—and they are far easier for me to get along with—who are so desensitized to disabling or handicapping conditions that they almost completely overlook them and are virtually unsympathetic to the real fears and anxieties which the disability or handicap causes. It is fine to have friends like this on the ordinary social level. They not only embrace large parts of your reality, but they also force you to think about subjects completely unrelated to yourself, which is absolutely necessary if you are to become a healthy, outgoing individual.

But it is vitally necessary that the severely handicapped person attempt to form a few really close and binding friendships with people who both understand him as a person and also comprehend the full significance of his disability or handicap, to whom he can easily and frankly vent the turbulent feelings about life situations which he must confront. Without such two-way, free-flowing relationships, one feels horribly shut off and lonely—and life soon becomes meaningless alone. There are, at least to my present knowledge, very few people who are sufficiently mature, stable, yet sensitive enough to fulfill the need, and who are also willing to be fully honest, not only about their fellow man, but also about themselves. Perhaps these friends are a rarity even for the nondisabled.

Identity Search

By the time I was well into high school I felt my difference to a tremendous degree, and furthermore, I felt that I was radically different not only physically but mentally. My parents and teachers recommended authors and books, and what I read had an added bearing on my feeling that I was mentally different from most other people. The young, severely handicapped person desperately searches for a normal person who feels the way he does about life. His search is so intensive that he is most apt to identify himself, though the image is vastly distorted, with whomever he is reading about.

Emily Dickinson, the recluse who wrote poetry, is a distant relative of mine. Because I already felt shut off from the world, because certain teachers encouraged me to become a poet, and finally because I began to speak in short, cryptic sentences—the full significance of which no one could have possibly understood—I was dead certain that I was to grow up to be just like Emily Dickinson. I imagined that I had inherited a family curse from her. It sounds laughable, but this line of thought was a most disturbing experience.

The lack of concern of my parents and teachers was in part my fault, for I was ashamed of my intense fear and apprehension concerning my future life, and therefore I did not try to express it often. On the rare occasions when I attempted to describe it to someone—and I always talked about it in a highly oblique manner—my listener would either look blank or else rapidly dismiss the idea as ridiculous. These light dismissals only compounded the problem. This example of a distorted self-image and distorted communications is most characteristic of my high school days.

After a few years I felt a great desire to assert my independence, but it was difficult because of my physical limitations. I began to choose my own books instead of reading only those which were recommended to me. One of the most memorable of these was John Updike's *The Centaur*. Updike writes very perceptively and honestly of the whole experience of being human—physiological, emotional, intellectual, and spiritual. What a tremendous comfort and revelation he was! The identity and unity that I suddenly felt with the human race after so long a period of isolation has to be experienced to be appreciated. To have been such an inestimable boon, the book had to start its reassurance on the animal level, a reassurance which had hitherto been neglected by those around me.

Another writer who meant a great deal to me for much the same reasons, but also for many others, was Thomas Wolfe. I was swept away by the vitality with which he described human experience.

Yet all these wondrous and newly discovered treasures brought me some worries as well as unhoped-for comfort. I fretted that I must be very queer indeed if I so desperately craved such basic affirmation that I shared something in common with the rest of humanity.

Fortunately, at this point I met some people who enjoyed the same sort of books which had so fired me. As we became acquainted, I found that because they were so honest and frank about the four main aspects of human existence—physiological, emotional, intellectual, and spiritual—I instinctively felt that these people perceived and comprehended both the person I was and the intricate and related ramifications of my handicap. I therefore spoke more freely to them of the fears and anxieties which had been pent up inside me for the major part of my life; and just as they had been fully open about the contingencies of universal human existence, so now they were most receptive to and accepting of (even shedding light on) the worries that appeared peculiar to being severely handicapped. Although our conversations covered a vast range of subjects, the full ramifications of my disability were so easily perceived and accepted by these people that none of us hesitated to discuss its consequences. I had finally formed with these nondisabled people some truly close friendships, which are the keystones of meaningful social living and without which all else fails and is scattered.

Privacy, Not Loneliness

Such experiences of being different which I have just related raise two important questions. First, how can we make the severely handicapped person feel that he shares the same basic experiences of existence with all humanity, and at the same time maintain his right to privacy? The reassurance of humanness must cover the physiological level as well as the others. This reassurance cuts through one's sense of personal isolation, which is even more strongly felt when severe disability renders one so different. When such isolation has been erased, one can begin to identify with the rest of mankind.

There is an intense satisfaction in some biological privacy, which has nothing to do with the conditioned shame fostered by a prudish society. Man needs to be entirely alone for certain periods in order to grow in self-knowledge and to get away from the pressures of his environment, and what better time is there for his self-renewal than when he is fully relaxed and aware of his whole person? To deprive anyone of any privacy which he values is to deprive him of one of the essential human dignities. Yet man's right to privacy must be balanced against the deep loneliness which results from doubts as to whether he has the same sensations as do all others. One happy solution to this rather touchy problem lies in books which deal with the entire range of human experience, with simplicity and unreservedness, for books may be read in private but may be shared with friends.

This brings us to the second question: How does one suggest books to a severely handicapped young person without his developing the "Emily Dickinson syndrome," as it were? The answer is simple, but terribly difficult to put into practice: Find out what the child himself is really thinking about, what his real concerns are, and what puzzles and really worries him. Obviously the process takes infinite patience, maturity, and time, for the child may be fearful, anxious, and reticent, and the effort has to be doubled if the child has a major speech defect that inhibits communication. Here again, the child's right to privacy must be respected, and it is a bad idea to push too hard. Respectful listening is also warranted when the child finally comes forth with an expression of his innermost feelings and needs. Make sure you understand what he means; otherwise the whole process is wasted. And then whatever you do, don't tell him his ideas are wrong or ridiculous; they do not seem so to him! Instead, help him to be frank and unashamed in all the aspects of being human.

Once you have discovered what is on the child's mind, tell him not only about your own experiences but also about any books that will speak to him personally, that will give him the experiences of others, and that will clarify his ideas and perhaps share some of his feelings. There are those who see the greatest value of literature as its capacity to broaden one's horizons; I am all for expanding one's viewpoint, but solutions to deep personal problems can never be alleviated through suppression and avoidance, and their resolution is prerequisite to the larger shared view of reality itself. I think the best books both offer a profile of the outer world and illuminate one's inner world.

The skillful recommendation of what to read requires a familiarity with numerous forms of literature and an alert and sensitive mind to put that familiarity to use. After the child has read a book, be sure to listen, just as attentively as before, to his reaction to it. Thus you will gain a clearer understanding of the direction his thought has taken. Books should be regarded as vehicles of communicating reality rather than as mere licenses to "join the fellowship of educated men."

I hope I have presented a few valid guidelines by which the severely handicapped but sensitive person and those around him can come to grips with and eventually overcome his deep-rooted fears and anxiety about being different, and partake of a larger, mutually shared reality, to the benefit of all.

Books That Help Children

RUTH E. HUTCHERSON

Today there is a new and tender regard for childhood. We recognize children, not as a classification of creature to be seen and not heard, but as individuals with feelings, desires, hurts and fears like our own—and, above all, great needs to grow freely and to be understood.

Children's feelings of insecurity, inferiority and fear of self and situations may bring about personal unhappiness which, if unrelieved, can develop into chronic undersirable personality traits or, in some instances, into mental and emotional illness.

Inasmuch as the building of a wholesome, self-confident, self-respecting, effective, and happy personality is one of the major goals of education, the teacher and librarian are constantly seeking ways to give each child the guidance he needs.

One of these ways is through telling stories which fit the developmental needs of a group of students, followed by group discussions of the characters in the story, why they reacted as they did and what social values may be found in the story. Defining these values is important for, as Virginia Woolf says in her essay on Defoe, "The impressions of childhood are those that last longest and cut deepest."

The librarian may also suggest books for recreational reading in which the child may receive mental and

Reprinted from *Library Journal*, May 15, 1963. Published by R. R. Bowker Co. (a Xerox company). Copyright © 1963 by R. R. Bowker Co.

emotional therapy through identification with a character in a book who faced a problem or situation similar to the child's own. The role of books in a child's emotional or intellectual development cannot be overestimated. Reading can and often does have a marked positive influence on personality. It can be used for promoting personal growth and furthering personal adjustment. To this use we attach the name bibliotherapy.

It is very important to know what books to place at a particular child's disposal, because a book will help a person only to the degree that it satisfies his particular need. "The right book for the right child at the right time," more than just a slogan, helps to lay the foundation and erect the framework of character in childhood.

As we know, each child reads with his store of knowledge rather than merely with his eyes. He takes his own needs and his own problems to the reading experience. He reads himself into the characters which he sees there, and he may come to see himself as others see him; the mirror image helps him to see his own weaknesses without directly threatening his ego.

Reading may give the child vicarious experiences. Through these he becomes better prepared to meet real problems because, through reading, he already has met similar problems. Vicarious experience is valuable to the child because it gives him an opportunity to carry on some of the trial-and-error process of choosing and rejecting behavior patterns, while avoiding the suffering and disaster such experimentation would involve if carried on in real life.

Five classifications of children's needs, and titles of books which the writer has used successfully in the elementary field to meet these needs, follow.

1. *Emotional security.* Children need to have emotional security. They need to love and be loved.

Normally, the development of emotional security begins in the home where the child learns his first lessons in human relations. When the relations in a home are normal and happy, children expect to find friendly relations with other people. Trust, integrity, fortitude, humor all flourish in the home (and in the classroom) where there is an atmosphere of emotional security.

Family antagonisms, on the other hand, breed suspicious, belligerent attitudes toward others. The child who is denied emotional security suffers serious handicaps. Books can help him.

In Ann Durrell's *Lost Bear*, a wicked dwarf tells Little Brown Bear that no one loves him. Then the other lost toy animals in the land of the Very Back of Beyond try to show him attention and be nice to him, but he still cries and cries. One day a kind dwarf tells the toy animals that toy love is not enough, that what Little Brown Bear needs is a real person to love him.

The Gift of Hawaii by Laura Bannon is the story of John-John, a little Hawaiian boy who wants to buy a big, big gift for his mother's birthday, because he has big aloha (love) for her. His few pennies turn out to be not enough, but his mother is proud of the lei which he made himself out of wildflowers. "This is the biggest gift I ever got," says his mother. "Every little flower is filled with big aloha and that's all that matters."

2. *Being accepted by peers.* Closely allied to the need for emotional security, and essential to it, is the need to belong, to be accepted as part of the group. Every child wants to be accepted; he achieves satisfaction and status as he contributes to the group. This form of emotional satisfaction is eagerly, sometimes desperately, sought by children. Those who are denied it often compensate in extreme ways.

There are many fine books which show the hurt that follows rejection and the different ways individuals react to being rejected.

In *The Beatinest Boy* by Jesse Stuart, David does not want to go to live with that tall, strange lady after the death of his parents, but he finds that his grandmother is the most wonderful woman in the world. He wants to make some money to buy her the grandest Christmas present, though they need all they have for bare necessities. She must feel that he is a help to her, also, for doesn't she often say that he is the beatinest boy in the world and she cannot get along without him?

Other fine stories of security through family togetherness are brought out in *All-of-a-Kind Family* by Sydney Taylor, Ruth Sawyer's *Maggie Rose* and Genevieve Foster's *Teddy Roosevelt.* These stories show not only the loneliness and isolation that an individual feels in being left out, but also how those social skills are built that can make him a contributing member of society.

M. E. Rey's *Spotty*, a blue-eyed, brown spotted little rabbit, runs away from home because his pink-eyed, white relatives are ashamed of him. (The children discuss ways that they can make all of their classmates feel wanted and loved.)

In *The Hundred Dresses* by Eleanor Estes, small, shabby Wanda is rejected and disbelieved by her schoolmates when she boasts of her hundred dresses. It is too late to make amends when she moves away and the children discover that her skill in art has given her honors greater than theirs. (This gives a vivid picture of how rejection affects a child's relationships in school.)

Little Gray Burro in Ann Nolan Clark's *Looking for Something* is not content to be a stray burro like his mother. He longs to belong to something or somebody. After searching throughout Ecuador, he succeeds.

Cyrano the Crow by Don Freeman learns the hard way that it pays to "just be yourself" rather than imitating others, when he performs on TV and forgets the simple call of a crow, after imitating nine other bird calls to perfection.

3. *Material security.* Desire for materials, or eco-

nomic security, is part of the drive toward comfort and well-being, goals which represent freedom from want and its accompanying anxiety. The child soon grasps the implications which society places on economic status and his attitudes are often conditioned by the position of his family on the socioeconomic scale.

Material security often satisfies in the child the desire to achieve. He gains self-respect as he feels that he and his family are contributing members of society. The child denied this security may suffer anxiety, fear, envy, resentment, frustration, despair, ill health, and neglect. His attempts to alleviate the accompanying tensions may take a wide variety of forms.

Elmo the giant, in the story *Lucky and the Giant* by Benjamin Elkin, has built a lake out of the brook so that it cannot come down the mountain to water the crops. Lucky, a small boy, outwits the giant, saves his parents from seven years of hard labor and retrieves the brook.

In discussing "giants" which individuals must learn to overcome, a child who never smiled nor took part in class activities suddenly exclaimed, "I have a big giant to overcome—fear. I am afraid of things trying to grab me at night." *Theodore Roosevelt* by Genevieve Foster showed her that others had the same "giant" to overcome. Teddy had just celebrated his seventh birthday and was sitting in bed reliving that wonderful day. He noticed that someone had forgotten to put his sister Connie's rag doll to bed. As he was getting back to bed, he saw a long, white, spooky something slither in from outside. He stood there shivering and shaking, too scared to move, until he suddenly realized that it was the window curtain. Teddy finally learned to overcome his fear by pretending to be brave just as he had read in a book. He would put his chest out, hold his shoulders back and say, "I'm not afraid." One day he realizes that he has not been afraid in a long time.

The next time that Mary came to the library, she came to me smiling, "I have only had two nightmares lately because I remember to do what Teddy did and I say real quickly, 'I am not afraid.'"

In *Something for the Medicine Man* by Flora Hood, April's first violet seems a poor gift for the revered old medicine man, and Ada is ashamed of her gift beside the nice gifts of the other children. But she learns that the heart needs more than food; since he could no longer go out into the woods to gather herbs, Ada had brought the beauty of the woods into him. "Beauty lives on long in the heart of man," this book tells us. The children learn that it is often not the most expensive gift that gives the greatest joy.

4. *Spiritual security*. Children need to see themselves in relation to all things; they need a sense of values and moral purpose. A child who has spiritual security is likely to be more tolerant, better able to withstand vicissitudes, better able to form valid judgments. He has a sense of direction and purpose in life. Denied this kind of security, a child may be confused, antisocial, egocentric, and unstable.

The ideals of children and young people should be broad enough to function in different emergencies. Books which discuss values and point out guideposts for courses of action are most valuable.

Maybe, like Shan in Jesse Stuart's *A Penny's Worth of Character*, in a moment of weakness we cheat just a little and then find that there is a heavy price to pay.

Jean Merrill's *The Superlative Horse* is full of values which help to light a child's dim path. A jealous disposition, such as that of the Chief Minister who constantly tried to berate Po Lo, never leads to happiness but to one's own downfall. In judging a superlative horse, like a superior or inferior person, one does not look for external details of color, sex, breed, or build. Excellence is a matter of the heart and spirit in a horse as in a man. Han Kan chooses a fine strong horse from the Imperial stables to run a race against his black stallion, for to race against an inferior horse holds no honor.

At the Christmas season, the *Christmas Tree Forest* is appropriate for children, for they see the value of an unselfish attitude on the part of Inge, who is concerned only with making his little crippled sister happy on Christmas Day. He is the only child who finds gifts in the Christmas tree forest where Grandfather Christmas put them only for children who were looking for gifts for others—not themselves.

The Little Juggler in Barbara Cooney's adaptation knows very little of anything except to juggle, but he finds that "doing his very best" is a far greater gift to the Christ Child and His Mother than are the seemingly finer gifts of the others.

Also, *Amahl and the Night Visitors, Why the Chimes Rang, Kickapoo,* and *The Terrible Mr. Twitmeyer* prove the values of unselfishness, kindness, love, and belonging.

Learning to accept responsibility and "how to listen" are brought out in the story of *Champ: The Gallant Collie* by Patricia Lauber. Champ knows how to take care of the sheep, but finds many things to distract his attention. However, during a storm he proves that he is worthy of his name.

Fear is something we all have sometimes. Courage is often something we talk about, but too seldom demonstrate. Mafatu is a Polynesian boy in *Call It Courage* by Armstrong Sperry. Mafatu fears the sea. Because of this fear, he hasn't the courage to be the kind of fisherman he, his father and others living on the island expect and hope he might become. How he comes to grips with his fear and earns the respect and admiration of his family, peers, and his society is truly inspiring.

5. *Physical handicaps.* This is one area that surely needs careful attention. Not all children can overcome their handicaps and become well and strong. Many children must learn not to feel sorry for themselves, and they must learn the important lesson of patience and perseverance.

Theodore Roosevelt had a strong mind, but his father told him that a strong mind could not go far unless he had a strong body. "You must make your body," said his father. This took patience and years of hard practice. Later, when he tries to enter college, Teddy finds that he is weak in some of his academic subjects. The children need no teacher-moralizing to realize the importance of studying to develop a strong mind to go with a strong body.

Bertie Poodle is a fat boy in *Bertie Comes Through* by Henry Felsen. He tries out for all the sports but fails in each one because of his weight and his slowness. He never gives up, but with courage and good humor he tries again.

Many children secretly suffer from freckles just as Ann in *Freckle Face*, until she discovers one day that many of the prettiest flowers have spots on them, just like freckles.

Thus the librarian can provide bibliotherapy—help through books that will influence personality and character. The books are of little value until the ideas in them are transferred to the minds of children and young people. The teacher and librarian have the job of bringing books and the reader together. If in our reading guidance we can encourage understanding for the way others feel, then we have had a part in broadening the adults of tomorrow.

BIBLIOGRAPHY

Alden, Raymond M. *Christmas Tree Forest.* Indianapolis, Ind.: Bobbs-Merrill, 1958.

Anderson, Neil. *Freckle Face.* New York: Crowell, 1957.

Bannon, Laura. *The Gift of Hawaii.* Chicago: Albert Whitman, 1961.

Clark, Ann Nolan. *Looking-For-Something.* New York: Viking, 1952.

Cooney, Barbara. *The Little Juggler.* New York: Hastings, 1961.

Durell, Ann. *Lost Bear.* New York: Doubleday, 1959.

Elkin, Benjamin. *Lucky and the Giant.* Chicago: Children's Press, 1962.

Estes, Eleanor. *The Hundred Dresses.* New York: Harcourt, 1944.

Felson, Gregor. *Bertie Comes Through.* New York: Dutton, 1947.

Foster, Genevieve. *Theodore Roosevelt.* New York: Scribner, 1954.

Freeman, Don. *Cyrano the Crow.* New York: Viking, 1960.

Hall, Natalie. *Zig-Zag Zeppo.* New York: Viking, 1961.

Hood, Flora M. *Something for the Medicine Man.* Chicago: Melmont, 1962.

Lauber, Patricia. *Champ: Gallant Collie.* New York: Random, 1960.

Menotti, Gian C. *Amahl and the Night Visitors.* New York: McGraw-Hill, 1952.

Merrill, Jean. *The Superlative Horse.* New York: W. R. Scott, 1961.

Miles, Miska. *Kickapoo.* Boston: Little, 1961.

Moore, Lilian, and Adelson, Leone. *The Terrible Mr. Twitmeyer.* New York: Random, 1952.

Rey, Margret, and Rey, H. A. *Spotty,* New York: Harper, 1945.

Sperry, Armstrong. *Call It Courage.* New York: Macmillan, 1940.

Stuart, Jesse. *The Beatinist Boy.* New York: McGraw-Hill, 1953.

———. *A Penny's Worth of Character.* New York: McGraw-Hill, 1954.

Williams, Gweneira. *Timid Timothy.* New York: W. R. Scott, 1958.

The Librarian in Bibliotherapy: Pharmacist or Bibliotherapist?

MARGARET C. HANNIGAN

Over the years since 1904, when the first hospital librarian in the United States was appointed to take charge of the patients' library at MacLean Hospital in Boston, the concepts of the library as a therapeutic agent and the librarian as bibliotherapist have been developing. In *Hospital Libraries*, E. Kathleen Jones[1] quotes two prominent hospital administrators of the early part of this century as considering a well conducted hospital library a therapeutic agent, useful in hastening convalescence and restoring health. Dr. Gordon R. Kamman,[2] in several notable articles written in the late 1930s and early 1940s, also endorsed bibliotherapy and stressed the necessity of a trained librarian as a contributing member of the therapeutic team.

Since World War II the concept of the librarian as the specialist whose responsibility is to bring books and people together for therapeutic reasons has gained acceptance. Dr. Maurice Floch made observations on the role of the librarian in group therapy with prisoners. These observations apply as well to the role of the librarian in a hospital. He says, "The librarian has an eminent and significant place in this type of treatment. He is the one who compiles the raw material for treatment, that is, the books. He is the one who determines what books can play what role in the process."[3] Later he adds, "The library is a crucial and integral part of the

Reprinted by permission from *Library Trends* 11:184–98 (1962).

corrective treatment setup. It can serve group therapy by expertly providing material for discussion and also by reenforcing and complementing the discussion through appropriate reading lists. The librarian, in turn, acts as an analyzer of the discussion material and provides the medicament, so to speak, for the use of the group therapists. As a librarian he necessarily becomes a specialist, that is, a specialist in correctional library work.''[4]

At the 1957 annual meeting of the Association of Hospital and Institution Libraries, in a panel discussion on bibliotherapy, Drs. Julius Griffin and Robert Zeitler showed no reluctance in saying that the librarians who worked with them in group bibliotherapy were therapists. They pointed out that the librarian with his knowledge of books and the psychiatrist with his knowledge of people generally and of his patients particularly, make an excellent team. Dr. Griffin reproved librarians for not taking the initiative in offering their specialty more widely; he charged them to see that what they have to offer patients and staff be exploited fully.

Of importance in establishing the role of the hospital librarian as bibliotherapist was the Veterans Administration *Position-Classification Guide*, July 1952,[5] even though it has now been superseded by new Civil Service standards. The *Guide*, in analyzing the functions of the Patients' Librarian, specifically listed the practice of bibliotherapy as a distinctive feature of this category of position and described its responsibility in this way:

Bibliotherapy

In carrying out the function of bibliotherapy the librarian, in consultation with the medical staff and as part of the total medical program, stimulates and develops reading interests and recommends and provides reading material through (1) readers' advisory service, (2) individual and/or group therapy, and (3) special library activities correlated with patients' interests. Individual and/or group therapy, as defined below, must be present for this function to be credited. This together with book selection represents the most difficult function associated with patients' library work and must be present to warrant allocation to the various classes of Librarian (Patients) described at the grade levels.

1. *Readers' Advisory Service*. The librarian stimulates and develops reading interest by recommending and providing reading materials through discussions with patients on the wards and ambulatory patients who come to the library. The librarian assists patients with book selection, and makes suggestions based on their requests, needs, reading habits, physical condition, and educational, social and occupational and language background.

2. *Individual and Group Therapy*. The objective of individual and group therapy is to lessen the mental and emotional strain and to motivate the patient toward normal living through professional guidance in the use of library materials. This function encompasses planned and directed reading and related activities planned from the ward surgeon's prescription to stimulate the patient's intellectual faculties, and the prevention of contact with harmful materials which tend to excite the patient's condition.

3. *Special Activities*. The librarian aids the patients' physical and mental recovery and adjustment by creating and stimulating their initiative, self-reliance, and confidence through projects leading to the use of library material. Hobby and vocational displays, nature study groups, library activities for special occasions, etc., correlated with the vocational, recreational, and cultural background of the patients, are organized and developed by the librarian to encourage the use of the library in connection with these projects. The primary purpose of these projects is to stimulate the patient to use his own initiative in engaging in activities which will aid in his adjustments.[6]

Here appears a clear understanding of the librarian's role as consultant in these matters. In the writer's experience, the stipulation, "in consultation with the medical staff and as part of the total medical program," is usually interpreted (both within and outside the Veterans Administration) in such a way as to place upon the librarian's shoulders the responsibility for conducting bibliotherapy programs, individual and group, to meet the aims of treatment and for cooperating with the methods being used by other therapists. This responsibility requires attendance at staff meetings where such aims and methods are discussed; acquiring knowledge of the patients through meetings, consultations with other staff members, the reading of case histories and reports, and interviews with the patients planning and conducting bibliotherapy programs; and reporting the results of the programs to the staff. In other words, once the librarian is accepted as a member of the therapy or treatment team, he is expected to assume responsibility for activities in his own field, under guidance of the medical staff and in cooperation with the other members of the team.

Concurrently there developed a second concept of the librarian's role in bibliotherapy, one in which the librarian fills the physicians' prescription for reading material for his patients and has varying degrees of responsibility for consulting with the doctor, suggesting titles, and discussing books with the patients. It reached its peak in the early 1940s and is still practiced in cases where the physician or psychotherapist himself prescribes specific reading matter for his patients. Representing this point of view is Dr. Ralph G. Ball,[7] who considers bibliotherapy an extremely valuable addition to the ever increasing therapeutic equipment of the physician and thinks of the librarian as the pharmacist who fills the prescriptions from his shelves for the bibliotherapist.

Some of the earlier writings in bibliotherapy presented this idea. For instance, in 1937 Dr. William C. Menninger reported on a five-year experiment in bibliotherapy at the Menninger Clinic which was directly under the physician's supervision. In discussing the technique of prescription of reading, he described the functions of physician and librarian in this way:

In the development of our program we have evolved a plan by which certain responsibilities are delegated to the physician and certain other responsibilities to the librarian. It is the established attitude that reading is a treatment method and, as such, must be directed by the physician. The librarian is the tool who carries out the mechanics and reports observations.

The physician is responsible for at least six functions with regard to the program. First, he is responsible for the contents of the library and must approve books before they are purchased. It is expected that the librarian will make herself familiar with new literature available, and prepare the recommended list of books to purchase . . . . Second, he must approve the weekly list of current reading assignments to the patients as submitted by the librarian. Third, he prescribes the first reading assignment given to a patient after having interviewed the patient; this is not only to insure a wise choice but also to enlist the patient's interest in it. Fourth, he holds weekly conferences with the librarian regarding problems that have arisen and the results that have been obtained. Fifth, it is his responsibility to communicate the historical data and the psychological status of each new patient, along with that patient's particular reading habits and interests, to the librarian for her aid and guidance. Last, he must express a personal interest in and carry on frequent discussions with the patient regarding his therapeutic reading.

The librarian's responsibilities include, first, the mechanics of purchasing and distributing the books. Second, she must have a personal acquaintance with the books she lends to the patients. Third, she interviews each patient as to the impressions and satisfaction gained from each assigned or chosen reading. Last, she is responsible for making a written report of the patients' comments and reactions to their reading for the physician's information.[8]

Fortunate is the librarian working with such a physician, and doubly fortunate the patient receiving bibliotherapy under these circumstances. But Dr. Menninger is, of course, describing a research study under the direct supervision of the physician, with his active participation in selecting and prescribing reading material. In the daily routine of a hospital, a physician can hardly be expected to assume all the duties listed. Unless, in fact, a doctor is well read and keenly interested in bibliotherapy, he will not attempt to personally prescribe reading for his patients. Many medical men confess, frankly and humbly, that they are not well enough

acquainted with general literature to select their patients' reading material. There is wide acceptance, however, of the idea that reading is a therapeutic aid to treatment. Physicians usually are eager to have their patients receive good library service and to trust the librarian with the details of bibliotherapy, if he is known to be interested and competent.

How then are we to produce librarians who are "interested and competent" in this important field?

The responsibility for establishing bibliotherapy as an accepted, vital part of treatment of the ill obviously rests squarely with librarians themselves. If we really believe what we say we do about the beneficial effects of bibliotherapy, then we must do something about making it generally available. Obstacles which seem insuperable must be overcome so that bibliotherapy will be practiced throughout the country. Its effectiveness, its economy, its very attractiveness must be demonstrated widely if it is to gain the recognition and acceptance of administrators and of the medical and allied professions.

Eventually we may have specialists to practice bibliotherapy, with no responsibility for administration of the library, for meeting bookcart schedules, or for other duties which consume the hospital librarian's time. At present, however, there is no one but the overworked librarian, who serves hundreds, even thousands, of patients with the help of untrained volunteers and patient workers, to lift the level of library service to include consciously practiced bibliotherapy. It will require a reevaluation of duties to rank bibliotherapy with such basic services as meeting of bookcart schedules to wards and the selection, acquisition, and processing of materials. It may demand streamlining or even abandoning of some routines presently performed by the librarian. It certainly will require shifting more duties to volunteers until additional staff can be added.

Even the most ardent advocate of bibliotherapy is realistic enough to recognize that full-blown programs will not spring up spontaneously. Most hospital librarians practice bibliotherapy in individual cases where the physician or perhaps the social worker has referred a patient to the library. Some conduct group bibliotherapy sessions as part of the therapeutic program of a ward. The recommendation here is that many more librarians start a project in individual or group bibliotherapy on a small, manageable scale with the cooperation of an interested staff member or team of workers. This program should be well planned, regularly conducted, and given priority on the librarian's schedule. It should be evaluated constantly and followed up frequently with reports to the proper authorities.

What better time is there than now to take the initiative, as individual librarians and as members of professional groups, in establishing bibliotherapy as a regular part of treatment and the bibliotherapist as an active member of the treatment team? For we are living in an age when the concepts of treatment, care, and rehabilitation of patients are based upon the idea of a team working together with one goal, the cure of the patient. Terms like "therapeutic community," "milieu therapy," and "treating the whole person" imply cooperation and coordination of functions on the part of all members of the staff.

The idea of treating the whole person and of considering more than the medical aspects of a patient's condition can be traced to ancient times, but its general acceptance and application are modern. Back in 1934, Dr. Kamman said, "We know that every illness has its mental component and we have long since come to regard the individual as a whole, as a unit. We no longer separate a person, as the Ancient Greeks did, into his various 'faculties' and treat each part of him as a separate entity. We recognize the unity of mind and body and realize that what affects one affects the other. Therefore, in the treatment of diseases we must see that the mental as well as the physical hygiene of the patient is taken into account."[9] In a recent article, Dr. Karl Menninger[10] noted that a great step forward had been taken when doctors began to concentrate some of their attention upon the individual himself apart from his affliction. Because his subject was "Reading as Therapy," he made special mention of the library as containing "many things needed by the patient to inform him, assist him, comfort him, inspire him, amuse him . . ."[11] and of the librarians who help maintain "the total therapeutic effectiveness of the hospital" by rendering "daily, patient, unobtrusive work of incalculable value."[12] But his emphasis upon the importance of the social and psychological factors in the life of the patient imply the need for the services and cooperation of many other people.

In attempting to visualize his own role on the therapy team, the librarian must understand the traditional roles of the hospital staff members and the changing roles of personnel in the modern hospital community where sociopsychological characteristics are the basis of treatment policies. With the evolution of the concept of the team, each group of workers has had to adapt itself to meet changing goals and relationships. This change requires the team to redefine its own scope and responsibilities and at the same time learn to work understandingly with many other persons for the good of the patient. Old-line staff members whose status is threatened by the assignment of new duties and the advent of new personnel may obstruct progress based upon ideals of diffusion and interdependence of roles in therapy, unless explanations are given and training for new roles carried on over a long preparatory period. Unless he thoroughly understands the old and the new situations, the librarian who has gone about his duties

of giving library service to all, patiently and unobtrusively as Dr. Menninger said, but more or less ignorant of the plans and coordinated efforts of the team, may meet resistance and unfriendliness when he tries to take an active part in the therapeutic program.

To help the librarian assume a more important and effective role, the writer recommends that he study modern hospital and institution organization and the philosophy of present-day treatment. Three pertinent books which explore current trends in the treatment of patients in mental hospitals demonstrate that traditional roles of hospital personnel can be redirected, that representatives of a variety of professions can be integrated into an effective team, and that a custodial-type hospital can be made into a therapeutic community characterized by the "open" door rather than the locked door. They are *The Therapeutic Community*, by Maxwell Jones;[13] *Research Conference on Therapeutic Community*, edited by Dr. Herman C. B. Denber;[14] and *The Patient and the Mental Hospital, Contributions of Research in the Science of Social Behavior*, edited by Dr. Milton Greenblatt.[15] All, while giving insight into the problems of introducing flexibility and new ideas into the rigid, traditional organization of a hospital, also demonstrate the effectiveness of such ideas in the treatment of the ill.

The librarian needs to know the purposes and objectives of other professional groups—nurses, social workers, occupational therapists, psychologists, psychiatrists, and others—whose work is integrated into the overall plan of treatment. Each profession is well represented by books and articles which give the aims and functions of the group and often the historical development as well. Only two texts will be named here as examples of writing in this field. *Principles and Technics of Rehabilitation Nursing*, edited by Deborah M. Jensen,[16] gives an enlightened explanation of rehabilitation, an excellent interpretation of teamwork, and helpful chapters on the techniques of rehabilitation of patients with many kinds of diseases and disabilities. The Fidlers' *Introduction to Psychiatric Occupational Therapy*,[17] concerned as it is with "techniques of teaching skills of living," presents experiences and case histories which will be of value to librarians. Of particular interest is the discussion of ways in which this specialty can be coordinated with more generally accepted treatment procedures in psychiatry since in many situations the position of the librarian parallels that of the occupational therapist.

Dominant ideas running through much of the writing on the therapeutic community and on hospitals using the team approach to treating the whole person are that these types of hospitals are operated along strongly democratic lines as opposed to authoritarianism; that present-day treatment must integrate all therapies available without particular emphasis upon any one; and that even the contributions of the nonmedical staff are essential in the total rehabilitative experience. Dr. Alexander Gralnick summarizes his remarks on the changing scene in psychiatric hospitals in this way, "It is believed that emphasis must be shifted towards 'total' treatment of the patient in an enlightened social setting. Here, active patient participation will be an index of healthy group interaction between various staff members and patients."[18] Dr. Henry Brill[19] notes that a marked diffusion of authority to personnel and to patients is the key characteristic of this system.

In this climate it seems that bibliotherapy would be recognized as one of the treatment procedures regularly used with patients. In some hospitals indeed this is already the case. It is from the experiences of librarians who practice bibliotherapy in conjunction with the treatment program that the role of bibliotherapist is here delineated.

The primary function of the librarian on the therapy team, as in other areas of library service, is based upon cognizance of the needs of the community and of the individual reader and upon knowledge of books available to meet those needs.

It is as bookman that the librarian is equipped to make his unique contribution. He must be a book specialist having a wide knowledge of literature, a love of books and reading, the ability to judge and evaluate books, and a proficiency in selecting them to meet the needs of his readers. Helen Haines, in the introduction to *Living with Books*, describes the special qualities of the librarian in this way, "The spirit of delight and confidence in books, the receptive and adventurous attitude toward the new and experimental, the catholicity of lifelong friendship and understanding for literature, are attributes of librarianship more than of any other calling."[20] She points out that the taste for books is not common to all. She says, "It is a spark latent in the individual, most often implanted by heredity, kindled by training or circumstance, and fed and tended by purpose and experience. But only those who possess this spark will draw from librarianship its full measure of inspiration and reward in the interpretation and enrichment of human life through books."[21] The spark Miss Haines talks about is an endowment essential for the librarian who would be bibliotherapist.

In common with other members of the team, the librarian must know the patients, their educational and vocational background, their interests, and enough about their illness and its characteristics to understand their behavior and some of their problems. He needs to know and understand the hospital community, the kinds of diseases treated, the goals of treatment, and the philosophy of administration.

Combining his knowledge of books and people, the bibliotherapist brings the two together for the therapeutic benefit of the patient. This skill is a refined application of his normal librarian's function as readers' advisor. Miss Haines also states that

Librarianship is the only calling that devotes itself to bringing books into the common life of the world. The materials librarians work with are the materials which furnish the understanding, knowledge, and reason that can inform the mind and direct the will to meet the challenge of the time, to fit ourselves to its compulsions, to discern and guide the forces that are shaping the future. The 'great trade' of publishing and bookselling, though it is the oldest and most universal agency for bringing together the reader and the printed word, has not the same range of opportunity nor the same variety and intimacy of relationship to readers of all tastes, capacities, needs, habits, and levels of education.[22]

The wisdom and the skill with which the bibliotherapist is able to select the right book for a patient at a given time depend upon the therapist's recognition of the range and potentialities of individual reading and upon his own intuition and insight into the problems of others.

But there is more than this. Supporting the major functions of bringing books and patients together is a variety of activities necessary to make the experience of bibliotherapy meaningful, beneficial, and pleasurable for the patients and satisfying to the therapist as well.

Since the librarian is in fact the chief therapist in the area of bibliotherapy, he will interview the patient regarding his reading, initially and from time to time. The technique of interviewing requires an interest in the patient as a person, an understanding point of view, an unhurried manner, and skill in conveying to the patient ideas which he should know about reading and the library and in obtaining needed information about his interests, reactions to reading, and any attitudes which might affect the guidance of his reading.

The stimulation of interest in reading is one of the functions of librarians in many types of libraries. When one is working with patients, this stimulation is especially important because of the apathetic attitude which frequently accompanies illness. In cases of patients who have not discovered the pleasures and benefits of reading, it requires ingenuity and imagination. When people are sick or worried they may need a lengthy period of exposure to books and ideas about reading before responding to suggestions. Experience shows that often the patience and tactful persistence of the librarian in continuing to keep in touch with such individuals results in time in grateful, interested readers.

The role of the librarian as leader of bibliotherapy group meetings is an effective one in situations involving long-term patients, both mental and medical, as well as inmates in correctional institutions, probably because it offers the benefits of both bibliotherapy and group therapy. In addition to stimulating reading interests and helping the individual to escape for a time from his preoccupation with himself and his problems, such groups have other important goals such as socialization, communication (significant even if limited to reading the words of an author with no comments of his own by a withdrawn or unsociable patient), and an increase of attention span. The devoted attendance by patients at group bibliotherapy meetings, even those patients who seldom speak or take part voluntarily in other activities, attests to the value of this kind of experience in the lives of the ill.

Basically the leader of group bibliotherapy uses the techniques of discussion group leaders, adjusting his methods and materials to meet the needs of his group. The writer, in previous articles,[23] has described experiences in group bibliotherapy with many types of neuropsychiatric patients. Since then she has conducted reading groups with chronic medical patients and is convinced that a relatively simple procedure can be adapted for use with any group if the materials are selected to meet the interests and condition of the members.

Once the librarian is established as bibliotherapist, he has to schedule his activities to include those which will enable him to function fully and responsibly on the team. Of major importance in this respect, as has been mentioned, is regular communication with other staff members for the purpose of mutual understanding of each one's part on the team, of learning as much as possible about the patient, his illness and the aims, methods, and progress of his treatment, and of receiving guidance in planning activities. It is worthwhile to take the initiative in attending orientation and in-service training classes given by the different professions for their members and in inviting heads of various departments to speak to the library staff about their work. Along with acquiring basic information about the functions of his coworkers, the librarian arranges to attend staff or team meetings regularly, participating appropriately by reporting generally on library services and programs and specifically about work with individual patients and groups. He makes sure that he understands the goals and general methods of treatment being employed; when necessary he seeks guidance in carrying out his functions and informs the staff of the services, aims, and procedures of the library.

The written record is of major importance in communication. The bibliotherapist will be wise to establish a system of reports to be routed to other team members and to be included in his own files. Although it is time-consuming to prepare these reports, they are essential because they establish a written record for future reference and comparisons. They also give other staff members an understanding of the potential of biblio-

therapy and its cumulative effect in a form that can be readily consulted. The Fidlers' chapter "Progress Reports" contains a helpful discussion of the value of written records kept by the occupational therapist. It points out that intelligently written reports containing pertinent material will be used by the psychiatrist and other professional personnel for diagnostic data and for handling the therapeutic situation. In addition, the actual writing of notes creates an excellent learning situation for the therapist. The bibliotherapist will find the entire chapter useful, especially this paragraph:

Current literature contains some information about the required contents of progress notes; and much concern seems in evidence in regard to the therapist's making evaluations, drawing conclusions, and generally playing the role of psychotherapist. The occupational therapist is a professional worker, and with this designation goes the responsibility for making certain intelligent evaluations. The psychiatrist expects professional, intelligent evaluations and observations, and would find fault only when these observations are neither professional nor intelligent. Descriptive adjectives with little understanding of their meanings, or a superficial evaluation of the situation without a clear understanding of its implications, are never justifiable. However, if the therapist has an understanding of psychiatry and understands what is going on in the clinical situation with the patient, it is a duty to make evaluations and record observations. There is a difference between an accurate evaluation and a postulation. The purpose of progress notes is to record data, and not to furnish a means for discussing theory or making questionable assumptions.[24]

In the writer's experience this observation is sound in the reporting of data on general medical patients and on psychiatric patients. The librarian's observations are needed if all aspects of the patient's activities are to be evaluated in determining his progress.

In the minds of the patients the librarian, the library, and books themselves share an advantageous position which should be exploited for the good of all concerned. The library is identified with the outside world, a place where well people go; reading is one of the few hospital activities which the patient associates with his life outside the hospital. Library experience then removes him from his sickness for a short while. In interpreting the reasons that the disturbed children at the National Institutes of Health loved to come to the library and were able to behave quite normally there, Dr. Fritz Redl (pp. 130–31) describes the library as a piece of the "outside world" safely smuggled into the children's lives, a high-status and high-structure situation in its own right with a purpose and a value system of its own. He uses expressions like "uncontaminated" and "therapeutically clean" to indicate that in the minds of his patients the library is free from the too "treatment orientated" excitement of the daily ward life.

The librarian, too, shares this favored position in the

minds of many patients, even when they know that he attends staff meetings and writes reports of their activities and interactions during library periods. As a result of this kind of relationship, in his reports to the staff the librarian is able frequently to supply information about the patient that is not evident in other hospital situations and hence is most important in total patient care.

Books have a high prestige value to many, the non-reader as well as the reader. Whatever the basis for this regard—as the embodiment of ideas, emotions, or the wisdom of the ages, as a means of education and self-improvement, or as a status symbol—it is true that patients are often reached through books when other means of communication fail.

Bibliotherapy prescribed for individuals can be carried on by a readers' advisor in any library—general hospital, correctional institution, college, school, or public—in cooperation with a physician, counselor, psychologist, or an interdisciplinary team. In the interests of mental health it is important that librarians be aware of the need of many people for bibliotherapy and that they take the responsibility for seeking out members of the medical profession equipped and willing to guide them in recommending books for such special readers in their community.

In summary, it would seem that there is a place for bibliotherapy wherever there are sick or disturbed people in or out of hospitals and institutions. The benefits of bibliotherapy have been observed and reported by reliable medical men and librarians throughout this century—throughout the ages, in fact, if we accept opinions about the effects of reading which antedate the modern term "bibliotherapy." The writer has described the role of the librarian in bibliotherapy as it is presently practiced in isolated cases, and as it may develop in the next ten or twenty years—as it must develop if the immense benefits of bibliotherapy are to be generally available. Of all those interested in the care, rehabilitation, and mental health of people, the librarian is the logical person to assume an important role in bringing books and people together, whether it be as pharmacist filling the reading prescriptions of the physician or as a consultant bibliotherapist prescribing reading and filling his own prescriptions.

Notes

1. E. Kathleen Jones, *Hospital Libraries* (Chicago: American Library Association, 1939).

2. Gordon R. Kamman, "The Doctor and the Patients' Library," *Transactions of the American Hospital Association* 36:374–84 (1934); "Future Aims of the Hospital Library," *Minnesota Medicine* 21:559–61 (August 1938); "The Role of Bibliotherapy in the Care of the Patient," *Bulletin of the American College of Surgeons* 24:183–84 (June 1939); "Balanced Reading Diet Prescribed for Mental Patients," *Modern Hospital* 55:79–80 (November 1940).

3. Maurice Floch, "Correctional Treatment and the Library," *Wilson Library Bulletin* 26:454 (February 1952).

4. Ibid., p. 455.

5. U.S. Veterans Administration, *Position Classification Guide* (Library Series, GS-1410-0) (July 1952).

6. Ibid., pp. 3–4.

7. Ralph G. Ball, "Prescription: Books," *ALA Bulletin* 48:145–57 (March 1954).

8. William C. Menninger, "Bibliotherapy," *Bulletin of the Menninger Clinic* 1:267–68 (November 1937).

9. Kamman, "The Doctor and the Patients' Library," p. 374.

10. Karl A. Menninger, "Reading as Therapy," *ALA Bulletin* 55:316–19 (April 1961).

11. Ibid., p. 316.

12. Ibid., p. 319.

13. Maxwell Jones and others, *The Therapeutic Community* (New York: Basic Books, 1953).

14. Herman C. B. Denber, ed., *Research Conference on Therapeutic Community: Proceedings* (Springfield, Ill.: Charles C. Thomas, 1960).

15. Milton Greenblatt and others, eds., *The Patient and the Mental Hospital* (New York: Free Pr., 1957).

16. Deborah M. Jensen, ed., *Principles and Technics of Rehabilitation Nursing*, 2nd ed. (St. Louis: Mosby, 1961).

17. Gail S. Fidler and J. W. Fidler, *Introduction to Psychiatric Occupational Therapy* (New York: Macmillan, 1954), pp. 102–3.

18. Alexander Gralnick, "Changing Relations of the Patient, Family and Practicing Psychiatrist to the Therapeutic Community," in Herman C. B. Denber, *Research Conference on Therapeutic Community: Proceedings* (Springfield, Ill.: Charles C. Thomas, 1960), p. 160.

19. Henry Brill, "Historical Background of the Therapeutic Community," in Herman C. B. Denber, *Research Conference on Therapeutic Community: Proceedings* (Springfield, Ill.: Charles C. Thomas, 1960), p. 6.

20. Helen E. Haines, *Living with Books: The Act of Book Selection* (Columbia University Studies in Library Service, no. 2, 2nd ed.; New York: Columbia University Press, 1950), p. 10.

21. Ibid.

22. Ibid.

23. Margaret C. Hannigan, "Experience in Group Bibliotherapy," *ALA Bulletin* 48:148–50 (March 1954); "Hospital-wide Group Bibliotherapy Program," *Bookmark* 13:203–10 (June 1954).

24. Fidler and Fidler, *Introduction*, p. 104.

PART 6

Supplementary Resources for Serving the Special Child

The library is the resource heart of the school. Given reasonable financial support, adequate time, and an energetic librarian, most school libraries will be self-contained and autonomous to a large degree. That is, the library serves as a repository theoretically capable of satisfying the standard informational demands of the school program.

However, as exceptional children and youth enter schools, the librarian will discover that the usual holdings are generally inadequate to meet the extraordinary requirements of these students. Although disabled children represent relatively small populations, they make highly specialized demands on the collection. Materials must be provided for them in adapted or alternative format. At the same time, they require access to as broad a spectrum of educational matter as their nonhandicapped peers. Acting responsively and in full measure to the needs of these newly integrated students would place on intolerable strain on the library budget. Yet the librarian feels a moral as well as a professional obligation to serve all patrons. Accordingly, the school library must expand its role and function as a borrowing as well as a lending agency. This, in effect, will exponentially increase access to the materials these children can consult. For example, brailled books are expensive to produce, occupy considerable storage space, and so are prohibitively costly for most schools to own and house in meaningful quantities. Moreover, the specialized nature of these materials makes them useful only to the relatively small population of blind students. There are, however, enormous collections of brailled and talking books available free to blind and physically handicapped students through agencies other than the public schools. It would be an unjustifiable extravagance for schools to attempt to provide an equivalent collection rather than take advantage of this excellent, readily available service.

Supported by private and governmental funds, special interest agencies have been identifying problems, developing materials, and providing service for selected disability populations for many years. Additional agencies have emerged recently to supplement the efforts of such long-established pioneers as the American Printing House for the Blind and the Library of Congress. These new instrumentalities are working to achieve the following objectives: provision of greater quantities of materials for partially served groups; design of instructional materials for unserved and multiply handicapped students; sponsorship of research to test the efficacy and impact of materials, technology, and teaching strategies; and coordination of programs provided by established organizations so as to reduce duplication and expand total service.

This chapter, then, represents a compendium of useful references the librarian will wish to consult in order to identify agencies which will provide backup services to augment the school's resources. Moreover, these articles provide guidance in locating probable sources for consultative and remediative assistance.

Specialized agencies and centers for the disabled have been placed in historical perspective by Miller. Building on the foundation developed by the Special Education Instructional Materials Centers, the newly formed Area Learning Resource Centers represent regional responses to the needs of exceptional individuals. A key problem has been that services originate on a national or regional level, yet the ultimate utilization must be with an individual child. Bottlenecks often exist in the delivery of these services from the generating agencies to personnel working directly with the special child. Using the state of New York as an example, this author details how one state designed a system to funnel information and support to disabled users. Although some readers may not have such extensive state-provided services, this program may suggest ideas for local planning.

The blind reader places heavy and varied demands for specialized services on the library. Fortunately, agencies which have developed extensive and high quality holdings will eagerly share their resources with personnel serving qualifying users. The following four articles reflect the variety of services available for this disability group.

For the librarian unfamiliar with the reading styles and techniques of blind and visually limited children, Berger and Kautz provide a succinct summary of background information. Their extensive article might be subtitled "Almost Everything the Librarian Needs to Know about the Visually Limited and Now No Longer Needs to Ask." The authors cram this article with essential data on informational input and output modes commonly employed by the visually impaired, point out instructional materials or methods which would address themselves to particularized learning problems, and suggest a deluge of periodicals, bibliographic references, and resources which librarians could tap to respond to the requirements of the blind patron.

Lappin speaks of the services provided by the American Printing House for the Blind (APHB), a clearinghouse for information about educational aids for the visually impaired. Through the Instructional Materials Reference Center, a subsidiary of APHB, didactic materials are developed, evaluated, and disseminated. Of particular interest is the central catalog, a comprehensive index of books in braille, large type, and recorded form. This one reference tool enables the librarian to discover the existence and location of books no matter which agency has transcribed or presently houses them. Lappin spells out procedures for access to this corpus of materials, defines user candidacy, and lists several key components of the collection.

The librarian working with visually impaired youth at the secondary level has the additional function of providing information to facilitate passage from school to extra-school and post-high school studies. In the totality of services available, the Hadley School, providing tuition-free correspondence courses, should be a resource well known to librarians, particularly those who work in rural or remote areas. Implicit in the article by Gearreald is the directive that the librarian share the knowledge about such opportunities with guidance counselors, language instructors, and other involved faculty.

Bray reveals the extent and thrust of services rendered by the Library of Congress, Division of Blind and Physically Handicapped. In addition to listing eligibility requirements and means for access to the collection, he also presents a capsule description of the myriad unique and specialized services of this agency. The librarian who is unfamiliar with this agency will be pleased with the summarization of the division's activities in Bray's information-packed article.

Many librarians may have heard of the federally funded Captioned Films for the Deaf project and concluded that titled movies were its sole product. Kundert enumerates the many functions of the program which include lending instructional materials in a variety of formats as well as conducting research and providing training. A critical byproduct of this effort was the realization that materials developed for usage with one disability group could successfully be employed with other special populations. The information in this article is important in that a key resource for the hearing impaired is identified. Perhaps even more vital is the assertion that materials need not be used only for their originally intended purpose but can have equal validity when used to respond to seemingly dissimilar problems manifested by other handicapped groups.

Because of the highly individualized needs of the physically handicapped, librarians who serve this group must provide an expanded reference function. Access to information, not only on the physiological, educational, and remediative implications of disabilities, but also on agencies and organizations providing a full range of special programs and supportive services, must be facilitated. Velleman supplies an annotated list of books, pamphlets, journals, and organizations which work toward minimizing the impact of physical disability.

Historically, individuals, foundations, or governmental bodies identified particular needs of handi-

capped persons which they were willing to meet. As a result, some groups, like the blind, had many organizations working on their behalf, and other populations, like the mentally retarded or emotionally disturbed, had far less in the way of specially designed instructional support. There was considerable duplication and overlap in some areas coexisting with large gaps or very minimal service in others. Coordination was perceived of as a necessity and a new organization, the National Center on Educational Media and Materials for the Handicapped (NCEMMH), was established. Belland explains the scope of the leadership responsibility of the NCEMMH in the development of instructional resources, technological competency programs, and informational delivery systems. To put this in perspective, he describes the interrelationships of the various components which together form a network of services for the handicapped. The listing of Area Learning Resource Centers and Regional Resource Centers should be especially useful to the librarian looking for nearby assistance in providing service to disabled youngsters.

Regionalized Support Services for Personnel Involved in the Education of the Handicapped

JOAN MILLER

Historical Perspectives

In 1964, an organizational structure sponsored through the United States Office of Education, Bureau of Education for the Handicapped took shape to form the nucleus of a network of centers whose activities were directed toward the provision of better and increased instructional options for the education of all children with handicapping conditions. It grew, expanded, and in 1969 merged with the federally sponsored Regional Media Centers for the Deaf to officially become the Special Education Instructional Materials Center/Regional Media Center Network.

From 1969 through August 1974, the network was composed of fourteen Special Education Instructional Materials Centers (SEIMCs), four Regional Media

Centers for the Deaf (RMCs), and a network Coordinating Office, all of which served specific geographic regions, blanketing the fifty states, Puerto Rico, and the Virgin Islands.

SEIMCs primarily served their clientele through the provision of instructional materials for use in the education of all youngsters with diagnosed handicapping conditions. RMCs focused their attention on the development of instructional materials for the deaf and hearing handicapped. The American Printing House for the Blind in Louisville, Kentucky, while not an SEIMC in the broadest scope of its activities, produced appropriate materials for the blind and visually handicapped. Included as an arm of the network and housed adjacent to the Special Education IMC/RMC Network Office was the Council for Exceptional Children Information Center, which is also the Educational Resources Information Center (ERIC) Clearinghouse for the Handicapped and Gifted. It supported the network through its professional reference and research services.

In an effort to further improve the network and

equalize the services provided throughout the United States, a restructuring of the components of the network was thought necessary by the Bureau of Education for the Handicapped and the United States Office of Education, and on August 31, 1974, the ten-year-old Special Education IMC/RMC Network was formally dissolved and reorganization begun.

Reorganization Pattern, 1974–1976

The basic need for provision of services to handicapped youngsters was still foremost in the thoughts of the "reorganizers," so in the place of the old network there arose a new configuration composed of thirteen Area Learning Resource Centers (ALRCs), thirteen Regional Resource Centers (RRCs), four Specialized Offices (SO), and coordinating offices for each (see Appendix). The thirteen regions again encompassed the United States, Puerto Rico, and the Virgin Islands, but were constructed using population densities, in order to maximize the service capabilities of the ALRCs and RRCs in each region.

The ALRCs are charged with the broad objective of responding to the educational media and materials technology needs of personnel involved in the education of all handicapped children within their respective regions. It is felt that this goal can best be reached through activities stressing demonstration and consultation concerning effective utilization of media technology services, as well as through the development of new or modified products to meet specific educational needs of the handicapped population.

It is the role of the Regional Resource Centers to establish a mechanism within these same regions to provide diagnostic, assessment, and prescriptive services for all children with handicapping conditions. Initially, this assessment is concentrating on small populations of handicapped youngsters and assistance will be provided to enable schools to implement the prescriptions developed by Regional Resource Center staff. Other activities of the RRCs are devoted to assisting the states in developing, refining, and replicating the various child assessment models at all levels of the educational process.

In support of the activities of the ALRCs and RRCs, the Specialized Offices perform certain distinctive tasks based upon work with specific handicapping conditions and the need for media materials which are appropriate to the educational needs of these populations. The S1 is assigned the area of the visually handicapped, the S2 deals primarily with the hearing handicapped, and the S3 with the mentally handicapped plus all other handicapping conditions. Specialized Office 4 functions as a depository and distribution center for those materials identified, adapted, or produced by the other Specialized

Offices as pertinent to the needs of handicapped learners and field tested through the network of Area Learning Resource Centers.

Coordinating the efforts of the ALRCs and RRCs are two units, the National Center on Educational Media and Materials for the Handicapped (NCEMMH) (see pp. 188–90), and the Coordinating Office for the Regional Resource Centers (CORRC). The two work together to insure the coordination of ALRC and RRC services through the development of procedures for sharing resources, communications, joint planning and management efforts, and program design and implementation. In addition, the CORRC conducts needs assessment studies and training related to educational assessment and NCEMMH operates a national information storage and retrieval system relative to child-directed instructional materials. This data base, the National Instructional Materials Information System (NIMIS) is accessed through the regional ALRCs and the Specialized Offices.

Learning Resource Center Program Objectives

In its totality, the organization structure is referred to as the Learning Resource Center (LRC) Program and is designed to utilize the best aspects of the earlier Special Education IMC/RMC Network projects, yet provide more uniformity of operation, structure, role definition, and program interpretation among the centers. It is expected that through the provision of both direct services and technical assistance to the states, each of the fifty states, Puerto Rico, and the Virgin Islands will be able to build an effective intrastate system of support centers and services which will replicate the LRC Program on a statewide, interactive basis.

The provision of these services at the state level will fulfill the commitment to maximize educational opportunities for all our nation's handicapped youngsters as well as insure the continuation of the components of the Learning Resource Center Program by each state.

Replication in New York State

It was the fortune of New York State, through the foresight of its Special Education administrative personnel, to have actively participated as a member of the original Special Education IMC/RMC Network from 1967 though 1974, and thus to have gained both philosophical insight and practical experience in provision of the support services previously discussed.

The New York State Education Department, Division for Handicapped Children, received funds in 1967 to develop Special Education Instructional Materials Center services for the geographic region "New York," one of only two original SEIMCs whose service region was limited geographically to one state. After the administrative office was established, it was recognized that regionalization and decentralization of services was the most viable way to assure that support centers would be readily accessible to personnel responsible for the education of the handicapped learner in programs throughout the state. Therefore, New York established three Regional Centers, the administrative center in the New York State Education Department in Albany, plus two subcontracting Regional Centers located at the State University College at Buffalo and the City University of New York at Hunter College.

Initially, these centers functioned as locations of short term loan collections of instructional and professional materials related to education of the handicapped, sources of information about programs and curricula for the handicapped, dissemination agents and training units for persons interested in learning newer techniques and methodologies to teach the handicapped learner.

It rapidly became apparent, however, that even further regionalization and decentralization of services would be necessary before essential materials and training needs of the user population could be adequately served. Therefore, procedures for the establishment of locally based, staffed, and operated centers were developed which would allow for the gradual growth and expansion of services as the capabilities of the centers increased.

Associate Special Education Instructional Materials Centers' Development

A variety of mechanisms designed to facilitate the regionalization of educational support services was already in place in New York State through Boards of Cooperative Educational Services (BOCES), "Big City" school systems, and state supported schools for the blind, deaf, and severely orthopedically handicapped. BOCES and "Big City" schools were offered the opportunity to participate in the expanding network by each establishing an Associate Special Education Instructional Materials Center (ASEIMC) which would serve its regional configuration. Thus, the widening range of support services offered to personnel working with the handicapped learner could be brought through the statewide network to the local level. In addition, the state supported schools were asked to participate in the network as Affiliate Centers, serving primarily their own school populations and their distinctive needs.

From January 1969, when the first ASEIMC officially joined the network, to the present (November 1974) the number of centers has risen to fifty-eight and the range of services available has expanded from "mailing list" operations to training and materials support centers staffed by specially prepared teachers, media

specialists, and other personnel whose combined expertise represents a valuable contribution in providing appropriate educational alternatives for handicapped youngsters.

Specialized Services of the New York SEIMC Network

Throughout the first seven years of growth and development of the statewide network, the Administrative Center in Albany and its two regional support centers provided extended direct services and assistance to teachers and parents of handicapped children across the state. The needs of this expanding user population were found to range in sophistication from a request for publishing information about a particular instructional material to a request for training in the latest curricular offerings for a specific group of handicapped youngsters. This centralized support was necessary in the early developmental stages of the network, since many local ASEIMCs were not yet prepared to provide this "across the board" assistance.

In an attempt to provide the resources and training essential before local centers could meet the expressed needs of their users and thus assure that the network would reach its goal of maximizing educational opportunities for the handicapped, an intensive training program was shaped by personnel at the Albany Center. This "training multiplier" method provided for a series of workshop sessions to be sponsored by the NYSEIMC Network each year through which ASEIMC staff would gain knowledge of and training in the use of current and innovative programs and materials of potential value in the education of the handicapped. ASEIMC staff would then return to their local service areas and conduct similar workshops for personnel throughout their regions. Utilizing this approach, new products and processes, both commercially and network developed, are now rapidly disseminated throughout the state and the merits of comparable equipment and materials can be quickly and more accurately evaluated prior to program implementation.

It has also been the function of the NYSEIMC Network to provide statewide support to assist local centers in filling user requests related to informational and researching needs. A centralized Information Services Unit is maintained by the Administrative Center in Albany where specialized reference and research materials in the field of handicapped education are utilized by a team of experienced personnel to respond to statewide needs. An extensive 16mm professional film collection geared toward preservice and in-service needs of educators of the handicapped is also maintained at this location, as well as source files of information concerning publishers of media and materials for the handicapped.

Consultative services are also available to assist local centers in determining appropriate methods for selecting, housing, and maintaining their collections of instructional and professional materials.

The Future Direction of the New York SEIMC Network

The New York SEIMC, during its past seven years as a member of the Special Education IMC/RMC Network, has been successful in establishing local educational support service centers for personnel working with handicapped children in each area of the state. These centers will continue to further define the needs of their service populations and to work together as a network dedicated to maximizing educational programming and opportunities for the handicapped.

The ALRC contract for the service area "New York," which was awarded to the New York State Education Department in September 1974, insures that the transition period from "SEIMC" to "ALRC" for New York, at least, will be rapid and will not result in loss of services to the handicapped. The continuation of this assistance from the LRC Program to the NYSEIMC Network hastens the time when the intrastate program will be self-sufficient and functioning optimally.

New York will continue to maintain its Administrative Center in Albany to coordinate the activities of the network and to act as the liaison to the ALRC and RRC services provided through the Learning Resource Center Program. Therefore, anyone in the state needing any of the types of support services available through these network efforts will find that help as close as a telephone or mailbox.

All persons working with handicapped learners are potential clientele of some portion of this federal-state-local effort and can reach into this network for answers to many questions concerning the handicapped and their educational needs. Through the efforts and dedication of many persons, the New York Special Education Instructional Materials Center Network is ready to fill those needs.

Sources of Information and Materials for Blind and Visually Limited Pupils

ALLEN BERGER
and
CONSTANCE R. KAUTZ

With the growing trend to have blind and visually limited pupils in regular school settings, an increasing number of elementary school teachers are having children with serious visual problems in their classrooms. The intent of this paper is to provide basic sources of information and materials so that children with visual handicaps will be helped in realizing their maximum potential.

Terminology

The terminology used to describe persons who do not see is often confusing. Many legally blind people use ordinary inkprint (or what you are now reading) in their reading and writing; that is, they practically operate as sighted individuals. For educational purposes, a legally blind person is one who has a visual acuity in the better eye of 20/200 or less after the best possible correction. A partially seeing person is one whose visual acuity is 20/70 or less in the better eye after correction.

Many students with usable vision wear low vision lenses and read regular print at close range, their eyes about two or three inches from the text. Other pupils who read inkprint use special large-print materials; an annotated listing of *Books for the Partially Sighted Child* appeared in *Elementary English* and is available as a separate publication from the National Council of Teachers of English.

In this paper, when making reference to both the totally blind and the visually limited, the term *visually handicapped* will be used.

As a result of federal appropriations many visually handicapped pupils are entitled to receive instructional materials at no cost. Information about free instructional materials for registered visually handicapped students may be obtained from your State Education Department.

School Programs

During the past two decades, school programs for the visually handicapped have expanded considerably. One type of program involves the residential school, of which there are now approximately 70 such schools for blind children in the United States and Canada. Many schools take steps to insure the integration of blind children into the sighted community.

In the public and private schools, there are two main kinds of programs. One involves the grouping of visually handicapped children into a special class which receives most of its instruction with a specially trained teacher. Another program growing in popularity involves the itinerant or resource teacher; in that program, the visually handicapped children are enrolled in regular classrooms and they receive instruction with their sighted peers for the major part of each school day. Special skills, such as reading and writing braille, as well as the reinforcement of certain learnings, are provided by the specially trained teacher in a resource room or by an itinerant teacher who travels among several schools.

The Braille System of Reading and Writing

A system of raised dots read by sensitive fingers makes extensive reading possible for blind persons. In 1784, Valentine Hauy devised books with raised letters. This was the first real step to educate persons who could not see, although the method proved to be slow and often confusing. In 1829 a young Frenchman, Louis Braille, devised the system now used by the blind throughout the world. Blinded by an awl while working in his father's leather shop, young Louis later remembered the marks left by the awl in the leather and used this idea as the basis for his system of combinations of dots to represent letters of the alphabet.

The braille system uses as its basis a cell composed of two vertical columns of three dots each, and numbered for convenience sake.

$$
\begin{array}{ccc}
1 & \bullet\ \bullet & 4 \\
2 & \bullet\ \bullet & 5 \\
3 & \bullet\ \bullet & 6 \\
\end{array}
$$

The *a* uses only dot one   the *b* is represented by one and two   the *c* by one and four   the *k* by one and three   The word *back* would appear

To save space and to facilitate reading, certain groups of letters appearing frequently are represented by special characters called contractions. For example,

is *and,* and   appears as *the.*

A special, highly contracted code of braille mathematics has been formulated by Abraham Nemeth. All signs used in modern mathematics are incorporated into this code. A braille music code uses sixty-three symbols for notes, rhythms, values, etc.

Methods used for transcribing printed material into braille include the slate and stylus, the braille writer, and the newly developed braille electric typewriter. In addition, copies of braille and similar materials can be made by a vacuum forming process.

For embossing braille by hand, a grooved board is used with a perforated metal or plastic guide. The points are impressed onto the paper with a small pointed tool called a stylus. This is slow and fatiguing, but useful for note-taking. A postcard size slate slips easily into the pocket or purse, and is readily available when needed.

The braille writer is a manual machine which has six keys corresponding to each braille dot in the cell. With this machine the student can write quickly and accurately. Braille can be transcribed at approximately fifty or sixty words per minute using this machine.

IBM developed an electric typewriter that types braille. Having a standard keyboard, it contains the configurations needed. Since the braille is embossed on the reverse side of the paper, the typist begins at the bottom of the page. An "erase" key will flatten any unwanted symbols and the correct one may be inserted. The copy may be proofread while still in the typewriter.

Methods and Materials for Blind and Visually Limited Pupils

The reader of braille and the reader of inkprint read for similar purposes: to obtain information, to solve problems, for pleasure. Similar methods of teaching reading apply to print and braille. Information about a *Braille Informal Reading Inventory,* which reveals strengths and weaknesses in the reading ability of a child who reads braille is available from either author or the American Printing House for the Blind.

In an integrated program, the blind pupil begins reading and writing with his sighted classmates. He uses the same texts and workbooks in braille that they use in print. Large type and braille dictionaries are also available as are encyclopedias which, however, may be too bulky and expensive for most schools; information from a print encyclopedia can be given by either the resource teacher or a volunteer to the visually handicapped.

Handwriting is often a laborious task for the visually limited. Writing paper with more vivid lines may be obtained, making it easier for the visually limited pupil to stay on the lines. About fourth grade he may be taught to type, using a regular or large-type machine. By the time that he enters junior high school, he will be able to type his assignments.

The blind pupil as well as the visually limited can use a pencil for workbook activities (e.g., underlining correct answers or making true and false items, etc.). In certain instances, using a pencil saves time. For the totally blind pupil, handwriting can be a profitable experience at the junior and senior high school levels. At certain times he will probably use a braille writer.

Specialized and adapted material can be provided by the resource or itinerant teacher, who will supplement the work of the classroom teacher; she will teach those skills needed for the pupil to function effectively in the classroom. Because the classroom teacher usually does not know braille, at the early reading levels the special teacher will write in ink over braille reading materials so that the regular classroom teacher can follow the pupil's progress and give assistance when needed. Though improvisations and adaptations are necessary at times, most of the items in the classroom are suitable for the visually handicapped.

Day-to-day materials, such as tests, duplicated exercises or blackboard work, can be provided to the classroom teacher. In addition, the special teacher can adapt or obtain maps, thermometers, "readable" flags (with different fabrics representing different colors) and other materials to assist in building concepts and experiential background. Along this line, alphabetized shoe boxes containing small items (shoestring, stamp, stocking, satin, sucker, etc., in the *s* box) may be used for beginning phonics, tactile discrimination, concept and vocabulary building. In addition, experience stories, descriptive phrases of things felt, smelled, tasted, and heard play an important part in beginning reading for the young child. Diaries also are of value personally as well as educationally.

Story books with attractive covers (cutout felt, rough burlap, etc.) and pictures (objects such as dime store items attached to the page) add interest for the beginning or early reader and further aid him in distinguishing between shapes and textures in preparation for reading the braille symbols.

Classroom teachers may be confronted with the problem involving the use of blackboards and duplicated materials. Some pupils with useful remaining vision can see the blackboard when a magnifier is attached to their glass lens. Pupils who cannot take notes can be helped by a classmate who will use a carbon paper with an extra sheet; the notes on the carbon can then be reproduced into large type or braille. At certain times a portable cassette tape recorder will assist the pupil in retaining information for a later date.

Of considerable interest and value to the visually handicapped are recorded and taped texts, books, and magazines. Periodicals available in braille include *My Weekly Reader* and *Current Events*. The recordings and tapes are profitable because of the amount of information a pupil may receive within a given amount of time. Of value here is the current interest in speeded speech, whereby the rate of taped speech is increased through computerized means, thereby avoiding the Donald Duck effect.

A reading machine which will be capable of presenting material in *spelled* speech is being developed at Massachusetts Institute of Technology. This machine would allow a visually handicapped person access to printed material, such as newspapers and periodicals, without the delay involved in obtaining a braille or recorded version.

A machine that will produce audible words from the coded information on the tapes used by publishers for typesetting is being developed by a professor of electrical engineering and supervisor of the Medical Systems Engineering Laboratory at Carnegie-Mellon University in Pittsburgh. According to Dr. Richard L. Longini, "the same tape, with minor modifications, that activates the production of Linotype, can be used in the reading machine, where it would operate a sound generator. The generator would translate the code into corresponding alphabetical sounds, or an audio code" called Spelltalk.[1]

Another machine, called an amauroscope ("blind seeing device") which will allow blind persons to see light, is in the research stages under the direction of Dr. Armando del Campo of Mexico City. Another electronic device which enables blind persons to see objects from a pattern of dots (resembling each object) felt on the skin is described in *Life*.[2]

Library Services

Through thirty-two regional libraries, the Division for the Blind of the Library of Congress circulates braille books, talking books, large type and taped editions. Any legally blind individual may receive the service by registering with the distributing library serving his area. Through federal legislation, those with other physical handicaps are also eligible for the services. The brailled or recorded material is sent through the mail in containers, free of charge. When the pupil wishes to return the material, he has only to turn over the address card and deposit the container in the post office.

Braille Book Review, published bimonthly for the Library of Congress by the American Foundation for the Blind, is distributed free to persons who borrow from regional libraries. It is a magazine of news about braille materials newly transcribed. *Talking Book Topics,* also a bimonthly magazine published under the same arrangement, contains news of recordings, magnetic tapes, book reviews, developments and activities in library services for blind and physically handicapped persons. A soundsheet, an experiment in producing a recorded version of this magazine, playable on the talking book machine at $16\frac{2}{3}$ rpm. is currently being tested.

The person wishing to receive recorded books will receive a Talking Book Machine to use with or without earphones. These play discs at $8\frac{1}{3}$, $16\frac{2}{3}$, or $33\frac{1}{3}$ rpm., and in many localities are repaired by members of the Telephone Pioneers. Records received are marked in braille as well as inkprint. Magnetic tapes are available to those who have access to a tape recorder. Recording for the Blind, Inc., is in the process of converting its library of discs to tapes. Recommended for the tapes is the adapted SONY 105, available from the American Printing House for the Blind.

Besides a huge variety of brailled volumes, the following magazines are available in braille from regional libraries: *American Girl, Boy's Life, Braille Book Review, Braille Mirror, Braille Musical Magazine, The Braille Musician, Braille Piano Technician, Braille Science Journal, Braille Technical Press, Braille Variety News, Catholic Review, Chess Magazine, The Children's Digest, Consumer Bulletin, Current Science, Galaxy, Horizon, International Journal for the Education of the Blind, Jack and Jill, Ladies Home Journal, Madam, National Geographic, Overtones, Popular Mechanics, Reader's Digest, Reporter, Seventeen,* and others.

Talking Books include: *American Heritage, The Atlantic, Braille Technical Press, Changing Times, Choice Magazine Listening, Dialogue, Ellery Queen Mystery Magazine, Farm Journal, Good Housekeeping, Harper's Magazine, Harvest Years, Holiday, Jack and Jill, Look, Natural History, New Outlook for the Blind, Newsweek Talking Magazine, Reader's Digest, Selecciones Del Reader's Digest, Sports Illustrated, True.*

Additional Selected Sources of Information and Materials

American Foundation for the Blind
15 W. 16th Street
New York, New York 10011

Consultation services, aids and appliance catalog; catalog of publications, films, posters; M. C. Migel Memorial Library contains 25,000 items available to students and general public. Publishes *The New Outlook for the Blind,* a monthly professional journal, available in inkprint, braille, and recorded editions; *Touch and Go,* a monthly news periodical in braille for deaf-blind persons.

American Library Association
50 East Huron Street
Chicago, Illinois 60611

Has a selective list of reading aids for the handicapped. The list includes information on commercially manufactured equipment, magnifiers, duplicating firms, page turners, projectors and readers, reading stands, talking book machines, talking books, and large-type books.

American Printing House for the Blind
P.O. Box 6085
1839 Frankfort Avenue
Louisville, Kentucky 40206

A major source of textbooks in braille and large print: Catalogs of braille publications, tangible materials (slates, maps, paper, etc.) large print publications, music publications, recorded aids, and vacuum-formed, plastic-plate braille. Information concerning texts located at other sources may be obtained from textbook consultant.

The Canadian National Institute for the Blind
929 Bayview Avenue
Toronto 17, Ontario

Provides pamphlets, booklets, and other information and services. Following are addresses of regional offices: 350 E. 36th Avenue, Vancouver, British Columbia; 12010 Jasper Avenue, Edmonton, Alberta; 1031 Portage Avenue, Winnipeg, Manitoba; 1425 Rue Crescent, Montreal, Quebec; 172 Almon Street, Halifax, Nova Scotia; and 1 Military Road, St. John's, Newfoundland.

Clovernook Printing House for the Blind
7000 Hamilton Avenue
Cincinnati, Ohio 45231

Prints books and magazines for children, young people and adults in braille. *American Girl, Boy's Life, Braille Variety News, Galaxy, Seventeen, Lion's International Juvenile Braille Monthly,* religious publications, calendars, cookbooks, paper, playing cards.

Dialogue Publications, Inc.
3132 Oak Park Avenue
Berwyn, Illinois 60402

National recording service; magazine issued quarterly on 10 inch records at $16\frac{2}{3}$ rpm.; contains items of interest to visually handicapped.

Division for the Blind and Physically Handicapped
Library of Congress
Washington, D.C. 20542

"That All May Read"—an information brochure describing program of books. Available to borrow is a talking book machine, listing of regional libraries serving each part of the U.S.

Educational Materials Coordinating Unit
Visually Handicapped
Office of the Superintendent of Public Instruction
410 South Michigan Avenue
Chicago, Illinois 60605

Through a contract with the United States Office of Education this project permits the Department of Special Education to demonstrate, among other things, how an office of the Superintendent of Public Instruction can coordinate, produce, and distribute educational materials for visually handicapped children and adults. (Director is Gloria Calovini, Instructional Materials Center for Handicapped Children and Youth, 316 S. Second Street, Springfield, Illinois 62701.)

Howe Press
Perkins School for the Blind
Watertown, Massachusetts 02172

Aids and appliances, mathematical devices, brailled games, embossed geographical maps are available.

Johanna Bureau for the Blind and Visually Handicapped, Inc.
410 S. Michigan Avenue
Chicago, Illinois 60605

Provides an excellent brailling service. Publishes braille tour guides for the Museum of Science and Industry, Chicago.

The Lighthouse (New York Association for the Blind)
111 E. 59th Street
New York, New York 10022

Low Vision Lens Service (e.g., 2.5 × magnifier).

Louis Braille Foundation for Blind Musicians, Inc.
112 E. 19th Street
New York, New York 10003

Nonprofit organization dedicated to advancement of

interests of blind persons in the field of music; transcription of music not otherwise available in braille, evaluations, scholarship aid, etc.

National Braille Book Bank
85 Godwin Avenue
Midland Park, New Jersey 07432
Brailled volumes of technical books in mathematics and science at college level.

National Braille Press, Inc.
88 St. Stephen Street
Boston, Massachusetts 02115
The New York Times "Week in Review," news recordings, wide range of selections.

The National Society for the Prevention of Blindness, Inc.
79 Madison Avenue
New York, New York 10002
Issues pamphlets and brochures on prevention of blindness.

Recording for the Blind, Inc.
215 East 58th Street
New York, New York 10022
Over 10,000 titles on discs 16⅔rpm. or tapes 3¾, 1⅞ips., 2 or 4 track to be borrowed at no cost by any blind elementary, high school, college, graduate student, or adult needing educational material. Qualified borrowers may request and have recorded any text not available.

Tactile Aids for the Blind, Inc.
2625 Forest Avenue
Des Moines, Iowa 50311
Catalog in print and braille of tangible apparatus, teaching aids.

Telephone Pioneers of America
195 Broadway
New York, New York 10007
Activities include making books with various objects attached to pages to illustrate the story which is written in braille and large type.

Tests for Handicapped Students
College Entrance Examination Board
Box 592
Princeton, New Jersey 08540
Information regarding college entrance examinations for visually handicapped students. Available also are some tests in large print and in braille.

U.S. Office of Education
Washington, D.C.
Various publications are available from Superintendent of Documents, U.S. Printing Office, Washington, D.C. 20402. One is *Educational Program for Visually Handicapped Children* (Bulletin 1966, No. 6-OE-35070).

Braille books are available from the following:

Cleveland Public Library
Library for the Blind
325 Superior Avenue
Cleveland, Ohio 44114

Free Library of Philadelphia
Library for the Blind
17th and Spring Garden Streets
Philadelphia, Pennsylvania 19130

Iowa Commission for the Blind
Library for the Blind
4th and Keosaqua
Des Moines, Iowa 50309

Jewish Guild for the Blind
1880 Broadway
New York, New York 10023

Nassau-Suffolk Braille Library
Industrial Home for the Blind
329 Hempstead Turnpike
West Hempstead, New York 11552

New York Public Library
Library for the Blind
116 Avenue of the Americas
New York, New York 10013

Large type materials are available from:

Amsco School Publications
P.O. Box 351
Cooper Station
New York, New York 10003
Enlarged books; will reproduce in large type any material.

Xerox
P.O. Box 3300
Grand Central Station
New York, New York 10017
Enlargement of complete books, magazines, sheet music and other printed material—approximately 2½ times size of ordinary print.

Harper and Row, Publishers
Department 61
49 East 33rd Street
New York, New York 10016
Harpercrest Large Type Editions from its book list; 18 point type.

Keith Jennison Books
575 Lexington Avenue
New York, New York 10022
Diversified titles, many of which are on high school reading lists; 18 point type.

Library Reproduction Service
Microfilm Company of California
1977 S. Los Angeles Street
Los Angeles, California 90011
Reproduction of large print textbooks, etc., to specific need of visually handicapped in extended or controlled size; five print sizes; catalog available.

Magnum Easy Eye Books
Lancer Books
1560 Broadway
New York, New York 10036
Paperbacks, 30% larger than ordinary paperback size, on glare-free paper; unabridged paperback classics—12 point type.

National Aid to Visually Handicapped
3201 Balboa Street
San Francisco, California 94121
   Catalog of materials available in large print—texts, testing and reading material; 18 point type.

New York Times, Large Type Edition
229 West 43rd Street
New York, New York 10036
   Twenty-four page, weekly edition with illustrations; 18 point type.

Scribner Large Type Editions
References Department
597 Fifth Avenue
New York, New York 10017
   First titles available in April 1968; clothbound volumes for visually limited or difficult readers; contemporary or classic works.

Sightext Publications
P.O. Box 1824
7015 Almeda Street
Houston, Texas 77001
   Has a variety of large type publications.

Stanwix House
3020 Chartiers Avenue
Pittsburgh, Pennsylvania 15204
   Catalog available on request; books are illustrated, some in color; 18 to 24 point type.

   Additional sources of large type materials include the American Printing House for the Blind and the Canadian National Institute for the Blind (addresses given previously) and the following:

Bell and Howell Co.
Micro Photo Division
Duopage Department
1700 Shaw Avenue
Cleveland, Ohio 44112

Dakota Microfilm Company
501 North Dales Street
St. Paul, Minnesota. 55103

Golden Press
850 Third Avenue
New York, New York 10022

Large Print Publications
11060 Fruitland Drive
North Hollywood, California 91604

Macmillan Company
866 Third Avenue
New York, New York 10022

Ulverscroft Large Print Books
F. A. Thorpe Ltd.
Artisan House, The Bridge, Anstey
Leicester, England

Viking Press
625 Madison Avenue
New York, New York 10022

Walker and Company
720 Fifth Avenue
New York, New York 10019

   To keep abreast of current trends and interests in the field of the blind and visually limited, the following periodicals are recommended:

The Braille Forum. Published bimonthly by American Council of the Blind, 106 N.E. Second Street, Oklahoma City, Oklahoma 73104.
   Designed to "inform its readers and to provide an impartial forum for discussion."

Fountainhead. Issued five times a year by the Association of the Visually Handicapped, 1604 Spruce Street, Philadelphia, Pennsylvania 19103.
   Contains much information on all phases of education of visually handicapped children.

The International Journal for the Education of the Blind. The official publication of the Association for the Education of the Visually Handicapped, 1839 Frankfort Avenue, Louisville, Kentucky 40206.
   Designed for teachers and parents of visually handicapped children.

The Lion. Published monthly by Lions International, 209 N. Michigan Avenue, Chicago, Illinois 60601.
   Contains articles and references to Lions-sponsored projects involving visually handicapped.

The New Outlook for the Blind. Published by the American Foundation for the Blind, 15 W. 16th Street, New York, New York 10011.
   Contains research reports and articles of current interest in the field of the blind. (*Cf.* October 1968, "Large Type Reading Materials for the Visually Handicapped.")

Perspective. Published by the Illinois Department of Children and Family Services, 404 State Office Building, Springfield, Illinois 62706.
   Contains articles of interest.

Rehabilitation Literature. Published by the National Easter Seal Society for Crippled Children and Adults, 2023 W, Ogden Street, Chicago, Illinois 60612.
   Includes research references relevant to visually handicapped.

The Seer. Pennsylvania Association for the Blind, 2843 N. Front Street, Harrisburg, Pennsylvania 17101.
   A quarterly bulletin.

The Sight-Saving Review. Quarterly of the National Society for the Prevention of Blindness, 79 Madison Avenue, New York, New York 10016.
   Contains articles relating to prevention of vision loss and other facets of interest involving the visually handicapped.

Talking Book Topics. Published for Library of Congress by the American Foundation for the Blind.
   Designed to inform readers of developments and activities in library service for blind and physically handicapped. (*Braille Book Review.* A magazine about braille materials is published under a similar arrangement by the American Foundation for the Blind.)

In addition, newsletters are published by many local community services for the blind in the United States and Canada.

NOTES

1. Richard L. Longini, "A New Kind of Reading Machine Being Developed," *The New Outlook for the Blind* 62, no. 4: 130 (April 1968).

2. "(Seeing) with the Skin of the Back," *Life* (December 19, 1969), pp. 59, 60.

At Your Service—The Instructional Materials Reference Center for the Visually Handicapped

CARL W. LAPPIN

Founded in 1858, the American Printing House for the Blind (APHB) is the oldest national agency for the blind in the United States. It is the only independent institution devoted solely to the publication of literature for the blind as well as the development and manufacture of tangible aids for their use.

For the first twenty years the Printing House supplied its materials on a cash basis, but with the need for a more adequate and permanent source of funds for books and instructional materials for all schools, the American Association of Instructors for the Blind asked Congress for an appropriation. In 1879 Congress passed the act to promote the education of the blind and to supply financial support for production of materials for the blind.

The present structure of the American Printing House includes such subunits as the editorial department, data processing department, recording department, educational research department, and production department.

The Instructional Materials Reference Center (IMRC) [now Specialty Office #1 of the Area Learning Resource Center (ALRC)] was created to facilitate dissemination, development, and evaluation of appropriate materials. The ALRC exists within the confines of an institution (APHB) which has a reputation for providing services far exceeding its role as a material producer. Now in its seventh year the center is meeting its purpose and disperses upon request lists of materials available from APHB and commercial businesses.

The Major Services of the Area Learning Resource Center

1. The center is the single national source of information about the availability of educational materials for the visually handicapped from all sources.

Reprinted from *Teaching Exceptional Children* 5: 74–76 (1973) by permission of The Council for Exceptional Children. Copyright 1972 by The Council for Exceptional Children.

2. The center provides a program for the development of additional materials when needed.

3. The center supplies a means of formally communicating and demonstrating the availability and method of use of such materials for educational programs and teacher training facilities.

The purpose of the Area Learning Resource Center is to provide educators of the visually handicapped and related personnel with ready references to valid materials and information pertaining to the education of visually handicapped children. Obtaining appropriate materials for the education of visually handicapped children is a long standing problem for educators. With the Instructional Materials Center as part of the American Printing House for the Blind, one of its objectives is to locate items, commercially produced or teacher devised, which are useful to the visually handicapped. Information is then disseminated to encourage wider use of such materials.

As of January 1, 1972, the registration of blind pupils in public, private, and parochial educational institutions of less than college level totaled 22,702. The total number of visually handicapped children is relatively small, and they are widely scattered among a variety of educational programs. As a result, only small numbers of textbooks of any given title are required and only small numbers of an educational aid are needed, making commercial manufacture of most of these items impractical. While many commercial materials are useful for education of the visually handicapped, the task of discovering and adapting these materials is great.

A Single, Coordinated Service—The Central Catalog

The Central Catalog of volunteer produced books is an integral part of the workings of ALRC. A comprehensive listing in card file form, the catalog lists titles of books in braille, large type, and recorded form. Compiled annually and now in its fourth edition, this collection is available in book form to large institutions concerned with the visually handicapped.

As one of its functions, the Central Catalog makes possible a single service coordinating the reporting efforts of all agencies, groups, and individuals producing literature for the visually impaired on a volunteer basis. The Central Catalog also serves as a valuable source of information for the benefit of transcribers, school administrators, teachers, librarians, students, parents, and all workers for the blind who need material in braille, large type, disc, or tape recorded form. This file contains some 40,000 completed titles with 10,000 titles in process. At the same time, the catalog is a single point of reference for schools, students, and visually handicapped readers needing a particular educational title. Finally, the catalog staff negotiates the clearance and recording of permission from ink print publishers through blanket agreements.

Some Simple Steps in Using the File

Those making use of the file maintained by the ALRC need first to check all available catalogs of materials for the visually impaired. If no listing is found from any of those sources in the form desired, an inquiry should be made at the Printing House concerning its availability elsewhere, always specifying the exact title, author, publisher, copyright date, and grade level. School grade level and the media needed are most important for elementary school textbook titles. Concise, immediate attention is given every inquiry. If the title has been previously transcribed, the Printing House staff provides the address of the depository, or if the book is currently being transcribed elsewhere, the name and address of the transcribing group.

Direct inquiries can be made as to whether the book is available for loan or for copying. The Central Catalog is in its fourth edition, 1972, and is available to residential schools, state departments, and large transcribing groups. The following materials are available from: Instructional Materials Reference Center, American Printing House for the Blind, 1839 Frankfort Avenue, P.O. Box 6085, Louisville, Kentucky 40206. If individual copies are desired of these publications they will be sent upon request with the exception of the Central Catalog. This is for residential schools, state departments, regional libraries, and large city school systems.

Central Catalog, 2nd ed. (February, 1970). Not available to individual teachers.
Central Catalog, 3rd ed. (October, 1971). Not available to individual teachers.
Commercial Aids That May Be Used or Adapted for Visually Handicapped (October, 1969).
Commercially Available Recorded Instuctional Materials for the Development of Communication Skills (September, 1970, published and distributed May, 1971).
Commercially Available Instructional Materials for Use in the Development of Elementary Readiness Skills in Young Visually Handicapped Students (January, 1972).
Educational Aids for the Visually Handicapped (February, 1969, revised September, 1971).
Handbook for Teachers of the Visually Handicapped (September, 1970).
Intention and Completion Report Forms for Volunteer Transcribers. Braille, tape, large type.
Materials Reference List (August, 1969, revised January, 1971).

Recorded Materials List (September, 1969).
Source of Materials for the Partially Sighted (August, 1967, revised February, 1972).
Utilization of Low Vision Bibliography and Materials List (Summer, 1970).
The Visually Impaired Child—Growth, Learning, Development—Infancy to School Age (1971). May be ordered through the General Business Office, American Printing House for the Blind, Catalog Number 8–5104. Price: 50¢.

A World of Knowledge through Sound— The Audio Program of the Hadley School

KAREN GEARREALD

"The senses are merely channels to the mind. We try to keep all channels open and knowledge flowing freely by every possible path." Thus, the executive vice-president summarizes the aims of the Hadley School for the Blind.

Founded 50 years ago as a nonprofit organization in Winnetka, Illinois, the Hadley School remains unique among the world's educational institutions. Hadley is devoted exclusively to providing correspondence courses for visually handicapped persons. The entire curriculum is taught by mail and is offered, tuition-free, to blind people everywhere, regardless of age or race or creed or geographical location. For support the school relies wholly on contributions from the public—from philanthropic foundations and individual donors.

Started in a living room, the school now occupies a two-story building in downtown Winnetka. This facility has become too small for Hadley's rapidly expanding program, and will soon be enlarged to double the present size. In addition, the school has established ten regional offices—for Latin America, Europe, Asia, and Africa.

The curriculum is growing even faster than the physical plant. More than 125 courses are offered, on levels ranging from the fifth grade through high school, college, vocational, and adult avocational. Two thousand students are currently enrolled, and inquiries from new applicants are received every day. The curriculum is fully accredited by the National Home Study Council and by the International Council on Correspondence Education.

Reprinted by permission of Association for Educational Communications and Technology from *Audiovisual Instruction* 14:31–33 (Nov. 1969).

Beginnings in Sound

During its early history the Hadley School taught mainly through braille, the time-proven international touch-reading system, which is used for textbooks as well as for teachers' letters of instruction. Experiments with supplementary recordings were begun two decades ago; but as recently as 1957, when the present headquarters were on the drawing boards, there was still grave doubt about the value and utility of recordings in the education of the blind. "We came so close to not having a studio at all," recalls Donald Wing Hathaway, president of the School. "In the final plans for the building, the site of the studio was marked 'unexcavated.'" Fortunately, eleventh-hour changes made space for an audio facility that now houses two reading rooms, a control room, duplicating equipment, and an amateur radio station.

First to be recorded was an elementary Spanish course, which was read and sung by volunteers from several Latin American countries. President Hathaway remembers how the group assembled on Sundays, working throughout the afternoons and on into the evenings. The initial sessions took place in a friend's studio, since the school's facilities were still under construction. The final dubbing, editing, and collating of the tapes was the inaugural project for Hadley's own new studio.

Since then the use of discs and tapes—as a supplement though not a substitute for braille—has become an integral part of the Hadley program. The first attempts with Spanish were so successful that they were followed by additional work in Spanish, as well as by tapes in French, German, Italian, Esperanto, and Hebrew. Recorded by native speakers and duplicated at Hadley headquarters, the tapes are mailed to the blind students, who may listen at leisure and repeat ad infinitum in the relaxed, unselfconscious atmosphere of home. Thus each student becomes the master of a "language laboratory." While braille textbooks provide the necessary instruction in spelling and writing and grammar, tapes enable the learner to achieve ease and accuracy in pronunciation and conversation.

Languages are only one aspect of the Hadley recording program. Braille—a basic skill which is difficult for the newly blinded adult to acquire—comes alive through a series of "talking braille" lessons. Using his fingers to feel the dots on the pages of the textbook, the student simultaneously listens to discs which explain the braille system. For the blind person who cannot read braille, other courses have been recorded in their entirety. They include literature, history, civics, psychology, salesmanship, amateur radio theory, and the use of the abacus.

Many of these courses have immediate practical and vocational value. Lessons in rehabilitation discuss the personal, social, intellectual, and psychological adjustments that enable the blind adult to function successfully in the world of the sighted. Another course, complete with sound effects, helps with orientation in both indoor and outdoor environments. For the person who is seeking "a secure and happy place in the world of work" vocational guidance is offered through lessons in career planning. Meanwhile the domestic scene is not forgotten. A tape-recorded course in home management explains techniques of cleaning, cooking, washing, ironing, sewing, entertaining, personal grooming, child care, household safety, and family finances.

Individualized Instruction

The textbooks for an ever-growing number of courses are being made available in recorded form. At the same time, recordings are being utilized for more and more contacts with individual students. Teachers have discovered that personalized, tape-recorded letters are an important means of explanation and encouragement. Recorded instruction is often speedier and more effective than bulky braille correspondence. Many students choose to submit some or all of their lessons on tape rather than in braille or typing; and the result is an exchange of tapes between student and instructor, who find that such voice-to-voice communication is almost like a face-to-face chat.

The school's corps of volunteer readers provides personalized help, too, by recording a wealth of collateral material for students and faculty members. Ink-print copies of books—in fields as varied as linguistics, sociology, and space exploration—are sent to the Hadley studio by individual requesters. Under the supervision of the recording engineer, the material is read on tape, word for word, by qualified readers who donate their time and skill. The finished tapes are then mailed to the individual requester. This service is a boon to the blind intellectual who, though unable to read the printed page, nevertheless longs to explore the treasures of past literature and to keep up with the current "knowledge explosion."

Present Projects

Attention is sometimes turned from the book explosion to the proliferation of magazines and newspapers. Hadley's "junior auxiliary," a group of interested young women, scans contemporary periodicals and chooses a variety of sophisticated articles on controversial aspects of politics, art, literature, science, and current events. The selections are recorded on tape by professional readers—actors and broadcasters from the Chicago area—who volunteer their voices. After being collated and duplicated, the tapes are circulated under the general title of *Focus*. Issued several times a year,

Focus is a popular periodical, enthusiastically received by hundreds of blind readers.

Meanwhile the production of textbooks goes on. *Direct English Conversation* and *College Typewriting* are two of the Hadley School's newest recorded courses. Complete with vocabularies, dialogues, and question-and-answer exercises, the lessons in *Direct English Conversation* will help foreign students take the first steps toward mastery of English. When the students have learned the language, they will be ready to enroll in all areas of the School's broad curriculum. *College Typewriting,* another basic communications course, is an experiment. The braille version of these lessons has proved unwieldy because it requires the student to move his hands back and forth again and again from the dots of the page to the keys of the typewriter. The result is clumsy, jerky typing, plus vast losses of time and patience. Featuring dictated exercises with pauses interspersed, the recorded format should help the learner establish a natural, relaxed rhythm of listening and writing.

In the area of personalized communication, a whole new field is being opened up through amateur radio. The chairman of Hadley's romance languages department has inaugurated the practice of scheduling radio contacts with students. Via the air waves he and the students converse in Spanish and discuss the technicalities of the language. Professor Eguiguren feels that the potential of the amateur radio station is just beginning to be tapped and that a well-established network will some day link faculty members around the globe. He also believes that radio contacts will help the school get up-to-date information about the activities of other organizations for the blind, particularly in remote overseas locations where postal service is uncertain.

Listening into the Future

From its unexcavated and unanticipated condition, the Hadley recording studio has grown into a thriving audio department where more space is urgently needed. The studio will have a large share in the planned expansion of Hadley headquarters. So it should, for the marvelous possibilities of audio instruction will keep on demanding room for experimentation and development.

Textbooks, tutorial letters, individually requested materials, and *Focus*—all of these will continue to be recorded and improved; but, in addition, a host of new ideas will be tried. Taped round-robin discussions may draw students and faculty members closer together. The use of compressed speech, still in the experimental stage but definitely a promising concept, may become standard for any recorded material that could or should be read rapidly. Tape cassettes, now coming into vogue, offer a handy supplement to the present store of standard discs and open-reel tapes. In the domain of broad-

casting, the school may ultimately have an FM transmitter as well as an enlarged version of the two-way amateur station.

In short, the Hadley School has accepted the challenge of modern technology. The school believes that education should be made accessible to all persons who earnestly seek it. Blind students have shown that, with the proper assistance, they can learn just as aptly and productively as their sighted contemporaries. Though the physical vision may be impaired or absent, the other channels to the mind are receptively, eagerly, available. Through an audio program that learns from the past and listens to the future, the Hadley School will continue working to utilize those channels so that knowledge may flow freely—"by every possible path."

Library of Congress Service through Tactile and Audio Senses

ROBERT S. BRAY

Personalized library service to the handicapped is the cornerstone of a unique program administered by the Library of Congress. Through the mail, or even by telephone, eligible readers can order books of their choice in a medium they prefer. The Library's Division for the Blind and Physically Handicapped (DBPH) produces complete books in braille and on records and tapes for free distribution through 42 regional libraries stretching from Hawaii to the Virgin Islands. DBPH also provides record players and catalogs of available titles.

DBPH does for the handicapped what many librarians are urging should be done for ghetto residents, migrant farmers, and other disadvantaged groups of readers and would-be readers. Reliance on the tactile and audio senses by persons whose visual or motor reflexes are weak illustrates the feasibility of a multimedia approach to library service.

To publicize the program and reach readers DBPH must rely on librarians, teachers, social workers, doctors, and others who may serve the handicapped and be in a position to turn them to books they can read. Talking books, which are books recorded on $16\frac{2}{3}$ rpm. discs, and talking-book machines, which are especially designed, easy-to-operate phonographs, are supplied free of charge to all eligible readers. If the reader prefers braille, he will be sent braille books, and, if he has a tape recorder, he can draw on the DBPH tape collection.

Reprinted by permission from *The Wisconsin Library Bulletin* 67:144–47, 164 (1967).

Collections

Talking-book records cover a wide scope of literature, including the best sellers *Couples* and *The Armies of the Night,* mysteries and science fiction, books for juveniles, poetry and great world classics from the plays of Aeschylus to the works of Shakespeare. The books are recorded in their entirety and are read by professional announcers and actors. Currently, over 600 talking-book titles are released each year. In addition, more than 20 different magazines are available on records, among them *The Atlantic Monthly, Newsweek, Sports Illustrated, Good Housekeeping, Jack and Jill* and *Ebony.*

Another facet of the talking-book program is the collection of over 3500 different titles produced by volunteers across the country on tapes. Works on magnetic tape are of a more specialized limited-interest nature. For instance, the tape collection includes approximately 200 different plays, including the great Greek dramas, medieval morality plays and works of the modern theatre of the absurd. Some recently produced tapes are Richard Hofstadter's *Anti-Intellectualism in American Life, Paradise Lost* by John Milton and Horst Janson's *The History of Art.* Besides books on tape, there are also nine magazines, including such special-interest publications as *Foreign Affairs* and *High Fidelity.* The Division for the Blind and Physically Handicapped does not provide tape recorders.

Complementing the DBPH talking-book program is its braille book service. DBPH issues approximately 300 braille titles a year. Braille books, like talking books, cover a wide area of literature and some technical materials. As with talking books, several magazines are available; for example, *National Geographic, Seventeen* and *Popular Mechanics.* Also available through the division and many of the cooperating regional libraries are books which have been brailled by volunteer transcribers in answer to individual requests.

Publications

Every other month the division publishes two magazines, *Talking Book Topics* and *Braille Book Review.* Both contain annotated listings of new book releases and news pertaining to library service for the blind and physically handicapped. *Talking Book Topics* also contains special subject bibliographies, articles about authors whose books have been recorded as talking books, and other special features, among them the "Soundsheet," a recording of the titles and annotations of the newly released books.

The Braille Musician, which contains selected articles from various music magazines and lists new musical score acquisitions, is published quarterly by the Music Section of the Division for the Blind and Physically Handicapped. DBPH also publishes (1) special subject bibliographies; (2) biennial catalogs with annotated listings of braille and talking-book releases; and (3) brochures describing the program, some especially for people with particular disabilities, such as multiple sclerosis or cerebral palsy.

Eligibility and Service

To be eligible for these services, an individual must obtain a statement from a professional staff member of a hospital, school or library or from a doctor, nurse or optometrist certifying and describing his disability. The statement should be sent either to the Division for the Blind and Physically Handicapped, Library of Congress, Washington, D.C. 20542, or to the nearest regional library. It is also possible to apply for the division's programs through certain private organizations working closely with the Library of Congress, such as the National Multiple Sclerosis Society and the United Cerebral Palsy Associations, Inc.

Once an individual has been certified by a competent authority and the statement has been sent to the division or regional library, he will be contacted by the regional library. Unless he has requested braille materials, the reader will automatically be sent a talking-book machine and some talking books. He will also receive an introductory packet with talking-book and tape catalogs, general information on the regional library's programs and a questionnaire designed to inform the librarian of his reading interests and preferences. Through *Talking Book Topics* and *Braille Book Review* each reader is able to keep up with his library's latest acquisitions and newest services.

Special Services

DBPH's Music Section makes both braille music scores and taped music textbooks available to handicapped music lovers. The music scores are produced both by professional printing houses and by volunteer transcribers, and the taped books are strictly volunteer-produced. The section trains the braille transcribers and coordinates their efforts and those of the tape volunteers.

The Student Services Unit attempts to locate school-related or job-related materials for those eligible to use the services of the division. If a requested book cannot be located the unit contacts a particular volunteer group to transcribe the work. The names and locations of all of the procured books are being added to a steadily growing union catalog.

Volunteers

Although most of its funds are directed toward professional publications of braille and talking books, the division is greatly concerned with stimulating and helping volunteers to produce both braille books and books on magnetic tape. The Volunteer Services Section trains volunteer braillists through correspondence courses. This section also trains blind persons to be braille proofreaders. Other services include coordinating work by volunteer groups, conducting workshops in various parts of the country on different phases of volunteer braille work and processing volunteer-produced books through the division.

The Tape Volunteers Section seeks out qualified volunteers who can produce books on magnetic tape for the Library of Congress. The section helps volunteers set up recording facilities and also conducts workshops on various phases of the production of taped books. Printed books and magnetic tapes are sent to the volunteers. After a group or an individual has taped a book, the Tape Section reviews it, making sure Library of Congress standards have been met by checking pronunciation, phonetics and sound quality.

The division is also indebted to the Telephone Pioneers of America, a group of veteran telephone workers who repair and maintain talking-book machines, both in readers' homes and in the libraries.

Throughout the country, DBPH depends on volunteer agencies serving the blind locally. Services range from the distribution of talking-book machines to the reference of new readers to the Library of Congress program.

Projections

When DBPH was set up in 1931, its total Congressional appropriation was $100,000, the emphasis was on braille books, and only legally blind adults were eligible for the programs. Today, the annual appropriation stands at over $6,000,000, and talking books have become the most important part of the division's services. Handicapped persons of all ages who are unable to read are now eligible to use talking books. If the division gains greater readership among those who do not know about the program, it will mean that those who know about it have spread the word.

Media Services and Captioned Films

JAMES J. KUNDERT

Despite the great technical sophistication of the modern motion picture, it has failed dismally in bridging the communication gap between the screen and a half million of the nation's total population—the deaf. The silent screen had managed this, however crudely, through the use of the printed word. "The Jazz Singer," the first "talkie," ushered in a new era with the industry's first talking picture, and in doing so tuned out an audience that had been one of the minor mainstays of the infant industry. It remained for the 1960s for the deaf to relate once more to the message and medium emanating from the film capital of the world.

In classrooms for the deaf throughout the nation, teachers are now availing themselves increasingly of the rich resources of commercially prepared instructional films once restricted for use in normal classroom situations. Now they can tap the tremendous potential of the motion picture to enlarge and enhance concepts introduced in the classroom with a thoroughness, ingenuity, and imagination that characterize the best in this particular film genre. Moreover, the materials provided supply some much needed earlier stimulation to reading readiness as well as auditory training.

The process of adapting films for use with the deaf is not new. Hollywood had long used it to prepare its products for the lucrative export market. Printed subtitles, or captions as they shall hereafter be called, were inserted along the bottom of the picture. Properly synchronized with the audio in the film, these captions rendered the dialogue and/or narration in visual form, asking but the substitution of one sense for another, from those in whom the sense of hearing was seriously impaired.

In much the same way that recordings are basic to the federal program of Talking Books for the Blind administered by the Library of Congress, the captioned film forms the nucleus of the federal program of Captioned Films for the Deaf.

The Captioned Films program is the cumulative result of years of effort on the part of educators of the deaf to alleviate the ever-widening educational, cultural, and social gulf that has long been the particular bane of the hearing handicapped. Originating from the idea of a film library for the deaf developed by Emerson Romero of New York, the program had its beginning in 1950 in Hartford, Connecticut. The Junior League of that city donated a sum of money to set up a captioned films program. Dr. Edmund B. Boatner, superintendent of the American School for the Deaf, took the initiative and was joined in this enterprise by Dr. Clarence D. O'Connor, superintendent of the Lexington School for the Deaf.

Although a success from the time of its inception as a private venture, the program needed more financial support than could be supplied through private sources. The possibilities of federal government support were explored, and through the efforts of the Vocational Rehabilitation Administration of the Department of

Reprinted from *Media Services*, Aug. 1970, pp. 10, 40–42.

Health, Education, and Welfare, Congress was convinced of the need of such a measure, and responded by passing special legislation. The National Association of the Deaf, the National Fraternal Society of the Deaf, the Conference of Executives of American Schools for the Deaf, the Alexander Graham Bell Association for the Deaf and other organizations, along with numerous individuals, gave their active support to the enactment of Public Law 85–905 in September 1958. This law provided that a loan service of captioned films for the deaf be instituted in the Department of Health, Education, and Welfare for the following specified objectives:

1. To bring to deaf persons understanding and appreciation of those films which play such an important part in the general and cultural advancement of hearing persons;
2. To provide, through these films, enriched educational and cultural experiences, through which deaf persons can be brought into better touch with the realities of their environment; and
3. To provide a wholesome and rewarding experience which deaf persons may share together.

To carry out the provisions of this law, the Secretary was authorized among other things to acquire films by purchase, lease or gift and to provide for their captioning and distribution. The U.S. Office of Education was appointed to administer the fledgling program.

Federal funds for the program did not become available until July 1959. Dr. John A. Gough, formerly principal of the Kendall School for the Deaf and director of the teacher training program at Gallaudet College, was selected to head the program. The voluntary dissolution of the private group, Captioned Films for the Deaf, Inc., and the donation of its entire film library to the Government did much to get the federal program started on October 1, 1959.

The service of supplying films was accepted at once. So great was the demand that Congress enlarged the program with several sizable pieces of legislation. Public Law 87–715, passed in 1963, increased the original authorization and broadened the scope of the program to include research and training activities. A second amendment, Public Law 89–258, which became effective October 1, 1965, raised the authorized budget ceiling for several consecutive fiscal years. The law also revamped the objectives specified in the original legislation, permitting the program to make progress in other areas where the needs of the deaf had not been met. These objectives are two-fold in nature:

1. To provide enriched educational and cultural experiences for deaf persons by means of a free loan service of acquired or specifically produced captioned films.
2. To promote the educational advancement of deaf persons by:
   a) Carrying on research in the use of educational media for the deaf;
   b) Producing and distributing educational media for the deaf and for parents of deaf children and other persons who are directly involved in work for the advancement of the deaf or who are actual or potential employers of the deaf; and
   c) Training persons in the use of educational media for the instruction of the deaf.

The transition from a limited film service to one that encompasses the sweeping area of multimedia utilization led Congress to consider the development of the program for an even greater role. On January 2, 1968, Public Law 90–247 came into effect, and authorized the program to provide media services to all areas of the handicapped, including the mentally retarded, hard of hearing, speech impaired, visually handicapped, seriously emotionally disturbed, crippled or other health-impaired children who by reason of their handicap require special education and related services. Because of the expanded role, over five million children became potential users of special media services as compared with the approximately 250,000 deaf population in the United States (of which 40,000 are of school age) previously served by the program. Captioned Films for the Deaf was changed to its present designation, Media Services and Captioned Films, to more clearly reflect this expansion of activities.

Congress tied up this legislative package by authorizing funds in the amounts of $8 and $10 million for fiscal years 1969 and 1970 respectively, although the actual funding did not come to this amount. However, significant strides were made by Media Services and Captioned Films during 1969 under an operating budget of $4.7 million. Due to this limited funding, $3.2 million of the budget enabled the program to continue its services for the deaf, with the remaining $1.5 million being utilized to support demonstrations of the applicability of new media to other areas of the handicapped. The following program developments evolved during fiscal year 1969.

Acquisitions included 65 general interest films, 54 educational films and one free film made available through government agencies and private enterprise. Through the Captioned Films Educational Media Distribution Center in Washington, D.C., the recreational films are sent to the three regional libraries maintained by the program in New York, Indiana, and Colorado. The program also maintains 60 film depositories, which circulate captioned educational films to meet educational needs in schools and classes for the deaf. More than 400 of these educational titles are available at each depository. In addition, schools for the deaf receive extended loan of other educational media, including filmstrips, transparencies, slides, overhead and filmstrip projectors, projection tables and screens, as well as miscellaneous instructional materials.

The program's captioned film service reached more than 2,375 groups of hearing impaired persons. Of these, 942 were schools or classes for the deaf. Total audience for recreational films numbered over 1,000,000, with a monthly average of 1,998 showings. Users receive these films on free loan, and are required to pay only return postage.

Film production carried on under contracts with private companies and with Regional Media Centers for the Deaf included 8mm loop films for training in lip-reading, as well as classroom instructional filmstrips, transparencies, and slides. These were reproduced in quantity and loaned to schools for the deaf. Videotapes for sign-language instruction via the national networks were also produced. Other film production activities include the development of a series of instructional films on defined problems and solutions in special education for teachers and self-help films that would contribute to the academic and social adjustment of special education children who are identified as emotionally maladjusted and/or educationally mentally handicapped. A study guide project produced teachers' guides for 182 educational films and another project supplied a special edition of the National Geographic Schools Bulletin entitled *World Traveler* for use with language handicapped children.

An intensive training program designed to instruct teachers in the use of the new media is closely coordinated with the loan service. The four Regional Media Centers for the Deaf conduct intensive summer institutes in educational technology. One of the centers concentrates on programmed instruction, and one is serving as an advanced institute for persons who will supervise media programs in schools for the deaf. A start was made during the year to integrate teachers from other areas of the handicapped into the institute program. Demonstration teams from the Regional Media Centers provide on-the-job training by conducting two- and three-day workshops in schools during the regular academic year. A national symposium on educational technology for administrators of schools for the deaf is an annual highlight of the University of Nebraska center in Lincoln. Other training projects funded include such widely diverse areas as work with teachers, early childhood education for parents via a multimedia program, and training of special education

teachers working with trainable mentally retarded children.

Research is designed to find practical solutions to the problems of the handicapped. Examples of these problems include difficulties in acquiring normal use of the English language, abnormalities in visual perception, behavioral problems of the retarded and emotional maladjustments common to handicapped children. Programmed instruction, individualizing of teaching, multimedia presentations and specially produced films and video tapes are among the techniques being explored to meet these problems.

Other research projects lend themselves to feasibility studies. Among these are captioned television programs for the deaf and a multimedia approach in the education of educable mentally retarded students.

Demonstration projects dealt with programmed language instruction to facilitate the education of the deaf, teaching speech to the deaf, a computer-based evaluation and development project for instructional materials, individualizing instruction for the deaf, educational media for the visually impaired child, audiovisual and instructional media services for mentally handicapped children and language development for the retarded child via instructional media.

The magnitude of media services and materials called forth under the program's expanded authority led Congress to enact Public Law 91–61 on August 20, 1969, providing for the establishment of a National Center on Educational Media and Materials for the Handicapped. This center will provide a comprehensive program of activities to facilitate the use of new educational technology in educational programs for the handicapped.

The program's growth since 1958, when a benevolent Congress acted to relieve the cultural and communication vacuum that is the special plight of the hearing impaired, has been most encouraging. Under its new banner, Media Services and Captioned Films has been conceived to fulfill a vital area of need and to generate broader benefits for the nation's handicapped children.

Rehabilitation Information—A Bibliography

RUTH A. VELLEMAN

In the United States today roughly 10 percent of the population is physically disabled. In many areas of

Reprinted from *Library Journal*, Oct. 15, 1973. Published by R. R. Bowker Co. (a Xerox company). Copyright © 1973 by Xerox Corporation.

the country, the disabled cannot obtain the information they require in order to reach their potential as human beings and lead lives as active and productive as possible. The needs of the disabled include information about assistive devices to aid their physical well being, legislative information, knowledge of special educational programs, travel information to aid them in surmounting ever present architectural barriers, vocational counselling, etc. This bibliography is presented in the hope that public libraries in areas where this type of information is not currently available to their patrons will acquire some of this material.

For the past ten years, the author has been engaged in building an extensive Rehabilitation Research Library in the areas of Medical and Vocational Rehabilitation and Special Education. Housed at the Human Resources Center in Albertson, Long Island, the library is open by appointment to professional personnel, students, and laymen in need of information in these specialized areas. Mail or telephone requests are also handled from all over the country, and questions addressed to the librarian are most welcome.

Human Resources Center is a private nonprofit organization dedicated to the service of the handicapped. It was founded by Dr. Henry Viscardi, Jr., who was born disabled and tells his life story in *A Man's Stature* (John Day, 1952). The Center is comprised of three coordinated units: Abilities Inc., a nonprofit demonstration industrial and clerical work center for the handicapped; Human Resources School, which offers tuition-free education to 200 severely disabled previously home-bound children from preschool through high school level; and Human Resources Research and Training Institute, which conducts research and training relating to the disabled, retarded, aged, disadvantaged, and emotionally restored. The Center also houses the Insurance Company of North America's MEND (Medical and Educational Needs of the Disabled) Institute which provides rehabilitation information to business and industry. Monographs, published by the Center in the areas of attitudes toward the disabled, employment of the disabled, and special education, are available free upon request.

Books: Medical and Vocational Rehabilitation; Special Education

The three medical rehabilitation texts listed below, although technical, are the principal texts in a small field, and large libraries might wish to include them in a medical or reference department. The two books on employment of the disabled would be useful to disabled public library patrons and their counselors. Dr. Riekehof's book is invaluable for anyone who must learn to communicate with the deaf. Dr. Spock has written a most useful book for parents of disabled children; and there are two written specifically for the handicapped teen-ager and parents.

Apgar, Virginia, M.D., M.P.H. and Joan Beck. *Is My Baby All Right?: a Guide to Birth Defects.* illus. by Ernest W. Beck. 492p. index. Trident, 1972. $9.95
An accurate and well-written account, in popular style, of the birth defects that can afflict infants, and how parents should cope with them. The chapter on genetic counseling will be helpful to young married couples who fear that their family history would indicate the birth of a disabled child. Dr. Apgar is the creator of the "Apgar Score" for evaluating the health of newborn babies. Mrs. Beck, a journalist with the *Chicago Tribune*, is the author of the syndicated column "You and Your Child."

Arthur, Julietta K. *Employment for the Handicapped: a Guide for the Disabled, Their Families and Their Counselors.* 272p. index. appendixes listing organizations. Abingdon, 1967. $5.95
Valuable information for the handicapped from the onset of disability right through employment. The development of abilities towards self-sufficiency are explored, as well as the resources which can help restore the patient to working ability.

Ayrault, Evelyn West. *Helping the Handicapped Teenager Mature.* 184p. appendixes. Association, 1971. $6.95
A very informative book for parents and their disabled teen-agers. Deals with all of the physical, psychological, social and sexual problems of growing up, including problems of education, recreation, and career fulfillment. Appendixes give directories of agencies providing services to the disabled, listing of special camps, and adapted college facilities. The college list, however, is taken from other available lists (see Directories), and is not updated.

Krusen, Frank H., M.D. and others. *Handbook of Physical Medicine and Rehabilitation.* 2d ed. 920p. index. Saunders, 1971. $22.50
A compilation of chapters by many authors. Subject matter includes evaluation of patient, techniques of management and evaluation and management of specific disorders. Diagrams, illustrations, and bibliographical listings at the end of each chapter. A comprehensive text for nurses, physical and occupational therapists, social workers, and psychologists.

Licht, Sidney, M.D. *Rehabilitation and Medicine.* 823p. index. Waverly, Baltimore, Md., 1968. $18
Rehabilitation Nursing, Social Work, Rehabilitation of Amputees, and Spinal Cord Injuries are some of the important chapters in this book which also contains diagrams, charts, and bibliography.

Malikin, David and Herbert Rusalem. *Vocational Rehabilitation of the Disabled: an Overview.* 326p. index. bibliog. New York Univ. Pr., 1969. $8.95
A good general review of the history of rehabilitation followed by chapters on psychosocial aspects of disability, referral, evaluation and treatment, training, job placement and follow up, and counseling.

Riekehof, Lottie. *Talk to the Deaf: a Manual of Approximately 1,000 Signs Used by the Deaf of North America.* illus. by Betty Stewart. 143p. index to signs. bibliog. Gospel Publishing House, 1445 Boonville Ave., Springfield, Mo. 65802. 1963. $4.95
This is considered to be one of the best texts available for the beginning student in sign language. Dr. Riekehof is the dean of women and associate professor at the world's only liberal arts college for the deaf, Gallaudet College, Washington, D.C. In his foreword, Stanley D. Roth, Litt.D., superintendent of the Kansas School for the Deaf, states, "The need for human beings to communicate is one of the most basic needs. There are a great number of deaf children who are not able to meet the pace required for oral speech." While some schools for the deaf believe in teaching only oral means of communication, others take cognizance of the fact that some profoundly deaf children are unable to attain this ideal. For the parents of these children and others who need to communicate with the profoundly deaf, this book is an excellent tool. (See also Alexander Graham Bell Association for the Deaf, under Directories, and the periodical, *Volta Review.*)

Rusk, Howard A., M.D. *Rehabilitation Medicine.* 3d rev. ed. 668p. index. Mosby, 1971. $22.50
Medical rehabilitation principles and clinical applications. Recent developments in research and experience in training the disabled homemaker, handling speech problems, prescribing prosthetics and orthotics. Photographs, case studies, and charts.

Splaver, Sarah, Ph. D. *Your Handicap, Don't Let It Handicap You.* 224p. index. bibliog. Messner, 1967. $3.95
Addressing herself to young people with physical handicaps, Dr. Splaver attempts to provide readers with the information they need to live active lives. The book is worth having if only for the excellent source listings at the end. Addresses are given for voluntary health agencies, professional associations, state agencies administering services for disabled children, state Easter Seal Society offices, State rehabilitation (OVR) agencies, U.S. Civil Service regions, U.S. Government agencies serving the disabled; bibliography of inspirational reading, and pamphlet materials on rehabilitation available from government and nongovernment sources.

Spock, Benjamin, M.D., and Marion O. Lerrigo, Ph.D. *Caring for Your Disabled Child.* 373p. index. bibliog. Macmillan, 1965. $4.95; 1966, pap. $1.95
A book for parents to help them care for their disabled children. General advice for family living, medical care, education, vocational future, recreation, and home management.

Directories and Bibliographies

Since it is impossible to list all of the agencies dealing with and publishing material for the handicapped, further information may be obtained from the directories listed below.

Directory of Organizations Interested in the Handicapped. 92p. index. Committee for the Handicapped. 1218 New Hampshire Avenue, N.W., Washington, D.C. 20036. 50¢
A handy directory listing organizations, both private and federal, concerned with the techniques, training, treatment, devices and procedures utilized in rehabilitating and employing the disabled. Since a number of the agencies listed in this directory have been engaged in research and demonstration projects supported by the Office of Vocational Rehabilitation, a selection of such projects has been included.

Directory of State Agencies for the Blind and *Directory of State Offices of Vocational Rehabilitation.* Department of Health, Education and Welfare, Rehabilitation Services Administration, Washington, D.C.
Periodically updated, these directories are available free from the Administration officer, Rehabilitation Services Administration, Room 3024, 330 C St. S.W., Washington, D.C. 20201. A valuable addition to a reference room, they list names, addresses, and phone numbers of the personnel employed by the State Offices of Vocational Rehabilitation and the Divisions of Rehabilitation for the visually impaired. Many disabled people are unaware of the law which entitles all blind and disabled persons 18 years of age or over to vocational counseling and/or financial government aid for study or work training.

Directory of Residential Camps for Persons with Special Health Needs. National Easter Seal Society. Annual. $1
Unfortunately, a similar directory of residences for the severely disabled is not available because of the shortage of such facilities in most areas of the country.

Directory for Exceptional Children. 7th ed. 1248p. index. Porter Sargent, 1972. $14
A listing of 3600 special schools, both private and public, day and residential. Separate sections for different disabilities, organized by state. Includes blind, deaf, retarded, emotionally disturbed, brain damaged, and

physically handicapped. Information regarding tuition, admission requirements, etc. Location maps, listings of associations, foundations, federal and state agency personnel. If only one reference book is purchased to assist library patrons seeking information about schools for children with special needs, let this be the book.

Ellingson, Careth and James Cass. *Directory of Facilities for the Learning Disabled and Handicapped.* 624p. Harper, 1972. pap. $6.95

A new directory of diagnostic facilities for children and adults, providing descriptions of remedial, therapeutic, and developmental programs. Costs, given for the 1969–70 school year, will be somewhat higher now. Facilities are listed for the United States (by state), British Columbia, Manitoba, Ontario, and Prince Edward Island. Listings include university and hospital facilities as well as private clinics in areas such as remedial reading, speech, and hearing.

Hall, Robert E. and Eileen F. Lehman. *Some Colleges and Universities with Special Facilities to Accommodate Handicapped Students.* Department of Health, Education and Welfare, Washington, D.C.; dist. by the National Easter Seal Society for Crippled Children and Adults (see National Easter Seal entry), 1967.

This directory is based on a survey conducted during a research program at the University of Kansas in 1961–63. It lists many colleges in the United States which have eliminated architectural barriers for disabled students and/or operate special programs for the disabled with varying degrees of success. Unfortunately, this is the most recent study available. The information is somewhat outdated and some fine programs have begun since it was completed. For programs which offer attendant care for the severely physically disabled who wish the experience of college away from home, contact the Human Resources Center Library.

Institute of Rehabilitation Medicine, New York University Medical Center, 400 East 34th St., New York, N.Y. 10016. Publications Catalog on request from the Publications Office.

IRM publishes monographs in the area of rehabilitation, some of which are listed in this bibliography. For additional titles, see their catalog.

National Easter Seal Society for Crippled Children and Adults. 2023 West Ogden Ave., Chicago, Ill. 60612. Publications Catalog, 1972.

The Easter Seal Society is probably the oldest voluntary organization in the United States, serving the disabled with a three-fold program of care and treatment, research, and education. Publications include monographs on such topics as architectural standards for buildings; vehicles for the severely disabled; careers in rehabilitation; pamphlets for parents of disabled children covering information about learning disabilities, brain injury, and other topics; long-term care of the multihandicapped; speech and physical therapy; and many more. Most of the pamphlets sell for 10–20 cents each.

Bibliographies issued by the Society and updated periodically list books and pamphlets in many areas such as vocational rehabilitation, fiction about the handicapped, inspirational literature, periodicals concerning the handicapped, directories of national organizations, etc. These must be requested periodically since the agency does not keep a regular mailing list.

Regular serial publications include *The Easter Seal Bulletin*, a free quarterly newsletter; *Rehabilitation Literature* (see Periodicals for full description); and *Employment Bulletin*, free, issued ten times a year to persons with professional degrees in the field of rehabilitation. Easter Seal branch offices in many U.S. cities have published travel guides for the disabled which include information about architectural barrier-free motels, restaurants, theaters, and other public places. A listing of these directories and the addresses of the organizations in the cities where they have been published is available from the Chicago office. Travel guides published by other agencies are listed below in the section on travel.

President's Committee on the Employment of the Handicapped, Washington, D.C. 20210.

Catalog of rehabilitation information available, on request, in both printed and audiovisual form. *Accessibility of Junior Colleges for the Handicapped*, undated, contains fairly recent information in tabulation form, based on questionnaires. List facilities for disabled students in junior colleges by state.

Registry of Private Schools for Children with Special Educational Needs. National Educational Consultants, 711 St. Paul St., Baltimore, Md., 1971. Microfiche copies available. Ring binder.

A listing of over 800 schools to answer special education needs. Information regarding fees, disabilities served, by state. Yearly supplements planned.

Special Education Teacher Education Directory. Council for Exceptional Children, 1920 Association Dr., Reston, Va., 1968–69.

This directory, in need of updating, is issued by the Council for Exceptional Children, the professional organization for teachers in the field of special education. It provides high school and college guidance counselors with information that will assist them in working with students who are interested in programs in higher education in this field. Belongs with other college materials such as Lovejoy and Barron.

Prosthetics and Orthotics

Although there are many adaptive devices to aid the disabled person in the activities of daily living, very often the knowledge of what is avilable and where to find it is difficult to obtain. The books and monographs listed below will aid considerably in this area.

Gutman, Ernest M. and Carolyn R. Gutman. *Wheelchair to Independence.* foreword by Howard Rusk. 136p. illus. index. bibliography. Thomas, 1968. $6.75

As Dr. Rusk states in his foreword, the greatest goal of a disabled person with impaired ambulation is mobility, the symbol of independence. This book offers a compact, informative study about adapted homes, adapted college facilities, telephone adaptations, and other information. Although somewhat outdated, it is useful for the listings of names and organizations provided.

Hofmann, Ruth B. *How To Build Special Furniture and Equipment for Handicapped Children.* 88p. illus. and diagrams with measurements, lists of tools. index. Thomas, 1970. $6.50

Parents of physically disabled children have always had to improvise special furniture and equipment for their children. Many inventive parents have used their ingenuity to create chairs, standing tables, tub seats, reading boards, sand tables, car seats, and many other necessary but unmanufactured items. This book fills a need for sharing this kind of information. It gives precise directions, with diagrams and illustrations, for making a number of useful items for the handicapped child at home.

Kamenetz, Herman L., M.D. *The Wheelchair Book; Mobility for the Disabled.* 267p. index. appendixes. bibliog. Thomas, 1969. $14.75

Comprehensive information on types of wheelchairs available to the disabled. It will be helpful to nurses, physical therapists, the disabled themselves, and their families. There is a medical glossary, and appendixes listing manufacturers and brand names of wheelchairs, lifts, home elevators and stair lifts, and hoists, all in the United States.

Lowman, Edward, M.D. and Judith Lannefeld Klinger, O.T.R., M.A. *Aids to Independent Living: Self-help for the Handicapped.* 796p. index. McGraw, 1969. $39

This book is expensive, but well worth the money. It is the latest and most definitive catalog of devices for independent living for the disabled. The authors are on the staff of the Institute of Rehabilitation Medicine, New York University Medical Center. Useful for groups who work with the disabled without benefit of medical centers, such as general practitioners, public health nurses, occupational and physical therapists,

vocational counselors, as well as the disabled themselves. Each category is expanded by the inclusion of bibliographies of agencies and periodicals. At the end of the book, there is a list of equipment sources with addresses and prices. Emphasis is on mail order availability, thus making many devices available for the first time to people who lack access to distributors in large metropolitan areas. Devices include everything on the market for the disabled at home, for equipping automobiles for handicapped drivers, and a myriad of other things.

Mealtime Manual for the Aged and Handicapped. 242p. index. S. & S., 1970. $5.95; pap. $2

This manual offers solutions for practical kitchen management problems for handicapped homemakers and should help millions of handicapped homemakers who have no contact with rehabilitation personnel or institutions. Hints on how to compensate for handicaps by modifying kitchen design, what appliances to choose, and easy menus.

Richardson, Nina K. *Type with One Hand.* 27p. Southwest Pub., 1959. pap. approx. $2

A very useful teaching or self-teaching tool to enable a one-handed person to learn to type. Instructions are given for left-handed or right-handed typing.

Sullivan, Richard, M.D. and others. *Telephone Services for the Handicapped.* 147p. Monograph No. 37. Available from the Institute of Rehabilitation Medicine. $2.50 prepaid.

This manual is directed toward the disabled person seeking ideas for adapting his telephone.

Zimmerman, Muriel. *Self-Help Devices for Rehabilitation.* Part I, 418p. $5.95; Part II, approx. 375p., $4.95. William C. Brown, Dubuque, Iowa.

Much less expensive than the Lowman and Klinger book and still a classic in the field, this book is a very good basic reference for self-help for the handicapped.

Periodicals

There are many professional periodicals in fields related to rehabilitation and special education, but very few general major periodicals in these areas. Those most basic and most general are listed below.

Accent on Living. Quarterly. $2.50. P.O. Box 726, Gillum Road and High Drive, Bloomington, Ind.

A small, useful magazine for the disabled and their families with inspirational stories and classified advertisements featuring prosthetic devices and other items of importance to the disabled.

Closer Look Newsletter. Box 19428, Washington, D.C. 20036.

Closer Look is an information service which was established by the U.S. Department of HEW, Office of Education, Bureau of the Education of the Handicapped. It is designed to help parents find services for children with mental, physical, emotional, and learning handicaps. All parents of exceptional children should be advised to have themselves put on the mailing list for this newsletter.

Exceptional Parent. Six times per year. $12. Published by Psy-Ed Corp. 264 Beacon St., Boston, Mass. 02116; correspondence to P.O. Box 101 Back Bay Annex, Boston, Mass. 02117.

A new publication addressed to parents of exceptional children, offering practical advice on daily problems as well as issues of long-range planning, care, and financing.

Journal of Rehabilitation. Bimonthly. $5; free to members of the National Rehabilitation Association. Published by the Association, 1522 K St. N.W., Washington, D.C.

General articles in the field of rehabilitation.

New Outlook for the Blind. Monthly except July and August. $6. In inkprint, braille, and recorded editions by Department of Information, American Foundation for the Blind, 15 West 16th St., New York, N.Y. 10011.

Research articles plus listings of current literature, books, directories, pamphlets, and other material of interest to the blind and those who work with them.

Paraplegia News. $3.50. Official organ of the Paralyzed Veterans of America and the National Paraplegia Foundation. 935 Coastline Drive, Seal Beach, Calif. 90740.

A popular magazine for the paraplegic, filled with newsy items about the paralympics, employment or educational opportunities, classified advertisements, and a column on legislation for the handicapped. A good magazine for a library with paraplegics among its clients.

Rehabilitation Gazette. 1972. (Formerly the "Toomey j. Gazette") Published once a year by a volunteer staff, both disabled and able-bodied. Donation per annual copy, $2 from the disabled; $4 from the able-bodied. 4502 Maryland Ave., St. Louis, Mo. 63108.

A fascinating mixture of personal stories of courage and useful information about available devices, tour guides, housing, etc. Back issues also available, each concerning itself mainly with one specific topic.

Rehabilitation Literature. Monthly. $10. National Easter Seal Society for Crippled Children and Adults, 2023 W. Ogden Avenue, Chicago, Ill. 60612.

One or two professional articles each month plus book reviews and abstracts of current literature. The most professional journal in the general field of rehabilitation.

Teaching Exceptional Children. Quarterly. $7.50. Published by the Council for Exceptional Children, 1920 Association Dr., Reston, Va.

Aimed at classroom teachers of exceptional children, this is a practical teaching guide which would also be helpful to parents. The CEC also publishes *Exceptional Children*, the professional periodical in the field which publishes technical research articles.

Volta Review. Journal of the Alexander Graham Bell Association for the Deaf, 3417 Volta Place N.W., Washington, D.C. Monthly except June, July, and August. With membership, $15 per year.

The Alexander Graham Bell Association is committed to the pro-oralist point of view in the education of the deaf, to the extent that they advocate that deaf children be educated to make the fullest use of any available hearing, receive auditory training, and improve language, speech, and speech reading. The position of the "oralists" is that the deaf cannot communicate with the hearing world without oral skills. A poignant letter in a recent issue of the magazine, written by the mother of a deaf child, deplores the lack of information in the public libraries for parents of the deaf and asks that this magazine be made widely available.

Travel Guides

For the traveling disabled there are many guides to help them overcome obstacles. Branches of the National Easter Seal Society and other public service organizations publish travel guides listing architecturally free accommodations of all kinds in many of the cities of the United States (see Directories: National Easter Seal Society). There are other special guides issued periodically in other areas of the world. New ones, as they appear, are announced in the rehabilitation periodicals.

Annand, Douglass R. *The Wheelchair Traveler.* 1972 ed. unpaged. Available from the author, Ball Hill Road, Milford, N.H. 03055. $3 postpaid.

This well known travel guide, written and issued yearly by a world traveling paraplegic, includes 2000 listings in 49 states, Canada and Mexico, of accessible motels, restaurants, and sightseeing areas. Annand also lists the cities for which the National Easter Seal Society has issued guides. He offers helpful hints about making travel easier for the disabled, such as how to narrow your wheelchair for those "slightly too narrow" doorways, how to handle air travel, how to summon medical aid, etc.

European Highways E1 and E4. Motel Guide for the Disabled. 16p. International Society for Rehabilitation of the Disabled, 219 East 44th St., New York, N.Y. 10017. 50¢

The International Society for Rehabilitation of the Disabled has member organizations in 65 countries. This pamphlet has been published by the subcommittee of ISRD, International Committee on Technical Aids, Housing and Transportation, which is housed by the Swedish Institute for the Handicapped, Fack. 161–03 Bromma 3, Sweden. It is an early attempt to list motels along Highway I (London-Palermo) and Highway 4 (Lisbon-Helsinki).

Hogsett, Stanley G. *Airline Transportation for the Handicapped and Disabled.* 45p. appendixes. National Easter Seal Society, 1971. $1.25

A survey of the policies of 22 domestic airlines, regarding their handling of disabled passengers. It includes many helpful hints for the handicapped traveler with a table of specific services offered by each airline and the person to contact for reservations and provision of special service.

Lockhart, Freda Bruce. *London for the Disabled.* rev. ed. 128p. Ward, Lock & Co., Ltd., 116 Baker St. London, W. 1 and at Sydney, 1967. 6/net.

Freda Lockhart, well known film critic, broadcaster, and victim of multiple sclerosis, has been wheelchair-bound for some years. She has compiled a directory of London shops, hotels, restaurants, galleries, museums, libraries, churches, theaters, transportation, and other ports of call that are accessible to the disabled.

National Park Guide for the Handicapped. National Park Service. U.S. Department of the Interior. U.S. Government Printing Office, 1971. For sale by Superintendent of Documents, Washington, D.C. 20402. Stock #2405–0286. 40¢

The National Park Service is working on a program of removing existing obstructions and building new facilities to accommodate the handicapped. This booklet will make it possible for the disabled to visit the National Parks and Monuments. Special provisions have been made for the blind as well as the wheelchair traveler. Parks are listed by state and accessible areas noted, as well as those which are inaccessible at the present time.

Schleichkorn, Jacob S. *Carriage of the Physically Handicapped on Domestic and International Airlines; a Report on the Policies, Rules and Regulations Affecting Travel of the Handicapped.* United Cerebral Palsy Association, 815 Second Ave., New York, N.Y. 10017, 1972. $1.25

Describes the viewpoint of each airline's procedures and recommendations in the transportation of the disabled. Includes a chart on physical and mental conditions which might require additional care or refusal by the airlines to transport.

Where Turning Wheels Stop. 76p. Paralyzed Veterans of America, 3636 16th St., N.W., Washington, D.C. 20010. $1

PVA works actively to encourage business establishments, predominantly hotels and motels, to build architecturally barrier-free units for the comfort of wheelchair travelers. This publication lists accessible restaurants, hotels, and motels by states of the U.S. and also Washington, D.C., Bermuda, Canada, Mexico, and Puerto Rico. It also includes a PVA chapter directory and a listing of accessible government buildings in Washington, D.C.

Women's Committee. President's Committee on the Employment of the Handicapped. *A List of Guidebooks for Handicapped Travellers.* 3d ed. 1972. 22p. Free.

This directory lists guidebooks prepared for cities in the U.S. and includes a section on foreign cities.

Special Tours

Many disabled people who could not travel alone are able to arrange for group trips to meet their needs. Addresses of organizations which provide such tours are listed below, along with other general information to enable the disabled to arrange to travel comfortably.

Evergreen Travel Service, Inc., 19429 44th St. West, Lynnwood, Wash. 98036.

Tours for the disabled, blind, and retarded. Brochures available in braille. Information on request.

Handi-cap Horizons. 3250 East Loretta Drive, Indianapolis, Ind.

Organized tours for the handicapped. Newsletter listing future tours will be sent for a small fee for subscription.

Pan American Tours for the Disabled. Information can be obtained at local Pan American ticket offices or write: Larry J. Chadwell, Sales Coordinator, Pan American World Airways, 1219 Main St., Houston, Tex. 77002.

Rambling Tours. P.O. Box 1304, Hallandale, Fla. 33009.

Guided tours for disabled travelers. Severely disabled persons requiring physical care may bring an attendant or request the tour directors to provide one for a fee which will be agreed upon in advance. A newsletter is issued about past and future tours and will be sent upon request.

For additional sources on tours, see the article on "Travel for the Handicapped," *New York Times,* August 24, 1973, p. 35.

Mission and Services of the National Center on Educational Media and Materials for the Handicapped

JOHN C. BELLAND

The National Center on Educational Media and Materials for the Handicapped is an organization established by the federal government. It exists to promote a range of media and materials services to all handicapped young people by working with a system of regional, state, and local centers which provide backup to those schools and libraries that have direct service responsibility to the handicapped person. In order to understand something of the nature of the National Center on Educational Media and Materials for the Handicapped, some historical perspective may be helpful; this is followed by a description of the services provided by the center in fiscal year 1975, and a projection of a potential long-range mission.

Historical Background

The National Center on Educational Media and Materials for the Handicapped was authorized by Public Law 91–61 in 1969. This law provides that the Secretary of the Department of Health, Education, and Welfare may enter into an agreement with an institution of higher education to provide for the establishment and operation of this center. Public Law 91–61 also provides that the center shall offer a comprehensive program of educational technology services to all handicapped people.

At the time of enactment, the Senate Committee on Labor and Public Welfare issued a report which described the purpose and meaning of Public Law 91–61 in more extensive terms. The report suggested that the National Media Center would provide coordination to the system of federally sponsored programs which were designed to bring the benefits of educational technology to handicapped people. This included: (1) the network of Regional Special Education Instructional Materials Centers and Regional Media Centers for the Deaf [The Regional Special Education Instructional Materials Centers and Regional Centers for the Deaf have been superseded by the Area Learning Resource Centers (see Appendix)], (2) components of special institutions such as the instructional materials activities of the American Printing House for the Blind and the pre-

This document was prepared pursuant to a contract with the Office of Education, U.S. Department of Health, Education, and Welfare. Contractors undertaking such projects under government sponsorship are encouraged to express freely their judgment in professional and technical matters. Points of view or opinions do not, therefore, necessarily represent official Office of Education position or policy.

college program educational technology services of Gallaudet College, and (3) various programmatic thrusts in other areas of the federal government, such as those in the office of Child Development. It was felt by the Senate Subcommittee that if the National Center on Educational Media and Materials for the Handicapped was able to provide these programs with some kind of coordinated effort, optimum use of relatively scarce resources would be accomplished.

In addition to the coordinating responsibilities, the Committee on Labor and Public Welfare suggested that the National Center on Educational Media and Materials for the Handicapped should serve as a collection point for reports on all instructional research into the design of appropriate instructional experiences for handicapped persons. In addition, the center should also serve as a demonstration and training center for all those persons who work with handicapped young people, providing them the opportunity to become as sophisticated in the use of media and materials as the state of the art allowed. Since considerable activity had already been generated by the Special Education Instructional Materials Centers, the Regional Media Centers for the Deaf, special centers for multiply handicapped children, the Council on Exceptional Children, many other professional and lay organizations, and many university departments of special education and/or educational technology, to the extent that at least 25,000,000 federal dollars were being spent on educational technology for the handicapped each year, the National Media Center was added to construct linkages among all the federally sponsored programs and agencies.

Even before Public Law 91–61 was enacted, the Bureau of Education for the Handicapped had supported planning projects in two institutions of higher education to prepare guidelines for the development of a National Center on Educational Media and Materials for the Handicapped. With passage of the law and receipt of the planning studies, a Request for Proposals (RFP) was generated in the Bureau of Education for the Handicapped, with the condition that institutions of higher education in the Washington, D.C. area would be qualified applicants. Of all the proposals submitted in response to the RFP, not one was found to meet the specified needs of the Bureau of Education for the Handicapped; therefore, none was accepted and a second request was generated with the geographic restriction removed and the mission substantially revised. In reponse to the second request, six institutions submitted responses, with Ohio State University eventually selected to establish the National Center on Educational Media and Materials for the Handicapped for an initial period of thirty-nine months ending August 31, 1975.

The National Center on Educational Media and Materials for the Handicapped was officially established at Ohio State University in June of 1972 and began operations with a symposium of representatives from Special Education Instructional Materials Centers, Regional Media Centers for the Deaf, special education, and Bureau of Education for the Handicapped. Several creative individuals were invited to describe innovative uses of media and materials for handicapped learners. During the first year of operation, the Center was involved largely in planning activities and gathering specific information on which to build center services and decision-making models.

Services

Three service areas are presently operational at the National Center on Educational Media and Materials for the Handicapped. They are: Coordination Services; Media, Materials, and Technology Services; and Information Services. In addition, there is a Research and Evaluation/Administrative component which supports, coordinates, and leads these three primary services.

Coordination Services. Coordinating the vast array of activities for the development and provision of instructional materials to the handicapped is an immense task. The National Media Center for the Handicapped will be involved most directly in providing services which will coordinate the Area Learning Resource Centers, which are the successors to the Regional Special Education Instructional Material Centers and Regional Media Centers for the Deaf. Those area learning resource centers are responsible for stimulating a comprehensive program of educational media and materials support to all handicapped children in their geographic territory. The National Media Center is concerned that each of the Area Learning Resource Centers provide strong links between the National Media Center and the local centers, known as Associate Instructional Materials Centers.

Four specialized national offices have also been established. The Special Office for the Visually Impaired, the Special Office for the Hearing Impaired, and the Special Office for Other Handicaps are primarily materials development and demonstration centers (see appendix). The Special Office for Materials Distribution maintains and circulates a national collection of materials to back up local collections and provide opportunities to try out innovative materials. The National Media Center will work with the Special Offices to stimulate the development or adaptation of needed materials, the testing and demonstration of the effectiveness of the developed or adapted materials, and will facilitate the dissemination of materials developed by Special Office personnel. In addition, the National Media Center will attempt to share successful practices and techniques for the solving of common problems among ALRCs, Specialized Offices, and other agencies.

Public Law 91–61 required that the National Media Center support the educational technology needs of the Model Secondary School for the Deaf at Gallaudet College in Washington, D.C. This mandate has been extended to the Kendall Demonstration Elementary School, at the same location. Services will be provided to the Model Secondary School and the Kendall School to facilitate the development and utilization of materials within that environment; to link the Specialized Office for the Hearing Impaired with the developmental activities at the model schools; and to facilitate dissemination of materials and information resulting from the efforts of the demonstration schools.

Media, Materials, and Technology Services (MMT). The Center's services in media, materials, and technology emphasize the placing of already developed instructional materials products into appropriate distribution channels. MMT personnel are developing and updating policies and procedures for a comprehensive system of product review, prioritization, refinement, and distribution channel selection. These policies and procedures will be implemented primarily with child-use products in the context of the network of Area Learning Resource Centers and Specialized Offices. The results of reviewing the materials will guide decisions about further development, testing, or dissemination of those materials. It is important that the National Media Center be confident that materials have a high probability of satisfying a learning need for a handicapped young person before investing resources in those materials.

The dissemination of materials, of course, is the goal of the technological efforts of the National Media Center. Since the number of handicapped young people is relatively small, those materials which are suitable only for a particular subgroup of the handicapped may not be commerically viable. Thus, the National Media Center is establishing noncommercial thin-market pathways for dissemination when commercial distribution is found to be unfeasible. One such pathway is through the National Audiovisual Center of the National Archives. The National Media Center will provide the necessary original materials to the National Audiovisual Center and will also provide information on the materials to the field. The National Audiovisual Center will, through its contracts with film laboratories, etc., provide multiple copies on demand at approximately the cost of reproduction. Of course, materials which are useful for more than one category of the handicapped or which are useful to general learners even though designed for handicapped learners may be commercially viable, and the National Media Center for the Handicapped will act as an advocate for those materials in the commercial marketplace, locating competent commerical producers and distributors and encouraging those distributors to market the materials.

Information Services. The building of a network of instructional materials centers requires considerable information interchange. The National Center on Educational Media and Materials for the Handicapped is developing a system which will provide on-line access to the file of materials appropriate for handicapped learners. This system can be accessed in a number of different ways; it is initially projected that field personnel will eventually be able to telephone the regional center personnel who will, in turn, conduct the on-line computer search using coordinate indexes or author/producer and title information. This system will provide information not only about the existence of the material, but will also identify the source of evaluative reviews and the sources for obtaining the materials. If the materials are within the collections in the system of instructional materials centers, the information system will also be able to accomplish a circulation transaction for those materials for demonstration or initial trial purposes regardless of the physical location of the materials. Operationalization of such an information system depends on the comprehensive coordination of the Area Learning Resource Centers and the Special Office for Materials Distribution.

The National Media Center for the Handicapped will also publish information about educational media and materials for the handicapped. At the present time, the center is producing a newsletter, *Apropos*, which includes an essay on some aspect of media and materials for the handicapped and the identification of newly available materials either for the learner or for training professionals. Various monographs will be issued by the center so that the field can be continually apprised of developments in the state of the art or of systems under development.

Mission

The National Center on Educational Media and Materials faces a major challenge in initiating the services described above, but those services should be understood to be only part of an evolving system of services which relate to a broadly defined mission. That mission requires that the National Center on Educational Media and Materials for the Handicapped, in cooperation with other agencies, bring the benefits of educational technology to all handicapped children and young people. This will involve the development of materials, training of personnel in the use of those materials, informing those personnel about materials which exist, and delivering materials through various channels to the learner who needs them.

The National Media Center seeks the best application of all information relevant to the development of materials for handicapped learners. In addition, the center will work to acquaint researchers with problems which need to be solved in the design and development of educational materials for the handicapped. Eventually, it will actively seek resources and work coperatively to conduct the necessary applied research experimentation. Taking the tightly controlled experimental findings from psychology and applying them within more typical instructional environments, the Center can attempt to ascertain whether theoretical principles can become design principles.

Naturally, if new techniques are developed or new systems of materials provided, personnel in the field will need to be systematically introduced to those materials; this, along with the materials development, the National Media Center for the Handicapped and the network will stimulate the development and dissemination of training materials, and will design dissemination training systems which will insure that field practitioners will be continually updated as new materials are made available.

The National Media Center will also work to provide educational technology support for the continuing education of handicapped adults. This effort will involve the use of mass media and will provide a location to which handicapped people and special educators can turn to gain access to mass communications systems. The National Media Center will work to support the effort of professionals and parents in integrating handicapped persons into the mainstream of American life. This means that while most of the initial services will be directed toward special educators and schools with special education programs, the services must be broadened as soon as possible to reach any public agency involved in the education of any person within the society, so that agency can adequately serve handicapped persons.

The mission of the National Media Center should become elaborated and refined as Congress, funding agencies, the ALRC/SO/NCEMMH network, state departments, organizations of and for the handicapped, and the special education profession continue an extensive dialog about the center. The National Media Center is a concept which belongs to no single organization or agency; rather it must evolve in the rich context of a pluralistic national concern. It will be a long-term developmental thrust which should truly increase the learning opportunities of handicapped young people.

Appendix: Learning Resource Centers Network

Regional Resource Center #1
Northwest Regional Resource Center
Telephone: (503) 686–3591
Address: University of Oregon
    Clinical Services Building, Third Floor
    Eugene, Oregon 97403
Contractor: University of Oregon

Area Learning Resource Center #1
Northwest Area Learning Resource Center
Telephone: (503) 686–3591
Address: University of Oregon
    Clinical Services Building, Third Floor
    Eugene, Oregon 97403
Contractor: University of Oregon

Regional Resource Center #2
California Regional Resource Center
Telephone: (213) 746–6188
Address: 1031 South Broadway, Suite 623
    Los Angeles, California 90015
Contractor: University of Southern California

Area Learning Resource Center #2
California Area Learning Resource Center
Telephone: (213) 747–9308
Address: 1031 South Broadway, Suite 623
    Los Angeles, California 90015
Contractor: University of Southern California

Regional Resource Center #3
Southwest Regional Resource Center
Telephone: (801) 581–6281
Address: 2363 Foot Hill Drive, Suite G
    Salt Lake City, Utah 84109
Contractor: University of Utah

Area Learning Resource Center #3
Southwest Area Learning Resource Center
Telephone: (505) 646–1017
Address: New Mexico State University
    Box 3AW
    Las Cruces, New Mexico 88003
Contractor: New Mexico State University

Regional Resource Center #4
Midwest Regional Resource Center
Telephone: (515) 271–3936
Address: Drake University
    1332 26th Street
    Des Moines, Iowa 50311
Contractor: Iowa Department of Public Instruction

Area Learning Resource Center #4
Midwest Area Learning Resource Center
Telephone: (515) 351–4361

States Served

Alaska, Hawaii, Samoa, Guam, Trust Territory, Washington, Oregon, Idaho, Montana, Wyoming

California

Nevada, Utah, Colorado, Arizona, New Mexico, B.I.A. Schools

North Dakota, South Dakota, Nebraska, Kansas, Oklahoma, Iowa, Missouri, Arkansas

Address: Drake University
    1336 26th Street
    Des Moines, Iowa 50311
Contractor: Iowa Department of Public Instruction

Regional Resource Center #5
Texas Regional Resource Center
Telephone: (512) 475–3527
Address: Texas Education Agency
    201 East 11th Street
    Austin, Texas 78701
Contractor: Texas Education Agency

Area Learning Resource Center #5
Texas Area Learning Resource Center
Telephone: (512) 471–3145
Address: Texas Area Learning Resource Center
    2613 Wichita Street
    Austin, Texas 78712
Contractor: Texas Education Agency

Regional Resource Center #6
Great Lakes Regional Resource Center
Telephone: (608) 266–1771
Address: Wisconsin State Department of
    Public Instruction
    126 Langdon Street
    Madison, Wisconsin 53702
Contractor: Wisconsin State Department of
    Public Instruction

Area Learning Resource Center #6
Great Lakes Area Learning Resource Center
Telephone: (517) 373–1695
Address: Michigan Department of Education
    P.O. Box 420
    Lansing, Michigan 48902
Contractor: Michigan Department of Education

Regional Resource Center #7
Illinois Regional Resource Center
Telephone: (309) 672–6717
Address: Peoria Public School District
    3202 North Wisconsin Avenue
    Peoria, Illinois 61603
Contractor: Peoria Public School District

Area Learning Resource Center #7
Illinois Area Learning Resource Center
Telephone: (217) 782–2263
Address: 1020 South Spring Street
    Springfield, Illinois 62706
Contractor: Office of Superintendent of
    Public Instruction

Regional Resource Center #8
Ohio Regional Resource Center
Telephone: (614) 466–2650
Address: Ohio State Department of Education
    Division of Special Education

States Served

Texas

Minnesota, Wisconsin,
Michigan, Indiana

Illinois

Ohio

933 High Street
Worthington, Ohio 43085
Contractor: Ohio State Department of Education

Area Learning Resource Center #8
Ohio Area Learning Resource Center
Telephone: (614) 466–2650
Address: Ohio State Department of Education
   Division of Special Education
   933 High Street
   Worthington, Ohio 43085
Contractor: Ohio Department of Education

Regional Resource Center #9
Northeast Regional Resource Center
Telephone: (609) 448–4773
Address: 384 Stockton Street
   Hightstown, New Jersey 08520
Contractor: New Jersey State Department
   of Education

Area Learning Resource Center #9
Northeast Area Learning Resource Center
Telephone: (609) 488–4773; (609) 443–5753
Address: 384 Stockton Street
   Hightstown, New Jersey 08520
Contractor: New Jersey State Department
   of Education

Regional Resource Center #10
New York Regional Resource Center
Telephone: (212) 866–9430
Address: City University of New York
   144 West 125th Street
   New York, New York 10027
Contractor: City University of New York

Area Learning Resource Center #10
New York Area Learning Resource Center
Telephone: (518) 474–2251
Address: New York State Education Department
   Division for Handicapped Children
   55 Elk Street, Room 117
   Albany, New York 12234
Contractor: University of New York

Regional Resource Center #11
National Learning Resource Center of Pennsylvania
Telephone: (215) 265–3706
Address: 443 South Gulph Road
   King of Prussia, Pennsylvania 19406
Contractor: Pennsylvania Department of Education

Area Learning Resource Center #11
Pennsylvania Area Learning Resource Center
Telephone: (215) 265–3706
Address: 443 South Gulph Road
   King of Prussia, Pennsylvania 19406
Contractor: Pennsylvania Department of Education

States Served

Maine, Vermont,
New Hampshire,
Massachusetts,
Rhode Island,
Connecticut,
New Jersey

New York

Pennsylvania

Regional Resource Center #12
Mideast Regional Resource Center
Telephone: (202) 676–7200
Address: 1901 Pennsylvania Avenue, N.W.
            Suite 505
            Washington, D.C. 20006
Contractor: George Washington University

Area Learning Resource Center #12
Mideast Area Learning Resource Center
Telephone: (606) 258–4921
Address: University of Kentucky
            Porter Building, Room 123
            Lexington, Kentucky 40506
Contractor: University of Kentucky
            Research Foundation

Regional Resource Center #13
Southeast Regional Resource Center
Telephone: (205) 279–9110, ext. 257 or 258
Address: Auburn University at Montgomery
            Montgomery, Alabama 36109
Contractor: Auburn University at Montgomery

Area Learning Resource Center #13
Southeast Learning Resource Center
Telephone: (205) 279–9110, ext. 257 or 258
Address: Auburn University at Montgomery
            Montgomery, Alabama 36109
Contractor: Auburn University at Montgomery

*Coordinating Office for the Regional
Resource Centers*
CORRC Project
Telephone: (606) 258–4671
Address: Bradley Hall
            University of Kentucky
            Lexington, Kentucky 40506
Contractor: University of Kentucky
            Research Foundation

*The National Center on Educational Media
and Materials for the Handicapped*
NCEMMH
Telephone: (614) 422–7596
Address: The Ohio State University
            220 West 12th Avenue
            Columbus, Ohio 43210
Contractor: The Ohio State University
            Research Foundation

Specialized Office #1
Specialized Office for Visual Impairment
Telephone: (512) 895–2405
Address: American Printing House for the Blind
            Box 6085
            Louisville, Kentucky 40206
Contractor: American Printing House for the Blind

States Served

Delaware, D.C.,
Maryland, Virginia,
West Virginia, Kentucky,
Tennessee, North
Carolina

Louisiana, Mississippi,
Alabama, Georgia, South
Carolina, Florida,
Puerto Rico, Virgin
Islands

National

Specialized Office #2
Specialized Office for the Deaf and Hard of Hearing
Telephone: (402) 472–2141
Address: University of Nebraska
       175 Nebraska Hall
       Lincoln, Nebraska 68508
Contractor: Board of Regents of the
       University of Nebraska

Specialized Office #3
Wisconsin Research and Development Center
for Cognitive Learning
Telephone: (608) 263–7850
Address: 1025 West Johnson Street
       Madison, Wisconsin 53706
Contractor: University of Wisconsin System

Specialized Office #4
Indiana University
Telephone: (812) 337–2853
Address: Audio-Visual Center
       Bloomington, Indiana 47401
Contractor: Indiana University Foundation

Index